A BIBLIOGRAPHICAL AND CRITICAL ACCOUNT OF THE RAREST BOOKS IN THE ENGLISH LANGUAGE

ALPHABETICALLY ARRANGED

WHICH DURING THE LAST FIFTY YEARS HAVE COME UNDER THE OBSERVATION OF

J. PAYNE COLLIER F. S. A.

IN FOUR VOLUMES

VOL. I

NEW YORK
DAVID G. FRANCIS 506 BROADWAY
CHARLES SCRIBNER & CO. 124 GRAND ST.
1866

PREFACE.

During my whole life, now rapidly approaching fourscore, I have been a diligent reader, and, as far as my means would allow, a greedy purchaser of all works connected with early English literature. It is nearly sixty years since I became possessor of my first really valuable old book of this kind, — Wilson's "Art of Logic," printed by Richard Grafton in 1551, — from which I ascertained the not unimportant facts that "Ralph Roister Doister" was an older play than "Gammer Gurton's Needle," and that it had been written by Nicholas Udall, Master of Eton School. I thus learned who was the author of the earliest comedy, properly so called, in our language. This was my first literary discovery, made several years anterior, although I had not occasion to render it public, until I printed my Notes upon "Dodsley's Old Plays" soon after 1820. My latest discovery, which occurred only a few months ago, is that "Tottel's Miscellany," 1557, the oldest and most interesting in our language, containing as it does the poems of the Earl of Surrey, Sir Thomas Wyat, and their contemporaries, has always, during the last three centuries, been reprinted, by Dr. Sewell, Bishop Percy, Dr. Nott, and their followers, from the second instead of the first edition. The differences between the two are not merely extremely curious, but very interesting and important.

Between the one discovery and the other there was an interval of perhaps fifty years; and whatever may appear to be new in the ensuing volumes has been the result of literary investigation during considerably more than that period. My early employments were irksome and wearisome; but, stimulated in some degree by my first success, and by my love for the best poetry the world has produced, I lightened my labors by the collection and perusal of old English books, and by making extracts from and criticisms upon them, whether in prose or verse; so that in time they formed a large body of manuscripts, consisting of separate articles alphabetically arranged.

The work in the hands of the reader has been mainly derived from this source, and not a few of the notices are of forty, or even fifty, years standing. Although I kept constantly adding to, altering and correcting them, both as to facts and opinions, some of them are, in the most material points, just as they came from my pen, soon after the perusal of the books to which they relate. It will be found that a few are reviews of productions altogether unknown to bibliographers, while others apply to publications of which only a single copy remains to us, or to separate tracts of the utmost rarity.

It is true that notices of a very few more common, but still scarce, books will be found interspersed, a circumstance arising from the fact that I have incorporated all the productions formerly embraced in what is generally known as the "Bridgewater Catalogue," which about thirty years ago I prepared for the first Earl of Ellesmere, and which was privately printed at the expense of that gifted, enlightened, and liberal nobleman. Through my hands in 1837 he dispersed, as presents, in different quarters of the globe, the fifty copies of which the whole impression consisted; but, some years after the completion of the undertaking, his Lordship expressed his regret, that the limitation in point of number much restricted the utility of that Catalogue. He therefore authorized me at any time to reprint it, if I thought it would answer as a pecuniary speculation. During Lord Ellesmere's life I never availed myself of this permission; but a proposal of the kind was made to me not long after his demise. I did not then listen to it, because I was still anxious to introduce corrections upon many of the pages; and because, even then, I contemplated a work upon a broader basis, and of a wider range, not limited to the contents of any single library, whether public or private.

It may be stated, nevertheless, that in the course of my four volumes, I have reprinted the whole of the "Bridgewater Catalogue." I refused to mutilate it by the omission of any article, however comparatively insignificant; but I have, at the same time, carefully inserted whatever information I subsequently procured, and the consequence is that there is no one piece of criticism, derived from the "Bridgewater Catalogue," that has not received improvements more or less important. Had I not been desirous of giving that work in its entirety, I might have discarded accounts of a few books of more ordinary occurrence, but which the autographs of the writers, in dedications or otherwise, had rendered of peculiar interest and value in the Ellesmere Library.

Before that memorable assemblage of books came into the possession of Lord Francis Egerton (afterwards the first Earl of Ellesmere) some highly important works had been turned out of it, in many instances under the mistaken impression that they were duplicates. These supposed duplicates, generally marked by John Earl of Bridgewater (who died in 1649) in a somewhat peculiar manner, were to be found on the shelves of several booksellers, or in private hands, and two or three occurred in sale-lists not long after the preparation of the "Bridgewater Catalogue." One of these may be specified as the finest copy of the sonnets of Shakspeare (4to. 1609) that has ever been seen, and I had the satisfaction of repurchasing it for Lord Ellesmere. Having also a noble collection of old plays, (though much impaired when imaginary duplicates were incautiously extruded,) his Lordship was at all times anxious to restore them to their ancient places at any price, and he commissioned me to secure such relics for him. He besides applied a considerable sum every year to the formation of a separate library, especially devoted to the illustration of Shakspeare and our early stage. This most agreeable duty Lord Ellesmere assigned to me; and had not the commission on the British Museum intervened, (on which I felt, most reluctantly, bound to take an independent course, in favor of a compendious catalogue which would enable readers instantly to find the book wanted without wading through a labyrinth of tediously extended titles,) this design might have advanced considerably farther towards completion. The difficulty was to procure the books, so rare and costly had the best of them become, but Lord Ellesmere did not hesitate to purchase any work I recommended. There never, perhaps, existed a more confiding or bountiful patron; and, after an intercourse of more than thirty years, I may venture to say, with affectionate humility, that the only fault of his character was having too high an estimate of those who were interested in misguiding him, and too little reliance upon his own unswayed convictions.

It is now above sixty years since I first obtained a ticket for the reading-room of the British Museum, and my own notions as to the easy possibility of procuring a short and useful catalogue of the books, have never undergone the slightest change. This is probably the last preface I shall ever be able to compose, and I therefore add, that if the Lord Ellesmere of 1847 and 1848 had only been as firm as, in my opinion, he was originally right, we might possibly (I only say possibly) long ago have obtained the easiest mode of reference to every printed volume in the library. The want of it has often kept me, and others, away from the reading-room, because, in the confused multitude of volumes over which the various catalogues are distributed, we never could be sure whether the books we were in search of were, or were not, upon the shelves of the Institution. It is, besides, the misfortune of the British Museum that it is peculiarly deficient in works of the class to which I was anxious expecially to refer. I willingly admit that this is not the fault of the present principal librarian. In our time, the books are not to be procured, except at enormous prices, particularly if it be known that the British Museum is in the market. My acquaintance with the head of that establishment is necessarily very slight. I am well aware, however, of his energy, ability and acquirements; but I must say, that the long-felt want of a concise and intelligible mean of reference to the books in the British Museum (which mean he has always resisted) much counterbalanced the other advantages derived from his position, when he had the control of the department of printed books. Such are my confirmed sentiments, after a life-long experience in the library, and when, in my seventy-seventh year, I am so near the end of my laborious course, that the existing state of the catalogues can make little difference to me.

I have reason to know that, nearly twenty years since, I injured my own prospects by the part I took upon this subject; because, if I were correctly informed, the commissioners had at one time a design to separate the printed book department into two portions — English and foreign. If this reasonable plan had been carried out, and I had accommodated myself to the views of those who were for a manuscript catalogue in five or six hundred huge folio volumes, I might, with the assistance of the Earl of Ellesmere, as head of the commission, and of the Duke of Devonshire, as one of the trustees, have had a chance of filling the appointment which would thus have been created. I am now, of course, too old for any such duties, but the trustees, after the close of the inquiry, did appoint a new and a most valuable officer in another overgrown department. All I wish now to do is to record, before I die, my ancient conviction in favor of the scheme I advocated in my two days' evidence before the commissioners, by whom, I fear, I was considered a very obstructive secretary.

For the reasons stated, I have obtained few of my materials from the British Museum, while from the Bodleian library, where the books are instantly accessible and the catalogue complete, I have from time to time derived important assistance. The head of that establishment and the other learned curators were never weary of giving me their readiest aid. My chief reliance, however, has been upon my own industry and vigilance, willingly encouraged, even from my outset, by the liberality of private individuals, who had fine collections of rare books, from the days of Sir Francis Freeling and Mr. Perry down to the later acquisitions of Mr. Heber and Mr. Miller. To collectors of a later period I have seldom been indebted; but I may mention the name of one bookseller who was always glad to contribute to my purpose — the late Thomas Rodd, a man as celebrated for his knowledge of books as for his fairness in dealing with them. Many and many a literary rarity has he purchased for my use and advantage, sometimes at my instance; and as the price of such commodities has been gradually rising during the whole of the present century, neither he nor I ever had to regret the dearness of our bargains. He was of a good family, but accidentally reduced, and my father and his father were at the same public school; they afterwards met in Spain, and it was in the year 1804, or 1805, that my father first took me to the old book-shop then kept by his worthy, though less fortunate schoolfellow. This was, in fact, my introduction to the early literature of our country; and it was not many years afterwards that I purchased my first old English book of any real value, Wilson's "Logic." Long subsequently I bought hundreds of other books from and through Rodd; but, as I never was rich enough to collect, and keep, what may be called a library, he sold them again, and very seldom at a loss.

Readers may imagine that I have obtained much in formation from such works as *Censura Literaria*, "The British Bibliographer," or *Restituta*, to say nothing of smaller productions of a similar character. This is a mistake. I have never referred to them without acknowledgment; but it will be found in the fourteen hundred pages that follow this preface that, excepting for the sake of illustration or for the correction of some important error, I have never criticised, or I may almost say, quoted a single volume noticed by others. It was generally enough to induce me to lay an old book aside to find that it had already passed through the hands of Brydges, Park, or Haslewood. To the taste and learning of the first I bear willing testimony. The second possessed knowledge, but without much discrimination; and the third was a man remarkable for his diligence, but remarkable also for the narrowness of his views, for his total want of judgment, and for the paucity of his information.

I can assert, without the chance of contradiction, that there is no one book, the merits or peculiarities of which are discussed in these volumes, that has not passed through my own hands and been carefully read by my own eyes. There is no extract, no line, that has not been copied by my own pen; and although I cannot for an instant suppose that I have altogether avoided mistakes, I hope that I have made as few as possible. In a case of this sort, where hundreds of names occur, and thousands of dates are given, errors must inevitably have crept in; but I am aware of none, whether relating to books or their authors, that I have not set right in the "Additions, Notes and Corrections," placed at the beginning of my book, as it were, to solicit the indulgence of the reader in the outset.[1] Even if this work be found to deserve reprinting, I can hardly hope to live to superintend a revised edition of it.

It may be necessary to add, that I have purposely avoided old English dramas and plays, because they form so distinct a subject that they ought to be separately treated. I have by me many details regarding the plots, characters, poetry and appliances of performances of this description, from the remotest dates, some of them relating to productions hitherto unrecorded; and if time, opportunity and eyesight should unexpectedly and graciously be allowed me, it will much add to my happiness to be able hereafter to put them into shape for publication. *Dum spiro spero.*

J. P. C.

MAIDENHEAD, 14*th April*, 1865.

[1] These "Additions, Notes and Corrections" have, in this edition, been inserted in their proper places, as foot-notes.

Bibliographical Account

OF

EARLY ENGLISH LITERATURE.

ABBOT, GEORGE. — A Sermon preached at Westminster, May 26, 1608, at the Funerall Solemnities of the Right Honorable Thomas Earle of Dorset, late High Treasurer of England. By George Abbot, Doctor of Divinitie and Deane of Winchester, one of his Lordships Chapleines, &c. — London: Printed by Melchisedech Bradwood for William Aspley. 1608. 8vo. 18 *leaves.*

This production, although upon the death of a man of the highest distinction as a Poet and Statesman, has sometimes been omitted in the list of the works of Archbishop Abbot. It has, of course, been mentioned, but we notice the sermon in some detail from the only copy we ever saw sold, (there is one in the Bodleian Library, and another at Cambridge,) chiefly on account of the biographical matter it contains. The text is from Isaiah xl. *v.* 6, 7; and after various moral observations and illustrations, of no great originality, the preacher proceeds to Lord Dorset's character in these terms: —

"Her Majestie (Q. Eliz.), not long before her death, being pleased, as it seemeth, with some speciall piece of service, which his Lordship had done unto her, grew at large to discourse touching this nobleman, as an honorable person, and a Counsellor of Estate, in writing hath advertised me. Her Highnesse was then pleased to decipher out his life by seven steps or degrees. The first was his yoonger daies, the time of his scholarship, when first in that famous Universitie of Oxford, and afterward in the Temple (where he took the degree of Barrister) he gave tokens of such pregnancie, such studiousnesse and judgement, that he was held no way inferiour to any of his time or standing. And of this there remain good tokens both in English and Latine published unto the world. The second was his travell, when being in France and Italy he profited very much in the languages in matter of story and state (whereof this Commonwealth found great benefit in his Lordship's elder yeares in the deepest consultations that belonged unto this kingdome). And being prisoner in Rome for the space of fourteene daies (which trouble was brought upon him by some who hated him for his love to religion, and his dutie to his Soveraigne) he so prudently bare himselfe that, by the blessing of God, and his temperate kind of carriage, he was freed out of that danger. The third step, which her Majestie did thinke good to observe was (upon returne into England) his comming unto her Court, where, on divers occasions, he bountifully feasted her Highnesse and her Nobles, and so he did to forren Ambassadors. At that time he entertained Musicians, the most curious which any where he could have, and therein his Lordship excelled unto his dying day. Then was his discourse judicious, but yet wittie and delightfull. Thus he was in his yoonger daies a scholar and a traveller, and a Courtier of speciall estimation."

Afterwards Abbot mentions the well-known gift of a ring by King James (Cooper's *Ath. Cantabr.* II. 487); but the Archbishop had no reason to plume himself on his own knowledge, or on the accuracy of his information, for in the margin, opposite the words where he had applauded the Earl's "pregnancy" both in English and Latin, he placed this note: — "The Life of Tresilian in the Mirrour of Magistr. — Epist. prefix. Aulic. Barth. Clerke." Lord Dorset unquestionably had written a Latin letter prefixed to Bartholomew Clerke's Latin translation of Castiglione's *Cortegiano*, but George Ferrers was the author of the "Life of Tresilian" in the "Mirror for Magistrates," while the Earl, when Mr. Sackville, had written a much superior portion of that work, "the Complaint of the Duke of Buckingham." More than all, he contributed the famous "Induction" [1] to that celebrated collection in

1 This "Induction," in what is called "The Seconde Parte of the Mirrour for Magistrates" (which, in the edition of 1563, was appended by W. Baldwin to the first part, originally published in 1559), precedes Sackville's "Complaynt of Henrye duke of Buckingham," and in a manner prepares the way for it. The "Induction" alone fills twenty pages, viz., from sig. P iii. to R iiii.

1563, which "Induction," it has been admitted by everybody, displays consummate ability in abstract impersonation, a department in which even Spenser, many years afterwards, scarcely went beyond him.

Sackville's English lines introductory to Hoby's version of the *Cortegiano* in 1561 were perhaps hardly worth mention, (as indeed they have often been passed over,) but Abbot says nothing of the authorship by the Earl of two entire acts in our earliest blank-verse tragedy "Gorboduc": we believe that it arose from his ignorance of the important fact, and not because he thought it a topic unbecoming the pulpit. The drama was acted before Queen Elizabeth at Whitehall in 1561, and it was printed in 1565 with the names of Norton (the joint author) and Sackville on the title-page, but we do not recollect that it was ever spoken of as theirs by contemporaries; and when once Lord Dorset had entered on his public career, he seems not to have been fond of recurring to his youthful literary performances. Nevertheless, his "Induction" to the "Mirror for Magistrates," and his two acts of "Gorboduc," so memorable for the effect ere long produced on our national drama by the introduction of blank-verse, must give him a more permanent claim to admiration than any of the great public duties in which he, for about half a century, was engaged.

The last three leaves are filled by an extract from Lord Dorset's will.

ABSOLOM. — A godly and profitable Treatise, intituled Absolom his fall, or the ruin of Roysters, &c. Imprinted at London by Thomas Orwin for N. L. and Iohn Busbie. 8vo. B. L. n. d. 44 *leaves*.

This small work, cited by Prynne in his "Histriomastix," 4to, 1633, p. 198, is included in only one public catalogue (that of the Bodleian Library), and is not, as far as we know, in the possession of any private collector. No tract of the time (1589) gives so concise and singular an account of the dress, &c. of both sexes; and these peculiarities, or absurdities, excited so strongly the bile of the puritanical writer, that he found it impossible to keep his language within the bounds of moderation, almost of decency.

It has no date, and only the initials of the author at the end of the dedication to Sir John Hart, Lord Mayor in 1589, in which W. T. calls upon him to exert his power for the correction of such gross abuses. He entitles his book "Absolom his Fall," because he especially directs his attack against "the vile and abominable abuse of curled long haire," which, if remedied, would happily be, in the words of his title, "the ruin of roysters." The subsequent specimen of his style refers to the ridiculous apparel of women: —

"As for their little copped crowne hats, which are so little and so light, that the smallest blast of winde would carie them away, which so artificially is, I thinke, pinned to their heads, or at least wise to the attire of their heads, are they not more comelie for little children, or babies that the children make, than for them? As for their deepe and great ruffes (wherein, I thinke, the diuell lieth in every set) are they not more fit for monsters and giants, than for such slender and tender creatures of God? As for their fardingales (which but for reverence sake we might otherwise term) which so like breeches stand about them, are they not better beseeming the state of fooles, than the corps of wise and discreete women? As for their truncke sleeves, made to their gownes, are not the sleeves thereof more fitter to weare in stead of men's Venetians, than the sleeves of women? And all this (for sooth) must be to preserue their tender carcasses from the weather."

Men also wore "copped crowne hats," and they are doubtless what Shakspeare refers to in "The Taming of the Shrew," Act V. sc. 1. They continued long in fashion.

The writer dwells likewise at considerable length, and with great animation, upon the pride and extravagance of servants, a point which till then had not attracted much attention. It was about this period that the old-fashioned blue coats, in which male attendants had usually been attired, began to be laid aside for varied and garded liveries.

ACHELLEY, THOMAS. — A most lamentable and Tragicall historie, conteyning the outrageous and horrible tyrannie which a Spanishe gentlewoman named Violenta executed upon her lover Didaco, because he espoused another beyng first betrothed unto her. Newly translated into

English meter, by T. A. 1576.—Imprinted at London by Iohn Charlewood for Thomas Butter dwelling in Paules Church-yarde neere to S. Austines gate at the Shippe. 1576. 8vo. 39 *leaves.*

Although Achelley professes to have translated this story anew in 1576, there is little doubt from comparison, that in putting it into " English metre " he availed himself of the tale, not so much as we find it in Bandello, but as it appears in Paynter's "Palace of Pleasure," which had then been published nearly ten years. Paynter tells us, at his conclusion, that he had varied from his original in saving the life of the guilty servant Janique, whom Bandello had represented as suffering with her more guilty mistress; and Achelley adopts the improvement, by allowing her to escape from Valencia, where the whole scene is laid, to Africa.

Whether Achelley had written anything in verse before this attempt we know not, but he displays considerable skill and freedom; and though, like Bandello, coarse in his epithets and strong in his expressions, he makes good use of his mother-tongue, and displays more ease and variety than some of his contemporaries. In 1572 he had published a work that does not seem to have especially qualified him for his Italian task, since it consists merely of " prayers and meditations " under the title of " The Key of Knowledge."[1] However, he was certainly a better versifyer than Lewicke or Partridge, although inferior, in some respects, to Garter and Brooke; but they all, though similar in style and subjects, wrote some years earlier than Achelley, and between 1562 and 1576 our language had made considerable advances. Watson printed his Εκατομπαθια in 1581, and Achelley was then of sufficient prominence to be called upon for commendatory verses, even of a poet whose reputation as a writer of sonnets became so distinguished. Watson's merits as a poet rest not so much upon the work we have named, as upon his " Tears of Fancy," (see

[1] Achelley's "Key of Knowledge" must have come out later than 1572, because, in the dedication of it to Lady Elizabeth Russell, he speaks of his " ragged verses whiche, about two yeares paste, I presumed to tender to your discreete judgement." It is probable that he refers to some other, and earlier, poetical production than his "Didaco and Violenta," published in 1576.

Watson, *post*,) which did not come from the press until 1593. Thomas Achelley the elder, who was perhaps the father of Thomas Achelley the younger, (see the next Art.,) must be judged by the work under consideration.

It is dedicated in prose " to the Right Worshipful Sir Thomas Gresham, Knight," and here the author, or translator, furnishes the argument of his work, upon which we need not enlarge, because the story will be gathered sufficiently from what follows. In imitation of the style of Bandello, Achelley talks of " the beastly Progne " and " the butcherly Medea," and subsequently opens his narrative, headed " The Tragicall Historie of Didaco and Violenta," with these lines: —

" Where Phœbus foming steedes
  Their restles race doo ende,
And leaving our Horizon to
  Th' Antipodes doo wende,
Right there dooth lye a famous soyle,
  Whose farthest bounds of land,
Environed with the brinish floods
  Of Ocean doo stand."

Here " doo ende," " doo wende," and " doo stand " give no favorable impression as to the writer's powers, merely eking out, as they do, the measure of his verse. By the above and some other similar lines he means to describe Spain, on the etymology of which name he is afterwards thus clumsily learned : —

" Our former auncetors have tearmde
  The same Hesperia hight,
But tract of time presound the name
  Iberia to write:
Both names, by great dexteritie
  And judgement, sound againe
Hispania; the same at last
  Was calde in Englishe Spaine."

The " dexterity " and " judgment " which derived " Spain " from " Iberia " may not be very apparent; but the extravagant laudation of Spanish soldiers, whose bravery and skill could, if they had then lived, have saved Troy, and defeated " the raging Macedonian routs," would be better tolerated in England in 1576 than ten or twelve years afterwards. Didaco, we are told, was a most accomplished soldier of Valencia, who had never yet yielded to the weakness of love: —

"Enjoying still his libertie,
Not knowyng Venus yoke,
Unexpert in the panges of love,
And cursed Cupides stroke,
He never haunted Venus Court,
Ne yet her carped troupe:
Such weaklinges he abhord; his mind
To no such thing would stoupe."

However, while "walking in the Goldsmithes Row" in Valencia, he sees Violenta, the daughter of one of the shop-keepers; and Venus in a long speech to Cupid, who replies with about equal prolixity, induces her son to wound Didaco. The hero is, of course, instantly and furiously passionate, and consoles himself by recounting the great men and deities who have yielded to Cupid's power, according to the representations of the Poets: —

"Yes, sure, if credit ought be due
To Poets learned lore;
If that their volumes be perusde
As gemmes of passing store,"

there could be no derogation in his submission. He is at first modestly put off by Violenta, to whom he had sent 500 ducats; but in the end he offers her marriage, she consents, and they are privately united, in order to keep the matter from the knowledge of his noble and wealthy relatives. After about a year, Didaco falls in love with another lady of great beauty, high birth, and large possessions, and, in spite of his former vows, marries her. Violenta hears of the event, and, among other things, exclaims: —

"O haples hap and dolefull chaunce,
That ever thy tangling tonge
Made breache into my Virginitie,
Which I preserved so long!
O caytife wretch! and can thine eyes
Sustaine for to behold
These raging panges and marterdome
Wherein I am enrold?
Is this the guerdon of my fayth,
Which I have usde alway,

Now, like a beast and reprobate,
Thus to be cast away?"

She vows revenge, and accomplishes it in a very brutal manner with the assistance of her maid Janique (always misspelt Jamque, to the ruin of the measure), and sends Didaco a letter (given in plain prose) treacherously entreating him to visit her once more, and to spend the night in her company. He consents, and attempts to pacify her by telling her, what, however, she does not believe, that he had married a second time by compulsion, and that ere long he would destroy the lady thus forced upon him by his kindred: —

"And when my practize once hath wrought
Her cursed finall end,
The remnant of my vitall race
With thee (my deare) Ile spend:
And then, in tearme of further time,
It plainely shall appeare
How that Didaco is the knight
That holdes thy love most deare."

They go to bed, and Janique, (who had previously fastened a rope which, when drawn tight, would keep Didaco from rising, and had removed his sword, as well as prepared "two chopping-knives" at the instance of Violenta,) when Didaco is asleep, pulls the rope which prevents him from resisting, while Violenta deliberately cuts his throat. She subsequently mangles the body most savagely, and with the help of Janique casts it out of window into the street, where it is found and recognized. The maid escapes to Africa with the connivance of her mistress; and Violenta, before the judges and officers, makes a bold confession of her guilt. The description of the murder is very revolting from the coarseness of the "butcherly" language; and the poem concludes, not with any moral reflections on the hideous brutality of the heroine, but upon the folly of those who allow themselves to be overcome by blind passion: —

"Hap glad or sad, hap weale or woe,
Hap hoped joy or payne,
Yet both in this one issue end,
In love nought is but vayne;"

the line being printed in Italic type, in order to enforce the axiom: the last words are —

"FINIS. (qd) Thomas Achelley."

The whole story is written much in the same style as Drout's "Gaulfrido and Bernardo," which had come out six years earlier; but, if anything, Achelley has the advantage in ease, as well as in variety of versification. We have dwelt the longer upon this novel of "Didaco and Violenta," because, although it is mentioned both by Warton and Ritson, no bibliographer has hitherto given any account of it.

ACHELLEY, THOMAS. — The Massacre of Money. *Terunteo seu vitiosa nuce non emitur.* — London: Printed by Thomas Creede for Thomas Bushell. 1602. 4to. 23 *leaves.*

It has been usual, upon no very sufficient grounds, to assign this work to a Thomas Achelley: the initials T. A. at the end of the Dedication (to M. William and M. Frauncis Bedles) form the only mark of authorship.

There can be little dispute that "The Massacre of Money" was not by the Thomas Achelley who, twenty-six years before, had written the subject of the preceding article; but he may have had a son of the same name, and of a similar poetical propensity. The later work, both in style and topic, more nearly resembles Barnfield's "Encomion of Lady Pecunia," (see hereafter,) which had come out in 1598, and was republished, with changes adapted to the altered circumstances of the times, in 1605. The initials T. A. belong to no other known writer of the period, and Achelley is a poet whose name occurs, not unfrequently, in "England's Parnassus," 1600.

As the extreme scarcity of the poem (we have heard of only two complete copies) has hitherto prevented the appearance of any specimens from it, we will make one or two quotations, which do not prove that the author was very original in his notions, or harmonious in the expression of them. In the following lines a simile has been caught from "Romeo and Juliet": Act I. sc. 5. Pecunia, who is the subject of a contest between Avarice, Prodigality, and Liberality, thus speaks: —

> "Whilst that my glory midst the clouds was hid,
> Like to a Jewell in an Æthiop's eare,
> Or as a spot upon a christal lid,
> So did my brightnes with more pride appeare."

The three candidates for the favor of Pecunia having abused each other abundantly, the strife is augmented by the arrival of Fortune, Vice, and Virtue: the two latter, after a formal challenge, have a vigorous struggle, which is about to end in the discomfiture of Virtue, when Jove decides the contest by striking down Vice with a thunderbolt. The production closes with an extravagant compliment to Queen Elizabeth, who was still on the throne when it was published: —

> "Jove now departing, Vertue did command
> In England to set up her chiefest rest;
> She should find favour at Eliza's hand,
> With whom faire wisdome builded hath his nest.
> The Gods ascend to heaven, Vertue departs
> T'our more then mortall Queene, ruler of harts.
>
> Fortune now frets to see her selfe throwne downe,
> And Vertue lifted to such dignitie;
> Truth at the last attained due renowne;
> Pecunia is disposed thriftily.
> England, thou art Pleasures-presenting stage,
> The perfect patterne of the golden age.
>
> Never be date of this felicitie;
> Never be alteration of this joy;
> Never, ah never! faile thy dignitie;
> Never let Fortune crosse thee with annoy:
> Never let Vertue by Vice suffer death;
> Never be absent our Elizabeth!
>
> Ever, for ever, Englands Beta bee,
> Feared of Forraines, honour'd of thine owne:
> Ever let treason stoope to sov'raigntie;
> Ever let Vice by truth be overthrowne!
> Ever, graunt Heavens Creator, of our Queene
> We still may say she is, not she hath beene!"

In the outset the writer informs the reader that the whole construction of his poem is the result of "a thought conceived dreame." The quotations ascribed to *Tho. Achely*, *Tho. Achlow*, and *Tho. Ach.* in "England's Parnassus," 1600, could not of course be from "The Massacre of Money," not published until two years afterwards.[1]

ADAGES. — Adagia Scotica, or a collection of Scotch Proverbs and Proverbial Phrases. Collected by R. B. Very usefull and delightfull. *Omne tulit punctum qui miscuit utile dulci.* — London. Printed for Nath Brooke, &c., 1668. 12mo. 30 *leaves.*

The Adages are alphabetically arranged, but the Collector, R. B., (possibly Richard Brathwaite, who was a north-countryman, although not a native of Scotland, and who did not die until 1673,) has not shown much skill in this respect, for all the Proverbs beginning with the definite and indefinite articles are placed under the letters A. and T.: thus the first proverb in the volume is, "A fair bride is soon buskt, and a short horse is soon wispt." The same objection applies to the Collection published by N. R., in 1659, 8vo, "Proverbs in English, French, Dutch, Italian, and Spanish;" from whence we might be led to conclude that they were inserted in those languages, but they are only translated, and miscellaneously printed. The work before us appears to be the earliest assemblage professedly of Scotch Proverbs, with the exception, perhaps, of that of R. Fergusson, said to have been first printed in 1598: the "Adagia in Latine and English," printed at Aberdeen in 1622, 8vo, is taken from the *Adagia* of Erasmus, with corresponding English Proverbs subjoined.

Although the work, of which the title is inserted at the head of this article, is called "Adagia Scotica," some of the proverbs are of a general kind, and belong to many countries, and to various states of society, while others are purely national. The following are a few specimens of the most characteristic: —

[1] Some of the quotations in "England's Parnassus" might be, and probably were, derived from MS.

"A teem purse makes a bleat merchant.
A man may wooe where he will, but wed where he is weard.
Biting and scarting is Scots folks wooing.
Curtesie is cumbersom to them that kens it not.
Drink and drouth comes sindle together.
Every man can rule an ill wife but he that hes her.
Fair words brake never bain, foul words many ane.
Good chear and good cheap garres many haunt the house.
He that is ill of his harbery is good of his way kenning.
Hap and a halfpennie is worlds geir enough.
It's na mair pity to see a woman greit, nor to see a goose go barefoot.
Knowledge is eith born about.
Little kens the wife that sits by the fire, how the wind blows cold in hurle-burle swyre.
Many masters, quod the Paddock to the harrow, when every tind took her a knock.
Neir is the kirtle, but neirer is the sark.
Of other men's leather men take large whangs.
Put your hand no farther nor your sleeve may reek.
Quhen thieves reckon leal men come to their geir.
Rhue and time grow both in ane garden.
Sooth bourd is na bourd.
There is little to the rake to get after the beisome.
They are good willy of their horse that hes none.
The next time ye dance wit whom ye take by the hand.
Wishers and woulders are poor householders.
Ye breed of the cat, ye would fain have fish, but ye have na will to wet your feet."

The earliest extant collection of proverbs in English is that made by John Heywood, the dramatist, printed in 1547, 4to, and many times afterwards. There are two distinct works, called "The Crossing of Proverbs," one by B. N., (probably Nicholas Breton,) in 8vo, with the date of 1616, and the other by B. R., also in 8vo, published about 1680: the latter is not a reprint of the former, but both consist of proverbs with answers to them immediately following, as:

"*Proverb.* No man can call againe yesterday.
Cross. Yes; hee may call till his heart ake, though it never come.
Proverb. Had-I-wist was a foole.
Cross. No; he was a foole that said so."

These are from "The Crossing of Proverbs," 1616, as well as the following:

"*Proverb.* The world is a long journey.
Cross. Not so; the Sunne goes it every day.
Proverb. It is a great way to the bottome of the sea.
Cross. Not so; it is but a stone's cast."

These two proverbs and crosses are found in the ballad of "King John and the Abbot of Canterbury," and in several old jest-books.

As no perfect copy of either part (for it was in two parts) of "Crossing of Proverbs" is known, we give a full transcript of the title of the first part: — "Crossing of Proverbs. Crosse-Answeres. And Crosse-Humours. By B. N. Gent. — At London, Printed by John Wright, and are to be solde at his Shop without Newgate, at the signe of the Bible. 1616." The date of the second part (imperfect, but sold in Heber's Sale, Part IV. p. 10) is the same, but it professes to have been compiled, not by B. N., but by N. B., (Nicholas Breton sometimes reversed his initials,) and was called "Crossing of Proverbs. The second part, with certaine briefe Questions and Answeres." The above will be sufficient for identification, should a complete copy ever be discovered: the popularity of the small work inevitably led to its destruction.

ADAM BELL. — Adam Bell, Clim of the Clough, and William of Cloudesle. London, Printed by A. M. for W. Thackeray at the Angel in Duck-Lane. 4to. B. L. 11 *leaves.*

There is no date to this impression of a most popular ballad in three parts, or "fits," as they were called of old, although the divisions are here marked only by spacing. A woodcut of three men occupies the centre of the title-page, the centre one with sword and target, while on his right and left stand a bow-man and a bill-man: it was used for various other pieces of the time.

It seems likely that the original edition of "Adam Bell, Clim of the Clough, and William of Cloudesley" was that, very incorrectly, printed by W. Copland: there is also an entry of it by John Kyng in the Stationers' Registers in the year 1557-58; but that impression has not come down to us, unless it be in a fragment of a single sheet, not long since discovered as the fly-leaf to another book. As far as it goes, it supplies a text vastly superior to that of Copland, which, however, has been usually adopted, and we find it repeated, more or less accurately, by James Roberts in 1605, 1616, and by Thackeray some thirty years later. Ritson, in his "Ancient Popular Poetry," 8vo, 1791, gave Copland's text, but how inferior it was to that which we may, perhaps, presume to be Kyng's, we will illustrate by a single example. Not far from the beginning of the second fit we read thus in Copland: —

"And as they loked them besyde
A paire of new galowes ther thei see,
And the justice with a quest of Squyers
That had judged Cloudesle there hanged to be."

Thackeray printed the last two lines thus: —

"And the Justice with a Quest of *Esquires*,
That judgeth William hang'd to be."

What we may call Kyng's text abolishes at once the "Quest of Squyers" and the "Quest of Esquires," and shows how the real word had been misread and misprinted: —

"And as they loked them besyde
A payre of newe galowes there they see,
And the justyce with a quest of *swerers*
That had judged Clowdysle there hanged to be."

The "swerers" were of course the *jurors*, by whom the verdict against Cloudesley had been pronounced. The other improvements, as far as the fragment extends, are so numerous and important that we cannot but lament that it goes no farther than a single sheet.

A comparison of Copland's version with Thackeray's sometimes shows the changes our language had undergone in the course of less than a century: as one proof, we may mention that when the ballad, as Copland printed it, tells us of the three heroes, that,

"They preced prestly into the hall,"

Thackeray did not understand it, and gave it

"They *proceeded presently* into the hall:"

the meaning is, that the archers *pressed instantly* into the hall. In the same way, Thackeray did not think another line would be easily understood, viz.: —

> "Where the people were most in prece,"

and therefore translated it,

> "Where the people *thickest* were."

"To prece" was of old to *press* as in a crowd, and a "prece" was a *crowd*. Not a few of Thackeray's changes seem, however, to have been purely arbitrary. He rightly added no "second part," which is very inferior and comparatively modern, having made its first appearance in the edition by J. Roberts in 1605. It is singular that nobody, not even the indefatigable Ritson, has adverted to Drayton's notice of this ballad, and of Robin Hood, in his "Idea: the Shepheard's Garland," 1593, 4to, where Gorbo tells his fellows (sign. D 3), —

> "Come, sit we downe under this Hawthorne tree;
> The morrowes light shall lend us daie enough,
> And tell a tale of Gawen or Sir Guy,
> Of Robin Hood, or of good Clem of the Clough."

Between the date of Copland's and Kyng's editions, and the date of Drayton's Pastorals, there must have been many reprints of "Adam Bell, Clim of the Clough, and William of Cloudesley," but they have probably perished. Heber (Cat. Part iv. p. 11) had an impression by T. and R. Cotes, dated 1632.

Affrican and Mensola. — A Famous tragicall discourse of two lovers, Affrican and Mensola, their lives, infortunate loves, and lamentable deaths, together with the offspring of the Florentines. A History no lesse pleasant then full of recreation and delight. Newly translated out of Tuscan into French by Anthony Guerin, domino Creste. And out of French into English by Jo. Goubourne. — At London Printed by Ja. R. for William

Blackman, dwelling neere the great North doore of Paules. 1597. 4to. B. L. 44 *leaves.*

We never saw nor heard of more than one copy of this prose romance, written in an affected style, and the languid story devoid of interest. A young shepherd named Affrican falls in love with a nymph of Diana, whom he long in vain pursues, but at length, in female attire, deflowers her, and finally kills himself. Of Mensola is born Pruneo, who is represented as the original, or "offspring," of the Florentines. The description of the half-willing and half-unwilling rape upon the heroine is sufficiently prurient, and must have constituted the chief attraction of the performance.

Of Jo. Goubourne we have no other trace, and at the close is printed "Thus endeth Maister John Bocace to his Flossolan: *Data fata secutus.*" It is dedicated by I. G. "to the vertuous gentleman Maister Fraunces Versaline": then comes an address "To the Reader health," and a page headed "The author disireth the favour of his Mistris." "A Table of Contents" gives the titles of the 18 tedious chapters of which the Romance consists. The whole merits notice only on account of its extreme rarity.

AGES OF SIN. — The Ages of Sin, or Sinnes Birth and groweth, with the stepps and degrees of Sin, from thought to finall Impenitencie. n. d. 4to. 9 *leaves.*

This work consists of nine well executed copperplates, to the last of which the initials "Ja. v. L. fecit," are attached; and, from the similarity of the style, we need not hesitate in assigning the other eight to the same engraver; perhaps Jacob van Lochem, a Dutch or Flemish artist, who produced other plates circulated in this country about the time of the Civil War, although the present series appears to be unknown. The first plate constitutes the title, which is inserted in an oval frame, and underneath it the representation of a large snake, with a number of smaller ones making their way out of its entrails. All the plates are in the nature of emblems, with engraved verses underneath, not always very intelligible, nor explanatory.

From the little connection between the engravings and some of the inscriptions, we might be led to imagine that the artist, having the plates by him, employed a person to write verses, who was not very ingenious in applying them to the subject. The following are the titles of the nine engravings: 1, Suggestion; 2, Rumination; 3, Delectation; 4, Consent; 5, Act; 6, Iteration; 7, Gloriation; 8, Obduration; 9, Finall Impenitency. No publisher's name is furnished.

AIMON, THE FOUR SONS OF. — The right plesaunt and goodly Historie of the foure sonnes of Aimon, the which for the excellent endytyng of it, and for the notable Prowes and great vertues that were in them, is no les pleasaunt to rede then worthy to be knowen of all estates bothe hyghe and lowe, n. d. fol. B. L. 197 *leaves.*

It will be seen by the following Colophon, that this copy, at least so far, differs from that described much at large by Dr. Dibdin in his "Typographical Antiquities," iii. 137. "Here finissheth the hystory of the noble and valiaunt Knyght Reynawde of Mountawban, and his three brethren. — Imprinted at London, by Wynkyn de worde, the viii. daye of Maye, and ye yere of our lorde, M,CCCCCiiii, at the request and commaundement of the noble and puissaunt erle, the Erle of Oxenforde, And now Imprinted in the yere of our Lorde, M,CCCCCliiii, the vi. daye of Maye, by Wylliam Copland, dwellyng in Fletestrete at the Signe of the Rose Garland, for John Waley."

If Dr. Dibdin be correct, in the Colophon of the copy he used, Copland omitted his place of residence as well as his sign, and it purported to have been printed for Thomas Peter, instead of John Waley. No doubt, as Dr. Dibdin suggests, a certain number of copies was struck off for particular stationers with their names appended. As in his citations Dr. Dibdin does not profess to follow the original spelling, it is impossible to ascertain from his work whether there are any other variations of typography. The Colophon certainly renders it quite clear that Wynkyn de Worde printed an edition of the Romance in 1504, although no copy of it is now known. Dr. Dibdin has not quoted the very interesting "Prologue," which gives an exact account of the origin of the undertaking, as well as of another book translated, probably, by Caxton. It is as follows, but in the second sentence there is an obvious misprint: "desyred and coveite to lerned," ought of course to be "desyred and coveited to lerne," the letter *d* having been added to the wrong word: —

"As the Philosopher in the fyrst booke of hys methafysyque sayth, y^t^ euery man naturally desireth to know and to con newe thynges. And therfore haue the Clerkes and people of great vnderstandynge desyred and coueite to lerned sciences, and to know vertues of thinges. Some by Phylosophy, other by Poetrye, and other by Historyes and cronyckes of thynges passed. And vpon these three they haue greatly laboured in suche y^t^ thanked bee God, by theyr good dylygence and laboures: they haue had greate knowledge by innumerable volumes of bookes, whiche haue be made and compyled by great studye and payne vnto thys day. And bycause that aboue all thinges the princes and lordes of hie estate and entendement desyre to see thystoryes of the ryght noble and hye vertues of the prodecessours whiche ben digne, and worthy of remembraunce of perpetuall recommendacion. Therfore, late at ye request and commaundement of the ryght noble and vertus Erle John Erle of Oxeforde my good synguler and especial lorde I reduced and translated out of Frenche into our maternall and Englyshe tongue, the lyfe of one of his predecessoures, named Robert Erle of Oxeforde tofore sayd w^t^ diuerse and many great myracles whiche God shewed for him as wel in his lyfe as after his death, as it is shewed all a longe in hys sayde booke. And also that my sayd Lorde desyreth to haue other Hystories of olde tyme passed of vertues chyualry reduced lykewyse into our Englishe tongue: he late sent to me a booke in Frenche, conteynyng thactes and faytes of warre doone and made agaynst ye great Emperour and king of Fraunce Charlemayne by ye iiii sonnes of Aymon, other wyse named in Frenche Les quatre fylz Aymon, whyche booke accordynge to hys request I haue endeuorde to accomplyshe and to reduce it into our englyshe, to my great coste and charges, as in the translatinge as in enprynting of the same, hopyng and not doubtyng but that hys good grace shall rewarde me in suche wise that I shal haue cause to pray for his good and prosperus welfare. And besechynge his said noble good grace to pardon me of ye rude and this simple worke, For accordynge to the coppy whyche he sent to me, I haue folowed as nigh as I can, and where as any defaute shall be founde I submyt me to the correccion of them that vnderstande the cronycle and hystory, besethying them to correcte it and amende there as they shall fynde faute. And I shall praye almighty God for them that so doo to rewarde them in suche wyse that after this shorte and transytory lyfe, we all may come to euerlastyng lyfe in heuen. Amen.

"Thus endeth the Prologue."

This introduction is followed by the Table of Contents, occupying seven pages, and the story commences on sign. A vi. Herbert remarked that the prologue savors strongly of the style and manner of Caxton: this is true, and it is very possible that he wrote it with a view to publication, and that he did not livo to print the work he had translated. We know that such was the case with the *Vitas Patrum*, printed by Wynkyn de Worde in 1495. This supposition will solve the whole difficulty, if we believe that Wynkyn de Worde kept Caxton's manuscript by him some years before he put it to press.

ALABASTER, WILLIAM. — A Booke of the Seuen Planets, or Seuen wandring Motiues of William Alablaster's wit, Retrograded or remoued by John Racster. — *Melius est claudicare in via quam currere extra viam.* August. — At London, Printed by Peter Short for Andrew Wise, dwelling in Paules Church-yard at the signe of the Angell. 1598. 4to. B. L. 47 *leaves.*

At the back of the title-page are the arms of Robert Earl of Essex, to whom the book is dedicated; and the writer informs us that he and Alabaster were at the same school, Westminster, and at the same university, Trin. Coll. Cambridge, under the tuition of Dr. Still (Bishop of Bath and Wells in 1598), the author of the famous early comedy, "Gammer Gurton's Needle."

The work before us is an answer to what had been published by Alabaster (or Alablaster, as the name was often spelt) on his seven motives for abandoning the Church of England, and becoming a Roman Catholic. He is the man whom Spenser has so highly lauded by name in his "Colin Clouts come home again," which was not published till 1595, although the dedication is dated 1591. Besides his "Eliseis," which Spenser mentions, and which was a Latin poem upon Queen Elizabeth, Alabaster wrote in

English some "Divine Meditations," (existing only in manuscript of the time,) consisting of seventeen Sonnets, one of which may be fitly quoted here, because it is entitled

"*Of his Conversion.*

"Away, Feare, with thy spirits! No falce fire
Which thou dost make can ought my corage quale,
Or cause me leeward come, and strike my saile.
What if the world doe frowne at my retire?
What if denial doth my wisht desire,
And purblind pittie doth my state bewayle,
And wonder crosse it selfe, and free speech rayle,
And greatnes take it not, and death sewe nigher?
Tell them, my soule, the feare that makes me quake
Is smouldering brimstone and the burning lake.
Life-feeding death, ever life devouringe,
Torments not movde, unheard, and yet still roaring,
God lost, hell found ever, never begonne,
Now bidd me into flame, from smoke to runn."

It may well be supposed that Alabaster's Latin verse was better than his English, but his intention is pretty obvious, and some corruption may be suspected. As the sonnet never found its way into print, and as no other MS. of it is known to exist, we are not in a condition either to correct the halting measure, or to elucidate the obscure meaning.

Besides Racster, of whom nothing is known beyond what he has himself told us, Dr. Roger Fenton, in 1599, published another reply to Alabaster's "Seven Motives"; and his perversion to Popery, considering his eminence and known attainments as a scholar, excited a sensation among clergy and laity. He had followed the Earl of Essex to Cadiz in the capacity of chaplain, and it was after his return that he went over to Rome. Racster's answer is entirely prose, with the exception of the following: —

"AD LECTOREM EPIGRAMMA AUTHORIS.

"*Pro captu lectoris habent sua fata libelli.*

"If Lippus read my bookes, they bleare-eyde be;
If Linx, all spots, such eiesight have those beasts.
One sees too much, another cannot see:
Mens tasts of wit be diverse, as of feasts."

Racster deals very fairly with Alabaster, for he first quotes the "Motive," and then replies to it in detail; but the argument is dull and dry, the most lively passage in the book being the following, which doubtless refers to Lord Chancellor Ellesmere, then Sir Thomas Egerton, Keeper of the Great Seal:—

"It is a rule in philosophy that *nihil agit extra sphæram activitatis suæ*, nothing by nature can worke without the circuit of his own shop or workehouse. The fishes cannot flie as birdes in the ayre; neither can the birds swim as the fishes within the water. And therefore it was pretily said of a learned lawyer of this land unto a noble warrier, when he was as loude and lusty in the Star-chamber as he used to be in the field, 'Sir, remember your selfe: we are not now in your element.'"

The date of Alabaster's birth has not been ascertained, but Racster, in 1598, calls him "a young master of artes," and we know that he was incorporated at Oxford in 1592. While he was at Cambridge, under Dr. Still, he wrote a Latin tragedy called "Roxana," which was acted in the hall of Trinity College, but not printed until 1632. After remaining some years in the Church of Rome, Alabaster reverted to his old faith, and died a Protestant, probably not long after he had printed his *Lexicon Pentaglotton* in 1637.

As Racster says that Alabaster and he were of the same College at Cambridge, we ought to meet with a notice of him in Cooper's *Athenæ Cantabrigienses*: Racster is there, II. 271, and Alabaster may have been postponed until the next volume.[1]

ALMANACKS.—Foure great Lyers, striuing who shall win the siluer Whetstone. Also a Resolution to the countriman, prouing it vtterly vnlawfull to buye, or vse our yeerly Prognostications. Written by W. P., &c.—At

[1] We once owned a valuable MS. which contained, at the end of it, various religious sonnets by Alabaster. Unfortunately we lent the MS. to a clergyman, and in some way, during the transit, Alabaster's sonnets accidentally escaped. If they should now be in the hands of any bibliographer, he will perhaps remember to whom they really belong: they were accompanied by some other rare unprinted poems of the time.

London, Printed by Robert Walde-graue, n. d. B. L. 8vo. 54 *leaves.*

Under a humorous title this is a serious attack upon the makers of Almanacs, then most frequently called Prognostications, whom Dekker and others subsequently turned into ridicule. (See *post*, Dekker's *Raven's Almanac.*) The "four great liars" are indicated by W. P., under the initials B. F. T. and D.; and he first shows their discordances by the juxtaposition of their predictions, and afterwards, under the title of "a Resolution to the countreyman," argues against the folly and impiety of such a pretended insight into the mysterious ways of Providence.

Perhaps the most remarkable production of this kind is a tract published by William Paynter, (editor of the collection of novels called *The Palace of Pleasure,*) under the title of *Antiprognosticon.* It is partly a translation from the Latin, and partly an original invective against the professors of the art of foretelling the events and prospects of the coming year. It was printed by Henry Sutton in 1560, 8vo, and is preceded by some verses by Paynter, and by "Henry Bennet Calesian." Paynter's lines are curious from the mention they make of Archbishop Grindall, as a fellow-laborer in this undertaking, although he fell under Queen Elizabeth's displeasure in 1576 for favoring such supposed prophecies. It is not at all improbable that the initials W. P., in the title-page at the head of the present article, are those of William Paynter, and that it was a renewed attack upon astrologers; but we observe that in Messrs. Cooper's *Ath. Cantab.* II. 529, it is stated that William Parys was the author of it. They, however, spell the title differently, and only say that they "suppose" him to have written it; whereas we know that in 1560 Paynter had published another tract in entire accordance with that the title of which forms the heading of the present article. We are therefore strongly inclined to give the "Foure great Lyers" also to Paynter.

AMYOT, JAMES. — The Lives of the noble Grecians and Romanes, compared together by that graue learned

Philosopher and Historiographer Plutarke of Chæronea. Translated out of Greeke into French by Iames Amyot, Abbot of Bellozane, Bishop of Auxerre, one of the Kings priuy counsel, and great Amner of Fraunce, and out of French into Englishe by Thomas North. — Imprinted at London by Thomas Vautroullier, dwelling in the Blacke Friers by Ludgate. 1579: folio, 595 *leaves.*

The first edition of the earliest English Plutarch is rare, and this copy of it is especially valuable, because it has upon the fly-leaf the only known autograph of John Offley, the friend of Izaac Walton, to whom the old fisherman dedicated his "Complete Angler" in 1653. It is supposed that Walton lived in Chancery Lane in 1632: he certainly was there in 1638, as appears by a record, not hitherto consulted, preserved in Lambeth Library: it is entitled, "The Valuation of the Rents and Tythes of the Parish of Saint Dunstants in the West, London, 7° May, 1638." We there find a return made by the clergyman of the parish, with this heading, followed by the names of the occupiers of each dwelling: —

"Chauncery Lane within the Liberties of London.

	The present Tithes.	The Annual Rent.
Isaac Walton	00. 11. 00	25. 00. 00"

With the exception of one George Tomlins, Walton lived in a house which paid the highest rent in that part of Chancery Lane. The clergyman states that in his valuation he had deducted a fourth part of the present rent, so that Izaac Walton's house really cost him £31. 5*s*. per annum. It seems that his immediate neighbors, as might be expected, were persons of no note, and the particular trades carried on are not specified. [See "Life of Spenser," 1862, I. cxxxvi.]

"North's Plutarch," as it is commonly called, (a handsome folio, published, as appears in MS. figures of the time, at 26*s*.,) was several times reprinted in the same form, with some additions, and with the same woodcuts of the heads of emperors, heroes, &c. It was dedicated to Queen Elizabeth, and North (afterwards knighted) does not profess to have gone farther than his French original: the date of the dedication is the 16th January, and of an address to the Reader the 24th January, 1579 (*i. e.* 1580), and in it North is again careful not to claim the merit of having made any part of his version from the Greek. His excellences as a translator are great, and his English is pure and vigorous. The value of the volume, in relation to Shakspeare, cannot be overstated.

It is a fine specimen of the press of Vautroullier, and he was no doubt assisted in it by Richard Field, (son to a tanner at Stratford-upon-Avon, and afterwards the printer of Shakspeare's "Venus and Adonis," 1593, and "Lucrece," 1594,) who, having been bound his apprentice in 1579, married his daughter in 1588, succeeded to his business in 1590, and used his device of the Anchor suspended by a hand from the clouds. [See Shakesp. Soc. Papers, iv. p. 36.]

Ritson omits the name of Sir Thomas North in his "Bibliographia Poetica," though well entitled to a place there for the many pieces of not ill translated poetry in his Plutarch.[1] He had produced a version of "The Morall Philosophie of Doni" in 1570: the last edition we have seen bears date in 1601, but it probably went through the press several times in the interval. (See *post*, under North.) His earliest performance was "The

[1] We quote the following specimen from his Life of Cimon, p. 533, — an inscription on a column: —

"The citizens which dwell in Athens stately towne
Have here set up these monuments and pictures of renowne,
To honour so the facts, and celebrate the fame,
Their valliant chieftaines did achieve in many a marshall game;
That such as after come, when they thereby perceive
How men of service for their deedes did rich rewards receive,
Encouraged may be such men for to resemble
In valliant acts and dreadfull deedes, which make their foes to tremble."

In an earlier Life, that of Alcibiades, p. 219, North thus quotes an attack by Aristophanes: —

"For state or common weale muche better should it be
To keepe within the countrie none suche lyons lookes as he:
But if they nedes will keepe a lyon to their cost,
Then must they nedes obeye his will, for he will rule the roste."

We have taken these specimens quite at random, as we happened to open the fine well printed volume.

Dial of Princes," from Antony Guevara, first printed in 1568, and again in 1582. Messrs. Cooper (*Ath. Cantab.* II. 350) by oversight state that the date of North's dedication of his "Plutarch" is 17 Jan. 1591, instead of 16 Jan. 1579.

ANAGRAMS. — Anagrammata Regia. In Honorem Maximi et Mansuetissimi Regis Caroli conscripta. Quibus Heroica quædam subnectuntur. Opusculum Regiis Nuptiis destinatum. Nunc verò Auctoris opera auctum et emandatum. 1626. 4to. 60 *leaves.*

This work is in Latin and English, and by an anagram upon the name of the author at the end, "I pen hony," we are led to suppose that it was John Peny, or perhaps Penny. By a chronogram at the foot of the title, it appears that it was printed in 1626, and by another on sign. E 3, that it was published by William Stansble: *Extant ista in ædibus Gulielmi Stansble.* [*Forsan* Stansbie.] The words *auctum et emendatum* seem to show that it had appeared earlier, but no other copy, even of this edition, has occurred. It is a very elaborate and tedious trifle, and could have had no sale, having been printed, probably, more for the gratification of the writer than of the reader.

The first eighteen leaves are filled by complimentary anagrams to the king and to the principal nobility, followed by this address: — "*Typographus Lectori:* Si placebunt quæ precedunt Anagrammata jucundissima, Auctoris Epigrammata tibi non invidebo." The epigrams are, however, far from meriting the praise bestowed upon the anagrams, and they are divided into *Religiosa*, *Officiosa*, and *Jocosa:* here the author makes the ordinary excuse for publication, viz., that he sent them to the press *propiorum amicorum jussu.* The religious epigrams are all of a pious character: those in the next division of the work are addressed to persons in office. One or two specimens of the *epigrammata jocosa*, most of which are in Latin only, others in Latin and English, and some in English, may be given: —

"*To a certaine Writer.*

"Halfe of your Booke is to an Index growne:
You giue your Booke *Contents*, your readers none."

"*Of Robertus.*

"Robertus when he saw Thieves hanged, then
Hee said, I 'le take *example* by those men;
And so he did, for at the next Assize
He mounts the *same* Tree for three robberies."

The following has often been repeated since, and probably was not new in 1626.

"*Of a Schoolemaster and his Scholler.*

"A Pedant ask'd a Puny, rife and bold,
In a hard frost, the Latin word for cold.
Ile tell you *out of hand*, (quoth he) for loe!
I have it at my fingers' ends, you know."

The two following are interesting on account of the poets to whom they relate. Hall was made Bishop of Exeter in 1627.

"*To Dr. Hall Dean of Worcester.*

"You in high straines have sung Gods Heavenly graces,
Which you shall sound in high and Heavenly places.
Sweet Hall, what Hallelujahs shall you sing
In Heavens high Quire to the eternall King."

"*Samuel Daniel.*

"Diceris egregius duplici tu nomine Vates;
Quam sanctus *Samuel*, quam sapiens *Daniel*.
Romanum superare potes, me Judice, Vatem;
Non tibi lasciva est Pagina, Vita proba est."

This must have been written before the death of Daniel, which happened at Beckington in October, 1619.

Anatomy of the World. — An Anatomy of the World. Wherein by occasion of the untimely death of Mistris Elizabeth Drury, the frailty and the decay of this whole world is represented. — London, Printed for Samuel

Macham, and are to be solde at his shop in Paules Church-yard, at the signe of the Bul-head. An. Dom. 1611. 8vo. 16 *leaves.*

This is an earlier edition than any hitherto discovered, that of 1612 being the first mentioned by bibliographers; and it was published anonymously in four distinct impressions, viz., of 1611, 1612, 1621, and 1625, before it was included in the 4to volume of the "Poems" of Dr. Donne, published in 1633, after his death. The subject of the tribute before us was the daughter of Sir Robert Drury, with whom Donne for some time resided, and whom he accompanied to Paris. In a letter dated from Paris, 14th April, 1612, Donne mentions that the "Anatomy of the World" had been printed. The copy at Bridgewater House consists of only 15 leaves; but sign. A is a fly-leaf, existing in another copy of 1611 very recently recovered, and making the whole tract 16 leaves, or two 8vo sheets.

Donne was at one period, before his marriage with the daughter of Sir George Moore, Secretary to Lord Chancellor Ellesmere; and some documents subscribed by Donne are preserved among the MSS. at Bridgewater House.

The variations between the first edition of these poems in 1611 (printed, perhaps, only for private distribution) and that in 1633 are not many, and they are rarely of importance; but there is an exception in the very last line of what is placed under the heading "The Anatomy of the World." In the edition of 1611 it runs thus: —

> "The grave keeps bodies, verse the same enroules;"

and the misprint, by mistaking the long *s* and *f*, might not be detected, if we did not refer to the 4to of 1633, where it stands as follows: —

> "The Grave keepes bodies, Verse the *Fame* enroules."

Dr. Donne was a poet before he had attained his twentieth year; for although his Satires are not known to have been printed until 1633, some of them were written forty years earlier, and a MS. copy dated 1593 is preserved in the British Museum — [MS. Harl. 5110]. From what he says in one of his letters dated in

1614, and from other circumstances, it may be doubted whether a now lost edition of his Satires was not then privately circulated. Francis Davison, editor of "The Poetical Rhapsody" (1602, 1608, 1611, and 1621), who died before 1620, records in an undated memorandum, that he had lent a copy of "J. Dun's Satyres" to his brother Christopher.[1] This copy might, however, have been a manuscript. They were sons to poor scape-goat William Davison, who was sacrificed for accomplishing the wish of Q. Elizabeth, as regarded the death of Mary of Scotland.

ANSWER. — An Aunswere to the Proclamation of the Rebels in the North. 1569. — Imprinted at London by Willyam Seres. Cum Privilegio. 8vo. B. L. 10 *leaves.*

We apprehend that we have to add a new name to the list of our early writers of verse, in the person of William Seres, the printer, who here put forth a production of his own on the subject of the Rebellion in the North in 1569 : it is of extreme rarity, and has hitherto been given to Thomas Norton, merely on the ground that he was unquestionably the author of an address, in prose, "To the Queene's Majesties poore deceiued Subjectes of the North Countrey." That, however, was printed by Bynneman, and not

1 In 1614 Thomas Freeman printed a collection of Epigrams, &c., under the title of "Rubbe and a great Cast," which contains the following upon Donne, (or Dunne, as the name is there spelt,) from which we may safely infer that, at that date, he had printed various poems, including some or all of his Satires, which Freeman complains were too brief.

"Epigram 84. To John Dunne.

"Thy Storme describ'd hath set thy name afloate ;
Thy Calme a gale of famous winde hath got ;
Thy Satyres short, too soone we them o'erlooke :
I prethee, Persius, write a bigger booke."

"The Storme," in the edition of 1633, p. 56, is dedicated "to Mr. Christopher Brooke," and it is immediately followed by "The Calme." The Satires contain many proofs that they were written while Elizabeth was on the throne. In a copy of the impression of 1633, now before us, the blanks are filled up in a handwriting of about the time.

by Seres, who, at the end of the piece before us, thus placed his own initials —

"FINIS qd (W. S.)
God saue the Queene."

William Seres, as the printer, would hardly have made his own initials thus conspicuous, if they had not been intended to prove that he was the author. He entered the "Answer" in his own name at Stationers' Hall, and it does no discredit to his skill as a versifier, or to his loyalty as a subject. It is not mentioned by Ames, Herbert, or Dibdin among works from the press of Seres, but in their time a copy of it was known : to present it as the work of so distinguished an early typographer gives it additional interest.

It opens, as follows, in lines of fourteen syllables divided, and with rhyme at the end of the eight-syllable line, as well as at the end of the six-syllable line.

"O Lorde! stretch out thy mightie hande
against this raging route,
And saue our Prince, our state and land,
which they doe go about
For to subuert and ouerthrowe,
and make this Realme a pray
For other Nations here to growe,
what so, like fooles, they say."

Seres does not keep up this inconvenient multiplication of rhymes, as may be seen in the subsequent portion of the "Answer" to the sixth Article of the Proclamation of the Rebels : —

"You say hir Grace is led by such
as wicked are and euill:
By whom, I pray you, are ye led?
I may say, by the Deuill.
Whom would ye poynt to leade hir Grace,
if ye might haue your choyse?
The Pope, I thinke, your father chiefe,
should haue your holy voyse;
And then she should be led, indeede,
as Lambe for to be slaine.
Wo worth such heades, as so would fee
hir Grace for all hir paine!"

Some twenty, or more, passages might be quoted from authors before Shakspeare, in illustration ot his concluding lines in "King John,"

> "Nought shall make us rue,
> If England to itself do rest but true;"

and Seres shows us that the sentiment, if not the expression, was, in fact, proverbial: —

> "A Proverbe olde, no lande there is
> that can this lande subdue,
> If we agree within our selues,
> and to our Realme be true."

The whole is written with facility, and the poem concludes quite as well as it began, continuing the address to the Rebels: —

> "Bethinke your selues, and take aduice,
> and speedily repent:
> Accept the pardon of the Prince,
> when it to you is sent.
> So may you saue your bodies yet,
> your soules, and eake your good,
> And stay the Deuill, that hopes by you
> to spill much Christian blood.
> God saue our Queene, and keepe in peace
> this Iland evermore,
> So shall we render vnto him
> eternall thanks therefore."

It is hardly to be wondered that Seres afterwards obtained for himself and his son, through the interest of Lord Burghley, the renewal of his patent (of which he had been deprived by Queen Mary) "for the printing of all primers and psalters."

ANTIDOTE AGAINST MELANCHOLY. — An Antidote against Melancholy: Made up in Pills. Compounded of Witty Ballads, Jovial Songs and Merry Catches.

These witty Poems though sometime may seem to halt on crutches,
Yet they'l all merrily please you for your charge, which not much is.

Printed by Mer. Melancholicus, to be sold in London and Westminster. 1661. 4to. 40 *leaves.*

This is clearly a Shakspearean book, not only because it mentions Falstaff by name, but because it contains two "Catches," one of which is as follows: part of it, as all will remember, is sung by Autolycus in "The Winter's Tale," A. IV. sc. 2.

"Jog on, jog on, the Foot path-way,
And merrily hen't the stile-a;
Your merry heart go'es all the day,
Your sad tires in a mile-a,
Your paltry mony bags of Gold
What need have we to stare for,
When little or nothing soon is told,
And we have the less to care for?
Cast care away; let sorrow cease,
A Figg for Melancholly!
Let's laugh and sing, or if you please,
We'l frolick with sweet Dolly."

Shakspeare only introduces the four first lines, but, as we see, there are eight others that belong to the same catch. Isaac Reed tells that the four first lines are found on p. 69 of "the Antidote against Melancholy"; but they occur in fact on p. 73.

The other Catch is mentioned in "Twelfth Night," A. II. sc. 3, where Sir Toby Belch says, "Malvolio 's a Peg-a-Ramsey, and three merry men be we:" there were several sets of words to the same tune, and in the work before us they are thus given: —

" The Wisemen were but seven, ne're more shall be for me;
The Muses were but nine, the Worthies three times three:
And three merry boyes, and three merry boyes are we.

The Vertues were but seven, and three the greater be;
The Cæsars they were twelve, and the fatal sisters three:
And three merry Girles, and three merry Girles are we."

Chappell, in his admirable work on "English Song and Ballad Music," gives different words on different authority, and does not there refer to the "Antidote against Melancholy," which, however, he had met with. The mention of Falstaff occurs on

p. 72 in a Catch, the first stanza of which runs thus characteristically: —

> " Wilt thou be fatt, Ile tell thee how
> Thou shalt quickly do the feat,
> And that so plump a thing as thou
> Was never yet made up of meat.
> Drink off thy Sack! 'twas onely that
> Made Bacchus and Jack Falstafe fatt, fatt."

We are without information by whom this collection of Poems, Ballads, Songs, and Catches was made; but Thomas Durfey, about sixty years afterwards, imitated the title, when he called his six volumes " Wit and Mirth, or Pills to purge Melancholy," 8vo, 1719–20. This " Antidote against Melancholy, made up in Pills," has not been anywhere correctly described: we shall therefore be more particular as to its contents, beginning by stating that on the title-page is a very pretty engraving in two compartments, one above the other, representing different classes, gentry and peasantry drinking and carousing, the first attended by two fiddlers, and the last by a bag-piper. No engraver's name is appended, but it is in a superior style of art, and quite as neat as anything by Marshall. Following the title-page is an address " To the Reader," in triplets subscribed N. D., at the back of which is a list of " Ballads, Songs, and Catches in this Book," twenty-three in number, besides " forty more merry Catches and Songs."

There are, in fact, only thirty-four " merry Catches and Songs," the last numbered thirty-three; but it is properly thirty-four, as twenty-two is twice repeated: they occupy the last twelve pages.

With reference to No. 5 in the list of Contents, " The Ballad on the Wedding of Arthur of Bradley," it may be remarked that nobody appears to have been aware of the great antiquity of it: it is older than the beginning of the reign of Elizabeth, and it is a scrap of a song introduced by Idleness, the Vice, in the Morality of " The Marriage of Wit and Wisdom," which has come down to us in a manuscript dated 1579: the character of the drama, however, carries us back to the reign of Edward VI., or even earlier, and " the *Kings* most royal Majesty " is mentioned in it. The oldest notice of " Arthur of Bradley " hitherto pointed out is in Dekker's " Honest Whore," 1604: Ben Jonson speaks of it in his " Bartholomew Fair," 1614; Brathwaite, in his "Strappado for the Devil," in 1615, and two lines from it are cited in Gayton's "Festivous Notes on Don Quixote," 1654. Ritson, when he printed it in his "Robin Hood" (Vol. ii. p. 210), was not aware what high claims it possesses as one of the most ancient productions of the kind in our language. Of course, in all the copies that have come down to us it is much modernized and corrupted, but the following words, from "The Marriage of Wit and Wisdom," show that no other popular production could there be intended: —

> "For the honour of Artre Bradle,
> This age wold make me swere madly."

These are words often repeated in the Ballad, as we find it in the "Antidote against Melancholy," p. 16, where it fills more than three pages. We wish that we had space for it.

If N. D., whose initials are at the end of the rhyming address "to the Reader," were the person who made the selection, we are without any other clue to his name. There is no ground for imputing it to Thomas Jordan, excepting that he was accustomed to deal in productions of this class; but the songs and ballads he printed were usually of his own composition, and not the works of anterior versifiers.

Ape, the English. — The English Ape, the Italian imitation, the Foote-steppes of Fraunce. Wherein is explaned the wilfull blindnesse of subtill mischiefe, the striuing for Starres, the catching of Mooneshine, and the secrete sounde of many hollowe heartes. By W. R. *Nulla pietas prauis.* — At London, Imprinted by Robert Robinson dwelling in Feter Lane neere Holborne, 1588. 4to. B. L. 16 *leaves.*

This extraordinarily scarce tract has been attributed to W. Rankin; but a copy (the only perfect one we ever saw) now before us, has the initials W. R., at the end of the dedication to Sir Christopher Hatton, filled up in old MS. with "W. Rowly." Now the earliest known work by Rowley bears date in 1609, whereas Rankin, or Rankins, (see *post*, under RANKIN,) was an author in 1587, and his first extant production is not, in style, very dissimilar to "The English Ape." In the dedication of it he mentions a still earlier performance, viz., "my roughcast Conceit of Hell," which he had also inscribed to Hatton, and of which we have no trace unless, as is possible, he means his "Mirrour of Monsters" under that singular title. Whether "The English Ape" be really by Rankin, or by any other writer with the same initials, we are therefore unable to decide. In the first page of it he refers to some work by him which had already failed to rouse "the generall sort" from their "dull silence," which could hardly have been the case with his "Mirrour of Monsters." Though Rankin was subsequently a writer of many verses, there is not a scrap of poetry from the beginning to the end of his "English Ape."

It is entirely directed against the proneness of the people of this country to imitate and adopt the peculiarities and fashions of continental nations, especially of the Italians: — "There is not," he says, "a vice particularly noted in any country, but the Englishman will be therein as exquisite, as if he had Nature at command for every enormity. If he be in Creete he can lye, if in Italy flatter, if in Fraunce boast, if in Scotland cloke the treachery of pretended treason; which having gathered, and fraught him selfe full of this wealthy treasure, he lovingly bringeth his merchandize into his native Country, and there storeth with instruction the false affectors of this tedious trash."

The invective is not so violent and vehement as it is affected, overwrought, and disjointed; from one end of the tract to the other we look in vain for anything but the most general abuse, illustrated by very commonplace examples drawn entirely from ancient history. In one paragraph, however, he breaks out against Englishwomen in these terms: —

"It is a woonder more than ordinary to beholde theyr periwigs of sundry collours, theyr paynting potts of perlesse perfumes, theyr boxes of slibber sauce, the sleaking of theyr faces, theyr strayned modesty and theyr counterfayte coynesse. In so much that they rather seeme Curtyzans of Venyce, then matrones of Englande, monsters of Ægypt then modest maydens of Europe, inchaunting Syrens of Syrtes then diligent searchers of vertue: these inchauntments charme away theyr modesty, and entrap fooles in folly; bewitcheth them selves wyth wanton wyles, and besotteth other with these bitter smyles."

We conclude that "these bitter smiles" ought to be "*their* bitter smiles," but it is not always easy to see at what the author is driving in his accumulation of accusations, and he does not pretend to offer any cure for the evils he points out. It may deserve remark, as a matter of language, that while he delights much in new-fangled words, he is old-fashioned enough to use the Saxon plural for houses, viz., *housen*, in several places. Before his conclusion, he cautiously admits that, notwithstanding all he has advanced, "there are in England many modest wise, godly virgines, wyves and widowes," and he especially directs admiration to Queen Elizabeth, "endelesse in glory, and matchlesse in mortall majesty." He winds up with an exhortation precisely in the same style as all the rest of the pamphlet, excepting that he intermixes a considerable spice of religious enthusiasm. There may have been two W. Rankins, one who wrote in 1587, and the other who wrote in 1598.

ARMIN, ROBERT. — A true Discourse of the practises of Elizabeth Caldwell, Ma. Ieffrey Bownd, Isabell Hall, widdow, and George Fernely, on the parson of Ma. Thomas Caldwell, in the County of Chester, to haue murdered and poysoned him with diuers others, &c. Written by one then present as witnes, their owne Country-man, Gilbert Dugdale. — At London, Printed by Iames Roberts for Iohn Busbie, and are to be sold at his shop vnder Saint Peters Church in Cornewell. 1604. 4to. B. L. 16 *leaves*.

There is no doubt that Armin, the actor, was really the author of this tract, and he prefixed an epistle stating as much, though he found it convenient to put the name of "his kinsman," Gilbert Dugdale, to it: Dugdale had been a witness on the remarkable trial to which it refers, in which a wife, Elizabeth Caldwell, was accused of attempting to murder her husband at the instigation of Jeffrey Bownd, her paramour, and with the aid of George Fernely.

We need not here enter into the circumstances of the case, but it was thought that if Armin (who had been "a common pamphleteer," as Gabriel Harvey called him, in 1593) wrote an epistolary preface to the statement of them, it would materially increase the sale. So much read and thumbed was it, that only a few copies of the tract have reached our day. Armin had been at one time (see his "Nest of Ninnies," 1608) a player in the company of Lord Chandos, (or Shandoys, as he spells it,) and it was to his widow, "Lady Mary Chandos," that he addressed his prefatory letter, regarding the crime and execution of Elizabeth Caldwell and others, in June, 1603. After briefly adverting to the facts, he proceeds thus, and it is the only passage that, for our purpose, is worth quoting: —

"We have many giddie pated Poets that coulde have published this Report with more eloquence, but truth in plaine attire is easier knowne: let fixion maske in Kendall greene. It is my qualitie to adde truth to truth, and not leasing to lyes. Your good Honour knowes Pinck's poore hart, who in all my services to your late deceased kind Lord never savoured of flatterie or fixion; and therefore am now the bolder to present to your vertues the view of this late truth, desiring you to thinke of it, that you may be an honourable mourner at these obsequies, and you shall no more doe then manie more have doone. So, with my tendered dutie, my true ensuing storie, and my euer wishing well, I do humbly commit your Ladiship to the prison of heauen, wherein is perfect freedome.

Your Ladiships ever in duty and service,

ROBERT ARMIN."

Here we see that he terms the narrative "*my* true ensuing storie," so that we are entitled to look upon the pamphlet as the production of one of Shakspeare's fellow-performers, who succeeded to Dogberry and to several of Kempe's other characters, after the latter, on the accession of James I., had gone over to the company calling itself "the Prince's Players." In the patent granted to Fletcher, Shakspeare, and others, in May, 1603, we find the name of Robert Armin substituted, as it were, for that of William Kempe.

ARNOLD'S CHRONICLE. — In this boke is conteined ye names of the baylyfs Custose mayers and sherefs of ye cyte of london from the tyme of kynge Richard the fyrst, & also the artycles of ye Chartour and lybartyes of the same Cyte, And of the chartour and lybartyes of England, with other dyuers maters good and necessary for euery cytezen to vnderstond and knowe. n. d. B. L. fol. 133 *leaves.*

This is the edition of Arnold's Chronicle, which, though without his name, came from the press of Peter Treveris, who is supposed to have been the first printer who carried on business in Southwark. Dr. Dibdin does not seem to have made up his mind whether this edition by Treveris was the earliest, or whether it had been previously printed by John Doesborowe at Antwerp; for, on p. 34, of Vol. III. of his "Typographical Antiquities," he speaks of Doesborowe's edition as "the second," and inserts, in a note on p. 35, the statement of the late Mr. Douce, that Treveris printed the second edition. There is little doubt that the latter is the correct conclusion.

It is only from similarity of type that it has been decided to be the work of Treveris, and not of Pynson, as Ames supposed. The date has been fixed in 1521, from the following paragraph at the end of the list of the mayors and sheriffs of London: —

"This yere Galy halfpens was banysshed out of england, & whete was worthe xviij. s. a quarter. And this yere one Luther was accowntyd an eretyck and on sonday that was the xii day of Maij, in the presence of the lorde legate and many other bysshops and lordys of england, the sayd Luther was openly declared an heretyck at powlys crosse, and all his bokes burnyd."

On sign. O vi., commences the celebrated ballad of "The Notbrowne Mayde," which Prior modernized, and which, with some inaccuracies, was inserted by Capel in his *Prolusions*, p. 3. Mr. Douce superintended a reprint of the whole chronicle from the edition of Doesborowe, but even he, with all his exactness, made trifling mistakes when giving the ballad. In the edition by Treveris, it frequently varies typographically from the impression by Doesborowe. Capel divided the lines differently, but in the original, and in the second edition before us, they stand precisely in this manner: —

"Be it right or wrōg, these mē amōg. on womā do complayne
Affyrmynge this, how that it is. A labour spent in vayne
To loue thē well, for neuer a dele. They loue a mā agayne.
For late a man, do what he can. theyr fauour to attayne
Yet yf a newe, to them pursue. theyr fyrst true louer than
Laboureth for nought, for from her tought he is a banysshed man."

This form of stanza is peculiar to this ballad, and no other poem which exactly adopts it is known. It seems agreed that "The Nut-brown Maid" is not older than the beginning of the sixteenth century, though Hearne, in one of his letters, printed in *Restituta*, i. p. 70, would carry it back to the time of Henry V., and Dr. Percy (*Reliques*, ii. p. 26, Edit. 1765) to the early part of the reign of Henry VII.

ARTHUR. — The storye of the most noble and worthy Kynge Arthur, the which was the fyrst of the worthyes Chrysten, and also of hys noble and valyaunt knyghtes of the rounde Table. Newly imprynted and corrected. — Imprynted at London by Thomas East. n. d. B. L. fol. 307 *leaves*.

A rare edition of the Mort Arthur, which work came originally from the press of Caxton in 1485. East's impression is without date, the Colophon running thus: "Imprinted at London, by Thomas East dwelling betweene Paules wharfe and Baynardes Castell," and it differs, as far as the text is concerned, in no material respect from the reprint previously made by William Copland from the text of Caxton: some of the woodcuts, which are placed at the head of every book, are also identical, and must have devolved into the hands of East; but others vary rather in design than in subject. On the title-page is a woodcut representing the conflict between St. George and the Dragon, but here the Knight of Cappadocia is made to pass for King Arthur. A reduced copy of it is inserted on the title-page of Southey's edition of the Mort Arthur, 4to, 1817.

A few of the woodcuts of East's edition are considerably older than the date when he printed: one of them was used by Wynkyn de Worde in 1520, before Christopher Goodwyn's poem, "The Chaunce of a Dolorous Lover." The block then came into the hands of W. Copland, and, having been used by him in his reprint of the Mort Arthur, it subsequently was in the possession of East, who applied it to the same purpose in the volume before us: it precedes the 15th book, "Of Syr Launcelot du lake," the chapter being thus headed: "Howe Sir Launcelot came into a Chappelle, where he founde dead in a whyte sherte a man of religion of an hundred wynter olde." Thus Wynkyn de Worde's "dolorous lover" served the turn, in the hands of Copland and East, to represent a dead man in a white shirt, an hundred winters old. At the time the block was employed by East it had been considerably worn and battered.

The "Prologus" is inserted on the next leaf after the title, and it is followed by "the Table" of the contents of each chapter of the twenty-one books into which the whole work is divided: it fills eleven leaves. These have distinct signatures, and the first chapter of the first book begins on A j., with a woodcut half-length of Arthur in armor, holding his sword and shield.

Somewhat less than a century after East's edition appeared, Martin Parker, the notorious ballad-poet, published an abridgment of the Mort Arthur, with the title of "The most admirable Historie of that most renowned Christian Worthy Arthur, King of Great Britaines;" (see "Parker, Martin," *post;*) and on the forefront of his life of this "Christian Worthy," he is represented as a Turkish hero, in a woodcut that had been intended, and used for the Soldan of Babylon, mounted on a plumed charger. It had also been pressed into the service of another publisher, and then it represented "the Scythian Tamerlane."

ARTHUR. — The most ancient and famous History of the renowned Prince Arthur, King of Britaine, wherein is declared his Life and Death &c. As also all the noble Acts &c. of his valiant Knights of the Round Table. Newly refined and published for the delight and profit of the Reader. — London, Printed by William Stansby for Jacob Bloome, 1634. B. L. 4to. 467 *leaves.*

This is a reprint of the Mort Arthur with certain modernizations, or, as it is worded in the title-page, "newly-refined." In an address to the reader, he is informed that the original history was written in French and Italian, and that in the ninth year of Edward IV. Sir Thomas Maleore [Malory] translated it into English. "In many places," adds the writer, "this volume is corrected, (not in language, but in phrase,) for here and there King Arthur or some of his knights were declared in their communication to sweare prophane, and use superstitious speeches, all (or the most part) of which is either amended or quite left out by the paines and industry of the compositor and corrector of the presse; so that, as it is now, it may passe for a famous piece of antiquity, revived almost from the gulph of oblivion, and renued for the pleasure and profit of present and future times." To this succeed Caxton's "Prologue" and his "Preface," and "The contents of the first part," in one hundred and fifty-three chapters. Facing the title-page is a coarse woodcut of Arthur and his Knights at the Round Table, the king making his appearance out of a large hole in the centre of it.

The second and third parts have each fresh title-pages, with a repetition of the woodcut to the first part. The second part consists of one hundred and seventy-four chapters, and the third part of one hundred and seventy-six chapters. A table of contents is prefixed to each division.

ASS. — The Noblenesse of the Asse. A worke rare, learned and excellent. By A. B. — London, Printed by Thomas Creede, and are to be sold by William Barley, at his shop in Gratious streete, 1595. 4to. B. L. 60 *leaves.*

A tract of which only three or four copies are known to be in existence. It is from beginning to end a prose burlesque in praise of the Ass, and it displays a great variety of learning and some drollery: the fault is that the joke is a little too long drawn out; for the writer seems to have been oppressed by the abundance of his materials. If it had been of an earlier date, A. B. might have been taken for the initials of Andrew Borde, the humorist and physician of the reign of Henry VIII., who called himself Andreas Perforatus, lest (as he said) any one else should call him Andreas *Assis.*

A woodcut of an Ass, with a wreath of laurel about his neck, ornaments the title-page, and is repeated in the body of the pamphlet: it is followed by an address from "Atabaliba of Peru to the Asse-favouring Readers," the reason for which is not very obvious, seeing that the Incas knew nothing of any beasts of burden but Lamas, until the arrival of the Spaniards, who, riding upon horses, were thought centaurs. Atabaliba speaks in his own person throughout, as if he were the author, and A. B. only the translator.

The production is divided into three parts, without any apparent necessity, unless to give the reader an opportunity of pausing. Several scraps of verse also lighten the page, but it is to be observed that more than one of them is derived from Berni's Italian burlesque capitolo, *In lode del Asino:* the subsequent is a specimen: —

"One other gift this beast hath of his owne,
Wherewith the rest could not be furnished;
On man himselfe the same was not bestowne:
To wit, on him is ne're engendered
The hatefull vermine that doth teare the skin,
And to the body make his passage in."

We have here amended a misprint in the last line, which runs "And to the *bode doth* make his passage in."

According to A. B. there is nothing about an Ass that is not superexcellent — even his voice comes in for an extravagant amount of praise, in the course of which the author makes use of an adjective that we have never met with elsewhere. The employment by Shakspeare and others of "modern," to indicate what is common or ordinary, is well known; but A. B. gives us *immodern* in the opposite sense. After noticing "the goodly sweete and continual brayings" of Asses, he adds, — "Nor thinke I that any of our *immoderne* musitians can deny, but that their song is full of exceeding pleasure to be heard; because therein is to be discerned both concord, discord, singing in the meane," &c. Certainly, it would require a very "immodern," or extraordinary, musician indeed to find harmony in the braying of an Ass. The allusion, at the close of the whole, to the choice by our Saviour of an ass, when he entered Jerusalem in triumph, rather smacks of the profane, and need not be quoted.

ASTROPHEL AND STELLA. — Syr P. S. His Astrophel and Stella. Wherein the excellence of sweete Poesie is concluded. To the end of which are added sundry other rare Sonnets of diuers Noblemen and Gentlemen. — At London, Printed for Thomas Newman. Anno Domini 1591. 4to. 44 *leaves.*

Newman published two impressions of Sir Philip Sidney's "Astrophel and Stella" in the same year, viz. 1591: the above is the title-page of the first, and the stationer mentions in the preliminary matter that the manuscript had come into his hands "much corrupted by ill writers." The fact is, that the corruptions are innumerable, and on this account Newman put forth his later impression. Where he obtained the corrected copy is not stated, but it seems not unlikely that the family would interpose, to rescue the memory of Sir Philip Sidney from the imputation of having produced so much nonsense as the blunders of transcribers had occasioned. Newman, however, was evidently delighted in the first instance to procure the work of so popular and famous a poet for his use, and dedicating it to "Ma. Frauncis Flower Esquire," (who perhaps had been instrumental in obtaining the MS. for him,) he employed the celebrated Thomas Nash, then, as usual, in poverty, to write an introductory epistle, and thus put forth the volume. This epistle, caustic and critical, is found nowhere else, and it will always render this edition remarkable. The later copy of the same year does not contain it, and why so readable and lively a production was excluded we can only conjecture: perhaps the Countess of Pembroke herself might object to the extravagant laudation heaped upon her in it: Nash is speaking of the Sidneys, and thus breaks out: —

"Amongst the which, fayre sister of Phœbus and eloquent secretary to the Muses, most rare Countess of Pembroke, thou art not to be omitted; whome Artes doe adore as a second Minerva, and our Poets extoll as the patronesse of their invention; for in thee the Lesbian Sappho with her lirick Harpe is disgraced, and the Laurel Garlande, which thy Brother so bravely advaunst on his Launce, is still kept greene in the Temple of Pallas. Thou only sacrificest thy soule to contemplation; thou only entertainest emptie handed Homer, and keepest the springs of Castalia from being dryed up. Learning, wisedom, beautie, and all other ornaments of Nobilitie, whatsoever, seek to approve themselves in thy sight, and get a further seale of felicity from the smiles of thy favour."

This might be rather too strong a dose of flattery even for those times of adulation, in spite of the known and admitted claims of "Sidney's sister." Various attacks upon his contemporaries were also inserted by Nash, and the Epistle opens with some severe ridicule even of his friend Robert Greene, who on his title-pages always added to his name the statement of the two Universities at which he had taken his degrees. The whole is headed,

"Somewhat to reade for them that list.

"*Tempus adest plausus aurea pompa venit:* so endes the Sceane of Idiots, and enter Astrophel in pompe. Gentlemen that have seene a thousand lines of folly drawn forth *ex uno puncto impudentiæ*, and two famous Mountains to goe to the conception of one Mouse; that have had your eares deafned with the eccho of Fame's brazen towres, when only they have been toucht with a leaden pen; that have seene Pan sitting in his bower of delights, and a number of Midasses to admire his miserable hornepipes, let not your surfeted sight, new come from such puppet play, think scorne to turn aside into this Theater of pleasure," &c.

Nash admits, however, that "his witless youth may be taxt with a margent note of presumption"; and as he was three years younger than Shakspeare, and therefore only twenty-four when he wrote the preceding epistle, we may perhaps allow his claim: still, it is to be recollected that four years earlier he had furnished the poet whom he here particularly assails, with an epistle introductory to "Menaphon," which epistle is written in a similar strain, and has given rise to as much literary speculation as some works of higher pretensions.

At the close of his Epistle, Nash leaves his readers to "the pleasures of Paphos" contained in the body of the work; but those pleasures are greatly diminished by the miserable condition of the text, with the preparation and correction of which, we may be confident, Nash had nothing to do, having left it entirely to Newman and his printer. Several sonnets by Sidney are omitted, and other poems, of a lyrical kind, are sadly mutilated and abridged. Still, much improved as was the reimpression of 1591, and the subsequent editions in folio of 1593, 1598, &c., there are defective passages in them, which even the garbled text of Newman's first edition of 1591 enables us to set right. Thus in Sonnet 64 we read in the authentic copy, —

"Nor hope, nor with another course to frame,"

where "with" ought to be *wish*, as it stands in what we may call Nash's edition. Again, in Sonnet 68, we are always told to read, —

"Seeking to quench in me the noble fire,
Fed by thy worth, and blinded by thy sight."

Here the "noble fire" was not "blinded" by the sight of Stella, but *kindled*; and it stands "kindled by thy sight" in Nash's edition. A third and more important instance occurs in Sonnet 91, where the usual text has been, —

"Milke hands, rose cheeks, or lips more sweet, more red,
Or seeing gets blacke, but in blacknesse bright."

Here "seeing gets" has been misprinted for *seeming jet*, the reference of the poet being to the brightness of polished jet.

However, these are rare instances; and if Sidney's poems had come down to us in no better condition than in Newman's earliest

4to of 1591, the loss would have been lamentable. We may partly judge from thence of the woful blunders transmitted to us in many of the productions of poets who did not enjoy, or neglected to avail themselves of, the opportunity of correcting the press of their effusions. Much was formerly left to ignorant and mechanical readers of proofs, and there is good reason to believe that many of the productions of our best versifiers came surreptitiously from the press.

Such was the case, not only with Sidney's "Astrophel and Stella," but with the whole of what follows in the impression to which Nash's epistle was prefixed. Samuel Daniel, who in 1591 had published nothing but a prose translation, had no fewer than 28 poems stolen from him, and printed without authority by Newman. Of these he inserted 23 in his "Delia," (twice printed in 1592,) where he complains of the injury thus done to him: the remaining five pieces by Daniel are only to be found in the volume under consideration.[1] Five other poems subscribed "Finis. Content," appear to be in the same predicament, and merit preservation in a more accurate state; as well as a production subscribed E. O. (Earl of Oxford), set to music in Dowland's "Second Booke of Songs or Ayres," fol. 1600. The two stanzas which wind up

[1] The reader may like to see a specimen of Daniel's subsequently excluded poems: one sonnet runs thus: —

"The slie Inchanter, when to worke his will,
And secret wrong, on some forespoken wight,
Frames waxe in forme to represent aright
The poore unwitting wretch he meanes to kill;
And prickes the image fram'd by magick's skill,
Whereby to vexe the partie day and night.
Like hath she done whose shewe bewitcht my sight,
To beauties charmes her Lover's bloud to spill;
For first like waxe she fram'd me by her eyes,
Whose rayes, sharp poynted, set upon my brest,
Martyrs my life, and plagues me in this wise,
With lingring paine to perish in unrest.
Naught could, save this, my sweetest faire suffice
To trie her arte on him that loves her best."

We are not sure whether the sprightly lines here imputed to the Earl of Oxford have ever been reprinted in modern times, (we suspect that they have been,) but we add them by way of illustration. This was the Earl

Nash's edition of "Astrophel and Stella," "If flouds of teares," &c., may be by Nash, but they are unquestionably found in a MS. in the Bodleian Library, preserved at the end of one of Bishop Tanner's curious volumes. There they would seem to belong not to Nash, but to Nicholas Breton.

AVALE, LEMEKE. — A Commemoration or Dirige of Bastarde Edmonde Boner, alias Sauage, vsurped Bisshoppe of London. Compiled by Lemeke Auale. *Episcopatum eius accipiet alter.* Anno Domini 1569. Imprinted by P. O. B. L. 8vo. 22 *leaves.*

of Oxford who had put the affront upon Sir Philip Sidney: he died in 1604. We divide the lines exactly as they stand in the original copy of 1591.

"Faction that ever dwelles in Court where wit excelles
hath set defiance:
Fortune and Love have sworne, that they were never borne
of one alliance.

Cupid, which doth aspire to be God of desire,
sweares he gives lawes;
That where his arrowes hit, some joy, some sorrow it,
Fortune no cause.

Fortune sweares weakest hearts, (the bookes of Cupids arts)
turnd with her wheele,
Senseles themselves shall prove: venter hath place in love,
aske them that feele.

This discord is begot Atheists that honor not:
Nature thought good
Fortune should ever dwell in Court where wits excell;
Love keepe the wood.

So to the wood went I, with Love to live and die,
Fortune's forlorne.
Experience of my youth made me thinke humble Truth
in desarts borne.

My Sainte I keepe to mee, and Joane her selfe is shee,
Joane faire and true:
She doth onely move passions of love with love.
Fortune, adieu! *Finis*, E. O."

Bishop Bonner died in the Marshalsea prison on the 5th of September, 1569, and this highly humorous and bitter attack upon him was doubtless published just afterwards. It is possible that the name of the author, Lemeke Avale, is only assumed. The tract is principally in verse, and in a biographical point of view extremely curious. It was obviously written and printed in haste, that the temporary interest occasioned by the death of Bonner might not subside before it was ready for publication.

"The Preface" of nine pages is chiefly directed to establish that Bonner, like Tunstal, by his bastardy was disqualified for being bishop. The *Dirige* then begins; and the rest of the tract, with the exception of about six pages at the end, is in verse of various measures, with Latin lines and half lines intermixed: thus the following is part of an address to Bonner: —

"*Custodiens parvulos dominus*, the Lorde hath helped Sion,
And taken awaie this mad dogge, this wolfe, and this Lion;
Qui erupit animam de morte, and my hart from sorowe,
Now, gentle maister Boner, God give you good morrowe.
Lorde, surely thou hast given them eternall rest
Whom Boner in prison moste sore opprest.
Placebo. Bo. Bo. Bo. Bo. Bo.
Heu me! beware of the bugge: out, quod Boner, alas!
De profundis clamavi, how is this matter come to passe?
Lævavi oculos meos from a darke deepe place.
Now, Lazarus helpe Dives with one droppe of grace.
Ne quando rapiat ut Leo animam meam, druggarde, druggarde,
To defende this matter came John Availe, and Miles Huggarde."

Miles Huggarde was a celebrated verse-maker in the reign of Mary, but of John Availe we recollect no record: he was perhaps some relation to Lemeke Avale, the supposed author of this tract. The whole is conducted in the form of Lessons and Responses, and "the fifth Lesson" commences in what has been called Skeltonic verse: —

"*Homo natus*
Came to heaven gatus.
Sir, you doe come to latus,
With your shorne patus. * * *
Thou art *filius populi*,
Go, go to Constantinopoli,

To your maister the Turke,
There shall you lurke,
Emong the heathen soules.
Sometime your shorne brethren of Poules
Were as blacke as Moules
With their cappes fower forked,
Their shoes warm corked;
Nosed like redde grapes,
Constant as she apes. * * *
Lo, lo! now is he dedde
That was so well fedde,
And had a softe bedde.
Estote fortis in bello;
Good Hardyng and thy fellowe,
If you be Papistes right
Come steale hym awaie by night,
And put him in a shrine;
He was the Popes devine."

This measure is continued for several pages. "The Eighth Lesson" opens thus: —

"My fleshe is consumed; there is but skinne and bone:
In sainct Georges Churche yarde my grave and I alone.
My tongue that used lewde woordes, and lippes awaie are rotten:
Take pitie upon me R. L., and H. let me not be forgotten."

Initials are here and elsewhere employed, when, perhaps, the writer could not venture to insert names at length. He is often coarse and abusive, and not a few of the allusions to persons and events are now unintelligible. Among other things it is said, that Crowley the printer, afterwards a preacher, delivered a sermon before the door of the Marshalsea where Bonner was confined, in hopes of converting him: —

"One morne betime I loked forth, as ofte as I did before,
And did se a pulpit, in churches wise, made by my prison dore.
A preacher there was, that Crowly hight, whiche preached in that place,
A meane, if God had loved me, to call me then to grace.
Hodie si vocem was his theme, and harden not thyne harte,
As did the fathers the rebbelles old, that perished in desarte."

In the next year was printed by John Day another tract of the same kind, called "A Recantation of Famous Pasquin of Rome," by R. W., from which it appears that John Heywood, the poet and dramatic author, was alive in 1570. It seems certain, indeed, that he was not dead even as late as 1576–77, because in a list made on 29th of January in that year, "of all such as are certified into the Exchequer to be fugitives over the seas, contrary to the stat. 13 Eliz.," the name of John Heywood is included, and he is described as "of the county of Kent." He was then resident in Louvaine, his sons, Ellis and Jasper, being with him. By mistaking the authority of Anthony Wood, (*Athenæ Oxonienses*, i. 394, edit. 1813,) it has been supposed that Heywood died in 1565. *Vide Biogr. Dram.* i. 329, and *Gen. Biogr. Dict.* xvii. 445. Wood only says that, after the decease of Queen Mary, Heywood "left the nation for religion sake, and settled at Mechlin in Brabant," and that he died there "about 1565." The earliest notice we have of him is in 1514, when he probably was one of the children of the Chapel Royal, of whom he afterwards seems to have become master. (*Hist. of Engl. Dram. Poetr. and the Stage*, i. 70.) In the King's Household Books, later in the reign of Henry VIII., he is sometimes termed "Singer," and at others, "Player on the Virginals."

BACON, FRANCIS. — The Translation of certaine Psalmes into English Verse: By the Right Honourable Francis Lo. Verulam, Viscount St. Alban. — London, Printed for Hanna Barret and Richard Whitaker &c. 1625. 4to. 11 *leaves*.

The dedication is "to his very good friend Mr. George Herbert," author of "The Temple," printed in 1633; and hence it appears that these translations had been "the exercise" of Lord Bacon's "sickness." He also thanks Herbert for "the pains it pleased you to take about some of my writings," referring to the translation by Herbert of part of the "Advancement of Learning" into Latin.

The Psalms versified are the 1st, the 12th, the 90th, the 104th, the 126th, the 137th, and the 149th, in various measures.

Among the MSS. at Bridgewater House are several letters from Lord Bacon to Lord Ellesmere, among them the celebrated epistle upon the want of a history of Great Britain, a work which Samuel Daniel afterwards undertook, but did not live to complete. (*Vide* DANIEL, *post.*) This letter has been printed in both editions of the "Cabala," but most imperfectly in all respects, and with the total omission of two very important passages. It is, therefore, here subjoined from the original, which is carefully and clearly penned, and is entirely in the handwriting of Lord Bacon. It is addressed "To the R. Hon. his very good L. the L. Ellesmere, L. Chancellor of England," and it is indorsed by Lord Ellesmere as follows: — "Sir Francis Bacon touching the story of England."

"Yt may pleas yor. good L.

Some late Act of his M. referred to some former speach which I have heard from yor. L. bredd in me a great desire, and by strength of desire a bouldnesse to make an humble proposition to yor L. such as in me can be no better than a wysh, but, if yor L. should apprehend it, may take some good and woorthy effect. The Act I speake of is the order giuen by his M. as I vnderstand, for the erection of a tomb or monument for o^{r} late Soueraine Lady Q. Elizabeth; whearin I may note much, but this at this tyme: That as her M. did alwaies right to his Highness hopes; so his M. doth in all things right to her memory — a very just and princely retribution. But from this occasion, by a very easy ascent, I passed furder; being put in mynd, by this Representative of her person, of the more true and more firm Representative which is of her life and gouvernm^{t}. For as Statuaes and Pictures are dumbe histories, so histories are speaking Pictures. Whearin if my affection be not to great, or my reading to small, I am of this opynion, that if Plutarque were aliue to write lyues by Paralleles, it would trouble him, for vertue and fortune both, to find for her a Parallele amongst wemen. And though she was of the passive sex, yet her gouvernmt was so actiue, as in my simple opynion it made more impression vpon the seuerall states of Europe, then it received from thence. But I confess vnto yor L. I could not stay hear; but went a littell furder, into the consideration of the tymes which have passed since K. Henry the 8th., whearin I find the strangest variety that in like number of Successions, of any hereditary Monarchy, hath euer been knowne: The Raign of a child, the offer of an vsurpation (though it were but as a Diary Ague) the Raign of a Lady maried to a forein Prince, and the Raign of a Lady solitary and vnmaried. So that as it cometh to pass in massive bodies, that they have certen trepidations and wauerings before they fix and settle, so it seameth that by the prouidence of God, this Monarchy, before it was to settle in his M. and his generations (in wch I hope it is now established for euer) it had these prælusive chaunges in these barren Princes. Neyther could I contein myself hear (as it is easier to produce then to stay a wysh) but calling to remembrance the vnwoorthiness of the History of England (in the main continuance thearof) and the partiality and obliquity of that of Scotland in the latest and largest Author that I have seen, I conceived it would be honor for his M. and a woorke very memorable, if this Iland of great Brittaine, as it is now joyned in Monarchy for the ages to come, so were joyned in History for the tymes passed, and that one just and complete History were compiled of both Nations. And if any man thinke it may refresh the memory of former discords, he may satisfie himself with the verse *Olim meminisse juuabit;* for the case being now altered, it is matter of comfort and gratulation to remember former troubles.

"Thus much, if it may pleas yor Lp, was in the optatiue moode. It is trew that I did looke a littell into the potentiall, whearin the hope wch I conceiued was grounded vpon three obseruations: The first of the tymes, which doe flourysh in learnyng both of art and language, wch giueth hope not onely that it may be doon, but that it may be well doon. For when good things are vndertaken in yll tymes it turneth but to losse; as in this very particular, we haue a fresh example of Polydore Virgile, who being designed to write the English History by K. Henry the 8th, (a straung choise to chuze a stranger) and for his better instruction hauing obteyned into his hands many registers and memorialls owt of the Monasteries, did indeed deface and suppresse better things then those he did collect and reduce. Secondly, I doe see that which all the world seeth in his M. both a wonderfull judgment in learnyng, and a singular affection towards learnyng and the workes of true honor, which are of the mynd and not of the hand. For thear cannot be the like honor sowght in the building of galleries, or the planting of elmes along high waies, and the like manufactures, things rather of magnificence then of magnanimity, as there is in the vniting of States, pacifying of controversies, nourishing and augmenting of learnyng and arts, and the particular actions apperteinyng vnto these; of which kynd Cicero judged trewly when he said to Cæsar, *Quantum operibus tuis detrahet vetustas, tantum addet laudibus.* And lastlie I called to mynd that yor L. at sometymes hath been pleased to express vnto me a great desire that some thing of this nature should be perfourmed, answerably indeed to yor other noble and woorthy courses and actions, whearin yor L. showeth yor self not onely an excellent Chauncello^r and Counsello^r, but also an exceeding fauorer and fosterer of all good learnyng and vertue, both in men and matters, persons and actions, joyning and adding vnto the great services towards his M. wch haue in small compass of tyme been accumulated vpon yor Lp. many other deseruings both of the Church and Commonwealth and particulars; so as the opynion of so great and wise a man doth seem vnto me a good warrant both of the possibility and woorth of this matter. But all this while I assure my self I cannot be mistaken by yor L. as if I sowght an office or imployment for myself; for no man knoweth better than your L. that (yf there were in me any faculty therevnto, as I am most vnable) yet neither my fortune nor profession would permytt it. But bycause thear be so many good paynters, both for hand and colors, it needeth but incouragement and instructions to giue life and light vnto it.

So in all humbleness I conclude my presenting to yor good L. of this wysh, wch if it perish, it is but a losse of that which is not. And thus crauing pardon, that I haue taken so much tyme from yor L. I allwaies remayn,

Your Lps very humbly and
much bounden

Graies Inne this 2d of Aprile 1605." FR. BACON.

It is very possible that Daniel was encouraged to write his history by Lord Ellesmere, in consequence of the preceding letter. The same task was subsequently assigned to Sir Henry Wotton, and a Privy Seal is extant in the Chapter House, Westminster, raising his annuity from £200 to £400 for the express purpose. This fact is not mentioned by the biographers of Wotton.

BACON, FRIAR. — The famous Historie of Fryer Bacon. Containing the wonderfull things that he did in his Life: Also the manner of his Death; with the Liues and Deaths of the two Conjurors Bungye and Vandermast. Very pleasant and delightfull to be read. *Bliidschap doet, het leuen yer Langhen.* Printed at London by E. A. for Francis Grove, &c. 1629. B. L. 4to. 26 *leaves.*

There is another edition of this production without a date, but probably posterior to the present, which itself can scarcely have been the first, inasmuch as Robert Greene made ample use of the story, in his play of *Friar Bacon and Friar Bongay*, originally printed in 1594, and written some years earlier: according to Henslowe's Diary, it was performed on the 19th of February, 1591. The tract was doubtless popular before 1590; and there is reason for supposing it to be of German invention. The motto on the title-page above inserted was omitted in the edition without date, and in subsequent reprints; but the woodcut, representing the two Friars, Miles, and the Brazen Head, was continued, and it was transferred to the title-page of Greene's play when it was republished in 1630. Miles, Friar Bacon's man, is a humorous personage, and in the woodcut he is exhibited playing on the pipe and tabor, as Tarleton and the theatrical Clowns of that day were wont to do: no doubt, this circumstance was adopted from the mode in which Greene's drama was got up and represented. Poetry and songs of a light humorous kind are interspersed with the prose, and the subsequent is no unfavorable specimen. It is sung by Miles, "to the tune of a rich Merchant man," when the Brazen Head, which he addresses, pronounces "Time was."

"Time was when thou a kettle
Wert fill'd with better matter;
But Fryer Bacon did the[e] spoyle,
When he thy sides did batter.

"Time was when conscience dwelled
With men of occupation:
Time was when Lawyers did not thrive
So well by mens vexation.

"Time was when Kings and Beggers
Of one poore stuffe had being.
Time was when office kept no knaves:
That time were worth the seeing.

"Time was a bowle of water
Did give the face reflection:
Time was when women knew no paint,
Which now they call complexion."

The tract begins with the birth of Friar Bacon, and ends with his burning his books of magic, his turning hermit, and his death. "Thus," says the author, "was the Life and Death of this famous Fryer, who lived most part of his life a Magician, and dyed a true penitent Sinner, and an Anchorite." In his *Pseudodoxia Epidemica*, Sir Thomas Brown contends that the brazen head of Bacon was "a mystical fable concerning the philosopher's great work," (p. 461, edit. 4to. 1658.)

Baldwin, William. — Beware the Cat. [Colophon] Imprinted at London at the long Shop adioyning unto Saint Mildreds Church in the Pultrie by Edward Allde. 1584. B. L. 8vo.

There were three impressions of this very singular tract, — one in 1561 (Ritson, *Bibl. Poet.* p. 118), another in 1570, and the third in 1584, which we have employed; but of the two first only fragments have come down to us, and of the last the title-page is deficient: we have therefore been obliged to derive our information respecting the printer and the date from the colophon on the last page. Although the work has been noticed by Ritson and Herbert, (*Typ. Ant.* p. 1238,) no mention is made of it in any other bibliographical work.

We are authorized in assigning it to no less an author than William Baldwin, the writer of "The Funerals of Edward VI." 1560, and of several other works, besides his contributions to "The Mirror for Magistrates," in the editions of 1559, 1563, 1574, &c. By whom the impression of "Beware the Cat" in 1561 was printed, cannot be ascertained, — perhaps by Baldwin himself, who, after having been at Oxford, became an assistant to Edward Whitchurch, the typographer, and printed, with his own name and Whitchurch's types, his translation of "The Balades of Solomon," in 1549: the edition of "Beware the Cat" in 1584 came, as we see, from the press of Edward Allde, and in some preliminary stanzas subscribed T. K. we are told that the first edition had been suppressed: —

"This little book, Beware the Cat,
Moste pleasantly compil'd,
In time obscured was, and so
Since then hath been exilde:

"Exilde because, perchaunce, at first
It shewed the toyes and drifts
Of such as then, by wiles and willes,
Maintained Popish shifts."

To nine other such stanzas succeeds a dedication "to the right worshipful Esquire John Yung," who was "maker of interludes, comedies and playes" to Henry VIII.; so that this inscription must have preceded the earliest copy of 1561. Here we meet with the first trace of authorship, for it is signed G. B., the initials of Gulielmus Baldwin; and that he wrote the volume we have the additional and conclusive evidence of a very early broadside, (in the library of the Society of Antiquaries,) but which has no date and no printer's name: it is not likely that any typographer of that day would have made himself responsible for the gross personal abuse there heaped upon William Baldwin, as an avowed enemy of Popery. This broadside must have made its appearance very soon after "Beware the Cat" was published in 1561, and in it we read as follows: —

"Where as there is a boke called Beware the Cat:
The veri truth is so, that Stremer made not that;
Nor no such false fabels fell ever from his pen,
Nor from his hart or mouth, as knoe mani honest men.
But wil ye gladli knoe who made that boke in dede?
One Wylliam Baldewine. God graunt him wel to spede!" &c.

In reference to the question of authorship it is also to be noted that there exists in the Register of the Stationers' Company an entry by Ireland, the publisher, of a "boke intituled 'Beware the Catt,'" which asserts without reserve that it was "by Wyllm Bawdwin." The entry bears the date of 1568–69, as if it were intended then to reprint it; and we know that it was actually republished by William Griffith in 1570.

We may therefore conclude without hesitation that William Baldwin was the author of "Beware the Cat," and not a person of the name of Stremer, or Streamer, who figures conspicuously all through it. The dedication to John Young, the dramatist and actor, *temp.* Henry VIII., signed G. B., opens thus: —

"I have penned for your maistership's pleasure one of the stories which M. Streamer tolde the last Christmas, and which you so faine would have had reported by M. Ferrers him selfe; and although I be unable to pen or speake the same so pleasantly as he coulde, yet have I so neerly used both the order and woords of him that spake them, which is not the least vertue of a reporter, that I dout not that he and M. Willot shall in the reading think they hear M. Streamer speak, and he him self, in the like action, shal dout whether he speaketh or readeth."

Ferrers, mentioned above, it may be remembered, was the other poet, besides Baldwin, to whom Sackville, afterwards Earl of Dorset, intrusted the completion of his design in "The Mirror for Magistrates": of Willot we know nothing, but we are led to believe that Streamer was one of those clever inventive jesters, like Skelton or Scoggin, whom Henry VIII. kept about his Court. It deserves remark also that the whole scene of "Beware the Cat" is laid in the office of John Day, the printer, over Aldersgate. Thus it curiously and interestingly carries us back to the very place, persons, and time, — the reign of Edward VI., when Baldwin, Streamer, Ferrers, Willot, Young, and others, met to spend their merry Christmas at John Day's house of business. Ferrers is expressly introduced in the book as "the Lord of Misrule," an office which we know, on other evidence, that he had filled under Edward VI. and his royal father.[1] The particular time fixed for the relation of Streamer's story is while Day's "Greeke Alphabets were in printing." Day was the great improver of Greek types.

The whole piece from end to end is nothing but a pleasant absurdity, the humor of which depends much upon personal and other allusions, which it is not easy now to explain. The attacks upon the Roman Catholics are frequent and fierce; but the main purpose of the book is to make out that Cats have speech and reason, and Streamer tells the others that he had nightly been disturbed by "catterwalling" while sleeping at Day's, the animals being attracted to Aldersgate by the savor of the many traitors' and malefactors' heads exposed upon it. By the assistance of Albertus Magnus, Streamer pretends that he compounded magical meat and drink, which enabled him to understand the language of Cats, but that afterwards he lost the faculty by returning to his old and usual diet. His narrative consists of prose and verse, but the verse is sometimes printed as prose, and in this latter form we find a singular enumeration of the confused sounds he hears and understands, while under the influence of the broths and unguents Albertus had taught him to employ: it begins, —

"Barking of dogges,
Grunting of hoggs,

[1] See, respecting George Ferrers and his employments, *Hist. Engl. Dram. Poetry and the Stage*, Vol. I. p. 151, &c.

Wauling of cats,
Rumbling of rats,
Gagling of geese,
Humming of bees,
Rousing of bucks,
Gagling of ducks,
Singing of swannes,
Ringing of pannes," &c. &c.

This is in the second part of the work, for it is divided into three portions: in the first part we meet with the subsequent remarkable passage respecting a belief, at that date, in the existence of werwolves in Ireland: —

"There is also in Ireland one nacion whereof some one man and woman are at every seven yeeres end turned into Wulves, and so continew in the woods the space of seven yeers; and if they happen to live out the time, they return to their own forme again, and other twain are turned for the like time into the same shape; which is penance (as they say) enjoyned that stock by Saint Patrick for some wickednes of their ancestors: and that this is true witnessed a man whom I left alive in Ireland, who had performed this seven yeeres penance, whose wife was slain while she was a wulf in her last yeer. This man told to many men whose cattel he had wooried, and whose bodyes he had assailed, while he was a wulf, so plain and evident tokens, and shewed such scars of wounds which other men had given him, both in his mannes shape before he was a wulf, and in his wulfes shape since, which all appered upon his skin, that it was evident to all men; yea, and to the Bishop too (upon whose grant it was recorded and registred) that the matter was undoubtedly past peradventure."

In fact, nothing was then too strange, in the shape of wildness and savagery, to be disbelieved of Ireland, and Streamer's auditors seem to have taken his assertions literally. The third part consists mainly of narratives made by Cats to each other, to which Streamer had listened; and here we are not unfrequently reminded of some portions of "Reynard the Fox," while one of the cats obtains the name of Isegrim: she seizes a man exactly in the same dangerous manner in which a cat in "Reynard" seizes a priest. The incidents are not to us very humorous, as they have lost their application, and a few of the stories seem borrowed from the Italian and French; otherwise we do not understan dhow an English cat could obtain the appellation of poylnoir, or black-skin.

One Italian tale relates to a religious old bawd, who employed herself in the seduction of the beautiful and virtuous wife of a citizen, which is accomplished, in part, by persuading the lady that the daughter of the old woman had by witchcraft been converted into a cat. The work is ended by sixteen stanzas, in ten-syllable couplets, of little merit or interest in our present state of information regarding the persons and events of the reign of Edward VI.: in one of these Streamer himself is punningly, but not very intelligibly, mentioned: the writer is addressing the Creator, —

> " Which hast given grace to Gregory, no Pope,
> No King, no Lord, whose treasures are their hope;
> But sily preest, which like a Streamer waves,
> In ghostely good, despisde of fools and knaves."

Besides the preceding important addition to William Baldwin's claims to authorship, there is a smaller one, in the shape of a ballad, (reprinted by the Percy Society in 1840,) which is subscribed G. B., and which bears the following title: —

> " A free Admonition, without any fees,
> To warne the Papistes to beware of three Trees;"

meaning the gallows, or " three-legged mare," as it was then familiarly called. This was printed by John Awdely, with the statement of the very day on which it was published, " the xij of December, 1571," about five months after the execution of Felton, who is expressly brought forward as a recent example of the crimes and punishments of Roman Catholic traitors.

BARNFIELD, RICHARD. — Lady Pecunia, or The praise of Money. Also a combat betwixt Conscience and Covetousnesse. Togither with The complaint of Poetry for the death of Liberality. Newly corrected and inlarged by Richard Barnfield, Graduate in Oxford. — Printed by W. I. and are to be sold by Ihon Hodgets, dwelling in Paules Church-yard, a little beneath Paules Schoole, 1605. 4to. 26 *leaves.*

It is no small tribute to Barnfield that two poems printed by him, or for him, in 1598, having in the next year been inserted in Shakspeare's "Passionate Pilgrim," were long thought by many to be the property of Barnfield, on account of his priority of claim. In 1598 the fine sonnet in praise of Dowland and Spenser, "If music and sweet poetry agree," and the beautiful lyric, "As it fell upon a day," were first published as Barnfield's, in a work which then bore the following title:—

"The Encomion of Lady Pecunia, or The praise of Money.—*quærenda pecunia primum est, Virtus post nummos.*—London, Printed by G. S. for Iohn Iaggard, and are to be solde at his shoppe neere Temple-barre, at the Signe of the Hand and starre. 1598." 4to.[1]

John Jaggard, who published the above, was brother to William Jaggard, who published Shakspeare's "Passionate Pilgrim," and in some unexplained manner the two poems we have designated, "If music and sweet poetry agree," and "As it fell upon a day," the authorship of our great dramatist, found their way out of the hands of W. Jaggard into those of John Jaggard; who, we may suppose, was, in 1598, on the point of publishing Barnfield's "Encomion of Lady Pecunia": there he inserted them; but they, nevertheless, made their appearance in 1599 in "The Passionate Pilgrim," by which it was made to seem as if W. Jaggard had stolen the poems from J. Jaggard, because the latter had printed them as Barnfield's in the year preceding. The reverse was, however, the fact; and the matter stood thus doubtfully until the year 1605, when Barnfield, (perhaps partly on this account,) putting forth a new impression of his "Encomion" under a different title, and with many important changes, expressly excluded from that reimpression the two poems, which he knew did not belong to him, and which he presumed were the property of Shakspeare.

[1] In giving the title of Barnfield's "Encomion of Lady Pecunia," the words "Horace. By Richard Barnfield, Graduate in Oxford," have by a strange accident been omitted. It may be questioned whether John Jaggard were brother or son to William Jaggard: there was an Isaac Jaggard, who followed the business of a stationer about the same date.

Hence the especial value of the second edition of the "Encomion," since it may be said to ascertain that John Jaggard, wishing to swell Barnfield's small volume in 1598, did so by inserting in it two pieces that did not belong to the author of the rest. The second edition of Barnfield's "Encomion," under the title of "Lady Pecunia, or the praise of Money," was not known at all until a comparatively recent date; and still more recently it was discovered that it did not contain the poems to which Barnfield seemed to have the earliest title. In 1605 Barnfield was too honest to retain what had been improperly attributed to him in 1598. The Sonnet and the Poem are therefore not to be traced in the volume in our hands, which forms part of the Library at Bridgewater House.

As the earliest impression was accurately reprinted for the Roxburghe Club in 1816, it is hardly necessary here to say more about it, than that in 1598 it was made especially applicable to Elizabeth and her reign. In 1605 all the lines mentioning or alluding to her were omitted or altered to suit the altered circumstances of the time: thus, for a passage, heaping well-worded adulation upon the queen, we meet with the following, which extravagantly applauds her successor, and forms the 37th and 38th stanzas of the main poem, which is headed "Lady Pecunia": —

"But now more Angels than on Earth yet weare
Her golden impresse, haue to Heaven attended
Her Virgin-soule: now, now, she sojornes there,
Tasting more joyes then may be comprehended.
Life she hath changde for life, (oh, countlesse gaine!)
An earthlie rule for an eternall Raigne.

"Such a Successor leaving in her stead,
So peerelesse worthie, and so Royall wise,
In him her vertues live, though she be dead:
Bounty and Zeale in him both soveranize.
To him alone Pecunia doth obay;
He ruling her that doth all others sway."

Barnfield proceeds in the same strain for three other stanzas. It is a very clever poem, and it is not surprising that it was popular, although no other copy of this edition is known, and those of 1598 are of the utmost rarity. The subsequent are four stanzas from an earlier part of "Lady Pecunia," numbered severally 16, 17, 18, and 19 : —

"But now unto her praise I will proceed,
Which is as ample as the world is wide.
What great Contentment doth her presence breed
In him that can his wealth with Wisdome guide!
She is the Soveraine Queene of all Delights:
For her the Lawyer pleads, the Souldier fights.

"For her the Merchant ventures on the seas;
For her the Scholler studies at his booke;
For her the Usurer (with greater ease)
For silly fishes lays a silver hooke;
For her the Townsman leaves the country village;
For her the Plowman gives himselfe to tillage.

"For her the Gentleman doth raise his rentes;
For her the Servingman attends his mayster;
For her the curious head new toyes invents;
For her to sores the Surgeon lays his playster:
In fine, for her each man in his Vocation
Applies himselfe in every sev'rall Nation.

"What can thy hart desire, but thou mayst have it,
If thou have ready money to disburse?
Then, thanke thy Fortune that so freely gave it,
For of all friends the surest is thy Pursse.
Friends may prove fals, and leave the in thy need,
But still thy purse will be thy friend indeed."

"Lady Pecunia" consists of 56 such stanzas, followed by "the Author's Prayer to Pecunia," and by "The Combat betwixt Conscience and Covetousness in the minde of Man," a sort of Dialogue, in couplets, occupying four leaves. "The Complaint of Poetry," &c. (which in the copy of 1598 precedes "The Combat," &c.) is in 45 stanzas, concluding with "A comparison of the Life of Man," in seven lines. On the last page, in 1605, is the following remarkable "Remembrance of some English Poets," viz., Spenser, Daniel, Drayton, and Shakspeare.

"Live Spenser ever, in thy Fairy Queene,
Whose like (for deepe Conceit) was never seene:

Crownd mayst thou be, unto thy more renowne,
(As King of Poets) with a Lawrell Crowne.

" And Daniell, praised for thy sweet-chast verse:
Whose Fame is grav'd on Rosamond's blacke Herse:
Still mayst thou live, and still be honoured,
For that rare worke, the White Rose and the Red.

" And Drayton, whose well-written Tragedies,
And sweet Epistles, soare thy fame to skies,
Thy learned Name is equall with the rest,
Whose stately Numbers are so well addrest.

" And Shakespeare, thou, whose hony flowing vaine,
(Pleasing the World) thy Praises doth containe;
Whose Venus, and whose Lucrece (sweet, and chast)
Thy name in Fame's immortall Booke have plac't,
Live ever you, at least in Fame live ever:
Well may the Body die, but Fame die never."

These verses vary only literally in the two editions of 1598 and 1605. The whole work is introduced by eight dedicatory lines, not addressed to any particular person, and by two pages of prose " to the gentlemen Readers," in which Barnfield mentions his " Cynthia." In the Epistle before that poem, printed in 1595, he speaks of his " Affectionate Shepherd " as his " first-fruit." " Cynthia " was his second production; and the tract under review his third. It is now ascertained that Barnfield was not the author of " Greene's Funerals," 1594, attributed to him by Ritson and others. In the introductory matter to his " Cynthia," he mentions that a second book had been falsely assigned to him, probably referring to " Orpheus his Journey to Hell," 1595, to which his initials R. B. seem to have been fraudulently affixed.[1]

Barnfield's " Praise of Money," in 1598, was, no doubt, the occasion of a poem called " The Massacre of Money," by Thomas Achelley, in 1602, for an account of which see p. 9.

[1] The full title of " Orpheus his Journey to Hell " is this, — " Orpheus, his Journey to Hell, and his Musicke to the Ghosts for the regaining of faire Eurydice, his Love and new spoused Wife. By R. B." 4to. 1595. We cannot say that the " music to the ghosts " is very seductive, and his

BARTHOLOMEW FAIR. — Bartholomew Faire, or

Variety of fancies, where you may find
a faire of wares, and all to please your mind.

With the severall Enormityes and misdemeanours, which are there seene and acted. — London, Printed for Richard Harper at the Bible and Harpe in Smithfield. 1641. 4to. 4 *leaves.*

Although very few of them have come down to us, the Registers of the Stationers' Company bear witness that, almost annually, some new publication was issued to attract buyers who frequented Bartholomew Fair: the title of one of these we have placed at the head of the present article; but we will first advert to another production of the same class, which was entered at Stationers' Hall as early as July 16th, 1607, in anticipation of the fair, which at that period commenced on the 24th August. Only a fragment of it has been preserved, which has no title-page (it is possible that it never had one) and no conclusion, but which is headed "Newes from Bartholomew Fayre," and is wholly in verse. Its existence has only recently been pointed out, and it has never been examined. In the entry at Stationers' Hall it is attributed to Richard West, who was also author of "The Court of Conscience, or Dick Whippers Sessions," 4to, 1607, — a piece *in pari materiâ*, though not especially addressed to the visitors of Bartholomew Fair. It is fortunate that this imperfect specimen has been saved from destruction, but it is a large fragment, consisting of 12 4to pages, and thus opens: —

"Those that will heare any London newes,
Where some be merrie, and some do muse,

---

song before Pluto and Proserpine is not much better, each stanza ending with *Quod Amor vincit omnia.* We quote a stanza, specially addressed to Pluto: —

"Thou great Commaunder of this Court,
Triumphant victor over Death,
To whom so manie soules resort,
When pale-fac'd death gins stop their breath,
Witnesse the trueth of this I say,
Quod Amor vincit omnia."

And who hath beene at Bartholomew Faire,
And what good stirring hath beene there,
Come but to mee, and you shall heare,
For among the thickest I have beene there."

And so West proceeds, in a different measure, to enumerate many of the commodities, sold in the fair more than 250 years ago, viz.: —

"There double beere and bottle-ale
In everie corner hath good sale:
Many a pig, and many a sow,
Many a jade, and many a cow:
Candle rushes, cloth, and leather,
And many things came in together:
Many a pound and penny told,
Many a bargain bought and sold,
And tavernes full in every place."

Taverns lead West to dissert upon noses, especially red ones, acquired in taverns; and he laments especially the loss by death of *Nos maximus omnium* in a merry jumble of nonsense, which however contains various popular and personal allusions: —

"The Can maker cried, as if he had bin mad:
O sticks and stones, brickbats and bones!
Briers and brambles,
Cookes shops and shambles!
O fishers of Kent,
Heycocks and bent!
O cockatrices and hernshawes that in woods do dwell!
O Colliers of Croydon,
O rusticks of Roydon!
O Devills of hell!
O pewterers and tinkers,
O swearers and swinkers,
O good ale drinkers!" &c.

He assigns different places, at the funeral of *Nos maximus omnium*, to noses of all descriptions, who, in spite of the sad ceremony, are to meet and be merry, exclaiming, —

"Hang him at Wapping
That will not tipple and be merry,
With a nose as red as a cherry.
Hey! over the ferry

Into Bucklers berry,
Where good men be dwelling,
That have sugar selling
To make claret wine
In the goblet to shine;
And make noses fine,
Like thy nose and mine."

The whole is a mere piece of Skeltonical drollery, calculated to please the frequenters of the fair; and it goes through the process of the mock funeral with spirit and vivacity, but with no great coherency or distinctness of purpose. We have stated that the fragment is unfinished, for although the word *Finis* is appended at the bottom of p. 12, it is very evident that it was not printed from types of the time, but is a comparatively modern insertion, to make some incautious buyer believe that the piece was perfect. The last line —

"With bromestalkes and bay berries, the Divell and all,"

has in fact nothing to rhyme with it, and the sense is left incomplete.

We believe the above to be unique; [1] but such is not the case

[1] Playford's "Pleasant Musical Companion," 1701, supplies us with two Bartholomew-Fair songs, showing the nature of some of the sights and entertainments there nearly two centuries ago. The earliest of these is called "The Second Part of Bartholomew Fair," and the music to it was by the famous Dr. John Blow. It runs as follows: —

"Here are the rarities of the whole fair!
Pimperle-Pimp, and the wise Dancing Mare.
Heres valiant St. George and the Dragon, a farce,
A girl of fifteen with strange moles on her ——
Here is Vienna besieg'd, a rare thing,
And here is Punchinello, shown thrice to the King.
Ladies mask'd to the Cloysters repair,
But there will be no raffling — a pox take the Mayor!"

This proves that at the commencement of the eighteenth century masked Ladies used to frequent the cloisters of Christ Church, and that the Lord Mayor had interposed to put an end to gambling there. The siege of Vienna, in a show, affords a curious note of time. The next piece is called merely "A Catch," and no author of the music is mentioned: its contents are still more singular and amusing: it carries us back to the date of Charles II., as is proved by the mention of Jacob with the quarto sheet, the title of which we have placed at the head of this article, but which title Lowndes, and his successor, (edit. 1834, p. 120, edit. 1857, p. 124,) have divided into two, as if the first portion belonged to one tract, and the last to another. They are in fact one and the same, as we have given them, with a woodcut in the centre of a conjuror about to swallow a serpent. It goes into a general description of the fair and of all that belonged to it in 1641, observing, "Bartholomew Fair begins on the twenty fourth day of August, and is then of so vast an extent, that it is contained in no lesse then foure severall parishes, namely, Christ Church, Great and Little Saint Bartholomewes, and Saint Sepulchres." Stow tells us that it was originally confined to the churchyard of St. Bartholomew, "closed in with walls, and gates locked every night, and watched for safety of men's goods and wares." ("Survey," 1599, p. 309.) We will only quote from the pamphlet before us what the anonymous writer says regarding the portion of the fair held in Smithfield: it is not deficient in humor:—

Hall, the famous rope-dancer, who was so great a favorite with the Duchess of Cleveland.

> "Here's that will challenge all the Fair!
> Come buy my nuts and damsons, my burgamy pear!
> Here's the *Whore of Babylon*, the Devil and the Pope!
> The Girl is just a going on the rope!
> Here's *Dives and Lazarus* and *the World's Creation!*
> Here's the Dutch woman; the like's not in the nation.
> Here is the booth where the tall Dutch Maid is!
> Here are bears that dance like any ladies!
> *To-ta, to-ta-tot* goes the little penny trumpet!
> Here's Jacob Hall that can jump it, jump it.
> Sound, Trumpet, sound! A silver spoon and fork:
> Come, here's your dainty Pig and Pork!"

Although it has no relation to Bartholomew Fair, we cannot refuse a place to the following bacchanalian Catch, "words by Mr. Otway," which may, however, have been elsewhere printed:—

> "Would you know how we meet o'er our jolly full bowls,
> As we mingle our liquors we mingle our souls,
> The sweet melts the sharp, and the kind sooths the strong,
> And nothing but friendship grows all the night long.
> We drink, laugh, and gratify every desire:
> Love only remains, our unquenchable fire."

"Let us now make a progresse into Smithfield, which is the heart of the Faire, where, in my heart I thinke, there are more motions in a day to be seene, then are in a terme in Westminster Hall to be heard. But whilst you take notice of the severall motions there, take this caution along with you: let one eye watch narrowly that no one's hand make a motion into your pocket, which is the next way to move you to impatience. The Faire is full of gold and silver drawers. Just as Lent is to the Fishmonger, so is Bartholomew Faire to the Pick-pocket. It is his high harvest, which is never bad, but when his cart goes up Holborne."

i. e., on its way from Newgate to Tyburn.

About this date, we may observe, that the word "pick-pocket" was superseding its equivalent *cut-purse;* for people began to carry their money in their pockets, instead of wearing their purses at their girdles. Both these tracts contain much that illustrates Ben Jonson's "Bartholomew Fair," which was acted in the interval between the publication of the one in 1607, and of the other in 1641.

BASKERVILLE AND SAVILE. — A Libell of Spanish Lies: Found at the Sacke of Cales; discoursing the fight in the West Indies, twixt the English Navie, being fourteene Ships and Pinasses, and a fleete of twentie saile of the king of Spaines; and of the death of Sir Francis Drake. With an answere briefely confuting the Spanish lies, and a shorte Relation of the fight according to truth, written by Henrie Savile Esquire, employed Captaine in one of her Majesties Shippes in the same service against the Spaniard. And also an Approbation of this discourse by Sir Thomas Baskervile, then Generall of the English fleete in that service: Avowing the maintenance thereof, personally in Armes, against Don Bernaldino, if hee shall take exceptions to that which is heere set downe, touching the fight twixt both Navies, or justifie that which he hath most falsely reported in his vaine Printed letter. Proverb 19, ver. 9, &c. — London Printed by John Windet, dwelling by Pauls

Wharfe at the signe of the Crosse Keyes, and are there to be solde. 1596. 4to. 27 *leaves.*

This is a very long title to a short widely printed pamphlet, of great rarity and of much historical importance. It relates to the voyage of Drake and Hawkins to the West Indies in 1595, during which they both died. Afterwards the command seems to have devolved upon Sir Thomas Baskerville, who had been appointed only "General at land." During the attack upon Cadiz, under the Earl of Essex and others, a printed letter from Don Bernaldino Dalgadillo de Avellaneda fell into the hands of the British forces: Don Bernaldino had commanded a Spanish fleet in the West Indies, while the English ships were there; and claiming a victory, or at least the merit of putting the fleet, then under Baskerville, to flight, he wrote to that effect to a friend in Spain, Don Pedro Florez, commencing with a statement which he had obtained, as he said, from an Indian, of the death of Drake of grief and disappointment at Nombre de Dios. Now, it happened that Drake died off Portobello, of a flux (or *flixe*, as Savile spells it) which "had growne uppon him eight days before"; it proved mortal.[1]

[1] Several pieces were published on the death of Sir Francis Drake; but the most popular, as well as the best, was by Charles Fitzgeffrey, under the title "Sir Francis Drake, his honorable Life's Commendation, and his tragicall Death's Lamentation," of which two editions appeared in 1596: in the second edition it is stated that it had been "newly printed with additions," the additions being to the commendatory poems. The work has been reprinted in modern times, but very unsatisfactorily, because not only is the spelling of nearly every word altered, but some are totally misrepresented; as, for instance, "all" is changed to *that*, "lightend" to *lighted*, when the poet's meaning is *enlightened;* and even the rhyme is sometimes deserted: when Fitzgeffrey wrote and printed,

> "For he that sings of matchlesse Drake hath neede
> To have all Helicon within his braine,"

the printer altered "neede" to *new*, making nonsense of the passage, and leaving the word "reede," at the close of the preceding line, without any rhyme. These errors are near the commencement, but we have not had patience to go through the whole of the 101 pages, of which the reprint consists. As Fitzgeffrey was a very ambitious, vigorous, and often striking poet, we will quote, in his own words, his address to the great

This letter of Don Bernaldino was most joyfully welcomed in Spain, and instantly printed; and coming to the knowledge of Captain Savile, who had commanded the Adventure in the West Indian voyage, he undertook to answer it, point by point, beginning with the false statement of the cause and place of death of Drake, and insisting further, that the Spanish ships of war were twenty, while the force of the English was far inferior, and that the latter had compelled the former to sheer off, and to avoid an action, which the English challenged.

At the back of the title is a woodcut of a sphere, and then comes a brief address "to the courteous Reader." Next we have an introduction, on one page, to a reprint of the letter of Don Bernaldino in Spanish, informing us that it had been "found at the sacking of Cales." The Spanish original fills eight pages, and its translation as many; and to them (after a page of farther

dramatists of his day, in which he calls upon them to abandon inferior subjects, and to celebrate the name and achievements of Drake.

"O you, the quaint Tragedians of our times,
Whose statelie shanks embuskend by the Muses
Draw all the world to wonder at your rimes,
Whose sad Melpomene robs Euripides
And wins the palme and price from Sophocles,
While Poe and Seine are sicke to thinke upon
How Thames doth ebbe and flowe pure Helicon:

"Who at your pleasures drawe, or else let downe
The floud-hatches of all spectators' eies,
Whose full braind temples, deckt with laurell crowne,
Ore worlds of harts with words doe tirannize,
To whom all Theaters sing plaudities,
While you with golden chaines of well-tun'd songes
Linke all mens eares and teares unto your tongues:

"Cease to eternize in your marble verse
The fals of fortune-tossed Venerists
And straine your tragicke Muses to rehearse
The high exploites of Jove-borne Martialists,
Where smoakie gun-shot clouds the air with mists,
Where groves of speares, pitch'd ready for the fight,
Dampe up the element from Eagles sight."

That Fitzgeffrey had Shakspeare in his mind when he wrote the above is evidenced by the fact that he almost quotes one of our great dramatist's lines, (1 Henry IV. A. II. sc. 1,) with the alteration of the word "flood-hatches" for *flood-gates*. It is the earliest allusion to the play.

explanation) is subjoined Savile's brief answers to each of the six Spanish lies. A narrative, headed, " The Meeting of our English Navie and the Spanish fleete, and the order of our encounter," follows upon seven pages, subscribed Henrie Savile; and the last four pages consist of " Thomas Baskervile, Knight, his approbation to this Booke."

This last is a composition of a singular character, and not inconsistent with the chivalrous nature of some of the incidents of warfare in those times; for, after Baskerville has borne testimony to the truth of Savile's representation, he ends with a challenge of Don Bernaldino to a personal encounter. " I then saye," he observes, " that hee falsely lyed; and that I will maintain against him, with whatsoever Armes he shall make choyce of," in any " indifferent kingdom." Baskerville adds that if he should be employed by the Queen in France, he sees no reason why Don Bernaldino should not meet him there to settle the question. This is signed " Finis. Tho. B.," and a ship of war in full sail fills up a blank near the bottom of the last page.

We have described this historical tract the more minutely, because we are not aware that the contents of it have been previously noticed — certainly not in the ordinary biographies of Drake and Hawkins.

BASSE, WILLIAM. — Great Brittaines Sunnes-set, bewailed with a shower of Teares. By William Basse. — At Oxford, Printed by Joseph Barnes. 1613. 8vo.

It is singular that a man who wrote lines on the death of Shakspeare, (not however printed in the folio 1623, as Dr. Bliss erroneously states in his edit. of Wood's *Ath. Oxon.* iv. 222,) who put forth the above poem on the demise of Prince Henry, who contributed verses in the "Annalia Dubrensia," 1636, and made a MS. collection of his poems under the title of " Polyhymnia," intending them for the press, should not have attracted more attention from bibliographers: even the title of his " Great Brittaines Sunnes-set " has been absurdly misquoted, and called " Summer-set," as if the island had taken to vaulting on the death of Prince Henry.

Wood informs us that Basse was "sometime a retainer to the Lord Wenman of Thame Park," Oxfordshire, and his poem, the title of which is at the head of the present article, is inscribed "to his honourable Master Sr Richard Wenman, Knight." It is merely a fragment, consisting of eight pages, but it is the whole that has been preserved: it is in what the Italians call *ottava rima*, only a single stanza on each page numbered 5, 6, 7, 8, 13, 14; but with the peculiarity, that the two lines which conclude the octave consist of twelve syllables each: thus, in st. 8 we read as follows, where Basse calls his Muse "young," as if he were inexperienced in poetry, though his lines are smooth enough: —

"Here then run forth, thou river of my woes,
In cease lesse currents of complaining verse;
Here weepe (young Muse) while elder pens compose
More solemn Rites unto his sacred Hearse:
And as when happy earth did here enclose
His heav'nly minde, his fame then Heav'n did pierce;
Now He in Heav'n doth rest, now let his Fame earth fill;
So both him then possess'd, so both possesse him still."

In fact, tolerably easy versification, with thoughts naturally becoming the subject, but without any great originality, are all we can discover in the relic before us, which terminates with this stanza: —

"Like a high Pyramis, in all his towers
Finish'd this morning, and laid prostrate soone;
Like as if Nights blacke and incestuous howers
Should force Apollo's beauty before noone:
Like as some strange change in the heav'nly powers
Should in hir full quench the refulgent Moone;
So He his daies, his light, and his life here expir'd,
New built most sun-like bright, ful man and most admir'd."

The preceding stanza, we are inclined to think, is about the worst of those that here remain to us. We have mentioned above that Basse collected some of his scattered pieces — apparently for the press, because they were regularly dedicated in MS. to Lady Bridget Countess of Lindsey, under the title of "Polyhymnia." This must have been late in Basse's life, as one of the poems is dated June 19, 1648, and another is addressed to Lady Falkland on her journey into Ireland. The volume was lent to us nearly forty years ago by its then owner, Mr. Heber, but it contained no production of any great merit or interest. The longest was a species of unexplained allegory, entitled "The Youth in the Boat," and what seemed its purpose was set out in the three following introductory stanzas: —

"When we our young and wanton houres
Have spent in vaine delight,
To shew you how celestiall powers
At length can set us right;

"How they can frame our mindes unfixt
Unto their just directions,
When waveringly we reele betwixt
Opinions or affections;

"How fatall it may sometimes prove
Unto our frayle estate,
Vainely to hate what we should love,
And love what we should hate."

The sonnet to Lady Falkland on her going to Ireland is ingenious, but far below excellence: it is this: —

"What happy song might my Muse take in hand,
Great Lady, to deserve your Muses care?
Or skill to hold you in this amorous land,
That held you first, and holds you still so deare?
Must needs your anchor taste another sand,
Cause you your praise are nobly loth to heare?
Be sure your praises are before you there,
How much your fame exceeds your Caracts sayle:
Nay, more than so; your selfe are every where
In worth, but where the world of worth doth fayle.
What boots it, then, to drive, or what to steere?
What doth the axle or the oare avayle,
Since whence you ride you cannot part away,
And may performe your voyage, though you stay."

This production savors more of an age of conceit than of genius, and the style is nearer the time of Charles II. than of Elizabeth. Basse seems to have been of a sporting, rather than of a sportive turn of mind, and he has several pieces of a racing character, both of bipeds and quadrupeds: one is upon a contention between two

Irish footmen, who executed twenty-four miles in three minutes less than three hours. In other poems, upon horse-racing, or horse-coursing, as it was then called, he mentions the names of many favorites of that day, — Crop-ear, Friskin, Kill-deer, Herring, Pegabrig, etc. He bears testimony to the pains, even then, taken with the breeding of horses: —

> "These prov'd themselves from Pegasus derived:
> There doth the northern spur oft draw a rayne
> From the fleet flanks of Barbary or Spayne,
> And wilde Arabia, whose tincture dyed
> Greene earth with purple staynes of bestiall pride."

Perhaps, in the second line above, we ought to read *vayne, i. e.* vein, for "rayne": the handwriting was obviously that of a copyist, and not of Basse himself. The following lines, near the end, show that such had been the early subjects of his verse, of which we do not find a printed trace, and it was hardly to be expected, in what he wrote in 1613 on the death of Prince Henry: —

> "Lo! but too ofte of man and horse, when young,
> The naked heele and hammered hoofe I sung;
> Which now to heare, or reade, might please some men,
> Perchance, as youthful now as I was then."

Basse's lines, headed "An Epitaph upon Shakespeare," were not printed until 1633, when they were erroneously assigned to Dr. Donne. (See Donne's Poems, 4to, 1633, p. 149.) They had then been long in circulation in MS., as by Basse, to whom they really belong; and they had the honor of being alluded to by Ben Jonson, in his noble poem, prefixed to the folio 1623, "To the Memory of my beloved, the Author, Mr. William Shakespeare." We apprehend that pieces attributed to William Bas, printed in 1602, (see Lowndes's B. M. edit. 1857, p. 126,) were not by Basse, who had spoken of his "young Muse" in 1613.

BASTARD, THOMAS. — Chrestoleros. Seven bookes of Epigrames written by T. B.

> Hunc novere modum nostri servare libelli,
> Parcere personis: dicere de vitiis.

Imprinted at London by Richard Bradocke for I. B. and are to be sold at her shop, &c. 1598. 8vo. 95 *leaves.*

The dedication to Sir Charles Blunt, Lord Mountjoy, is subscribed at length "Thomas Bastard"; and, consistently with the motto on his title-page, the author says of his work, "I have taught Epigrams to speak chastlie; besides, I have acquainted them with more gravity of sense, and barring them of their olde libertie, not onelie forbidden them to be personall, but turned all their bitternesse rather into sharpnesse." According to an Epigram upon Bastard by Sir John Harington, printed in 1615, but no doubt written soon after *Chrestoleros* first appeared, the author was at the time in orders, and credit is there given to him both for his design and execution: —

> "And this I note, your verses have intendment,
> Still kept within the lists of good sobriety,
> To work in men's ill manners good amendment."

These lines and others are addressed to "Master Bastard, a Minister, that made a pleasant Book of English Epigrams." In 1615, Bastard published some Sermons, he then having the living of Bere-Regis, Dorsetshire; but it seems that he subsequently was imprisoned for debt, and died in 1618. No doubt, he brought out his *Chrestoleros* in 1598, to relieve his present necessity, although he complains that he could find no printer who would give him a fair price for it. The Epigram (21 Liber i.), in which he mentions this fact, is one of the best in the volume.

> "*De Typographo.*
> "The Printer, when I askt a little summe,
> Huckt with me for my booke and came not nere;
> Ne could my reason or perswasion
> Move him a whit, though all things now were deere.
> Hath my conceipt no helpe to set it forth?
> Are all things deere, and is wit nothing worth?"

The Epigrams extend over a considerable space of time, from about the year 1580 downwards; but there is some reason to think that Ritson erred when (Bibl. Poet. 126) he noticed an edition of 1584. None such is now known; and if it ever existed, it could not have contained much that was printed in 1598, referring to events long subsequent to 1584. It appears from Epigr. 4 of Liber ii., inscribed to Sir Henry Wotton, that Bastard resided and wrote chiefly in the country. Epigr. 6 of Liber vi. is addressed —

"*Ad Thomam Egerton, equitem, Custodem Magni Sigilli.*

"Egerton, all the artes whom thou dost cherish
Sing to thy praises most melodiously,
And register thee to eternitie,
Forbidding thee, as thou dost them, to perish:
And artes praise the[e] and she which is above,
Whom thou above all artes dost so protect,
And for her sake all sciences respect;
Arts soveraigne mistresse, whom thy soule doth love.
Thus you as stars in earth and heaven shine,
Thou hers on earth, and she in heaven thine."

The following is addressed to a poet of considerable celebrity in his day, of whom we have no printed remains: it shows the nature of his productions. It is Epigr. 27 of Liber iii.:

"*Ad Richardum Eeds.*

"Eeds, onely thou an Epigram dost season
With a sweete taste and relish of enditing;
With sharpes of sense and delicates of reason,
With salt of witt and wonderfull delighting;
For, in my judgement, him thou hast exprest
In whose sweet mouth hony did build her nest."

BAXTER, NICHOLAS. — Sir Philip Sydneys Ourania, That is Endimions Song and Tragedie Containing all Philosophie. Written by N. B. — London Printed by Ed. Allde, for Edward White, and are to be solde at the little North doore of Saint Paules Church, at the signe of the Gun. 1606. 4to. 52 *leaves.*

Our main object in speaking of this very dull and elaborate work is to prove that it does not belong to Nicholas Breton, to whom it has always been attributed, but to Nicholas Baxter; and our authority (which we, many years ago, communicated to the late Rev. Joseph Hunter) is a copy of the work signed, and throughout corrected, by the author, now before us.[1] In different places he also puns upon his own name as *Tergaster*, and calls an adversary Baxtero-mastix.

He claims at one time to have been tutor to Sir Philip Sidney, and to have been in favor with the Countess of Pembroke and her family; but, for some unexplained cause, having forfeited her patronage, he had penned some portion of his "Ourania" in Wood-street Counter. We apprehend that he was in the Church, although he nowhere states the fact distinctly: under his pastoral name of *Endimion* he admits his obligations to John Stone, Esq., "Secondary of the Counter in Wood-street," while he was in confinement there for debt.

The main body of Baxter's poem is an explanation, in couplets, of all branches of natural philosophy; and he informs us that while he was piping as a shepherd in some part of Wales, he was accosted by Cynthia (*i. e.* Lady Pembroke) and her attendant Nymphs, who asked him to sing them a song, which lasts through 76 pages. He had rather a strange notion of harmony of versification, although he seems to have been well acquainted not only with Sidney, but with Spenser and Drayton. Of the last he was a special admirer, twice praises his "Owl," 1604, and, what is more remarkable, gives us the information that Drayton had written a poem on the death of Sidney. It has, we apprehend, been lost with various other similar elegies, and must have preceded anything by Drayton that has come down to us. Speaking of Sidney's fate, Baxter's words are,

"O, noble Drayton! well didst thou rehearse
Our damages in dryrie sable verse,"

adding as a note in the margin, "Drayton upon the death of S. P. S." This novel fact alone is sufficient to give value to Baxter's "Ourania." As may be supposed, he is extremely discursive in

[1] It is but fair to the memory of that excellent antiquary, the Rev. Joseph Hunter, to say, that we are not sure whether he was not the first to point out the fact that Nicholas Baxter was the author of the work entitled "Sir Philip Sidney's Ourania," 1606. We think that we confirmed his statement by the production of our volume, signed and corrected by Baxter, which we subsequently lent to him.

his long-drawn-out philosophical dissertation, or "song," and in many places attempts to be severe and satirical: thus, to Usurers, he says:—

"You dampne your selves and sweare that money's scant,
But rich commodities you shall not want,
That certaine money presently will yeeld
If he be skilfull to marshall the field:
Silks and velvets at intollerable price,
Embroydered Hangars, Pepper and Rice,
Browne paper, Lute-strings, buckles for a saddle,
Periwigs, Tiffany paramours to waddle," &c.

This is only the old story, told in prose long before by Nash and other sufferers. The main body of the tract is introduced by nine pages of seven-line stanzas, and as many stanzas and pages follow it, but we cannot say that the stanzas are any improvement upon the couplets. About the middle of the work we meet with a notice of Dr. Muffet by name, together with high praise of his poem, "Silkworms and their Flies," 1599, for which see *post*, under MUFFET.

BEAUMONT, FRANCIS.—Salmasis and Hermaphroditus. *Salmacida spolia sine sanguine et sudore.*—Imprinted at London for Iohn Hodgets: And are to be sold at his shop in Fleete-street, at the signe of the Flowre de Luce, neere Fetter-lane. 1602. 4to. 20 *leaves.*

Only two copies of this edition are known: one of them is in the Bodleian Library, and the other before us. The Rev. Mr. Dyce, in his edition of Beaumont and Fletcher's Works, admits that he had never seen it, (xi. p. 441,) and contented himself with the later impressions. The name of Beaumont nowhere appears in the first edition of 1602; and an examination of it, compared with impressions of 1640 (see the next article), 1653, and 1660, leads to the belief that he was in no way, and at no time, concerned in it.

The attribution of it to him seems to have been merely a bookseller's trick, for the purpose of securing a more ready sale. "Salmasis and Hermaphroditus" was, we see, originally published in 1602, and without the slightest mark of authorship; but when it appeared again in 1640, "printed by Richard Hodgkinson for W. W. and Laurence Blaikelocke," it was accompanied by various other pieces, all stated on the title-page to be "by Francis Beaumont, Gent." In order to give an appearance of truth to this statement, the initials F. B. were appended to the anonymous verses which in 1602 introduce "Salmasis and Hermaphroditus"; and not only so, but other preliminary verses "to the Author," signed A. F. in 1602, were altered in 1640 to I. F., as if to show that Beaumont's friend, John Fletcher, had borne testimony to their authorship and excellence. Another edition, much enlarged, was published by Blaikelocke in 1653; and the trick against Beaumont having been played with success in 1640 and 1653, in 1660 a farther and bolder experiment, of the same kind, was tried by the same bookseller; for then the very same poems, not even reprinted, were put forth with a new title-page, as "the golden Remains of those so much admired Dramatick Poets, Francis Beaumont and John Fletcher." "Salmasis and Hermaphroditus" was then accompanied by many additional poems, which, though assigned to Beaumont and Fletcher, were in fact by other authors of the time, from Ben Jonson to Waller.

Francis Beaumont is stated to have been born in 1586, so that at the date when "Salmasis and Hermaphroditus" first appeared he was only sixteen; and although it is by no means impossible, it seems improbable that at so early an age he should have written so elaborate a production. We are to bear in mind also, that it was originally printed without claim on the part of anybody to have been the author of it.

In the edition of 1602 the introductory and commendatory verses are thus arranged: 1. A Sonnet "To the true patronesse of all Poetrie, Calliope," which has no initials at the end of it. 2. Another Sonnet, *In laudem Authoris*, subscribed W. B. 3. A third Sonnet, "To the Author," with the initials I. B. 4. Three six-line stanzas, "To the Author," by A. F. 5. Ten lines, "The Author to the Reader," without signature. These, with the title-page, occupy the four first leaves, and "Salmasis and Hermaphroditus" commences sheet B. We are, of course, not prepared to assert definitively that it is not by Beaumont, and perhaps in a note to Shakspeare (edit. 1858, I. cxvi.) too positive an opinion is expressed against its authenticity.

Without touching further upon the preliminary matter, in which there are several important blunders in Blaikelocke's editions, such as "half-mad" for *half-maid*, &c., we will notice a few of the gross misprints in the body of the poem. First of all, the copy of 1602 enables us to restore the following couplet, entirely omitted in all subsequent impressions: —

> "Nor took she painted quivers, nor a dart,
> Nor put her lazy idlenesse apart."

They occur on sign. C 2 b of the copy of 1602. In a subsequent line two errors have obscured, or altered, the poet's meaning, for instead of reprinting

> "That should proceed from thy thrice radiant sight,"

Blaikelocke gave it —

> That should proceed from thy *chief* radiant *light;*

and no later editor has seen, or attempted to correct, the nonsense. Further on, the line —

> "If any wife with thy sweet bed be blest,"

is altered to

> If *any's wish* with thy sweet bed be blest.

Elsewhere we have *tippling* substituted for "tickling," *lively* for "shamefac'd," *white* for "moist," *mere* for "neare," and many other blunders, which render the impressions of 1640, 1653, and 1660 not only trustless, but worthless; independently of the original and unscrupulous fraud of imputing the poem to Beaumont, who, most likely, never had anything to do with it.

BEAUMONT, FRANCIS. — Poems: by Francis Beaumont, Gent. viz. The Hermaphrodite, The Remedie of Love, Elegies, Sonnets, with other Poems. — London, Printed by Richard Hodgkinson for W. W. and Laurence Blaikelocke, and are to be sold at the signe of the Sugar-loafe next Temple-Bar in Fleet-street. 1640. 4to. 39 *leaves.*

This is the fraudulent edition to which we have referred in the preceding article, and in which certain changes were made in the preliminary matter, in order to induce the belief that Beaumont was really the author of the volume. This is impossible, since it includes several pieces written by King, Randolph, &c.; and two others, upon indisputable evidence now first afforded, do not belong to Beaumont.

After two Elegies, one "on the Lady Markham," the other anonymous, we arrive at certain miscellaneous poems, the first of which is called "A Charme," in six four-line stanzas, beginning,

"Sleepe, old man, let silence charme thee," &c.;

and at the end of it Henry Lawes (who gave the book, with notes and a MS. inscription, to the Earl of Bridgewater) has placed the initials H. H., with this addition in his own handwriting: "this coppy of verses was made by Henry Harrington, and set by Henry Lawes, 1636." Again, on sign. 1. 4, we meet with a poem called "Loves freedome," at the end of which Lawes wrote "H. H.: this song was made by Henry Harrington, and set by Henry Lawes, 1636." As far, therefore, as these pieces are concerned, the evidence is conclusive. On sign. K is Bishop Earle's, Elegy on Beaumont, which seems to have been designed to end the volume; but, as there were still a few spare pages, the printer added two other poems, one of them "an Epitaph" on a lady who had married a relative, and the other the celebrated piece headed "a Sonnet," and commencing, —

"Like a ring without a finger
Or a bell without a ringer," &c.

We have a MS. copy of this poem, presenting some curious variations from the printed text.

BENDISH, SIR THOMAS.—Newes from Turkie or a true Relation of the passages of the Right Honourable Sir Tho. Bendish, Baronet, Lord Ambassadour with the Grand Signieur at Constantinople, his entertainment and reception there. Also a true discourse of the unjust proceedings of Sir Sackville Crow, former Ambassadour there &c.—London, Printed for Humphrey Blunden &c. 1648. 4to. 19 *leaves.*

This is an attack upon Sir Sackvile Crow for making exactions from the British merchants, for producing pretended credentials from the king, &c., until he was superseded at Constantinople by Sir Thomas Bendish. The address to the reader is subscribed W. L., who had access to the original but uninteresting documents, which he prints in the body of the tract.

BERNERS, LORD.—Arthur of Brytayn. The hystory of the moost noble and valyaunt knyght Authur of lytell brytayne, translated out of frensshe in to englushe by the noble Johan bourghcher knyght lorde Barners, newly Imprynted, n. d. B. L. fol. 179 *leaves.*

The words "Arthur of Brytayn" are upon a scroll, immediately under which is the title more at large, and, beneath that, the figure of a knight and his esquire, both armed and on horseback. The colophon is as follows: "Here endeth the hystory of Arthur of lytell Brytayne. Imprynted at London in Powles churche yeard at the sygne of the Cocke by Roberte Redborne."

Only one other perfect copy of this romance appears to exist, and the late Mr. Utterson made his reprint of it in 1814, partly from his own defective exemplar, and partly from Lord Spencer's complete one. No other work bears the name of Robert Redbourne as the printer, and it is impossible to fix the date of it with any precision. The types are old and worn, the execution slovenly, and the woodcuts, which are numerous, coarse and uncouth. The best of the latter represents the hero on the title-page, which had also been used by Wynkyn de Worde for "Richard Cœur de Lion," in the romance of that name, printed in 1528.

The Prologue, headed "Here foloweth the translatours prologue," is at the back of the title-page, in which Lord Berners says: — "Wherefore after that I had begon this sayd processe, I haue determined to haue left and gyuen vp my laboure, for I thoughte it sholde haue be reputed but a folye in me to translate beseming such a fayned mater, wherin semeth to be so many vnpossybylytees." However, he called to mind the numerous volumes of the same kind that he had read, and concluding "that this present treatyse myght as well be reputed for trouth as some of those," he finished his undertaking, "not presumynge," he adds, "that I haue reduced it into fresshe, ornate, polysshed englysshe, for I knowe my selfe insuffycyent in the facondyous arte of rethoryke, nor also I am but a lerner of the language of frensshe."

The *Tabula*, or heads of the one hundred and seventeen chapters into which the work is divided, fills the next five leaves, when we arrive at the romance itself, beginning with the birth of Arthur, who was the son of a Duke of Britain, (or Brittany,) by a daughter of the Earl of Leicester. "Afterward," we are told, "he grew to be the moost fayre creature that than was founde in all crystendome." The woodcut representations of him do not exactly accord with this description of the hero.

The last folio in the volume should be clxxiv, but it is, in fact, only numbered lxix, and other errors of the same kind occur.

Best, George. — A true Discovrse of the late voyages of discouerie, for the finding of a passage to Cathaya, by the Northweast, vnder the conduct of Martin Frobisher Generall: Deuided into three Bookes. &c. — At London, Imprinted by Henry Bynnyman, seruant to the right Honourable Sir Christopher Hatton Vizchamberlaine. *Anno Domini* 1578. 4to. B. L. 88 *leaves.*

The extreme scarcity of copies of this work, and the want, therefore, of the means of comparison, have prevented bibliographers from noting a singular circumstance connected with its original publication.

The fact is, that the dedication by George Best to Sir Christopher Hatton, as it was first printed, was cancelled, and in the copy we have used the cancelled dedication has been preserved, and no other substituted. There, one passage, beginning "name of God hath not once bin hearde of," and ending "and of governement good for any good place of service," consisting of fifteen lines, has been inserted twice over, making utter nonsense of the whole. This blunder rendered it necessary that the dedication should be reprinted; and in the Grenville copy in the British Museum, and in one other we have had an opportunity of examining, it has been reprinted. In a single paragraph no fewer than eighteen variations, of more or less importance, exist, one of them being the insertion of the epithet "notable" before "discoveries," where it is said, in the first copy, "wee may truely inferre that the Englishman, in these our dayes, in his discoveries to the Spaniarde and Portingale is nothing inferior."

As we have mentioned the book chiefly for the sake of recording this peculiarity, we may take the opportunity of describing the copy in our hands, in order that others may be able to make the comparison, if an exemplar should ever fall in their way. At the back of the title-page begins an account of "What commodities and instructions may be reaped by diligent reading of this Discourse": it occupies two pages, and at the back of sign. A ij are the Hatton arms, faced by the commencement of the dedication filling 8 pages, the third page, by mistake, being marked Aiij, instead of Aiiij. An address, "The Printer to the Reader," begins upon b iij, and occupies four pages, "The fyrst Booke of the first voyage of Martin Frobisher" commencing sign. C and numbered p. 1. This part of the volume runs on to p. 52, when we arrive at "A true Reporte of such things as hapned in the second voyage of Captayne Frobysher," &c. It runs on, with a fresh pagination, to p. 39, after which comes a map; and then "The thirde voyage" begins, also with a fresh pagination, from 1 to 68, at the bottom of which is the printer's colophon, "At London, Printed by Henry Bynnyman. Anno Domini. 1578. Decembris 10." A second map is unfortunately wanting in our copy.

Bevis, of Hampton. — Syr Beuis of Hampton. Newly Corrected and amended. — London, Printed by William Stansby. n. d. B. L. 4to. 34 *leaves.*

This romance was originally printed by Pynson, afterwards by William Copland, and thirdly by Thomas East: the edition before us, (of which no other exemplar seems to be known,) like the three which preceded it, has no date, but made its appearance about 1620. In "Henry VIII." Act I. Scene i., Shakspeare mentions Bevis, and it is not unlikely that the allusion was occasioned by the recent appearance of an edition of the romance, — not, of course, the present, because it is considerably more modern than the time when, according to plausible conjecture, "Henry VIII." was originally brought out.

Fourteen woodcuts are inserted in different parts of the volume. The edition by Copland is in many respects a modernization of that of Pynson, which came out perhaps thirty or forty years before it; and this edition by Stansby is a further modernization of Copland's text, which preceded it perhaps sixty or seventy years. To save room, Stansby printed two of Copland's lines as only one, thus, —

"Listen, Lordlings, and hold you still, of doubtie men tell you I will."

Sometimes, apparently from oversight, he left out couplets, as in the first page, where Copland says, —

"While Sir Guy was younge and light
Knowen he was a doughty knight."

Similar omissions by Stansby are not unfrequent. The manner in which the romance was altered, to suit the taste of readers of the day, may best be seen by comparing one or two passages, which will at the same time afford specimens of the poem itself. When Sir Guy, the father of Bevis, goes out to kill a wild boar in a wood, where he is treacherously slain by Sir Murdure, Copland describes it as in our first column, and Stansby as in our second: —

"The Erle a courser gan stryde,
His swerde he hanged by his side:
There myght no man with him rynne
He was the formest man therin.

"The Earle a Courser gan bestride,
His Sword he hanged by his side:
There might no man with him rin
He was the formost man therein.
Alas, that he had beene aware

Alas, that he had beware
Of his enemies that there were!
Whan he came to the forest
He gan chase after the beest,
That him herde syr Murdure,
And escryed Guy as a traytoure,
And pricked out before the hoost
For pompyng pryde to make great boost;
And to syr Guy gan he saye,
Yelde thee, traytoure, for by my faye,
Thou and thy sonne both dede shalbe
For the love of my lady free;
For I her loved or thou her knewe:
Yf thou her haue it shall the rewe."

Of his enemies that were there!
But when he came to the Forrest
And was in chase after the beast,
Him thought he heard Sir Murdure
Cry aloud, Sir Guy, thou Traytor!
And pricked out before his hoast
With promping pride and great boast:
And to Sir Guy thus did he say,
Yeeld thee, Traytor, for by my fay,
Thou and thy sonne both dead shall be
For the love of thy Lady free:
For I her loved or thou her knew,
Yet thou her hast and shalt it rew."

We take, as another extract from Copland, the description of Josian, the beautiful daughter of the Pagan King Ermine, who fell in love with Sir Bevis; and, as before, we place opposite to it Stansby's modernization.

"The kinge Ermine of that land
His wife was dead I understand:
He had a doughter fayre and bryght,
Josian that fayre mayde hight.
Her visage was whight as lylly floure,
Therin ranne the rede coloure,
With bright browes and eyes shene,
With heare as golde wire on the grene,
With comly nose and lyppes swete,
With louely mouth and fayre fete,
With tethe white and euen sette,
Here handes were swete as vyolet;
With gentell body withouten lacke,
Well shapen both belly and backe,
With smale handes and fingers longe;
Nothing of her was shapen wronge."

"The King Ermine of that land
His wife was dead, I understand:
He had a daughter faire and bright;
Josian that faire maiden hight.
Her visage was white as lilly flower,
Therein ranne the red colour,
With bright browes and eyes sheene,
Her haire as gold-wire was seene:
With comely nose and lips full sweete,
Lovely mouth and fine feete:
Her teeth white and even set;
Her hands were white as violet:
With strait body withouten lacke,
Well shapen both of belly and backe,
With small hands and fingers long;
Nothing of her was shapen wrong."

Stansby keeps about the same distance, in point of style, from Copland that Copland kept from Pynson; so that, notwithstanding the changes, and the frequent substitution of known for obsolete words, the romance of Sir Bevis, as printed by Stansby, must have read with "a considerable smack of antiquity," even in 1620, if we suppose it to have been printed about that year. The divisions of the chapters, and the titles of them, are nearly the same in Copland's and Stansby's editions. How both vary from Pynson, and from the MS. in Caius College, may be seen by comparing what is above given with the extracts in vol. ii. p. 95 of Ellis's "Specimens of English Metrical Romances," edit. 1811.

BIESTON, ROGER. — The bayte & snare of Fortune. Wherin may be seen that money is not the only cause of mischefe and vnfortunate endes, but a necessary mean to mayntayne a vertuous quiet lyfe. Treated in a dialoge betwene man and money. — Imprinted at London by Iohn Wayland at the signe of the Sunne ouer against the Conduite in Flete-strete. *Cum priuilegio per Septennium.* Fo. B. L. n. d. 10 *leaves.*

Wayland seems to have ceased business in the year that Elizabeth came to the throne; at least no book by him, with a date, is later than 1558, and he did not begin before 1537: in that interval "The bayte and snare of Fortune" made its appearance. The name of the writer is given on the last page in an acrostic, Rogerus Bieston, and he was possibly the ancestor of the family of Beeston, some members of which were connected with our poets, plays, and theatres until the Restoration. The acrostic has no other value than to give the author's name, but the dialogue between Man and Money is not without shrewdness and humor; and though the rhyme is complex, the eight-line stanza Bieston employs runs easily. Money says of herself: —

> "No lorde there is, lady, nor chorle of kynde,
> What for my power and wyse circumspeccion,

That they ne beare to me a lovinge mynde,
And gladly wold lyve under my proteccion.
What man of hym selfe, by myght or wise inspeccion,
Without my mean can wurke a worthy deede?
None doubtles, for I set all in good direccion:
Who lacketh money is not lyke to spede."

To which, among other things, Man replies: —

"In all the lawes and bookes many one,
I fynde how thou art roote of all mischief:
Through thee many a wyght hath misgone,
For unto man thou art so deare and lyef,
That he becummeth a robber, and a thyef,
For thee, forsaking God and all goodnes,
And hanged is at last for thee, with great repryef:
This wage he winneth by thy worthynes."

"Repryef" here, of course, does not mean what we now call *reprieve*, but *reproof*—the shame that attends merited punishment by the gallows. We ought to have mentioned that the poem is preceded by the author's "Prologue," in prose, where he maintains that avarice is the beginning of all the mischief in the world: it is placed, to save room, at the back of the title-page. Barnfield's "Encomion of Lady Pecunia" (*ante*, p. 58) and Achelley's "Massacre of Money" (*ante*, p. 9), respectively printed in 1598 and 1602, followed up the same subject, but in a somewhat different spirit and purpose.

Blenerhasset, Thomas. — A Direction for the Plantation in Ulster. Contayning in it sixe principall thinges: viz. 1. The securing of that wilde Countrye to the Crowne of England. 2. The withdrawing of all the charge of the Garrison of men of warre. 3. The rewarding of the olde Servitors to their good content. 4. The meanes how to increase the Revenue to the Crowne with a yearely very great somme. 5 How to establish the Puritie of Religion there. 6. And how the undertakers may with securitie be enriched.

Imprinted at London by Ed. Allde for John Budge, dwelling at the great South doore of S. Paules Church. 1610. 4to. 16 *leaves.*

In both editions of Lowndes the title only consists of the first line, and that is incorrectly given; and in both it is said that "Blenerhasset was one of the writers in the 'Mirror for Magistrates.'" This is true, but it was not the same Blenerhasset who wrote the above tract; but a much older man, who in 1582 had published what he called "A Revelation of the true Minerva."[1] The younger Blenerhasset tells us himself that he was "a playne Country-man and one of the Undertakers in Fermannagh." It is not necessary to enter into his project for "securing the wild Countrye" of Ireland to the Crown, further than to say that he recommends (like Spenser, some fifteen years earlier) the employment of bodies of soldiers to protect the settlers, "which soldiers at stated times should issue out, and scour the country round for many miles." By a note in the margin it appears that he wishes this proceeding to be called "Hassets Hunt." He divides his name, at the end of the dedication to Prince Henry, into two portions, Blener Hasset —Thomas Blener Hasset.

BODENHAM, JOHN. — Bel-vedére, or The Garden of the Muses.

Quem referent Musæ viuet dum robora tellus,
Dum cœlum stellas, dum vehet amnis aquas.

Imprinted at London by F. K. for Hugh Astley, dwelling at Saint Magnus corner. 1600. 8vo. 137 *leaves.*

[1] The fact is, that, as early as 1578, Thomas Blenerhasset, or Blener Hasset, published his "second part" of the work, and we give the full title of this separate contribution to the same design: "The Seconde part of the Mirrour for Magistrates, conteining the falles of the infortunate Princes of this Lande. From the Conquest of Cæsar, unto the commyng of Duke William the Conquerour. — Imprinted by Richard Webster, *Anno Domini*, 1578. Goe straight and feare not." This motto is at the bottom of an architectural compartment; and the author's Epistle to his unnamed friend is dated 15th May, 1577. The work contains twelve Legends.

The chief collector of the materials for this work was John Bodenham, of whom little more is known than that he also exercised his taste in the selection of the productions contained in "England's Helicon," 1600 and 1614, (reprinted in 1812.) They are, however, essentially different; for "England's Helicon" consists of entire poems, by various authors whose names are given, while "Bel-védere" is made up of single lines and couplets (more being studiously avoided) taken from the works of a long list of poets, whose names are not found in connection with any of the extracts. Bodenham confined himself to productions in ten-syllable verse, for none longer, nor shorter, are to be found in his volume. In what he calls "the Conclusion," which precedes the index, he gives a hint that he was assisted in the undertaking: — "The Gentleman who was the cause of this collection (taking therein no meane paines him-selfe, besides his friends labour) could not be perswaded, but determinately aimed at this observation," viz., the rejection of anything that could not be brought into a line or a couplet.

In order to adhere to this plan, if sometimes four consecutive lines presented themselves, forming two complete couplets, Bodenham did not scruple absurdly to separate them by lines from a different author. We have a remarkable instance of this practice (not hitherto pointed out) on pp. 178, 179, where we meet with the following: —

> " *There's nought so vile that on the earth doth live,*
> *But to the earth some speciall good doth give.*
> Good is the end that cannot be amended.
> Where good is found, we should not quit with ill.
> *There's nought so good, but strain'd from that faire use*
> *Revolts to vice, and stumbles on abuse.*"

The four lines in Italic everybody will recollect in "Romeo and Juliet," Act II. sc. 3, and they are consecutive, both in reason and in fact, but it did not suit Bodenham's friend's views so to print them. Now and then he took similar pains to avoid even a couplet, so that lines, intended by the author to run together, are separated. On p. 29, for instance, we read, —

"Where both deliberate, the love is light.
True love is mute, and oft amazed stands.
Who ever lov'd, that lov'd not at first sight?"

Here the first and third lines form a consecutive couplet, which will be easily recognized, not only because they are by Marlow ("Hero and Leander," Sest. 1), but because the last line is quoted by Shakspeare in "As you like it," Act III. sc. 5.

"Dead shepherd! now I find thy saw of might;
Who ever lov'd, that lov'd not at first sight."

The poets to whom Bodenham, in his preface, admits his obligations are these: — Thomas [Henry] Earl of Surrey, Marquess of Winchester, Countess of Pembroke, Sir Philip Sidney, Earl of Oxford, Ferdinando Earl of Derby, Sir Walter Raleigh, Sir Edward Dyer, Fulke Greville, Sir John Harrington, Edmund Spenser, Henry Constable, Samuel Daniel, Thomas Lodge, Thomas Watson, Michael Drayton, Sir John Davies, Thomas Hudson, Henry Locke, John Marston, Christopher Marlow, Benjamin Jonson, William Shakspeare, Thomas Churchyard, Thomas Nash, Thomas Kidde, George Peele, Robert Greene, Joshua Sylvester, Nicholas Breton, Gervase Markham, Thomas Storer, Robert Wilmot, Christopher Middleton, Richard Barnfield, Thomas Norton, George Gascoigne, Francis Kindlemarsh, Thomas Atchlow, George Whetstone. He adds that the last five are "deceased," but others whom he calls "modern and extant Poets," such as Spenser, Constable, Watson, Marlow, Peele, and Greene, were also dead before 1600, when "Bel-vedére" was published.[1]

The work came to a second edition in 1610, but the first part of the title, "Bel-vedére," was then, for some unexplained reason, dropped.

BODENHAM, JOHN. — Englands Helicon. —

Casta placent superis, pura cum veste venite,
Et manibus puris sumite fontis aquam.

[1] This is a mistake as regards Constable, who did not die until after 1604, when he wrote to the Earl of Shrewsbury from the Tower. See Mr. W. C. Hazlitt's edit. of Constable's "Diana," 1859, p. xiv.

At London, Printed by I. R. for Iohn Flasket, and are to be sold in Paules Church-yard, at the signe of the Beare. 1600. 4to. 95 *leaves.*

This first edition of an admirable and popular poetical miscellany is extremely rare, especially in the state of the copy before us; in which several names upon printed slips have been pasted over others for which they were substituted after the book came from the press, showing that mistakes had been discovered in the first instance, which were detected, and rather clumsily corrected, in some of the later copies.

We know that the collection was edited by John Bodenham from a preliminary sonnet addressed to him by a person who subscribes it A. B., which in terms imputes to him also "Wits Commonwealth," 1598, "Wits Theatre," 1598, "The Garden of the Muses," 1600, and, finally, "Englands Helicon," 1600.

Although the second edition of "Englands Helicon," in 1614, was reprinted by Sir E. Brydges and Haslewood in 1812, the first impression has never been sufficiently noted. As our copy differs in some respects from others, (as far as we have had an opportunity of examining them,) a few words may be acceptable on some of the separate poems; with the aid, moreover, of MS. Harl. 280, (in the handwriting of Francis Davison, editor of "The Poetical Rhapsody," 1602,) containing a list of the productions with the names of the authors, which does not seem to have been made out either from the first or second edition of "England's Helicon," but probably from some independent authority. Nevertheless, it accords in many cases.

In the first place, and without resort to this source of information, we may doubt whether E. B. (subscribed to poems on sign. B 2 and B 4) mean Edmund Bolton, because on sign. C 4 we have "a Canzon Pastorall in honour of her Majestie," which has his name at length. Why should initials have been used in the former instances, if they were intended to denote a poet who did not object to see his name at length?

Again, with reference to two poems on sign. E 3 b, subscribed I. M., it seems to have been forgotten that those initials are much more likely to belong to John Marston, than to Gervase or

Jervis Markham. Markham could hardly be equal to the later of the two; and Marston, much his superior as a poet, in 1600 was in the zenith of his reputation and popularity.

It has escaped notice also, that both the pieces attributed to "T. Howard Earle of Surrie" in the editions of 1600 and 1614, were in fact by H. Howard Earl of Surrey. Bodenham committed the same oversight in his "Bel-vedére," 1600, and it was not corrected in 1812.

On sign. G 3 occurs a production thus headed, "To Phillis the faire Sheepheardesse," with the initials S. E. D. at the end of it; and Ellis (Specimens II. 186, edit. 1811) gives it unhesitatingly to Sir Edward Dyer. Sir E. Brydges and Haslewood, in their reprint of the second edition of "England's Helicon," 1614, repeat the blunder. The poem is by Thomas Lodge, and is contained in his "Phillis," 1593, (see *post.*) Moreover, they make nonsense of the two last lines by printing *will* for "nill," (i. e. *ne will*, or will not,) as it stands in the original impressions both of "Phillis" and of "England's Helicon."

On sign. H 2 we meet with the celebrated ode, "As it fell upon a day," which we now know was by Shakspeare, and not by Barnfield, in whose name it had been published in 1598, but assigned to its true owner in "The Passionate Pilgrim" of 1599. In "England's Helicon," 1600, the word *Ignoto* is at the close of it, as if Bodenham had not been able to decide as to the real authorship. On the other hand, when he inserted "the Sheepheard's Ode" on sign. K 4, he gave it at once to Barnfield, because it was indisputably his. Sir E. Brydges and Haslewood did not know from whence it had been procured, but it was from Barnfield's "Cynthia," 1595.

The list of authors in MS. Harl. 280, assigns "The Sheepheards description of his Love" (sign. L 2 b) to Sir Walter Raleigh, and the initials S. W. R. were originally placed after it; but a slip pasted over it, on which is printed *Ignoto*, shows that Bodenham had early seen reason to alter the ascription of it.[1] Precisely the

[1] This was written about 1840; after which date the writer lent his copy of "England's Helicon," 1600; and the old paste having given way, the minute slip came off, and the book was returned without it, but the place where it, and others, were stuck on is clearly discernible.

same observation applies to "The Sheepheard's praise of his sacred Diana," on sign. N 3 b.

Fulke Greville, Lord Brooke's claims are confirmed by Davison's list; and a piece on sign. X b, which has no name nor initials, clearly belongs to the same noble poet on the authority of Dowland's "First Booke of Songs," 1597. Davison (MS. Harl. 280) gives "Another to his Cinthia," on sign. X b, to the Earl of Cumberland: Bodenham inserted it anonymously.

The additions made to the number of poems in the impression of "England's Helicon," in 1614, occur principally towards the close, some of them being by William Browne, and others by Christopher Brooke, who were not known as early as 1600. A few were transferred from Davison's "Poetical Rhapsody."

BOOK, A NEW. — A newe boke Conteyninge. An exortaciō to the sicke. The sycke mans prayer. A prayer with thankes at the purificaciō of women. A Consolatiō at buriall. [Colossi. iii. What soeuer ye do in worde or dede, &c.] MDLXI. 8vo. B. L. 27 *leaves.*

This little work was printed by William Copland, but it is nowhere enumerated among productions of his careless press. The colophon runs thus: "Imprinted at London in saynt Martines in the Vintry upon the thre craned wharfe by Wyllyam Copland."

It must have been published at a time when the metropolis was visited by what was called the Plague, and the tract is wound up with the following clever mock-prescription for its cure: —

"Take a pond of good hard penaunce, and washe it wel with the water of youre eyes, and let it ly a good whyle at your hert. Take also of the best fyne fayth, hope and charyte y[t] you can get, a like quantite of al mixed together, your soule even full, and use this confection every day in your lyfe, whiles the plages of god reigneth. Then, take both your handes ful of good workes commaunded of God, and kepe them close in a clene conscience from the duste of vayne glory, and ever as you are able and se necessite so to use them. This medicine was found wryten in an olde byble boke, and it hath been practised and proved true of mani, both men and women."

Brathwaite, Richard. — A Strappado for the Diuell. Epigrams and Satyres alluding to the time, with diuers measures of no lesse Delight. By Μυσοσυκος to his friend Φιλοκρατες. *Nemo me impune lacessit.* — At London printed by J. B. for Richard Redmer, &c. at the Starre. 1615. 8vo. 182 *leaves.*

There is, perhaps, no work in English which illustrates more fully and amusingly the manners, occupations, and opinions of the time when it was written, than the present volume by Richard Brathwaite; but it is a strange, undigested, and ill arranged collection of poems, of various kinds, and of different degrees of merit, some of them composed considerably before the rest, but few without claims to notice. The principal part consists of satires and epigrams, although the author purposely confounds the distinction between the two, telling "the captious Reader,"

> "My answer's this to him that saies I wrong
> Our art to make my Epigrams so long: —
> I dare not bite — therefore to change my nature,
> I call't an *Epigram* which is a *Satire.*"

Yet that he dared bite may be seen from the following, among other preliminary lines "to his Booke."

> "Which to prevent let this be understood —
> Great men, though ill, they must be stiled good:
> Their blacke is white, their vice is vertue made;
> But 'mongst the base call still a spade a spade."

He never scruples to use the plainest terms, and though he seldom inserts real names, he spares neither rank nor condition.

The title-page is followed by "the Author's Anagram," viz., *Vertu hath bar[e] credit;* and, after a double dedication to Sir Thomas Gainsford and Mr. Thomas Posthumus Diggs, we come to "another Anagram," and a prose address "to the gentle Reader," in which the author apologizes for typographical errors, by stating that he was absent when his book was printed. Then succeed lines "to his Booke," a third dedication "to all Usurers, Broakers and Promoters &c. Ladies, Monkies, Parachitoes, Marmosites," &c. and a note "upon the Errata," again mentioning the absence of the author, as well as "the intricacy of the copy." To these are added "Errata," some "Embleames," as they are termed, and separate addresses to the "equal" and "captious" Readers. The preliminary matter thus terminated, we arrive at the substance of the volume, commencing with a poem to "Mounsieur Bacchus, sole Soveraigne of the Ivy-bush," &c.

Brathwaite was an admirer of George Wither, (who had published his Satires two years before,) and of William Browne; and in a poem entitled "Upon the general Sciolists or Poetasters of Britannie," after abusing the low versifiers of the day, he thus distinguishes them:

"Yet ranke I not (as some men doe suppose)
These worthlesse swaines amongst the laies of those
Time-honour'd Shepheards (for they still shall be,
As they well merit, honoured of mee)
Who beare a part, like honest faithfull swaines
On witty *Wither* never-withring plaines:
For these (though seeming Shepheards) have deserv'd
To have their names in lasting marble carv'd.
Yea, this I know, I may be bold to say
Thames n'ere had swans that song more sweet than they.
It 's true, I may avow 't, that nere was song
Chanted in any age by swains so young
With more delight then was perform'd by them,
Pretily shadow'd in a borrow'd name.
And long may England's Thespian springs be known
By lovely Wither and by bonny Browne;
Whilest solid Seldon, and their Cuddy too,
Sing what our Swaines of old could never doe."

The latter part of this quotation refers to "The Shepherd's Pipe," printed in 1614, which, on the authority of Wither, is known to have been written by himself and Browne. "Solid Seldon" is, of course, "the learned Selden," who wrote some lines prefixed to Browne's "Brittannia's Pastorals," but who was meant by "their Cuddy" is not, we believe, ascertained.

One of the most amusing pieces in the collection, partly from its humor, but more from its allusions, is entitled "Upon a Poets Palfrey, lying in lavander for the discharge of his Provender": it reminds us in some degree of the Italian artist Bronzino's stanzas upon a horse given to him by one of his patrons, but never delivered: the latter, however, is in a higher strain of fancy. Brathwaite begins by a quotation from Shakspeare's "Richard the Third":

"If I had liv'd but in King Richard's dayes,
Who in his heat of passion, midst the force
Of his Assailants troubled many waies,
Crying 'A horse, a kingdome for a horse,'
O! then my horse, which now at livery stayes,
Had beene set free, where now he 's forc't to stand,
And like to fall into the Ostler's hand."

King Richard's exclamation had been parodied by John Marston, in his "Scourge of Villanie," two years after Shakspeare's play was published.[1] Farther on, we have the following allusion to Marlow's "Tamburlaine," and to the very passage Shakspeare had previously ridiculed:

"If I had liv'd when fame-spred Tamberlaine
Displaid his purple signals in the East,
'Hallow, ye pamphred Jades!' had been in vaine;
For mines not pamphred, nor was ere at feast
But once, which once 's nere like to be againe;
How, methinks, would hee haue scour'd the wheeles,
Having brave Tamberlaine whipping at 's heeles."

The same poem contains references to Shelton's translation of "Don Quixote," the first part of which was printed in 1612; to Banks's famous horse that ascended to the top of St. Paul's; to Vennar's "Englands Joy," played at the Hope Theatre in 1603;[2]

[1] He quotes it in one of his comedies; and in his "Parasitaster," 1606, he introduces another line from "Richard III."

"Plots ha' you laid, inductions dangerous?"

In the same comedy he again thus parodies Richard's exclamation, "A foole, a foole! my coxcombe for a foole!" Here, too, we meet with a couplet that more than reminds us of the two lines in "The M. W. of W." Act II. sc. 2, —

"Love like a shadow flies, when substance love pursues,
Pursuing that that flies, and flying what pursues."

Marston's lines are, —

"So may we learn that nicer love's a shade;
It follows fled, pursued flies as afraid."

[2] See article VENNAR, Vol. IV.

to Bartholomew Fair, as then celebrated, and to other matters of curiosity. In another long and not very lively poem, to the cotton manufacturers of the North of England, Brathwaite mentions "Wilson's Delight," "Arthur-a-Bradly," (see p. 33,) and "Mall, Dixon's Round," as celebrated tunes. The first was, perhaps, derived from Wilson the comic actor, who was famous before the time of Shakspeare, and who has left at least one play behind him. "Arthur-a-Bradly" is well known, but "Mall Dixon's Round" has perished, at all events by that name.

The last part of the volume has a new title-page, "Love's Labyrinth, or the true-Lover's knot: including the disastrous fals of two star-crost Lovers, Pyramus and Thisbe;" a subject, as the author adds, "heeretofore handled." He alludes, perhaps, to Dunstan Gale's "Pyramus and Thisbe," which originally appeared in 1596, and of which what purports to be a new edition came out in 1617: it may be doubted, however, whether more was done to it than giving it a fresh title-page. The story of Pyramus and Thisbe had also been told in Dr. Muffet's "Silkworms and their Flies," 4to, 1599, which see hereafter. An "Epistle of Hyppolitus to Phædra," in octave stanzas, in imitation of Drayton, and five pages of illustrative notes, conclude Brathwayte's volume.

BRATHWAITE, RICHARD. — The Arcadian Princesse or the Triumph of Justice. Prescribing excellent rules of Physicke for a sicke Justice. Digested into fowre Bookes and faithfully rendered to the originall Italian Copy. By Ri. Brathwait Esq. &c. — London Printed by Th. Harper for Robert Bostocke &c. 1635. 8vo. 269 *leaves.*

Besides the printed title, there is an engraved one by Marshall, representing Justice weighing the rich and poor, with the following lines opposite to it: —

"Hee that in words explaines a Frontispice
Betrayes the secret trust of his device:
Who cannot gesse, where Motts and Emblemes be,
The drift, may still be ignorant for me."

At the back of the printed title is the license, dated "Junij 7. 1634." The dedication is to the Earl of Worcester, followed by an address "to the deserving Reader," and certain testimonies in favor of Mariano Silesio, the author of the original work. To these are added, "a Summary of the Contents." At the end of the work is inserted a short life of Mariano Silesio, but it is not stated from what authority it is derived, and it may be doubted. Many pieces of poetry are interspersed, and some of them are harmoniously rendered.

BRATHWAITE, RICHARD. — The two Lancashire Lovers: or the Excellent History of Philocles and Doriclea. Expressing the faithfull constancy and mutuall fidelity of two loyall Lovers &c. By Musæus Palatinus. *Pereo, si taceo.* — London, Printed by Edward Griffin for R. B. or his Assignes. 1640. 8vo. 132 *leaves.*

The printed title is preceded by an engraved one, by which it appears that the initials R. B., in the imprint, are those of R. Best, the publisher, and not of Richard Brathwaite, the supposed author; — "printed by E. G. for R. Best, and are to be sould at his shop neare Graies Inn gate in Houlburne." How much of the story of this novel is founded upon facts, it is impossible now to ascertain, but many of the incidents read as if they had actually occurred. Facing p. 246 is an engraving of two hearts burning upon an altar, Cupid blowing the fire, while two lovers kneel below, the man saying, "What wouldst thou desire? Cupid retire;" and the lady, "Our flaming hearts are both a-fire." This plate is also employed in another production, assigned to Brathwaite, called "Art asleepe Husband," printed in 1640.

BRETON, NICHOLAS. — The Passionate Shepheard, or The Shepheardes Love: set downe in Passions to his Shepheardesse Aglaia. With many excellent conceited

Poems and pleasant Sonnets, fit for young heads to passe away idle houres. — London Imprinted by E. Allde, for John Tappe, and are to bee solde at his Shop, at the Tower-Hill neere the Bulwarke Gate. 1604. 4to. 19 *leaves.*

This production is an entire novelty in our poetical annals: it is not to be traced in any catalogue or work on bibliography.

It is all in verse excepting the dedication, which is thus headed: "Bonerto, the faithfull Shepheard, to Aglaia his faire Shepheard-esse, wisheth more wealth then the Sheepes-wooll, and a better Garland then the Bay-leafe." This is signed

> "Your poore Shephard
> BONERTO."

Against which name is written, in a hand of about the time, "Nicolao Bretono," the letters forming Bonerto, with a slight change, making Bretono, *i. e.* Nicholas Breton. In 1604 the name of Nicholas Breton was so well known on title-pages, either at length, or as N. B. and B. N., that in this instance, perhaps for novelty's sake, he preferred to vary it, and came before the world as Bonerto. The dedication is remarkable for nothing, but that it contains an allusion to a popular production by Samuel Rowlands, called "The letting of Humours Blood in the head Vein," which had been first published in 1600. Some of the pieces in the body of "The Passionate Shepherd" bear a considerable resemblance to Breton's earlier performances: his "Farewell to Town" (Ellis's Spec. II. 270, edit. 1811) is not very dissimilar to his "Farewell to the World," in the work before us.

Shakspeare's "Passionate Pilgrim" had come out in 1599, and "The Passionate Shepherd," as an imitation in title, seems also to have been intended, in various respects, as an imitation in style. The pieces it contains are many of them in short lines, such as, —

> "On a day (alack the day !)
> Love whose month was ever May;"

and, which is also in "The Passionate Pilgrim,"

> "As it foll upon a day
> In the merry month of May;"

while in "England's Helicon," 1600, sign. D 3, Breton himself has a poem in precisely the same metre: —

> "In the merry month of May,
> In a morne by breake of day," &c.

A variety of lyrical measures are employed, but none of them such as are not to be found in other productions by Breton. As "The Passionate Shepherd" is undoubtedly a literary curiosity, as well as a collection of meritorious poems by one of the most popular authors of that day, we will describe it with more particularity than usual. The title-page forms sign. A 1, and the back of it is blank: the dedication is on the next page, with the back also blank, and the "Pastorall Verses, written by the Shepheard Bonerto, to his beloved Shepheardesse Aglaia," commence on sign. A 3, the first piece being assigned to *Pastor Primus:* —

> "Tell me, all yee Shepheards swaines
> On Minervas Mountaine plaines,
> Yee that only sit and keepe
> Flockes (but of the fairest sheepe)
> Did you see this blessed day
> Faire Aglaia walke this way?
> If yee did, oh, tell me then,
> If yee be true meaning men,
> How she fareth with her health,
> All the world of all your wealth," &c.

It should be observed that the lines being generally short, and the page 4to, each outer margin is occupied throughout by an arabesque border. "Past. 2" and "Past. 3" (meaning probably *Pastor* 2 and 3) are in the same kind of verse, and the latter opens with a very sprightly description of a shepherd's life: —

> "Who can live in heart so glad
> As the merrie countrie lad,
> Who upon a faire greene balke
> May at pleasures sit and walke,
> And amidde the Azure skies
> See the morning Sunne arise?
> While he heares in every spring
> How the Birdes doe chirpe and sing;
> Or before the houndes in crie,
> See the Hare goe stealing by;

Or along the shallow brooke,
Angling with a baited hooke,
See the fishes leape and play
In a blessed sunny day," &c.

And so he proceeds, enumerating a variety of rural sights and sounds, and ending thus passionately regarding his shepherdess:

"For whose sake I say and sweare,
By the passions that I beare,
Had I got a kinglie grace,
I would leaue my kinglie place,
And in heart be truelie glad
To become a country lad,
Hard to lie and goe full bare,
And to feede on hungry fare,
So I might but live to bee
Where I might but sit and see,
Once a day, or all day long,
The sweet subject of my song;
In Aglaias onely eyes
All my worldly paradise."

We hardly know how such thought and language, in this graceful and fanciful department of poetry, are to be improved. It seems clear that some real person, who had an accidental mark, was intended by Aglaia, or why this couplet in what is headed "Past. 4"?

"And that skarre upon thy throate:
No such starre on Stellas coate."

In the same division the author shows his acquaintance, not only with classical poets, but with Petrarch, Tasso, Ariosto, Dante, and Guarini, and enumerates them in that somewhat defective order. "Past. 5" is short, and ends on the reverse of sign. C, when we arrive at a new heading, "Sundry sweet Sonnets and Passionated Poems;" but among them there is not a single "sonnet" strictly so called, but a number of miscellaneous love-poems, beginning with "A farewell to the world and the pleasures thereof." Here the measure changes to ten-syllable lines in quatrains, and it opens:—

"Now, for the last farewell I meane to make
To all the troubles of my tired thought:
This leave at last, and this last leave I take
Of some, and all, that have my sorrowe sought."

This piece is more in Breton's didactic style than any of the preceding pastorals, and in succession he bids farewell to youth, beauty, friendship, love, power, hope, fortune, art, and time. Still, he reverts to Aglaia, and to a rustic life, declaring —

"Thus will I sit, and set my pipe in tune,
And plaie as merry as the day is long;
And as in Aprill, so againe in June,
Fit both my spring and harvest with a song."

This production occupies about five pages, but we extract another stanza from it, because it accords so well with some lines in a poem attributed to Breton in "England's Helicon": —

"The filed tongue of fayning eloquence
Shall now no more abuse my simple trust:
In yea and nay I find that excellence,
Where perfect judgment cannot prove unjust."

The corresponding passage in "England's Helicon" is —

"Then with many a pretty oath,
Yea and nay, and faith and troth,
Such as silly shepherds use
When they will not love abuse."

Breton's "passionated poem," which may be termed his "Farewell," contains 35 stanzas of four lines each, with the exception of one stanza which has six lines. "Sonnet 2," as he calls it, is "The description and praise of his fairest Love," and is in some places rather warm and minute: it occupies 32 stanzas, ending on sign. D 3 b. "Sonnet 3" is very lively and brief, consisting of twenty-four short lines in couplets, divided as if they were stanzas. "Sonnet 4" is in the same measure, and commences thus: —

"Tell me, tell me, pretty Muse,
Canst thou neither will nor chuse,
But be busie with my braine,
Still to put my wits to paine?
Shall my heart within my breast
Never have an hower of rest?"

Still he is ready to endure, if Aglaia approve his lines, as the result of his pain and toil. Passing over "Sonnet 5," which does not claim particular notice, we quote "Sonnet 6" exactly as it stands: —

"Fooles cannot know what fancie is,
Where wisdome findes true wit;
And who can ever ayme at blisse
That hath no thought of it?

"A shallow braine can never judge
The sweet or sower between,
For Vulcan was but held a drudge,
While Venus was a Queene.

"A muddie spirit dwells in drosse,
While pure affections fire
Enflames the heart that feeles no crosse
To compasse his desire,
And sweetly doth conseale his griefe,
Who rather dies then begges reliefe."

We pass over "Sonnets" 7 and 8, in order to direct attention to a passage from "Sonnet 9," which is precisely in Breton's manner: —

"Youth but a blaze of time,
Whome Age to ashes bringes;
Time but a weary chime
That death to sorrow ringes,
While wealth the weight of care doth proove
The world hath little what to love.

"Beautie is sildome wise,
Nor wit hath fortune friend;
And love in Argus eyes
Findes Jealouzie a fiend:
While truth doth gaine so little grace
As makes the world a woefull place."

"Sonnet 9" is misprinted for Sonnet 10. The last poem in the volume (which ends on sign. E 3 b) deserves to be extracted, if only for its gayety and the felicity of its expression: it is as lively as it is lovely; and we are, of course, to conclude that it is addressed to Aglaia: —

"Pretty twinkling starry eyes,
How did Nature first devise
Such a sparkling in your sight
As to give love such delight,

As to make him, like a flye,
Play with lookes untill he die?

"Sure, yee were not made at first
For such mischief to be curst,
As to kill affections care
That doth onely truth declare:
Where worthes wonders never wither,
Love and Beauty live together.

"Blessed eyes, then give your blessing,
That in passions best expressing,
Love, that onely lives to grace yee,
May not suffer pride deface yee;
But in gentle thoughtes directions
Shew the praise of your perfections."

If "The Passionate Shepherd" had been a book of almost every-day occurrence, it would well have deserved notice for its indisputable merits; but when it is for the first time introduced to notice, and no other copy has ever been heard of, it would be idle to apologize for the length and minuteness of our criticism. Perhaps Breton was led to his title by the fact that Marlowe's ballad in "England's Helicon," 1600, (sign. A a b,) is headed "The Passionate Sheepheard to his Love." We need scarcely add, that in the reigns of Elizabeth and James I., the words "Poet" and "Shepherd" were often used synonymously.

BRETON, NICHOLAS. — The Pilgrimage to Paradise, joyned with the Countesse of Pembrookes loue, compiled in Verse by Nicholas Breton, Gentleman. *Cælum virtutis patria.* — At Oxford printed by Joseph Barnes, and are to be solde in Paules Church-yaard at the signe of the Tygres head. 1592. 4to. B. L.

Unquestionably one of the rarest of Breton's many productions: we believe that only one or two copies of it are known.

It is dedicated "to the Ladie Mary Countesse of Pembrooke," followed by an address "to the Gentlemen studients and Scholars of Oxforde," dated "this 12th of Aprill, 1592." To this address is appended a singular note, regarding the frauds of booksellers, or stationers, of that day: it is this: —

"Gentlemen, there hath been of late printed in London by one Richarde Joanes, a printer, a booke of englishe verses entituled *Bretons bower of delights.* I protest it was donne altogether without my consent or knowledge, and many thinges of other mens mingled with a few of mine; for, except *Amoris Lachrimæ*, an epitaphe upon Sir Phillip Sydney, and one or two other toies, which I know not how he unhappily came by, I have no part with any of them: and so, I beseech you, assuredly beleeve."

Now, it so happens that this "one Richard Jones" had printed and published Breton's earliest work, "A small Handfull of Fragrant Flowers," in 1575; his second work, "A Flourish upon Fancie," in 1577 (again in 1582); as well as his "Bowre of Delights," in 1591 (again in 1597): so that it should seem as if Breton, at all events until 1591, had employed this "one Richard Jones," though he afterwards resorted to others. Jones may have surreptitiously obtained the MS. of the "Bowre of Delights," calling it *Brittons* instead of "Bretons" for a fraudulent purpose, and may have mingled pieces by a then very popular author with others of less excellence and notoriety, for the sake of forming a substantial volume. Breton's popularity afterwards declined in some degree, and fluctuated considerably: he continued a writer until long after Charles I. came to the throne, and in 1625 appears to have lived in the parish of St. Giles, Cripplegate, for in the Register of that church, under date of the 27th July, 1625, we find that "Matilda the daughter of Nicholas Brittaine" was buried. His own marriage with Annes Sutton is recorded there, 14th Jan. 1592. The person we take to have been his father, or possibly grandfather, named also Nicholas Brittayne, was buried at St. James, Garlickhithe, on 24th May, 1564. Formerly we confidently believed that the Nicholas Breton, Esq., who was buried at Norton, Staffordshire, on 22d June, 1624, was the poet, but we have since found the preceding registrations, and an entry in a MS. (Cotton. Galba, D I. 135) showing that a "Capt. Nich. Breton" went with Lord Leicester to the Low Countries, who was doubtless the person buried at Norton. Nicholas Breton, the poet and pamphleteer, is twice mentioned in Beaumont and Fletcher, viz., in "The Scornful Lady," edit. Dyce, III. 28, and in "Wit without Money," ibid. IV. 150.

Reverting from these biographical particulars to Breton's productions, we may repeat that he sometimes published under his own name, sometimes under his initials N. B., sometimes reversing them as B. N., and sometimes anonymously. Under the last, however, in the list given in the new edition of Lowndes' Bibl. Man. I. 263, "Pleasant Quippes for Upstart New-fangled Gentlewomen," 1595 and 1596, is assigned to him by mistake, because (as is stated elsewhere, B. M. p. 2030) it belongs to Stephen Gosson, who had a vein for poetry and satire. Breton often put only his initials upon the title-pages, or at the end of the dedications of his pieces; but we do not believe that he ever resorted to Richard Jones as a publisher after 1591, although Jones of his own authority put forth a second edition of what he still called "*Brittons* Bowre of Delights" in 1597.

The dedication and address by Breton before his "Pilgrimage to Paradise" are followed by a prose letter from John Case, M. D., in praise of the book, and in laudation of the Countess of Pembroke; and by a copy of Latin verses, *Gulielmi Gageri, Legum Doctoris*, the defender of dramatic performances against the celebrated Dr. John Rainoldes. The body of the book is a somewhat tedious allegory, Spenser having rendered that species of composition popular by the publication of the three first books of his "Fairy Queen" in 1590. We need not delay to describe the construction attempted by Breton, but we may quote with approbation the following stanza, where he rather humorously draws the portrait of a fantastical lover: —

"After all these upon the right hand went
A silly foole, for so I tearme him right,
With wringing hands, that seemed to lament
Some crossing humor to a vaine delight:
For love, forsooth, and nought but love it was,
That made a woman make a man an Asse.

"Of Venus frailty and of Cupids blindenes
He cried out, Oh! that ever they were borne!
And of his mistres more then most unkindnes,
That did so much his truest service skorne:

Yet still he lovde her, and he did so love her,
It was his death: he never could recover.

"And then he sight, and sobde, and hong the head,
And wept and wailde, and cast up both his eies,
And in a trance, as if a man were dead,
Or did some dying kinde of fit devise;
Untill he wakte, and then he cried, Oh love!
That ever lover should such sorrowe prove!

"And then he redde his verses and his rimes,
Wherein he praisde her, too too out of reason;
And then he sight to thinke how many times
He watcht the day, the night, the hower, the season,
To finde some fruite of his deserved favoure,
But al his flowers were weedes that had no savour."

"The Countess of Pembroke's Love" is merely a religious poem, which has also been mistakenly called "The Countess of Pembroke's Passion." It is an easy piece of versification, but it makes no pretension to originality: the "love" treated of is holy love, but bears no sort of resemblance, excepting in the mere subject, to Spenser's "Hymn to Heavenly Love."

BRETON, NICHOLAS. — Pasquils Mad-cap and his Message. — London. Printed by V. S. for Thomas Bushell, and are to bee solde at his shop at the great North doore of Paules. 1600. 4to. 24 *leaves.*

There were certainly two editions of this performance in the same year, differing not only in title, but in typography, showing that the second edition was a reprint, and not merely a reissue with a new forefront. This circumstance is nowhere noticed: in one copy the tract is called "Pasquils Mad-cap and his Message," and in the other, "Pasquils Mad-cap and Mad-cappes Message:" both were by the same printer and publisher, and there is no doubt that the poem was popular. We assign it to Breton on the strength of his own acknowledgment in "the second part," of which we shall next speak; for "Pasquils Mad-cap" was in the first instance anonymous, the author waiting, perhaps, to ascertain how it was liked.

The main, if not the whole, purpose of the writer seems to have been to show the great advantage of being rich, and he runs over all classes and descriptions of persons: —

"The wealthy Rascal, be he ne're so base,
Filthy, ill-favoured, ugly to behold,
Mowle-eie, Plaise-mouth, Dogges-tooth and Camels face,
Blind, dumbe and deafe, diseased rotten, old;
Yet, if he have his coffers full of gold,
He shall have reverence, curtsie, cappe and knee,
And worship, like a man of high degree.

"He shall have Ballads written in his praise,
Bookes dedicate unto his patronage;
Wittes working for his pleasure many waies,
Petigrees sought to mend his parentage,
And linckt, perhaps, in noble marriage:
He shall have all that this vile world can give him,
That into Pride, the Divels mouth, may drive him."

This is certainly not so new as true; and Breton goes on in a similar strain to lecture players, poets, and authors of tragedies and comedies, for the manner in which they flattered the wealthy and powerful: nevertheless, he was himself quite as apt as other writers to offend in this respect. "Mad-cappes Message," which begins on p. 29, is in six-line stanzas, and the following is one of them: —

"Tell country Players, that old paltry jests,
Pronounced in a painted motley coate,
Fill all the world so full of Cuckoes nests,
That Nightingales can scarcely sing a note;
Or bid them turne their minds to better meanings:
Fields are ill sowne that give no better gleanings."

If particular and personal allusions were intended, as is most likely, they are not now intelligible: we therefore pass them over.

Breton, Nicholas. — The second part of Pasquil's Mad-cap, intituled The Fooles-Cap. With Pasquils Passion. Begun by himself, and finished by his Friend Marphorius. — Imprinted at London, for Thomas Johnes, dwelling neere Holborne Conduit, 1600. 4to. 19 *leaves.*

This poem was dedicated by Breton to Master Edward Conquest; and, in some preliminary lines, he complains that a "second part" had been published of which he was not the author. The fact is, that the success of the first part, which Breton had not owned until he saw how it was received, had encouraged imitation; but that imitation has not survived. This "second part" is hardly as good as the first; and here the author attacks some classes of the female, as well as of the male, sex, as in the subsequent stanza: —

"Shee that doth keepe an Inne for every Guest,
And makes no care what winde blows up her skirt,
And ready is to breake a Chaucers jeast,
To make a smocke even measure with a shirt;
If such a one be call'd a foolish flirt,
Twas not for nothing that she had her name,
When all the world is witnesse to her shame."

Breton often changed his publisher, and this "second part" of "Pasquil's Mad-cap" was not brought out by the same stationer who issued the first part.

Breton, Nicholas. — The Passion of a Discontented Minde. — London. Printed by T. C. for John Baily, and are to be sold at his shop at the doore of the Office of the Sixe Clarkes in Chancerie Lane. 1602, 4to. 12 *leaves.*

This piece has always been attributed to Breton, but it has nowhere any distinct mark of his authorship, (neither name nor initials,) and it was not put forth by any one of his previous publishers. The fifth stanza begins as follows: —

"O that the learned Poets of our time
(Who in a love-sick line so well endite)
Would not consume good wit in hateful Rime,
But would with care some better subject write:
For, if their musicke please in earthly things,
Well would it sound if straind with heavenly strings."

It would apply to Breton quite as well as to others of his day. The writer is far from consistent, for in one place he gives himself over to despair, and in another thus exclaims: —

"I might as others (Lord) have perished
Amid my sinnes and damnable delights,
But thou (good God) with care my soule hast cherished,
And brought it home to taste on heavenly lights.
Aye me! what thankes, what service can I render
To thee that of my safetie art so tender?"

The last stanza is this: —

"I sing not I of wanton love-sicke laies,
Of trickling toyes to feede fantasticke eares,
My Muse respects no flattering tatling praise;
A guiltie conscience this sad passion beares.
My sinne-sicke soule, with sorrow woe begonne,
Lamenting thus a wretched deed misdone."

If the poem were composed in consequence of some particular crime, that circumstance is not specified. Above we ought to read, not "trickling," but "*tickling* toyes." We doubt Breton's authorship.

BRETON, NICHOLAS.— Strange Newes out of Divers Countries, never discovered till of late by a strange Pilgrime in those parts.— London, Printed by W. Jones for George Fayerbeard &c. 1622. B. L. 4to. 14 *leaves.*

This also is one of the numerous performances of Nicholas Breton, his initials reversed being at the end of the short preface. He began his career of authorship, as we have already stated, in 1575, and he did not conclude it until 1636, — at least that is the date of "The Figure of Foure," his latest known work. The pamphlet before us has little merit, and much of it is now unintelligible, purporting to give a rambling, satirical, and, we must say, nonsensical account of the manners of a supposed people. The last part of it is in verse, consisting of eleven apologues in the shape of dreams: the following is one of the best, — best because shortest:

"*A Dreame of an Oister and a Crab.*

"Upon the shore neere to the Sea an Oister, gaping wide,
Lay looking for a little food to come in with the Tide;
But hard by lay a crauling Crab, who watcht his time before,
And threw a stone betweene the shels, that they could shut no more.
The Oister cride, Ho, neighbours! theeves! but ere the neighbours came,
The Crab had murtherd the poore fish and fed upon the same,
When wondring that such craft did live with creatures in the deepe,
With troubling of my braines withall, I wakt out of my sleepe."

It is very possible that this is only a reimpression of an earlier, but now lost, edition, and the verses are of a kind, and in a form, popular about thirty years earlier. On the title-page is a woodcut (or, rather, separate woodcuts) of two figures, one a knight in armor, and the other a man in a cloak, and over them the words "The Pilgrimes."

We may add that in 1597 was published by N. Ling a very rare piece by Breton, his names being at length upon the title-page, which he called "Wits Trenchmour in a Conference had betwixt a Scholar and an Angler": it is not to be supposed that it has any connection with fishing, an "angler" meaning at that time a person who lived by his wits. The tract occupies only two sheets 4to.

It is out of the question to impute to Breton (as is done by error in the last edit. of Lowndes' Bibl. Man. p. 264) the "Plot of the Play called England's Joy": it was the production of Vennar, or Vennard: see "Hist. Engl. Dram. Poetry and the Stage," III. 405.

BREWER, THOMAS. —

A knot of Fooles. But
Fooles or Knaves, or both, I care not,
Here they are; Come laugh and spare not.

Printed at London for Francis Grove &c. 1624. 4to. 14 *leaves.*

The only edition of this satirical poem mentioned by bibliographers is dated 1658;[1] but, as the author, Thomas Brewer, printed "The Weeping Lady," in 1625, on the plague in that year, it seemed improbable that there should have been so wide an interval of time between his productions. This first impression of the "Knot of Fooles" has a rude woodcut on the title, with seven figures, one female, and six male, in various habits, meant to represent characters spoken of in the body of the tract. Three lively stanzas "to the Reader" are signed "Tho. Brewer," and the production is introduced by a dialogue between a number of Fools, in which they display their several humors. We then come to the body of the work, consisting of satirical and sometimes abusive remarks, in couplets, upon the vices of the time and their professors, under separate and quaint titles, such as "Much adoe about nothing;" "Tomble downe Dicke;" "A Foole and his money is soon parted;" "Wit, whither wilt thou," &c. The conclusion, called "Pride teaching Humility," in seven-line stanzas, is, perhaps, the best part of the whole. It relates to the reproof of Sesostris, for his pride and vainglory, by one of the kings who was compelled to draw the conqueror's triumphant chariot into Memphis. The two last stanzas may be quoted as a specimen: —

"He now can see they (like himselfe) are men,
And so much being, had their blood been base,
It yet had beene more pure, more precious then
For such low duties: how much more disgrace
Impos'd on greatnesse — men whose birth and place
Were as his owne was. This he now can see;
For this he grieves, for this he sets them free,

"Takes to his Chariot horses; and these Kings
As men, his fellowes and his dearest friends,
To whom in notes concordant now he sings
The dulcet part of kindnesse, that transcends

[1] The edit. of 1624 is noticed by Mr. Bohn in his 2d edit. of Lowndes' B. M. p. 269, from the copy in the Bridgw. Catalogue.

A common friendship; noting Fortune lends
By fits her favours. In our Christian phrase,
Heaven hates the haughty, doth the humble raise."

Browne, William. — Britannia's Pastorals. Lond: print: for Geo: Norton dwell: at Temple barr. Fol. 134 *leaves.*

The above title is an engraved frontispiece of two Cupids supporting a scroll, and below it a shepherd and shepherdess. The dedication, to the Lord Zouch, Saint Maure, and Cantelupe, is without date, but the address "to the Reader" is "From the Inner Temple, June the 18. 1613," and here Browne speaks of this work as "the first bloomes of his Poesie." Latin and English commendatory verses by "I. Selden Iuris. C.," Michael Drayton, Edward Heyward, Christopher Brooke, Fr. Dynne, Tho. Gardiner, W. Ferrar, and Fr. Oulde, introduce the five songs of which the first part of "Britannia's Pastorals" consists. "The second book" has a new title-page: "Britannia's Pastorals. The second Booke: Horat. *Carmine Dii superi placantur, carmine Manes.* London Printed by Thomas Snodham for George Norton &c. 1616." This has a distinct dedication to the Earl of Pembroke, and laudatory Latin and English verses by John Glanvill; Tho. Wenman; W. Herbert; John Davies, of Heref; Carolus Croke; Unton Croke; Anth: Vincent; John Morgan; Thomas Heygate; Augustus Cæsar; G. Wither; W. B. and Ben Jonson. The second book, also, consists of five songs, or pastorals. The latter part of the first song contains Browne's beautiful and grateful tribute to Spenser:

——— "all their pipes were still,
And Colin Clout began to tune his quill
With such deep art, that every one was given
To think Apollo (newly slid from heaven)
Had tane a human shape to win his love,
Or with the westerne Swains for glory strove.
He sung th' heroicke Knights of Faiery Land
In lines so elegant, of such command,
That had the Thracian play'd but half so well
He had not left Eurydice in hell.

But ere he ended his melodious song,
An host of Angels flew the clouds among,
And rapt this Swan from his attentive mates
To make him one of their associates
In heavens fair Quire, where now he sings the praise
Of him that is the first and last of days.
Divinest Spenser! heaven-bred, happy muse!
Would any power into my brain infuse
Thy worth, or all that poets had before,
I could not praise 'till thou deserv'st no more."

In the second song of Book II., Browne introduces laudatory notices of George Chapman, Michael Drayton, Ben Jonson, Samuel Daniel, Christopher Brooke, John Davies, and George Wither. With the latter, as has been already noticed, (see p. 95,) he wrote "The Shepherds Pipe": in fact, when it was reprinted in 1620, 8vo, it was included among "The Workes of Master George Wither," the volume being introduced by Wither's "Satire to the King," and his "Epithalamia," and followed by his "Shepherds Hunting," "Fidelia," &c. "Britannia's Pastorals" were again printed in 8vo in 1623 and 1625.

Christopher Brooke, above mentioned, was partner with Browne in "Elegies" on the death of Henry Prince of Wales, 4to, 1613; but in 1614 he published a separate poem of great merit, entitled, "The Ghost of Richard the Third." The dedication to Sir John Crompton is only subscribed C. B., but there can be no hesitation in assigning those initials to Christopher Brooke, whose production was ushered by commendatory verses from several eminent poets of the day, viz., George Chapman, W. Browne, (whose name might of course be looked for,) George Wither, Robert Daborne, and Ben Jonson. Only two copies of it are, we believe, in existence, but its interest and importance may at once be established by the following stanzas, directly referring to Shakspeare and to his popular tragedy, put into the mouth of Richard's Ghost: —

"To him that impt my fame with Clio's quill,
Whose magick rais'd me from Oblivion's den,
That writ my storie on the Muses' hill,
And with my actions dignifi'd his pen;
He that from Helicon sends many a rill,
Whose nectared veines are drunke by thirstie men,

Crown'd be his stile with fame, his head with bayes,
And none detract, but gratulate his praise!

"Yet if his scænes have not engrost all grace,
The much fam'd action could extend on stage;
If time or memory have left a place
For me to fill, t' enforme this ignorant age,
To that intent I shew my horrid face,
Imprest with feare and characters of rage:
Nor wits nor chronicles could ere containe
The hell-deepe reaches of my soundlesse braine."

The piece is divided into two portions, and the above commences the second; but throughout, Brooke had Shakspeare's historical drama in his eye and memory, and could not avoid making many allusions to, and quotations from it. Of the author we may add that he was educated for the Bar, to which he was called about the year 1610, and that he attained eminence, especially as a real-property lawyer: he enjoyed the patronage of Lord Chancellor Ellesmere, who possessed several of his legal MSS., including opinions upon cases submitted to him. Still Brooke did not altogether relinquish poetry or its professors, and as late as 1625 he wrote a funereal tribute to the memory of Sir Arthur Chichester, reviewed, at more length than its real merits claim, in Brit. Bibl. II. 235.

BROUGHTON, ROWLAND. — A briefe discourse of the lyfe and death of the late right high and honorable Sir William Pawlet, Knight, Lord Saint John, Erle of Wilshire, Marques of Winchester, Knight of the honorable order of the Garter, one of the Queenes Maiesties priuie Counsel, and Lorde high Treasourer of Englande. Which deceased the tenth day of March. 1571. And was buried at Basing the 28 day of Aprill, Anno M.D.LXXII. — Printed at London by Richarde Iohnes, Anno 1572. 8vo. B. L. 16 *leaves.*

While Wolsey, More, Cromwell, and other statesmen, lost their lives in the service of Henry VIII., Sir William Pawlet, who was employed by the same sovereign, though not with equal distinction, was fortunate enough to survive far into the reign of Elizabeth. He was born in 1465, and did not die until the spring of 1572. Although we may presume that this tribute to his memory, written by an old servant who had worn his livery, was published, we find no trace of it in the Registers of the Stationers' Company, and only a single copy of it has been preserved. Of the author nothing is recorded but what he himself supplies, although it is clear that other rhyming productions had come from his pen.

Broughton supposes himself to be seated in his study, on 12th March, 1571–72, when the spirit of his late noble master, who had died two days before, appeared to him, and reproached him with neglecting to lament his loss in verse:—

" Canst thou (quoth he), with clownish cluche
  benumbde, forget thy pen?
Wilt thou untyll so idle state
  transforme thy fingers ten?

" What hath bee witched late thy powers,
  which thou wast wont to use?
Or where is now becom the fruite
  of thy acquainted Muse?"

This establishes that Broughton was not a novice in the art and mystery; but when he came to state the great age of the Marquis in rhyme, with the exact days of his birth and death, his ingenuity was put to the test, and, we must add, not very successfully:—

"*An.* a thousande, iiij hundreth, sixtie five,
  he was borne on Whitson night;
And lived a C. sixe, three quarter and od,
  by computacion right.

"*An.* thousand, five hundreth seventie one,
  the tenth of March last past,
He vaded as a Candell doth,
  when weeke and all is past."

We may suspect that in the second line of the preceding stanza "last" and "past" ought to change places for the sake of the rhyme. It was no great compliment to say that his Lord went out like the snuff of a candle. Camden informs us that the Marquis was only 97 years old. Broughton touches the chief points of his master's career, (admitting that he "had worne his clothing" and as a "servant" had enjoyed his "countenance,") and winds up thus: —

> "To finer heads, whose fyled verse
> in hauty style abounde,
> Belongeth this most famous facte
> his honour for to sounde:
>
> "Where floweth the sweet distilling drops
> of fresh Minerva's power,
> To those that on Mount Helicon
> have bathde in silver shower. * * *
>
> "My hermonye, much lyke to Pan,
> the cuntrye tourne may ease;
> But fine Apollo's musicke muste
> the learned people please."

Three Latin epitaphs, following an English one in six long lines, fill the two last pages, and show that Broughton (who signs them R. Br.) was not altogether deficient in scholarship: he probably acted in some superior capacity in the household of the Marquis of Winchester. As poetry, his production possesses no merit, even for the time when it was written.

BUCK, SIR GEORGE. — Δαφνις Πολυστεφανος. An Eclog treating of Crownes, and of Garlandes, and to whom of right they appertaine. Addressed, and consecrated to the Kings Majestie. By G. B. Knight. &c. — At London Printed by G. Eld for Thomas Adams. 1605. 4to. 29 *leaves.*

Sir George Buck, or Buc, as he sometimes spelt his name, having been knighted in 1603, became Master of the Revels in 1610. In the interval he printed this poetical tract, his earliest production, dedicating it, in a Latin inscription and in an English epistle, to King James, and subscribing it Georgius Bucus, Eq. Here he states that he had begun the poem "long since," but "could not finish it (according to my project) untill such time as he which should be sent (Expectatio gentium Britannicarum) should come, who was ordained from above to weare all these crownes and garlands, and to reduce this whole Isle (with the hereditary Kingdomes and Provinces thereof) to one monarchie and entire Empire." He then proceeds to deduce the genealogy of King James from the earliest period, adding an engraved table, entitled *Angliæ Regum Prosapia a tempore quo Anglia appellari cœpit &c.* The plate bears date in 1602, with the engraver's name, Joan. Woutneel: but in this copy it is altered by pen and ink to 1605. Probably Sir George Buck originally contemplated the publication of the work in 1602. "The Preface or Argument of this Poësy" succeeds upon seven leaves, when we come to the text of the work, in fifty-seven eight-line stanzas, besides "L'Envoy au Roy," in one more stanza, and "Πολυχρονιον: the Hymne inauguratory for his Majesty," in eight-syllable couplets, filling one page. The last page is occupied by a Latin epigram, offered to the King at Hampton, and two lines in Latin, headed *Aliud de symbolo nummi novi.* The following stanza is quoted on account of its accordance with the notion upon which Sir George Buck afterwards enlarged in the "History of the Life and Reign of Richard the Third," published in 1646, about twenty years after the death of the author: —

> "Two Richards more succeed, the one a Prince
> Whose goodly presence men to woonder moved,
> And was as bountefull as any since.
> Fame hath been sharp to th' other; yet bicause
> All accusations of him are not proved,
> And he built Churches, and made good laws,
> And all men held him wise and valiant,
> Who may deny him then his Genest plante?"

The copy before us was presented by the author to Lord Ellesmere, and on the fly-leaf is a poetical inscription in Sir George Buck's handwriting. It is very clear that he was under obligations of some kind to his lordship in 1605, and it is not unlikely that the Chancellor subsequently assisted him in obtaining the office of Master of the Revels, which he held until 1622. In the last line the writer plays upon his own name, and, as we may guess, upon that of a person of the name of Griffin, who possibly had been his adversary in a Chancery suit, which Lord Ellesmere decided in favor of Sir George Buck. Of this we hear nothing in his scanty biography. The autograph inscription of this copy of Δαφνις Πολυστεφανος to Lord Ellesmere is addressed "To the right honourable the greatest counsellor, Sir Tho. Egerton, knight, baron of Ellesmere, Lord Chancellour of England, my very good Lord," in the following terms: —

"Great & graue Lord, my mind hath longed long
In any thankfull maner to declare,
By act or woord, or were it in a song,
How great to you my obligations are,
Who did so nobly and so timely pluck
From Griffins talons your distressed Buck."

A comparison with this specimen of the penmanship of the Master of the Revels leaves no doubt that the inscription on an existing copy of the play of "Locrine," 4to, 1595, assigning the authorship of it to Charles Tylney, is the handwriting of Sir George Buck. He adds the information, that he himself had written the "dumb shews" by which it was illustrated, and that it was originally called "Elstrild." Charles Tylney was brother to Edmond Tylney, who had preceded Sir George Buck as Master of the Revels. The interesting question of the authorship of "Locrine,' falsely imputed to Shakspeare, is thus decided.

Buckler Against Death. — A Buckler agaynst the feare of Death, or Pyous and Proffitable Observations, Medytations and Consolations on Mans Mortality by E. B. minister in G. B. — London Printed for Mi. Sparkes Junior. 1640. 8vo. 68 *leaves.*

The above title is engraved, and represents Death and Time, with a skull and hour-glass at their feet, standing on each side of a tablet, holding a book between them, and above them is a buckler, with " T. R. fe : " at the corner: opposite are fourteen lines, headed " The mind of the Frontispiece." It is followed by a printed title-page, stating that the work was " By E. B.," without any addition, and that it was " printed by Roger Daniel, Printer to the University of Cambridge."

The dedication is " to the right worshipfull Mris Helena Phelips, and Mris Agneta Gorges, grand children" to the "late Marchioness of Northampton, now with God." The author nowhere gives more than his initials, but he was perhaps Edward Browne, who in 1642 published " A rare Paterne of Justice and Mercy," &c. The author writes in a peculiar kind of stanza, and in Part 1, Meditation 7, (for his work is divided into three Parts,) thus speaks of himself: —

> " I have been oft abroad, yet ne'r could find
> Half the contentment which I found at home:
> Methought that nothing suited to my mind
> Into what place soever I did come.
> Though I nothing needed there,
> Neither clothes, nor drink, nor meat,
> Nor fit recreations, yet
> Methought home exceeded farre."

Considering that he dedicates his poems to two ladies, E. B. is often gross in his allusions and indelicate in his expressions; and it seems to have been rather a matter of vanity with him to speak plainly. In one place, he fancies a rich lady at the point of death, whose attendant endeavors to console her mistress by pointing out her worldly pleasures and possessions: —

> " Here for your feet are tinkling ornaments:
> Here are your bonnets, and your net-work cauls:
> Fine linen, too, that every eye contents,
> Your head-bands, tablets, eare-rings, chains & falls:
> Your nose-jewels and your rings,
> Your hoods, crisping-pinnes & wimples,
> Glasses that bewray your pimples,
> Vails, and other pretty things * * *
>
> " Rich chains of pearl to tie your hair together,
> And others to adorn your snowie breast;
> Silk-stockings, starre-like shoes of Spanish leather;
> And that which farre excelleth all the rest,

And begets most admiration
Of your clothes is not their matter,
Though the world affords not better,
But it is their Frenchest fashion."

The author certainly displays suspicious learning upon all matters connected with a lady's toilet and bed-room.

It is worth noting, that Thomas Jordan made use of some waste copies of this book to defraud such as would pay him for dedications: he printed a new title to it without date, calling it "Death Dissected, or a Fort against Misfortune," and palmed it off upon the unsuspecting as his own composition. A copy with this peculiarity was sold in Heber's library, Part VIII., No. 1369. Jordan was unquestionably a great trickster in these matters; but he had usually the excuse of what Chaucer calls "a hateful good"—poverty.

BULLEIN, WILLIAM.—A Dialogue both pleasaunt and pietifull, wherein is a godlie regiment against the Fever Pestilence, with a consolation and comforte against death.—Newlie corrected by William Bullein, the authour thereof.—Imprinted at London by Ihon Kingston. Julij 1573. 8vo. B. L. 111 *leaves.*

There was an earlier impression of this work in 1564, but the edition of 1573 was "corrected by the author," the last work on which he probably was engaged, as he died in 1576. It is of no value at this time of day as a medical treatise, though the author was very eminent; but we advert to it because Bullein, for the sake of variety and amusement, introduces notices of Chaucer, Gower, Lidgate, Skelton, and Barclay, which, coming from a man who was contemporary with two of them, (for Bullein was born very early in the reign of Henry VIII.,) may be accepted as generally accurate representations. They are put into the mouth of an apothecary, whom he names Crispine, and who is describing Parnassus. Having spoken of Homer, Hesiod, Ennius, and Lucan, as favorites of the Muses, he proceeds:—

"And nere theim satte old morall Goore, with pleasaunte penne in hande, commendyng honeste love without luste, and pleasure without pride. Holinesse in the Cleargy without hypocrisie, no tyrannie in rulers, no falshode in Lawiers, no usurie in Marchauntes, no rebellion in the Commons, and unitie emong kyngdomes." &c.

"Skelton satte in the corner of a piller, with a frostie bitten face, frowning, and is scante yet cleane cooled of the hotte burnyng cholour kindeled against the cankered Cardinall Wolsey, writing many a sharpe disticon with bloudie penne againste hym; and sente them by the infernall rivers Styx, Flegiton and Acheron, by the Feriman of helle, called Charon, to the said Cardinall.

"How the Cardinall came of nought,
And his Prelacie solde and bought,
And where such Prelates bee
Sprong of lowe degree:
And spirituall dignitee,
Farewell benignitee,
Farewell simplicitee,
Farewell humanitee,
Farewell good charitee.
Thus parvum literatus
Came from Rome gatus,
Doctor dawpatus,
Scante a bachelaratus.
And thus Skelton did ende
With Wolsey his friende."

The Rev. Mr. Dyce, in his "Skelton's Works," I. p. lxxxvj, cites only the two first lines, adding that the rest were "chiefly made up from Skelton's Works," not being aware that they were a parody, and one of the oldest in our language. Of Chaucer, who comes next, Bullein says: —

"Wittie Chaucer satte in a Chaire of gold covered with Roses, writing prose and risme, accompanied with the Spirites of many kynges, knightes and faire ladies, whom he pleasauntly besprinkeled with the sweete water of the welle consecrated unto the Muses; and as the heavenly spirite commended his deare Brigham for the worthie entombyng of his bones, worthie of memorie, in the long slepyng chamber of most famous kinges, even so in tragedie he bewailed the sodaine resurrection of many a noble man before their time, in spoilyng of Epitaphes; whereby many have lost their inheritannce." &c.

Here again, as in the address to the Reader before Warner's "Continuance of Albion's England," 1606, we see Brigham justly applauded, for the cost he incurred in the " worthy emtombing " of Chaucer's bones in Westminster Abbey. Of Lidgate, Bullein speaks as follows : —

" Lamentyng Lidgate, lurking emong the lillie[s], with a bald skons, with a garlande of willowes about his pate: booted he was after sainct Benets guise, and a blacke stamell robe, with a lothlie monsterous hoode hangyng backwarde, he stoopyng forward, bewailyng every estate with the spirite of prouidence; forseyng the falles of wicked men, and the slipprie seates of Princes; the ebbyng and flowyng, the risyng and falling of men in auctoritie, and how vertue do advaunce the simple, and vice overthrow the most noble of the worlde."

Alexander Barclay Dr. Bullein calls Bartlet, in the irregular spelling of those times; and, asserting that he was " born beyond the cold river of Tweed," we see no sufficient reason for disbelieving that he was a native of Scotland. Barclay, after writing his Pastorals, &c., did not die until 1552, so that Bullein was his contemporary, and most likely knew him and the fact. He observes : —

" Then Bartlet, with an hoopyng russet long coate, with a pretie hoode in his necke, and five knottes upon his girdle, after Francis tricks. He was borne beyonde the cold river of Twede. He lodged upon a swete bed of Chamomill, under the Sinamum tree: about hym many Shepherdes and shepe, with pleasaunte pipes; greatly abhorring the life of Courtiers, Citizens, Usurers and Banckruptes &c. whose olde daies are miserable. And the estate of Shepherdes and countrie people he accoumpted moste happie and sure."

Whether Barclay were or were not a Scot, certain it is that he lived most of his time in Devonshire, far from the metropolis ; and continuing a rigid Catholic, as we see, of the order of St. Francis, he was sure to be abused by the Protestants. The later portion of Bullein's book is a ridicule of travellers' wonders, with an ironical description of Great Britain (called " Taerg Natrib ") as a country where the inhabitants were perfectly holy and virtuous. Everybody, even Ritson, has called this work " A Dialogue both pleasant and pitifull," but the last word really is *pietifull*, *i. e.* full of piety.

BULWER, JOHN. — Anthropometamorphosis: Man transform'd, or the Artificiall Changling historically presented in the mad and cruell Gallantry, foolish Bravery, ridiculous Beauty, filthy Finenesse, and loathsome Loveliness of most Nations, fashioning and altering their bodies from the mould intended by Nature; with Figures of those Transfigurations, &c. And an Appendix of the Pedigree of the English Gallant. Scripsit J. B. Cognomento Chirosophus. M. D. &c. — London, Printed by William Hunt, Anno Dom 1653. 4to. 323 *leaves.*

There was an edition in 1650, 8vo, of this singular and learned work, but it is here much augmented and improved. The title-page is preceded by a portrait of the author, by W. Faithorne, and the portrait by a "frontispiece," representing persons of various nations, with their peculiar and absurd transformations, brought to trial before Nature, who engages Adam and Eve for her assessors.

After five pages of verse, describing many of the monstrous changes men undergo by their own consent, we arrive at a dedication to Thomas Dickinson, Esq., in which the author states that the present was the fifth time "the heroic disease of writing" had attacked him: to this are appended six copies of commendatory verses in Latin and English, followed by a letter to the author in prose, "a hint of the use of this treatise," *Diploma Appollinis* in Latin hexameters, a list of authors quoted or mentioned, Errata, "a Table of the Scenes of Mans Transformation," and a general "Introduction." The body of the work occupies five hundred and fifty-nine pages, upon which are many coarsely executed woodcuts, representing some of the most striking "transfigurations." On p. 20 is given the representation of one of

"such men
Whose heads stood in their breasts,"

a race in the existence of which the author states his implicit belief, and this at a date fifty years subsequent to the time when Shakspeare wrote his "Tempest" and "Othello," where also "men whose heads do grow beneath their shoulders" are spoken of. Our great dramatist availed himself of the popular notion on the subject, warranted by "Hackluyt's Voyages," and by the translation of Pliny, B. v., ch. 8., where "the Blemmii, who have no heads, but mouth and eyes, both in their breasts," are mentioned. At the end of Bulwer's work is an unusually complete index of the contents of a volume, which displays a great deal of curious knowledge, and elaborately illustrates many vulgar opinions and superstitions.

BUTTES, SIR WILLIAM. — A Booke of Epitaphes made on the death of Sir William Buttes, Knight, who deceased the third day of September, Anno 1583. — Imprinted at London by Henrie Midleton. 4to. 28 *leaves.*

We notice this small and unique volume, not for any intrinsic worth it possesses, but because it contains several specimens of English versification by men whose names have not hitherto found their way into Ritson's Bibl. Poet., or into any other production of the kind. Of the subject of the Epitaphs we know nothing, unless Sir William Buttes were descended from Dr. Buttes, Physician to Henry VIII., and father of the Dr. Buttes who in 1599 published a work called "Dyet's Dry Dinner," more singular in its title than meritorious in its contents. The English versifiers on the death of Sir William Buttes are his relative T. Buttes, Henry Gosnold, Thomas Corbold, Samuel Stalon, and Robert Lawes, while the Latin contributions are by Richard Harvey, William Bourne, Henry Gosnold, Francis Burleigh, and Thomas Corbold. In none of these can we find a line that is worth quoting; but we gather, from particular expressions and allusions, that Sir William Buttes died rich, and that he had acquired his wealth by mercantile pursuits.

CAMBRIDGE JESTS. — Cambridge Jests, or Witty Alarums for Melancholy Spirits. By a Lover of Ha, Ha, He. —

London, Printed for Samuel Lowndes &c. 1674. 12mo. 76 *leaves*.

This collection consists of the usual stock of such merry miscellanies, and one additional story, so to call it, which shows how little people were acquainted, even in the reign of Charles II., with Shakspeare's "Merchant of Venice." For this reason only we notice "Cambridge Jests." When Lord Lansdowne, in 1701, made Shylock a comic character and a modern Israelite, introducing it by the line,

"To day we punish a stock-jobbing Jew,"

the original had been entirely forgotten on the stage, and few people knew what Shakspeare had really written, and how he had drawn the character, until the appearance of Rowe's edition of "the Works of Mr. William Shakespear" in 1709. The incident of the pound of flesh is thus told in "Cambridge Jests," even the scene having been transferred from Venice to Constantinople.

"In the City of Constantinople a certain Christian desired to borrow of a Jew the sum of five hundred Duckets. The Jew lent them unto him with condition that for the use of the money he should, at the end of the term, give him two ounces of his flesh, cut off in some one of his members. The day of payment being come, the Christian repayed the five hundred Duckets to the Jew, but refused to give him any part of his flesh. The Jew, not willing to lose his interest, convented the Christian before Sultan Soliman, Emperour of the Turks, who having heard the wicked demand of the one, and the answer of the other, commanded a Razor to be brought and to be given to the Jew, to whom he said: 'Because thou shalt know that justice is done thee, take there the Razor, and cut from the flesh of the Christian two ounces which thou demandest; but take heed thou cut neither more nor less, for if thou dost, thou shalt surely die.' The Jew, holding that to be a thing impossible, durst not adventure, but acquitted the Christian his interest."

It seems out of the question to suppose that, if Shakspeare's play had at this time been popularly known, the incident could have been thus related in a common jest-book: it occurs in it on p. 148. Dogget, as most people are aware, performed the part of Lord Lansdowne's Jew in 1701, in the dialect of an Anglo-German Hebrew.

Campion, Edmund. — A true reporte of the death & martyrdome of M. Campion, Jesuite and preiste, & M. Sherwin & M. Bryan, preistes, at Tiborne the first of December 1581. Obseruid and written by a Catholike preist, which was present therat. Wherunto is annexid certayne verses made by sundrie persons. B. L. 4to. 26 *leaves*.

This title is followed by a text from Apoca. vii., under the symbol of the Society of Jesus; and there is no doubt that the tract was either printed abroad, or secretly, in this country, without any printer's name. It is a vindication of Campion, Sherwin, and Bryan, and an attack upon "Charke, Hanmer, Whitakers, Fyld, Keltrigh, Eliot, kogging Munday, riming Elderton and John Nichols, the disciple of bawdy Bale, all worshipfull writers at this time against Preistes & Jesuites." After detailing the circumstances of the execution, at which Sir Francis Knowles, Lord Charles Howard, Sir Henry Lee, and others were present, "a caveat to the reader touching A. M. his discovery" is added, which supplies some interesting particulars regarding that celebrated pamphleteer, poet, and dramatist, Anthony Munday.

It asserts that he "first was a stage player (no doubt a calling of some creditt), after, an aprentise, which tyme he well served with deceaving of his master, then wandring towards Italy, by his owne report became a coosener in his journey. Comming to Rome in his short abode there was charitably relieved, but never admitted in the Seminary, as he pleseth to lye in the title of his booke, and, being wery of well doing, returned home to his first vomite againe. I omite to declare how this scholler, new come out of Italy, did play extempore; those gentlemen and others whiche were present can best give witnes of his dexterity, who, being wery of his folly, hissed him from his stage. Then, being therby discouraged, he set forth a balet against playes, but yet (O constant youth) he now beginnes againe to ruffle upon the stage. I omit, among other places, his behavior in Barbican with his good mistres and mother, from whence our superintendent might fetch him to his court, were it not for love (I would saye slaunder) to their gospel. Yet I thinke it not amiss to remember thee of this boyes infelicitie two several wayes of late notorious."

Hence the writer (supposed without much evidence to be Robert Parsons) proceeds to notice two publications by Munday: one upon the death of Everard Haunce, a copy of which was sold among Heber's books, and the other his tract entitled "A Discoverie of Edmond Campion and his Confederates," which also includes an account of their execution, and was published in 8vo by Edward White, with the date of 1582. Munday claimed to have been very instrumental, not only in the detection, but in the capture of Campion, and having been a witness at his trial, was present at his execution for the purpose of confronting him. The latter part of Munday's tract is "A breefe Discourse concerning the deathes of Edmond Campion, Jesuit, Raphe Shirwin and Alexander Brian, on 1 Dec. 1581"; and in the next year Munday wrote, and printed, a reply to the publication before us. (See MUNDAY, *post.*)

At the close of the small volume in our hands are four poems upon Campion and his fellow-sufferers. The first contains the following stanza against Munday: —

"The witnesse false, Sledd, Munday & the rest,
Which had your slanders noted in your booke,
Confesse your fault beforehand; it were best,
Lest God do find it written, when he doth looke
In dreadfull doome upon the soules of men:
It will be late (alas) to mend it then."

Elderton excited the author's wrath by ballads he had published, in the usual course of his calling, upon the execution of Campion. He attacks him thus: —

"Fonde Elderton, call in thy foolish rime:
Thy scurile balates are to bad to sell:
Let good men rest, and mend thy self in time.
Confesse in prose thou hast not meetred well;
Or if thy folly can not choose but fayne,
Write alehouse toys — blaspheme not in thy vain."

No ballad by Elderton on this subject has come down to us: he was a noted writer of poems upon temporary topics, and the laughing-stock of Thomas Nash and other younger contemporaries: he had been a player as early as 1552, (Kempe's Loseley MSS. p. 47,) and twenty years afterwards we find him at the head of a company of actors. It must have been subsequently to this date that he subsisted mainly by "balladìng," though some of his extant productions of that class bear an earlier date, as, for instance, his Epitaph upon Bishop Jewell in 1571. His "Lamentation of Follie," printed by Edward Allde without date, is probably still older, and, from expressions it contains, may be assigned to the very commencement of the reign of Elizabeth.[1]

CAP AND THE HEAD. — A Pleasaunt Dialogue or disputation betweene the Cap and the Head. — Imprinted at London by Henry Denham for Lucas Harrison &c. Anno 1564. Novembris 11. B. L. 12mo. 23 *leaves.*

This highly amusing and curious tract is anonymous, and it was so popular that it came to a second edition very early in 1565, a copy bearing the date of 19th Feb. in that year being known, and preserved in the library at Bridgewater House. It consists entirely of a conversation between a Cap and a Head that was about to put it on, the former remonstrating against the fantastic fashions of the early part of the reign of Elizabeth, and illustrating very minutely, and entertainingly, many of the prevailing peculiarities in attire, but especially in the ornaments and coverings for the head. It opens as follows: —

[1] It was reprinted by the Percy Society in 1840, with a more interesting, but not more curious ballad, entitled "The Panges of Love and Lover's Fittes," which is quoted by Shakspeare in "Twelfth Night," and in "Romeo and Juliet." It is also mentioned in the old play, "The Triumphs of Love and Fortune," 1589, and in the interlude of "The Trial of Treasure," 1567. We quote a single stanza relating to Troilus and Cressida: —

> "Knowe ye not how Troylus
> Languished, and lost his joye,
> With fittes and fevers mervailous,
> For Cressida that dwelt in Troye?
> Tyll pytie planted in hir brest,
> Ladie! Ladie!
> To slepe with him and graunt him rest,
> My deare Ladie!"

"*The Cap.* O, how undiscretely doth Fortune deale with many in this world! cursed be the time that ever I was appoynted to cover thee.

"*The Head.* What the Divel aylest thou? thou doest nothing now a dayes but murmure and grudge.

"*The Cap.* I would the Wolle that I was made of and the Sheepe that bare it had been devoured wyth Dogges, or that it had beene burned in the filthy fyngers of the ilfavoured olde queane that spunne it.

"*The Head.* Why, what meanest thou by this Cursing? I never did thee any harme."

Afterwards the Cap enters into particulars of his grievances; and this and other passages would have afforded amusing illustrations to the author of the articles on ancient head-dresses in Vol. xxiv. of the Archæologia: —

"*The Cap.* Who is able to beare suche injurye at thy hande? thou art never contented to weare me after one fashion; but one while thou wearest me like a Garlande; by and by lyke a Steeple; another whyle a Barber's Bason; anone after lyke a Boll whelmed upsyde downe; sometyme lyke a Royster; sometime lyke a Souldiour, and sometime like an Antique; sometyme plited, and anone after unplited; and not being contented with that, thou byndest mee wyth garishe bandes, one while of one colour, and another while of an other, and sometyme wyth many coloures at once, as if I were mad: howe is it possible to suffer so many chaunges?"

The Cap is sometimes very severe and satirical in his censures: —

"For how many are paynted wyth Diademe for Saincts, that in time of their lyfe have bene false Traytoures to their King and Countrye? howe many crowned wyth Golde, that haue better deserved to be crowned with perpetuall shame? how many paynted wyth precious Myters that, if their lives were wel examined, might more worthily weare an infamous Pyllory paper? so that their head attyre honoureth not them, but they rather dishonour their attyre: whereby thou maist perceave that it is not possyble for me to hyde the faultes of the understanding, as I hyde the scurfe of thy scalde Pate."

The Cap further complains that he is sometimes ridiculously "stuck with Ostridge, Cranes, Parrats, Bittons, Cockes and Capons feathers," signifying nothing but the lightness of the brain of the wearer. At last Cap and Head go out into the street together, and Cap questions Head very closely why he pulls him off so frequently to salute different people as they pass.

"*The Cap.* * * * But tell me why diddest thou put me of to him that passed by?

"*The Head.* Wouldest thou not have me shew obeyscence to him? looke what a fayre chayne he hath on.

"*The Cap.* Then madest thou curtesy to hys chayne, and not to him.

"*The Head.* Nay, I did it to him bycause of hys chaine.

"*The Cap.* What is hee.

"*The Head.* I can not tell; but well I wote he hath a fayre chayne.

"*The Cap.* But if he had had none, thou wouldest have let him passe.

"*The Head.* Yea: but sawest thou not, when hee perceaved that I made no accoumpte of hym, howe he opened his Cloake of purpose that I might see his chayne? and then, thou knowest, I can doe no lesse."

This leads to various shrewd remarks upon persons of different stations and professions: one of the persons they pass is a Catholic bishop, and in the course of the conversation the Head tells an anecdote how he escaped being considered a heretic. Throughout the discussion the Cap has by far the best of the "disputation," which terminates in this manner: —

"*The Head.* I cannot deny but thou haste spoken reason, but bycause I will not seeme to bee selfe willed, I minde to frame myselfe according to the time and company; and therfore beare with mee tyll I haue money to bye a new Cap, at which time I minde to let thee rest in quiet.

"*The Cap.* Well, syth it wyll be no better, I minde no more to trouble thee; but wyll arme my selfe paciently to beare all these Injuries, in hope that a time will come that thou shalte both remember my wordes, and I also shall bee in quiet: therefore, doe what thou wilte, I wyll say no more."

The last leaf is occupied only by the printer's colophon, with the same date as on the title-page.

CAREW, RICHARD. — Godfrey of Bulloigne or the Recouerie of Hierusalem. An heroicall poeme written in Italian by Sieg. Torquato Tasso and translated into English by R. C. Esquire. And now the first part containing fiue Cantos imprinted in both Languages. — London, Imprinted by John Windet for Thomas Man. 1594. 4to. 120 *leaves.*

This very faithful version was made by Richard Carew of

Anthony, author of the "Survey of Cornwall." There are not two editions in 1594, but the title-pages of some copies differ in the imprint, purporting to have been "printed by John Windet for Christopher Hunt of Exceter"; and an address, subscribed C. H., informs the reader that the MS. had got abroad without Carew's knowledge, and that, after five cantos had been printed, he forbade the publication of more, at least for the present. The address to this copy, instead of being dated, as usual with others we have seen, "From Exceter the last of Februarie 1594," is "From Exceter the last of Februarie 1593." In one case, no doubt, the commencement of the year was calculated from 1st January, and in the other from 25th March.

As Fairefax in 1600 (see FAIREFAX, *post*) availed himself of Carew's version, especially in the first draught of the first stanza of his translation, without much improving upon it, we may subjoin it here for the sake of comparison. Carew renders it, —

"I sing the godly armes and that Chieftaine,
Who great sepulchre of our Lord did free;
Much with his hande, much wrought he with his braine;
Much in his glorious conquest suffred hee.
And hell in vain it selfe opposde, in vaine
The mixed troops, Asian and Libick, flee
To armes; for heaven him favour'd, and he drew
To sacred ensignes his straid mates anew."

Perhaps one reason why Fairefax afterwards made changes in his first stanza was, that he was accused of having copied Carew. Carew's translation was never completed, and, as far as it goes, it is rather remarkable for fidelity than for freedom: his versification is always regular, and in the Italian form of stanza. If Carew were too faithful, certainly Fairefax was too free.

CAREW, RICHARD. — A Herrings Tayle: Contayning a Poeticall fiction of diuers matters worthie the reading. — At London Printed for Matthew Lownes. 1598. 4to. 18 *leaves.*

On the authority of Guillim's Heraldry, p. 154, edit. 1610, it has been supposed that this rhyming rigmarole, for it is nothing better, was written by Richard Carew of Anthony, the author of the preceding work, and of the "Survey of Cornwall," 1602. The internal evidence is all the other way; for, allowing much for discursiveness and intended obscurity, it is clear that the writer knew nothing of metre, and his meaning, when discoverable, is anything but such as would proceed from a man of good sense, elegant mind, and refined attainments. We think, therefore, that Guillim, who was himself no good judge of such matters, was misinformed: in deference, however, to his statement we have placed the tract under Carew's name. That the real writer, whoever he may have been, was a man of some classical learning, the many allusions to ancient history and mythology sufficiently establish; but even in this respect the piece is certainly not worthy of Carew, and it is very properly not assigned to him in either edition of Lowndes' Bibl. Man., while Fry, in his Bibl. Mem., 1816, 4to, p. 156, though he gives the writer far more than deserved credit, does not pretend to have ascertained who he was. It has been said that an allegory was intended, and that "A Herring's Tayle" was a sort of satire upon two eminent personages of the time; but we can discern nothing of the kind, although somebody may possibly have been personified under the figure of a snail in its futile endeavor to climb. That the author did not understand the commonest rules of metre, as then practised by Carew himself and so many great poets, we may prove by the first six miserably lame lines:—

"I sing the strange adventures of the hardie Snayle
Who durst (unlikely match) the weathercock assayle:
A bold attempt, at first by fortune flattered
With boote, but at the last to bale abandoned.
Helpe, sportfull Muse, to tune my gander-keaking quill,
And with inck blotles of sad merriments it fill." &c.

No person with the slightest ear for rhythm could possibly have produced such lines, and many others equally lamentable; yet the writer, if we understand him, professes admiration for Spenser and Sidney, the latter by his name and the former as the "Muses despencier":—

"But neither can I tell, ne can I stay to tell
This pallace architecture, where perfections dwell.
Who list such know, let him *Muses despencier* reede,
Or thee whom England sole did since the Conquest breed
To conquer ignorance, *Sidney*, like whom endite
Euen Plato would, as Jove (they say) like Plato write."

We conjecture that by *Muses despencier* (printed in Italics in the original) the author of "The Faery Queene" must have been intended, but the pun is as bad as the poetry, and we can trace no other allusion to any writer of the period. If the riddle of the whole piece were ever worth solving, we are not in a condition to explain it now, and such lines as those that follow could surely never have been considered tolerable:—

"For when the god of puffes, great master of the ayre,
Saw the base Snayle of his sonnes spoyles a Trophee reare,
Choler enflam'd his heart, revenge tickled his fist,
Disdaine wrinckled his face to smile of little list,
And up his throte bole staires climbd words of threatening,
Which to effects of deedes thus wise he sought to bring.
Poste through his large Dominions are writs out sent
To warne his windie vassals to a parliament:
So whizzing, blustring, peeping, whisking, there came in
First lithie Eurus with his parchie rivild skin;
Next Boreas armd in ice," &c.

Some humor seems here to have been meditated, but most ineffectually, as far as moderns are concerned; and when, in his last words, the author tells us that his "pen is worne to the stumpe," it is much in the same condition as the reader's patience.

CARRE, JOHN.—A Larume Belle for London, with a caueat or warning to England: also a pitiful complaint of the penitente synner, newlie set forthe by Ihon Carre, Citizein of London.—Imprinted at London by Henry Kirckham at the signe of the blacke Boie at the little North doore of Poules. 1573. 8vo. B. L. 11 *leaves*.

In this small unique tract we introduce two new names into

the annals of our popular poetical literature, — John Carre, the editor of the book, and W. Phillippes, who had a share in its composition. The main subject is the pride, vanity, and general vices of the metropolis, which they attack in a strongly puritanical spirit, warning the inhabitants to repent, ere they be overwhelmed by the judgments of heaven. We know nothing of the writer beyond the fact stated upon the title-page, that, whatever his coadjutor Phillippes may have been, Carre was free of the city: a John Phillips subsequently wrote upon the death of Sir P. Sidney and other topics, and his religious opinions were similar to those of his namesake.

The first poem subscribed "Finis qd Ihon Carre," begins immediately after the title-page, —

"For thee, O London! I lament,
And wring my hands with mourning chere,
Because that thou will not repent,
Seyng thy destruction draweth nere.
If it be true, as scriptures tell,
Thy sinnes will sincke thee doune to hell.

"The vices which in thee are used
To[o] tedious are for me to tell:
Thy noble fame is sore abused
By those whiche in thee now doe dwell:
Whereby I see thy great decaie,
That God doth threaten thee eche daie."

He observes the same measure through sixteen stanzas, especially attacking pride, "a weed that it is no boot to tread down, since it must be plucked up by the root:" —

"So likewise pride in London now
Doeth florishe in suche goodly sorte,
That thei invent whiche waie and how
Thereby augmented it might be;
And nothyng doe regarde at all
That pride in the ende will have a fall."

Here the defective rhyme "sorte" and "be" shows a clear misprint, which may be easily remedied if we read "in such high *degree*" for "in such goodly sort." We need hardly mention that Carre instances the fate of Sodom and Gomorrah; but with more novelty he goes on to refer to the destruction of Alexandria, Nineveh, Jerusalem, and even Troy, as warnings to London: he exclaims, —

> "O London! thou hast cause to weepe,
> For to consider thine estate:
> Thou art in synne now drounde so deepe,
> That from hell mouthe thou canst not scape:
> Except repentance thou embrace,
> At Gods hande thou shalt finde no grace."

In his last stanza he again reminds his fellow-citizens that "pride must have a fall," after which Phillippes takes up the song to a very similar tune, but in a different measure — fourteen-syllable lines, divided in order to come into the small page. He entitles his poem "A Caveat or warning to Englande," and it begins thus tautologously: —

> "The present plagues that now we fele
> our joyes doeth muche encroche,
> And feare of forrein foes besides
> who seeke for to approche
>
> "To worke annoye to Britaine soile,
> but Jove be thankte therefore,
> That hath dislodgde the treason now
> which Curia kept in store."

Here the substitution of Jove for the name of the Creator, and the use of the word Curia, in order, perhaps, to avoid more particular and personal allusion, are remarkable. Thence, affecting a classical style, he talks of Iris and Rhamnusius, and diverges to a wolf "in lambs array," finally arriving at a horticultural figure, representing Queen Elizabeth as the gardener: —

> "The gardner hath her sickle sharpte [1]
> to plucke up all suche seedes
> As to the eye do fruitfull seme,
> and yet are stincking weedes;
>
> "Whose barrein braunche as fertile semde,
> to those that simple were,

[1] The figure, resembling a garden to a kingdom, will bring to mind A. III. sc. 4, of Shakspeare's "Richard II."

In eche respect, as did the tree
  that yerely fruict did beare.

"But he whiche first did plant those trees
  in this our Englishe lande,
And did assigne the Gardener, she
  to take the charge in hande,

"Hath showne her Grace where she shall graft,
  and where that she shall roote,
According as affection serves
  to suche as yelde no fruite."

He advises the Queen to use her sickle in time "to crop such imps," and "not to stay as erst she did," until they had clomb too high. He, not very charitably, thus invokes her: —

"Renowned Prince, even so I crave,
  foresee thy subjectes woes,
And yelde revenge for such as wishe
  thy Croune to forrein foes;"

and at last addresses himself to the divine power by his proper appellation. While praying for the Queen, he does not forget the Lord Mayor and Aldermen of London; from whence we may, perhaps, infer that Phillippes also was a member of the corporation.

"And to this citie graunt (O God!)
  lorde Maior and his fraternitie
Degresse nothyng from Princes will,
  but joyne as one in unitie.

"God prosper her! God length her raigne!
  from harmes her grace God save!
Poore Phillippes he with gushyng teares
  doth thus desire to have.
      Finis. per W. Phillippes."

So, lest his name should be passed over in the text, he adds it immediately afterwards at the conclusion. To these two productions is added an anonymous third, in a different form and measure, but otherwise possessing no features calling for observation.

Cartwright, John. — The Preachers Travels. Wherein is set downe a true Iournall to the confines of the East Indies, through the great Countreyes of Syria, Mesopotamia &c. With the Authors returne by the way of Persia, Susiana, &c. Containing a full survew of the Kingdom of Persia, &c. Also a true relation of Sir Anthonie Sherley's entertainment there: &c. With the description of a Port in the Persian gulf commodious for our East Indian Merchants &c. Penned by I. C. sometimes student in Magdalen College in Oxford. — London Printed for Thomas Thorppe, and are to bee sold by Walter Burre. 1611. 4to. 56 *leaves.*

The author does not state his reason for undertaking this long and perilous journey, the account of which is dedicated to Sir Thomas Hunt (a Justice of the Peace of Surrey), "from mine House in Southwarke, this 18 of October. Anno Dom. 1611." On the next page he tells the "gentle Reader" that he had intended to have added some observations to show the great probability of a Northwest Passage, but he had delayed it, until he had ascertained whether the then current news were true that it had been discovered.

Cartwright narrates at considerable length the chief incidents of his travels through the various countries named on his title-page, and, on p. 67, adverts to Sir Anthony Sherley, and his mission to Persia, to stir the sovereign up against the Turks. He admits that Robert Sherley was left in Persia by his brother as a sort of pledge, and bears witness to the great favor in which he maintained himself in the court at Ispahan. The following is a remarkable allusion to the play, by Day, Rowley, and Wilkins, called "The Travels of three English Brothers," often acted, and printed in 1607, about four years before Cartwright's return to England. "And farther, the King, to manifest his love, gave him (Robert Sherley) out of his Seraglion in marriage a Circassian lady of great esteeme and regard. But that he should have a child in Persia, and that the King (a professed enemie to the name of our blessed Saviour) should be the God-father, this certainely is more fit for a Stage, for the common people to wonder at, then for any mans private studies."

It was on the author's return that he went to Mosul and surveyed the neighboring remains of Nineveh. He says, and the passage in our day is curious, — "It is agreed by all prophane writers, and confirmed by the Scriptures, that this cittie exceeded all other citties in circuit and answerable magnificence. For it seems by the ruinous foundation (which I thoroughly viewed) that it was built with foure sides, but not equall or square; for the two longer sides had each of them (as we gesse) an hundreth and fifty furlongs; the two shorter sides ninty furlongs, which amounteth to foure hundred and eighty furlongs of ground, which makes three score miles, accounting eight furlongs to an Italian mile." Whether this statement and calculation accords with modern measurements and computations we know not, but it is very possible that 250 years ago more of the proportions of Nineveh could be ascertained than at present. The practice of conveying goods and passengers down the Tigris upon air-filled goat-skins prevailed then as now, for Cartwright tells us, —

"From the Island of Eden we returned to Mosul, we staied there eight daies, and so went down the river Tigris to Bagdat, or New Babilon, being carried not on boat, as down the river Euphrates, but upon certaine Zataires or rafts, borne upon goates skins blowne full of winde like bladders. Which rafts they sell at Bagdat for fire, and carry their skins againe home upon Asses by land, to make other voyages down the said river."

The above, as might be expected, exactly accords with the present practice. The author is here and there too tedious and minute, while in other places he is too brief and general in his descriptions. On the whole, his book is rather a dull one, but there is less on the subject of religion than we should have looked for in "The Preacher's Travels." The work is not especially rare, but it touches some points not adverted to by other writers.

CAUMPEDEN, HUGH. — The History of Kyng Boccus and Sydracke how he confounded his lerned men and in the syght of them dronke strong venym in the Name of the Trinite and dyd him no hurt. Also his dyuynyte that he lerned of the Boke of Noe. Also his profycye that he had by Reuelacyon of the Aungell. Also the aunsweris to the questions of wisdome both morall and naturall with much worldly wysdome contayned in number ccclxij. Translated by Hugo of Caumpeden out of Frenche in to Englisshe. — [Colophon] Thus endeth the hystory and questyōs of kynge Boccus and Sydracke. — Prynted at London by Thomas Godfray. At the coste and charge of dan Robert Saltwode mōke of saynt Austens at Cantorbury. *Cum priuilegio regali.*

Warton (H. E. P. II. 408, edit. 8vo), Dibdin (Typ. Ant. III. 65), and others, have inconsiderately given 1510 as the date when this religious romance was printed, while the fact is that Godfray, whose name it bears in the colophon, did not begin to employ a press until 1522: the type serves also to show that it was similar to that he used for his Chaucer in 1532.

There is a confusion in the title-page which has sometimes misled those who have spoken of the work without reading it, for it was not Kyng Boccus who "confounded his learned men," but Sydracke; and it was Sydracke who drank the poison which, by the blessing of the Trinity, did him no injury: Sydracke too, of whose origin little or nothing is said, answered so satisfactorily the 362 questions in divinity, morality, natural history, &c., put to him by King Boccus. This he accomplished by the aid of the Holy Ghost, in addition to the conversion of all India to Christianity, although it afterwards relapsed to its ancient idolatry. Warton quotes from a MS. (Laud. G. 57) which materially differs from the printed copy, to which we have confined ourselves. It thus opens: —

"Men may fynde in olde bokys,
Who so therin lokys,
Actes worthy of memory
Full of knowledge and mystery;
Wherof I shall shew a lytell jeste
That be fell ons in the Eest.

"Ther was a Kynge that Boccus hyght,
And was a man of moche myght:
His land lay by the greate ynde
Bactorye hyght it as we fynde,
After the tyme of Noe even
Eyght hundred yere fourty and seuen.
The Kynge Boccus hym be thought
That he wolde haue a cytye wrought,
His enmyes ther with to fere
And agayn them to mayntayne his were.
Chefly for a kynge that was his foo
That moche of ynde longed vnto;
His name was Garaab: the Kynge
Boccus tho purueyed all thynge
And shortly a towre began he:
There he wolde make a cytye,
And was ryght in the incomynge
Of Garabys lande the Kynge."

By "Garaby's land" we are, perhaps, to understand Araby; but the author's chronology is a little defective, since he makes all that he relates occur only 847 years after the time of Noah. Boccus began his tower, but every night what he had done in the day was demolished, and "foure score and ix maysters," whom he consulted, could not discover the cause. He casts them all into prison and sends for Sydracke, an old man who professes to be able to carry out the completion of the tower. He converts Boccus to the true faith by showing him "the umbre of the Trinity" in a vessel of water; but as his people are thereby enraged, they insist that Sydracke shall drink "stronge venym": he consents to do so, and "it dyd him no hurt." Then follow the 362 questions which Boccus proposes to Sydracke, and the answers to them open the King's mind to the whole history of man's creation, and to the mystery of his redemption. Some of the doubts suggested by Boccus are only upon points of natural philosophy, as question 59,—

"May eny woman bere mo
Chyldren in her at onys than two?"

and question 74,—

"Why are some men blake in towne,
Some whyt and some browne?"

Other questions regard music and the sciences, as, —

"The fyrst instrument who made it,
And how came it in his wyt?"

to which Sydracke's answer is worth giving for its true poetry, in conception more than in words: —

"Of the chyldren of Noe
Japhet, the yongest of the thre,
He contryved it, and wrought
As God it sent in his thought:
And of the sound he it toke
Of trees that the wynde shoke;
And also of waters soune
That ran harde from hylles doune.
Some soune was lowe and some hye,
And therof found he melody.
An instrument he made anone
That melody to worke upon."

We cannot at all agree with Warton that there is "no sort of elegance in the diction," when we read a passage like the above. Question 207 reads like a puzzler, but Sydracke answers it in terms that would have not been at all relished in the time of the Stuarts: the question is, —

"Whether is hyer, as thou doyst undarstand,
The Kynge, or the lawe of the lande?"

To which the sage replies, —

"If the Kynge do agayne the lawe,
Lawe shal hym deme with skyl and ryght:
Than is the lawe above his myght,
And breke he the lawe in eny thyng,
He is not worthy to be kynge."

Afterwards the questions again become religious and polemical, as to whether Christ's disciples could work miracles; when Christ shall come to redeem the world, &c.? and under the last answer to question 362, we read "The ende of the hystory." Here it is related that Boccus completed the tower in the name of the Trinity; that Garaab submitted and was converted, but that after the deaths of Boccus and Sydracke all went wrong again, and the people of India reverted to their old pagan faith and worship. At the close, "Hughe of Caumpeden" claims the whole as his translation ; but, as far as English is concerned, it does not read as if the materials had been derived from any foreign source. Dibdin speaks of an "Epilogue," but there is nothing so called by the writer, and the word "Finis" precedes the colophon. This romance is not noticed by Ellis in his "Specimens."

CENTURION.—The valiant and most laudable fight performed in the Straights, by the Centurion of London, against five Spanish Gallies. Who is safely returned this present Moneth of May. Anno D. 1591. 4to. B. L. 3 *leaves.*

This tract, small as it is, was considered of sufficient importance to be entered at Stationer's Hall on the 15th May, 1591, by Andrewe White, who, on the same day, also registered "a ballad of the same vyctorye." There is a woodcut of a ship under sail on the title-page, and it occupies so much room that, if there were ever any stationer's name under it, it has been cut away. The terms of the entry in the Registers are these:—

"Andrewe White. Entred unto him &c. The wonderfull vyctorie obteyned by the Centuryon of London againste fyve Spanishe gallies, the iiijth. of April, beinge Ester daye, 1591."

The tract itself gives the date of the fight "upon Ester day last, in the straights of Iebualtare," where the Centurion, of 45 men and boys, in company with three smaller vessels, which left her to her fate, was attacked during a calm by five galleys full of Spaniards: "in every of the gallies," says the account, "there was about five or sixe hundreth souldiours," but the meaning must surely be that there were 500 or 600 Spaniards in the whole, and not in each galley. The enemy was beaten off with considerable loss, after a determined resistance of five hours and a half.

The name of the Captain of the Centurion was Robert Bradshawe, and at the end of the pamphlet, after the word "Finis," we meet with the subsequent sort of attestation to the truth of the narrative: "Present at this fight, Maister John Hawes, Marchant, and sundry other of good account." One of the companions of the Centurion, the Dolphin, was afterwards attacked by the Spaniards and blown up.

We are enabled to give three stanzas of the ballad from a broadside fragment: the whole, though we have never met with it, may be in existence, and what follows will be sufficient for identification: —

"Come listen noble mariners
And I a tale will tell
Of how the bold Centurion
The Spaniards did refell.
Rowe well ye mariners.

"She had but five and forty men,
The Spaniards many hunderd,
And if they gain'd the victory,
The ship they would have plunderd.
Rowe well, &c.

"The Spaniards rowd in gallies five;
No breath of wind did blow,
But still the bolde Centurion
Most boldly met the foe.
Rowe well, &c.

The above must have been sung to the popular old tune[1] of "Row well, ye Mariners," but we have seen various sea-songs, of different measures, to the same air.

CHALKHILL, JOHN. — Thealma and Clearchus. A Pastoral History in smooth and easie Verse. Written long since by John Chalkhill Esq. an Acquaintant and Friend of Edward Spencer. — London: Printed for Benj. Tooke &c. 1683. 8vo. 87 *leaves.*

This poem, in couplets, was edited by Izaac Walton, and his brief preface is dated May 7, 1678, but the work did not come from the press until five years afterwards. It is a circumstance

[1] Regarding this tune, see Chappell's admirable work "Popular Music of the olden Time," pp. 712, 770.

not noticed by Sir John Hawkins in his Life of Walton, nor in other authorities, that Spenser's Christian name is sometimes mistakenly given on the title-page, Edward instead of *Edmund*: such is the case with the copy before us. The volume is preceded by lines from the pen of Thomas Flatman, dated June 5, 1683, about six months before Walton's death, on the 15th of December, 1683, in his ninety-first year. The second Earl of Bridgewater seems to have been an attentive and an admiring reader of Chalkhill's poem, and has corrected errors of the press in various parts of it.

There is some reason for assigning to Chalkhill a collection of small poems under the title of "Alcilia, Philoparthens loving Folly," which was first printed in 4to, 1613,[1] in a volume with Marston's "Pygmalion's Image," and "The Love of Amos and Laura." The last of these is dedicated to Iz. Wa., or Izaac Walton, which connects him with the publication; and at the end of the first piece are the initials I. C., which perhaps were those of John Chalkhill. There were subsequent editions of "Alcilia" in 8vo, 1619, and 4to, 1628, and it certainly deserved considerable popularity for the "smooth and easy verse" in which it is written, — a quality imputed by Walton to Chalkhill's poetry. The author of "Alcilia" gives himself Philoparthen as his poetical name, and to him an epistle preceding the poems is addressed, headed, "A Letter written by a Gentleman to the Author his Friend," signed Philaretes: this may possibly have been Walton, who, nearly sixty years afterwards, edited "Thealma and Clearchus." The principal part of "Alcilia" consists of what I. C. is pleased to call "Sonnets," or short pieces in six-line stanzas, often unconnected excepting in the general subject. A specimen or two may be not improperly subjoined: —

"What thing is Love? A Tyrant of the minde,
Begot by hate of youth, brought forth by sloth,
Nurst with vain thoughts and changing as the wind;
A deepe dissembler void of faith and troth;

[1] See also, respecting this work and the edition of 1613, (which we never saw until sometime after the appearance of the Bridgw. Catalogue,) the Rev. T. Corser's valuable *Collectanea Anglo-poetica*, printed for the Chetham Society in 1860, p. 15.

Fraught with fond errors, doubts, despite, disdain,
And all the plagues that earth and hell containe.

"What thing is Beauty? Natures dearest minion,
The snare of youth; like the inconstant Moone
Waxing and wayning; error of opinion,
A mornings flowre that withereth ere noone:
A swelling fruit, no sooner ripe than rotten,
Which sicknesse makes forlorne, and time forgotten."

Not a very inconsiderable portion of "Alcilia" is in couplets, and the style, in more than one respect, reminds us of the versification of "Thealma and Clearchus." The following lines are from a division of the work called "Love's accusation at the Judgment-seat of Reason": it forms part of "the Author's evidence against Love": —

"It's now two yeares (as I remember well)
Since first this wretch, sent from the neather hell
To plague the world with new-found cruelties,
Under the shadow of two christall eyes
Betraid my sense; and as I slumbring lay
Felloniously convay'd my heart away,
Which most unjustly he detain'd from mee,
And exercis'd thereon strange tyranny.
Sometime his manner was to sport and game,
With bry'rs and thorns to raise and pricke the same;
Sometime with nettles of desire to sting it;
Sometime with pinsons of despaire to wring it:
Sometime againe he would anoynt the sore
And heale the place that he had hurt before;
But hurtfull helps and ministred in vaine,
Which served only to renew my paine:
For, after that, more wounds he added still,
Which pierced deepe, but had no power to kill.
Unhappy med'cine, which, in stead of cure,
Gives strength to make the patient more indure!"

Although, perhaps, no particular resemblance can be pointed out, yet in "Thealma and Clearchus" we observe the same flow of the verse, and so great a similarity of pause and rhythm, as, combined with other circumstances, to make it probable that both that work and "Alcilia" were from one pen.

Chamberlain, Robert. — Jocabella, or a Cabinet of Conceits. Whereunto are added Epigrams and other Poems by R. C. &c. — London, Printed by R. Hodgkinson for Daniel Frere &c. 1640. 12mo.

A jest-book of very rare occurrence, and especially recommended to notice by one of the "Conceits" applying to, and naming, Shakspeare.

The above printed title-page is preceded by an engraved one, "J. R. fecit," representing Mercury and the Fates in the foreground, and a champaign country with a river in the background: underneath the plate is this couplet: —

> "The Featherd God doth by his mirth betray
> The Fatall huswifes of or. lives to play."

The dedication to Mr. John Wild is subscribed Robert Chamberlain, probably the author of "Nocturnal Lucubrations," 1638, and "The Swaggering Damsel," a comedy, 1640, of whom little is known, excepting that he was of Exeter College. After a short address "to the Reader," begins, "Jocabella, or the Cabinet of Conceits," numbered from 1 to 459, followed by a few poems, only interesting on account of their temporary application. One is, "On the new fashion'd coats without sleeves, called Rockets;" another, "On the new fashion'd high-crown'd hats;" a third, "On the new fashion'd long cuffes;" a fourth, "On Mr. Nabbes his Comedie called the Bride;" and a fifth, "On the Swines-fac't Lady." Two commendatory copies of verses, signed "C. G. Oxon." and "T. R.," most unusually placed at the end, conclude the small volume.

The mention of Shakspeare is met with in the Conceit numbered 391, and it is this: —

> "One asked another what Shakespeares workes were worth, all being bound together? hee answered, not a farthing: not worth a farthing, said he, why so? He answered, that his playes were worth a great deale of money, but he never heard that his workes were worth anything at all."

At the time the above was printed, Shakspeare's Plays had been published twice "bound together," viz., in 1623 and 1632. All the "Conceits" are necessarily short, but some of them, as might be expected, have little point. The following illustrates a well-remembered passage in Butler's "Hudibras," published more than twenty years afterwards: it is numbered 69:—

"A gentleman going to take horse was observed to have but one spur; and being asked the reason, answered, that if he could make one side of his horse goe, he made no question but the other side would goe along with it."

Number 83 only gives in prose what on a previous page (21) we have seen in verse:—

"A Schoole-master, upon a bitter cold day, seeing one of his Scollers extreamly benumb'd, asked him what was the Latin for cold? he answered, ô Sir, I have it at my fingers ends."

The next we shall quote has little point, but it relates to an interesting topic—the employment, until the Restoration, of male actors on the stage to sustain the parts of women. It is numbered 122:—

"A Gentleman meeting a stage player in a great sicknes time, who had formerly plaid womens parts, told him he was growne grave, and that he began to have a beard: the other answered, while the grasse growes the horse did starve; meaning, because there was then no playing, and therefore he did let his beard grow."

While the plague prevailed in London, no performances were allowed at the theatres. These are a fair specimen of the whole work. According to Anthony Wood, Chamberlain did not go to Oxford until 1637, when he was thirty years old: if so, "Jocabella" must have been collected, and perhaps printed while he was still at college.

CHAPMAN, GEORGE.—Petrarchs seven Penitentiall Psalms, paraphrastically translated. With other Philosophicall Poems, and a Hymne to Christ upon the Crosse. Written by George Chapman. [Mottos from Arri. Epict.] —London, Imprinted by Matthew Selman dwelling in Fleete-streete neare Chancerie Lane. 1612. 8vo. 50 *leaves.*

This is one of the scarcest of Chapman's productions, and we have never seen more than three perfect copies of it. Warton (H. E. P. iv. 275) only knew of it from the Stationers' Registers, where it was entered the year before it was published; and Dr. Bliss (Ath. *Oxon.* II. 579), supplying the omissions of Wood, was obviously not aware of the existence of a most beautiful exemplar in the Bodleian Library: he cited the entry at Stationers' Hall exactly as he found it in Warton. The title-page above quoted gives us no information respecting what is, on some accounts, the most interesting portion of the small volume, namely, a number of miscellaneous original poems, of which we shall speak presently.

The dedication is to the then Master of the Rolls, Sir Edward Phillips, requesting him to read the book " at his emptiest leisure," Chapman excusing himself for not addressing it " to his most gracious and sacred patron " Prince Henry, on the ground that he destined for him his great work, the translation of Homer. Then begin the paraphrastical versions of Petrarch's seven penitential Psalms: I. *Heu mihi misero.* II. *Invocabo quem offendi.* III. *Miserere Domine.* IV. *Recordari libet.* V. *Noctes meæ in mœrore transeunt.* VI. *Circumvallarunt me inimici.* VII. *Cogitabam stare.*

He gives another, and what he terms a stricter, version of the first Psalm, but it is the only one he so treats. The paraphrase of the first stanza is this: —

" O me wretch! I have enrag'd
My Redeemer, and engag'd
My life, on death's slow foote presuming:
I have broke his blessed lawes,
Turning, with accursed cause,
Saving love to wrath consuming."

" More strictly translated," it stands as follows: —

" O me accurst! since I have set on me
(Incenst so sternely) my so meeke Redeemer,
And have bene proud, in prides supreme degree,
Of his so serious law a sleight esteemer."

Chapman admits, as all must allow, that his style is sometimes "harsh," and we may add that it is often obscure, from a struggle to bring his weighty and expansive thoughts into as small a compass of words as possible. His "Hymne to our Saviour on the Cross" begins,

> "Haile, great Redeemer! man and God all haile!
> Whose fervent agonie tore temples vaile,
> Let sacrifices out, darke Prophesies
> And miracles: and let in for all these
> A simple pietie, a naked heart
> And humble spirit, that no lesse impart
> And prove thy Godhead to us, being as rare,
> And in all sacred powre as circulare."

In reference to the words "A simple pietie," Chapman adds this note: — "Simplicitie of pietie, and good life answerable to such doctrine, in men, now as rare as miracles in other times; and require as much divinitie of supportation." The divines of his day were not much in favor with him, for he proceeds afterwards, —

> "Thou couldst have come in glorie past them all,
> With powre to force thy pleasure, and empale
> Thy Church with brasse and Adamant, that no swine,
> Nor theeves, nor hypocrites, nor fiends divine,
> Could have broke in, or rooted, or put on
> Vestments of pietie, when their hearts had none;"

upon which he subjoins this note: — "Such as are our divines in possession, and in fact devils, or wolves in sheepes clothing."

Elsewhere he thus applies the mythological fable of Narcissus:

> "Hence came the cruell fate that Orpheus
> Sings of Narcissus; who being amorous
> Of his shade in the water (which denotes
> Beautie in bodies that like water flotes)
> Despis'd himselfe, his soule, and so let fade
> His substance for a never-purchast shade:
> Since soules of their use ignorant are still
> With this vile bodies use, men never fill."

This is obscure. He draws up the moral of his whole hymn in the following couplet, placed at the end, and marked by Italic type: —

> "*Complaine not, whatsoever Need invades,*
> *But heaviest fortunes beare as lightest shades.*"

We must now make a few quotations from the third portion of the book, consisting chiefly of original pieces, which Chapman was too modest to announce on the title-page. After translating "Virgil's Epigram of a good man" and others, he gives a few epigrams of his own; as, —

Of Learning.

"Learning is the Art of good life: they, then,
That lead not good lives are not learned men."

Rather too severe a test, but a logical conclusion, admitting the premise.

Of Attire.

"In habite, nor in any ill to th'eie,
Affright the vulgar from Philosophie;
But as in lookes, words, workes men witnesse thee
Comely and checklesse, so in habite be."

We conclude with a piece entitled,

Of great Men.

"When Homer made Achilles passionate,
Wrathfull, revengefull, and insatiate
In his affections, what man will denie
He did compose all that of industrie?
To let man see that men of most renowne,
Strongst, noblest, fairest, if they set not downe
Decrees within them for disposing these
Of judgement, resolution, uprightnesse,
And vertuous knowledge of their use and ends
Mishaps and miseries no lesse extends
To their destruction, with all that they prisde
Then to the poorest and the most despisde."

As no bibliographer has ever made an extract from this rare volume, and some have not even mentioned it, we have thought it right to go more into detail regarding it.

Chapman, George. — Homer Prince of Poets: Translated according to the Greeke, in twelue Bookes of his Iliads. By Geo. Chapman. *Qui nil molitur ineptè.* — At London printed for Samuel Macham. n. d. fol. 126 *leaves.*

The title-page is engraved by W. Hole: on either side i: figure of Achilles and Hector, and at the top a head of Hom supported by Vulcan and Apollo, with this motto, —

Mulciber in Trojam, pro Troja stabat Apollo.

At what precise date these twelve first books of the Iliad ca out cannot be ascertained, as no year is mentioned in any part the volume. " Seven Books of the Iliads " and " The Shield Achilles" appeared in 1598, and the remaining five books w(not added to the seven and printed, at all events, till 1603, they are dedicated in verse, and at length, to Prince Henry: this in some copies (as in the present) a sonnet to Queen An is subjoined, but the leaf does not belong to the regular series the signatures. It is followed by an interesting address "to t Reader," where Chapman thus adverts to the general principl of translation: —

" Which how I have in my conversion prov'd,
I must confesse, I hardly dare referre
To reading judgements, since so generally
Custome hath made even th' ablest agents erre
In these translations: all so much apply
Their paines and cunnings word for word to render
Their patient Authors; when they may as well
Make fish with foule, camels with whales engender,
Or their tongues speech in other mouths compell.
For even as different a production
Asks Greeke and English; since, as they, in sounds
And letters shun one form and unison,
So have their sense and elegancie bounds
In their distinguisht natures, and require
Onely a judgement to make both consent
In sense and elocution; and aspire
As well to reach the spirit that was spent
In his example, as with art to pierse
His grammar and etymologie of words."

Of the capabilities of English he remarks farther on: —

" And for our tongue, that still is so empayrde
By travailing linguists, I can prove it cleere
That no tongue hath the Muses utterance heyrde
For verse, and that sweet musique to the eare

Strooke out of rime, so naturally as this:
  Our monosyllables so kindly fall
And meete, opposde in rime, as they did kisse.
  French and Italian, most immetricall:
Their many syllables in harsh collision
  Fall as they brake their necks: their bastard rimes
Saluting as they justl'd in transition,
  And set our teeth on edge, nor tunes nor times
Kept in their falls. And, methinkes, their long words
  Shewe in shorte verse, as in a narrow place
Two opposites should meet with two-hand swords,
  Unwieldily, without or use or grace."

What he says of English is certainly in a great degree true, but few will agree in this extraordinary opinion of Italian for the purposes of poetry. It is to be observed that, in 1598, Chapman employed the ten-syllable heroic measure, but he subsequently unfortunately adopted the fourteen-syllable long verse. The reason for the change he does not explain, but the consequence of it was the addition of epithets and expletives to make out the verse, sometimes without strengthening the sense. The volume is terminated by fourteen sonnets, addressed to the Duke of Lennox; Lord Chancellor Ellesmere; the Earl of Salisbury; the Earl of Suffolk; the Earl of Northampton; Lady Arabella Stuart; the Countess of Bedford; the Earl of Sussex; the Earl of Pembroke; the Earl of Montgomery; Lord Lisle; Lord Wotton; the Earl of Southampton; and Prince Henry. They are here enumerated, because sometimes there is a difference in this respect, and one copy now before us has two additional sonnets to Lady Montgomery and Lady Wroth: it was presented by the author to Sir Henry Crofts, and contains some emendations in the handwriting of the poet, such as the misprint of "a dance" for *advance*, in the first line of p. 215.

The two sonnets to Lady Montgomery and Lady Wroth, which do not usually occur, possess no greater merit than the other complimentary poems of the same kind. They were inserted on a separate leaf, each sonnet occupying a whole page, and were probably an after-thought by the translator. Spenser was the beginner of this practice of adding supplementary sonnets.

Chapman, George. — The Iliads of Homer, Prince of Poets. Never before in any languag truely translated. With a comment on some of his chiefe places. Donne according to the Greeke by Geo. Chapman. At London printed for Nathaniell Butter. n. d. fol. 189 *leaves.*

This title-page is a larger engraving, but of the same design (with trifling variations) as that to the twelve books. It is also by W. Hole.

The date of publication is here again a matter of conjecture, but it may be assigned to the year 1611 or 1612. The volume consists of the whole of the Iliad, and the dedication to the twelve books to Prince Henry is republished. To it succeeds a sonnet, printed for the first time, upon the anagram of Henry Prince of Wales, and the sonnet to the Queen. Next we have the address in verse to the Reader, as before the twelve books, with a prose preface, which contains the following remarkable passage : —

"If I have not turned him in any place falsly (as all other his interpreters have in many, and most of his chiefe places): if I have not left behind me any of his sentence, elegancie, height, intention and invention: if in some few places (especially in my first edition, being done so long since, and following the common tract) I be something paraphrasticall and faulty, is it justice in that poore fault (if they will needs have it so) to drowne all the rest of my labour? But there is a certaine envious Windsucker that hovers up and downe, laboriously engrossing al the aire with his luxurious ambition, and buzzing into every eare my detraction; affirming I turne Homer out of the Latine onely &c. that sets all his associates, and the whole rabble of my maligners on their wings with him to beare about my empaire, and poyson my reputation: One that, as he thinkes whatsoever he gives to others he takes from himselfe, so whatsoever he takes from others he addes to himselfe: One, that in this kinde of robberie doth, like Mercurie, that stole good and supplied it with counterfeit bad still: One, like the two gluttons, Phyloxenus and Gnatho, that would still emptie their noses in the dishes they loved, that no man might eate but themselves; for so this Castrill, with too hote a liver and lust after his owne glorie, and to devoure all himselfe, discourageth all appetites to the fame of another. I have stricken — single him as you can."

Some of the critics upon Ben Jonson would have "singled

him"; but the sonnet to Lady Montgomery, referred to in the preceding article, shows incontestably that Chapman and Jonson were on the most friendly terms. It seems likely that Marston was the poet alluded to, because he was afflicted with an envious turn of mind. Chapman apologizes for the imperfectness of his "first edition," by which we are perhaps to understand the twelve books published after 1603, and not the seven books printed in 1598. In this complete translation of the Iliad he very materially altered the first book, and the second as far as the catalogue of ships, after which Chapman adhered pretty closely to his earlier (not earliest) version. To every book he added a "Commentarius," partly perhaps to counteract the assertion of the "envious windsucker," that he had "turned Homer out of Latin only." He terminates the whole with the following brief address to his book, which, in the subsequent edition of the Iliad and Odyssey together, was omitted:—

> "Thus farre the Ilian Ruines I have laid
> Open to English eyes: in which (repaid
> With thine owne value) go, unvalu'd Booke,
> Live and be lov'd. If any envious looke
> Hurt thy cleare fame, learne that no state more hie
> Attends on vertue, then pin'd Envies eye.
> Would thou wert worth it that the best doth wound,
> Which this age feedes, and which the last shall bound."

It appears by what Chapman says in prose afterwards, that he translated the last twelve books in less than fifteen weeks. From a passage in his "*Euthymiæ Raptus*, or the Tears of Peace," 4to, 1609, we learn that Prince Henry had laid his injunctions upon the poet to complete his version of the Iliad.

> "In venturing this delay of your command
> To end his Iliads," &c.,

are his words, in what Chapman entitles *Corrolarium ad Principem*. For the purpose of finishing the undertaking with as little delay as possible, Chapman retired to Hitching, where his family appears to have been settled; and W. Browne, in his "Britannia's Pastorals" (1616), Book II. Song 2, calls him

> "The learned Shepherd of fair Hitching Hill."

In his address to the reader, before his translation, Chapman promises a separate "Poem of the Mysteries revealed in Homer." We are not aware that anything of the kind was published by him, but perhaps it afforded him pleasant occupation in his old age.

CHAPMAN, GEORGE.—The Crowne of all Homers Worckes, Batrachomyomachia, or the Battaile of Frogs and Mise. His Hymns and Epigrams. Translated according to the originall by George Chapman. — London, Printed by John Bill, &c. n. d. folio. 101 *leaves.*

The high reverence Chapman felt for the art in which he spent a long life seems to have increased with his age, and probably one of the latest undertakings upon which he was engaged was this completion of the translation of the works of the greatest Grecian poet. He tells the Earl of Somerset in the dedication: —

"Kings may, perhaps, wish even your beggars voice
To their eternities — how skornd a choice
Soever now it lies; and, dead, I may
Extend your life to light's extreamest raie.
If not, your Homer yet, past doubt, shall make
Immortall, like himself, your bounties stake
Put in my hands to propagate your fame: —
Such virtue reigns in such united name."

The preceding lines, with others not always so intelligible, follow an engraved title-page by Will: Pass, containing a portrait of Chapman at the bottom, and above, Homer crowned by Apollo and Minerva, with Mercury standing between them, at the back of the chair in which Homer is seated. To the dedication is added in prose, "The occasion of this impos'd Crowne," after which the version of Batrachomyomachia commences, followed by Hymns to Apollo, Hermes, Venus, Bacchus, Mars, Diana, &c. After these come "Certaine Epigramms and other Poems of Homer," including the various imputed fragments. Four lines, to the Fisher-boys who pleased Homer with riddles, terminate the whole; and we there read, "The end of all the endlesse works of Homer." Four pages are subjoined in which Chapman speaks in his own person:—

"The worke that I was borne to doe is done.
Glory to him, that the conclusion
Makes the beginning of my life! and never
Let me be said to live, 'till I live ever." &c.

It thus concludes:—

"For me, let just men judge, by what I show
In Acts expos'd, how much I erre or knowe;
And let not Envie make all worse then nought
With her meare headstrong and quite braineles thought:
Others for doing nothing giving all,
And bounding all worth in her bursten gall.

"God and my deare Redeemer rescue me
From men's immane and mad impietie;
And by my life and soule (sole knowne to them)
Make me of Palme or Yew an anadem.
And so, my sole God, the thrice sacred Trine,
Beare all th' ascription of all me and mine."

Chapman winds up by a short Latin prayer in a similar spirit. It is to be observed that in his version of the Batrachomyomachia he uses the Greek names given to the Frogs and Mice, inserting literal translations of them in the margin.

It is conjectured that this work was printed about 1624. Chapman was then sixty-five years old, having been born in 1559, five years before Shakspeare: he died in 1634.

We have already mentioned Chapman's retirement to Hitching, Herts: he must have had relations resident there, for in Nov. 1619 Thomas Chapman presented a petition to Prince Charles for the Bailywick of Hitching, of which he had been deprived by the Earl of Salisbury. On 30th Nov. this petition was referred to the Chancellor and Commissioners of the Prince's revenue. See Harl. MS. No. 781. At an earlier period of his life, George Chapman "poet" had lived in Southwark: he was then, 1598, writing plays for the theatres in the neighborhood.

Charles the First. — The true Effigies of our most Illustrious Soveraigne Lord, King Charles, Queene Mary, with the rest of the Royall Progenie. Also a Compendium or Abstract of their most famous Geneologies and Pedegrees, expressed in Prose and Verse. With the Times and Places of their Births. — Printed at London for John Sweeting &c. 1641. 4to. 10 *leaves.*

This production contains eight portraits, viz.: 1, Charles I., a kit-cat in an oval, without any engraver's name, but probably by Hollar; 2, Henrietta Maria, a kit-cat in an oval, by Hollar; 3, Prince Charles, a half-length in an oval, without any engraver's name, but dated 1641, and perhaps by Hollar; 4, Mary, Princess of Orange, a whole length, by Hollar; 5, Prince James, playing at tennis, a whole length, by M. Meisan; 6, Princess Elizabeth, a whole length, by Ro. Vaughan; 7, Princess Anna, a whole length, with "J. v. L. f." at the corner; 8, a plate, representing at the top the infant Prince Charles dead, and at the bottom Prince Henry Duke of Gloucester in long clothes, without the name of any engraver.

The work is without preface, dedication, or any kind of introduction, and to the verses belonging to the portraits no name is attached; in truth, they were not worth owning. The following, entitled *Maria Regina*, are a favorable sample of the rest: —

"Within the substance of this figure here
The Graces and the Vertue[s] do shine cleare:
The Godesses, the Muses, all agree
That in her brest their residence must be.
From Juno her majestique mind she gain'd;
From Citherea beauty she attain'd;
Minerva (Pallas) hath inspir'd her heart
With courage in regarding armes and art:
Apollo with his radient rayes divine
Inclin'd hir favour to the Sisters Nine,
And for a blessing to this happy land
Shee's largely graced by th' Almighties hand
To be a fruitful vine, whose branches may
Spread gloriously, as farre as Phœbus raie.
In goodnesse, greatnesse, and in true content
May she and they be supereminent."

The verses face the portraits, with the exception of the last lines upon Prince Charles, who was born and died on the 13th of May, 1629.

CHAUCER, GEOFFREY. — The woorkes of Geffrey Chaucer, newly printed with diuers addicions, whiche were neuer in printe before: With the siege and destruccion of the worthie citee of Thebes, compiled by Ihon Lidgate, Monke of Berie. As in the table more plainly doeth appere. 1561. fol. B. L. 388 *leaves.*

This edition, said to have been edited by Stow although his name is nowhere found in it, was printed by John Kyngston in 1561, the colophon being, "Imprinted at London, by Ihon Kyngston, for Ihon Wight, dwellyng in Poules Churchyarde. Anno 1561." On the title-page is a large shield of Chaucer's arms, with this couplet underneath it:

"Vertue florisheth in Chaucer still,
Though Death of hym hath wrought his will."

This is followed by Thynne's dedication to Henry VIII., and the Table with "eight goodlie questions, with their answers," &c. "The Caunterburie tales," and "The Romaunt of the Rose," have distinct titles in this impression.

CHAUCER, GEOFFREY. — The Workes of our Ancient and learned English Poet, Geffrey Chaucer, newly Printed, &c. — London, Printed by Adam Islip. Ann Dom. 1602. fol. 414 *leaves.*

This is Thomas Speght's second edition, (the first had appeared in 1598,) and his dedication to Sir Robert Cecil follows a plate headed, "The Progenie of Geffrey Chaucer," with the full length of the poet in the centre. In an address "to the Readers" Speght acknowledges his obligations to Francis Thynne, who, besides his aid in preparing the work, contributed some lines "Upon the picture of Chaucer," which precede the life. After the life comes a new general title to "The Workes of Geffrey Chaucer," &c., with the identical woodcut of Chaucer's arms which had been used by John Kyngston in 1561. On the earliest title is given a list thus headed: "To that which was done in the former Impression, thus much is now added," containing a statement of the improvements in this impression. The principal of these is the addition of "the Treatise called Iacke Upland," and "Chaucer's A.B.C., called La Priere de Nostre Dame."

CHETTLE, HENRY. — Englands Mourning Garment: Worne heere by plaine Shepheards, in memorie of their sacred Mistresse, Elizabeth &c. To which is added the true manner of her Emperiall Funerall. With many new additions, being now againe the second time reprinted &c. After which followeth the Shepheard's Spring-Song for entertainment of King James &c. — Imprinted at London for Thomas Millington &c. 1603. 4to. 24 *leaves.*

The variations between the present and the first impression (which came out without date) are not very material: the principal addition consists of a list (preceding "the Shepherd's Spring Song") of the twelve barons who carried "bannerols" at the funeral of Queen Elizabeth. There is, however, an omission of some importance, for in the first edition (without date), on sign. F 3, is found a note "to the Reader," signed by the author, Henry Chettle: it relates to the errors of the press, which, being subsequently corrected, it was probably considered not necessary to reprint.

The dedication is "to all true lovers of the right generous Queene Elizabeth"; and the tract commences with a dialogue in verse between Thenot and Colin, the author figuring himself under the latter name, although, as he mentions (when quoting Spenser on sign. D), it had been borne by Spenser. A sort of laudatory historical discourse follows, and forms the principal subject; but near the centre is a very interesting poem, in which Chettle reproaches all the principal poets of the day with their silence in offering tribute to the dead Queen, while some of them were so eager to pay their court to the living King. Daniel, Warner, Chapman, Ben Jonson, Shakspeare, Drayton, and Dekker, are all distinctly pointed at, although their names are not inserted. Of Shakspeare he speaks as follows by the name of Melicert, whom, on sign. B 3, he had already introduced: —

"Nor doth the silver tongued Melicert[1]
Drop from his honied Muse one sable teare
To mourne her death that graced his desert,
And to his laies open'd her royal eare.
Shepheard, remember our Elizabeth,
And sing her rape done by that Tarquin Death."

Chapman is spoken of as Corin "that finish'd dead Musæus gracious song"; Ben Jonson is called "our English Horace"; and Dekker, (Ben Jonson's adversary,) "quick Anti-Horace": with the last he couples "young Mœlibee his friend," a name not easily appropriated; and Henry Petowe, who, in 1598, had printed "the second part of Hero and Leander," and is, therefore, styled by Chettle "Hero's last Musæus." Daniel is distinguished as "the sweetest song-man of all English Swains," and Warner, author of "Albion's England," as having "sung forty years the life and birth" of Queen Elizabeth. Drayton is distinctly charged with having welcomed James on his accession, before he had deplored the loss of Elizabeth.

"The Shepherd's Spring Song," in gratulation of James I., occupies the four last pages, and is smoothly written, but it has little other recommendation: the following is one of the earlier stanzas, where Colin is endeavoring to rouse the sleeping shepherds.

"The gray eyde morning with a blushing cheeke,
Like England's royal rose, mixt red and white,
Summons all eies to pleasure and delight.
Behold, the evenings deaws doe upward reeke,

[1] We may here notice that Melicertus is one of the heroes in R. Greene's "Menaphon," 1587: we never saw any edition of it earlier than 1589.

> Drawn by the Sun, which now doth gild the skie
> With his light-giving and world-cheering eie."

In both editions the word "blushing" in the first of these lines is printed "blustring," but it is an easy and an obvious error.

Besides the two editions bearing the name of Millington, it appears from the books at Stationers' Hall, that Matthew Lawe had pirated "England's Mourning Garment," in consequence of which he was ordered by the Court of the Company to bring all the copies in, and to pay a fine of 20*s*. This circumstance has only recently come to our knowledge, but we copy the following from the original record.

"7 Junij 1603. Math. Lawe. Yt is ordered that he shall presently pay xx*s* for a fine for printinge, contrary to order, a book called England's mourning Garment, beinge Thomas Millington's copie; and that he shall bring into the hall, as forfayted by thordonance, all such numbers of the said bookes as now remayne in his hand unsold, which he say are 100 ——— xx*s* : pd. xv*s*."

In a note to the above it is added, that Lawe "brought in three quarterns, or thereabouts," and that "five shillings of the fine had been given back to him." No copy bearing Lawe's name is known, so that we may presume they were all destroyed.

CHRIST'S BLOODY SWEAT. — Christ's Bloodie Sweat, or the Sonne of God in his Agonie. By I. F. — London. Printed by Ralph Blower, and are to be sold at his house upon Lambert Hill. 1613. 34 *leaves*.

We are unable to speculate who was the pious author of this very rare poem: his initials I. F. might belong either to Ford or Fletcher, but the style is altogether unlike theirs; and the writer's minute acquaintance with Scripture (constantly quoted in his margin), together with the general force of his expressions, and unhesitating creed, would lead to the supposition that he was a zealous puritanical divine. The dedication is to the Earl of Pembroke, but it contains nothing to clear up the doubt; and the address "to such as shall peruse this booke" only speaks of the manner in which, in his day, "poetry was in every way made the herauld of wantonnesse," so that "there is not now any thing too uncleane for lascivious rime." Yet I. F. owns, near the commencement of his poem, that he had himself "spent his best days in thriftless verse," and, being so practised, we may be surprised at the number of his faulty measures. These defects may in part be owing to the printer, whom he blames; and in the very passage we have last quoted "thriftless" is misprinted *thirstless*: in other places we have *sinns* for "sums," *anger* for "angry," and *wrath* for "breath," which, and more, are left for the discovery of the reader, no list of errata being furnished. I. F. represents the Saviour as thus explaining to him personally the cause of the "bloody sweat," which gives title to the poem: he is speaking of his divine Father;

"The charge of whose hot wrath so fearefull was,
As against Nature chang'd my sweate to bloud;
Which, trickling downe my cheekes uppon the grasse,
Well tould the agony wherein I stood:
An agony, indeed, whose trembling heate
Powr'd out the wonder of a bloudy sweate."

The whole production consists of 319 such stanzas as the above; and we must own, in spite of the talents and ingenuity of the author, that many parts are wofully wearisome: he does not attempt any flights of imagination, but ties himself down to the language and incidents of the New Testament, with various references to the Old. When we read the following stanza, with its allusions to the stage, we fancied for the moment that the poem might have been by John Ford, the dramatist, but it was later in his career that he wrote productions of a pious and moral character, and in other respects the language is unlike that which he would have been likely to employ:—

"He died, indeed, not as an actor dies,
To die to-day and live again to-morrow,
In shew to please the audience, or disguise
The idle habit of inforced sorrow:
The Crosse his stage was, and he plaid the part
Of one that for his friend did pawne his heart."

Near the close the author supposes a parent to relate to his child the story of God's mercy and man's salvation, introducing it thus simply and prettily: —

"In after-times, when in the winters cold
Folkes use to warme them by their nightly fires,
Such parents as the time of life termes old,
Wasting the season, as the night requires,
In stead of tales, may to their children tell
What to the Lord of Glorie once befell."

The writer has not Father Southwell's impassioned fervor and eloquence; but his convictions, of a different character, are as strong, and his faith as courageous.

CHURCHYARD, THOMAS.—A Myrrour for man where in he shall see the myserable state of thys worlde.[1]

[1] In 1594, Churchyard published another work under a similar title, and of a similar character: he called it "The Mirror of Man, and manners of Men," and it was printed "by Arnold Hatfield for W. Holme." In it he refers to "a little booke almost fifty years ago made by me," of which we might suppose that that of 1594 was a reprint; but they are entirely different, and the "Mirror" is there succeeded by what is thus entitled, —

"Heere follows a glance, and dash with a pen
On worlds great mischance, and maners of men."

It was dedicated to Sir Robert Cecil, and is not by any means so offensive to the great as the production under the same name printed in the reign of Edward VI. The method is the same, but the matter different, as may be seen by a brief quotation: —

"Who safely will goe, or surely would stand,
Dwels in some low place, and walks on playne land.
These mountaynes are hye, and hard for to clime,
Where tempests and stormes blowes roughly some time.
Great trees have weake bowes, that bends at each blast;
Small graffs do grow long and stands in stock fast.
The poore sleeps in peace, and rise in great rest,
And thinks at their meate ynough is a feast.
Brown bread unto them is sweeter, God knowes,
Then manchet to some that goes in gay cloes."

Churchyard, like many other writers of that day, was apparently altogether careless of his concords.

The above is the whole of the heading, for the three leaves of which the piece consists have no title-page; but the following is the colophon, showing that it was printed in the reign of Edward VI.: —

"God save the Kyng,

"Imprynted at London by Roberte Toye, dwellynge in Paules churche yarde at the sygne of the Bell. *Cum privilegio ad Imprimendum Solum.*"

Neither Ames, Herbert, nor Dibdin include it among the productions of Toy's Press. The author, in his old age, claimed to have commenced writing while Edward VI. was on the throne, and he continued it until two years after the accession of James I., exceeding half a century of authorship. He seems nearly all his life to have been a struggler against poverty, and much of what he says in this, his earliest known performance, is directed against the great and wealthy. Such is the case with the two following stanzas, which we insert as a specimen of a work of only 172 lines: —

"Some men have treasure and hartes ease at wyll,
  Yet ever wyshing, and neare hath theyr fyll:
Soch fylthy lucre enbraceth theyr hartes,
  So that thei may have, thei force not who smartes;
And though they have all, yet for more they gape:
  They drinke both the wyne, and lokes for the grape,
Whych maketh the poore ryght sore to lament,
  For they haue nothing but dobble rent.

"They wold wyn theyr fode wyth labour and sweat,
  Yet all wyll not helpe, theyr rent is so great;
And where they were wont to upholde a plowe,
  Now scarce can they fynd the grasse for a cowe.
Theyr childrē do watche as haukes for their praye,
  Yet can they not get one good meale a daye.
Soch woful morninge as is in Englande
  Was never before, I dare take in hande."

The lines, as the reader will perceive, are couplets, but they were printed by Toye as eight-line stanzas: "Finis quod Thomas Churschard" is misprinted at the end, for, with all his subsequent peculiarity of spelling, he never so wrote his name.

Churchyard, Thomas. — The Contention bettwyxte Churchyeard and Camell, vpon Dauid Dycers Dreame sett out in suche order, that it is bothe wyttye and profytable for all degryes. Rede this littell comunication betwene Churchyarde: Camell: and others mo. Newlye Imprinted and sett furthe for thy profyt gentyll Reader. — Imprinted at London by Owen Rogers for Mychell Loblee dwelynge in Paulls churchyeard. Anno M.D.LX. 4to. 28 *leaves.*

Nobody has yet given, at all correctly, either the title or contents of this rare book: it was reprinted in 1565, but we never heard of more than one copy of each edition. In his "Chance," printed in 1580, Churchyard informs us that many of these productions were "written in the beginnyng of Kyng Edwardes raigne," and most of the original broadsides (for in that form the various pieces first appeared) are in the library of the Society of Antiquaries. The subjoined is an accurate list of all that were republished in a collected form in the work under consideration: —

1. The Preface (probably by Churchyard, but without signature).
2. Dauy Dycars Dreame.
3. To Dauid dicars when.
4. A Replication vnto Camels Obiection.
5. Camels Reioindre to Churchyarde.
6. The Surreioindre vnto Camels reioindre.
7. A Decree betwene Churchyarde and Camell.
8. Westerne Wyll vpon the debate betwyxte Churchyarde and Camell.
9. Dauye Dikers dreme (an enlargement of No. 1, adding to it twice as much).
10. Of such as on fantesye decree and discus: on other mens workes, lo Ovides tale thus (This is the contest of Pan and Apollo, subscribed T. Hedley).
11. A supplication vnto mast. Camell (subscribed "Your daily Belman at your maundement, Good man Gefferay Chappell of whipstable").

12. To goodman Chappels supplication (signed Thomas Camell).
13. Steuen Steple to mast. Camell.
14. Camelles Conclusion (signed Thomas Camell).
15. Westerne will to Camell and for him selfe alone, although hee leudly lust to knitte vp three in one (signed W. Watreman).
16. A plain and fynall confutation of camelles corlyke oblatraoion.
17. Camelles crosse rowe.

Such are the contents of the 4to of 1560, but to these is to be added a broadside of greater interest and importance, but upon the same subject, which seems to have employed many of the wits and versifiers of the time. It is by no less a person than the famous ballad-maker, William Elderton (here called Ilderton), and it is upon a unique broadside: it seems to have been Elderton's earliest appearance in print, which renders it additionally curious. It has for title the same as No. 7 in the preceding enumeration, namely, "A Decree betwene Churchyarde and Camell," and the imprint is, "Imprinted at London by Richard Haruy, dwellyng in Fosterlane," without date; and possibly it did not come out until after the publication of the volume the title-page of which stands at the head of this article. It consists of 133 lines, all printed upon one side of a large sheet, the back of which is blank. It begins thus: —

" A decree vpon the dreame made by Dauy Dicar
Wyth answer to Camell, whose taũtes be more quicker."

This couplet forms a sort of title, after which we read as follows: —

" Wher Dicar hath dreamed of things out of frame,
And Churchyard by writing affirmeth the same,
And Camell contendeth the same to deface,
And therfore hath put hys doynges in place,
Sythe both of those twayne hath set foorth in myter
The wordes of the Authour, the skyl of the wryghter,
And runne in thys race, styl chaffyng the bytte,
I thynke in this case much more then is fytte."

Elderton then proceeds to state the case, and after quoting

Cato, and translating the passage, we come to a new heading, —

"The iudgement of the Authour,"

which ends with these lines and the signature of the writer: —

"Take me to the best, as one to you vnknowen
Whose worthy wyts I do com̄end & wold w[t] you be one:
Not mindyng so assuredly to spende and waste the daye
To make the people laugh at me, & here I make astaye.
Finis quod W. Ilderton."

Although, perhaps, all the productions forming this celebrated "flyting" may have been preserved, much of the humor which belonged to the contest has certainly not survived the day when it took place.

CHURCHYARD, THOMAS. — A sad and solemne Funerall of the right Honorable sir Francis Knowles knight, treasorer of the Queenes Maiesties houshold, one of her priuie councell, and knight of the most honorable order of the Garter. Written by Thomas Churchyard Esquier. — Imprinted at London by Ar. Hatfield, for William Holme. 1596. 4to. 4 *leaves.*

This unique tract is dedicated to Lord Delawarr, whom Churchyard calls the son-in-law to Sir Francis Knowles: the poet here speaks of his own "aged years," and refers to the number of distinguished persons who had died within a very short period before he wrote. On this point he places the following remarkable obituary [1] in a marginal note opposite his first, second, and third

[1] We may add a list of no fewer than 18 "Epitaphs" upon different individuals, which Churchyard had written before 1580: it is taken from his "Pleasant Laborinth, called Churchyardes Chance framed in Fancies," published in that year: he states that they were "alreadie printed," but could not be inserted in his book as they were "out of his handes."

1. "The Epitaph of Kyng Henry the eight.
2. The Earle of Surries Epitaphe.
3. The Lord Cromwell's Epitaphe.
4. The Ladie Wentworth's Epitaphe.

stanzas:—"In the compasse of one yeere there died of the cleargy, of the wars, and honorable councellers, so many Byshops, Captaines and Governours whose names follow heerafter. Bishop of London D. Fletcher. Bishop of Winchester. Bishop of Chichester D. Bycklie. Bishop of Chester D. Byllyt. D. Whitakers Master of S. Johns in Cambridge. Captaines, Sir Martyn Furbyshar. Sir Roger Williams. Sir T. Morgan. Sir Fr. Drake. Sir I. Hawkins. Sir N. Clifford. The Earle of Huntingdon. The Lord Delaware. Honorable Councellers, Sir T. Henneage. Sir I. Wolley. Sir I. Puckering L. Keeper. Sir Francis Knowles. The L. Chamberlaine."

Churchyard is not a poet who possessed any imagination, nor are his thoughts novel or striking: his language is often below his

5. The Lorde Graies of Wilton his Epitaphe.
6. The Lorde Poinynges Epitaphe.
7. Maister Audleis, the greate Souldiours Epitaphe.
8. The worthie Captaine Randall's Epitaphe.
9. Sir Edmond Peckham's Epitaphe.
10. Sir James Wilforde's Epitaphe.
11. Sir John Wallope's Epitaphe.
12. Sir George Peckham's first wives Epitaphe.
13. The Erle of Penbrokes Epitaphe.
14. The Counteis of Penbrokes Epitaphe.
15. The Lord Henry Dudleis Epitaphe.
16. Sir John Pollardes Epitaphe.
17. The Lorde of Delvins Epitaphe.
18. The Epitaphe of Maistresse Pennes daghter, called Maistresse Gifforde.

"And many other gentilmen's and gentilwomen's Epitaphes that presently I neither can remember, nor get into my handes againe."

Doubtless nearly all these had originally come out as broadsides, and were scattered beyond the reach of the author. He adds some "Verses that weare given to a moste mightie personage," meaning the Queen, and they are solely devoted to his own actions and disappointments: they begin,—

"O pearless Prince! if penne had purchast praise,
My parte was plaid long since on publicke stage,
Sith leaden worlde disdaines the golden daies:
With face of brasse men must go through this age.
Though Poetts prate like parret in a cage,
Poore Tom maie sitte like crowe upon a stone,
And cracke harde nuttes, for almonds sure are gone."

The whole is very lugubrious and pitiful, but the author remained poor and penniless (not penless) for many long years afterwards.

subject, but his versification is usually flowing, and his reflections frequently just and natural. The subsequent stanza is as good as any in this production : —

" But yet, good knight, the lamp and torch of troeth,
Sir Francis Knowles, I can not so forget.
Thogh corse to church, and soule to heaven goeth,
And body needs must pay the earth his det,
Good will of men shall wait upon thy toem,
And Fame hir selfe thy funerall shall make,
And register thy name till day of doem
In booke of life for thy great vertues sake.
Thy frends shall mourne, not with long clokes of black,
But with sad looks of doell behinde thy back."

Eight other similar stanzas compose the whole of the tract, of which, probably, only a very few copies were printed for presentation to the nobility, or persons in office, who were likely to reward the author.

CHURCHYARD, THOMAS. — A wished Reformation of wicked Rebellion. Newly set foorth by Thomas Churchyard Esquier. — Imprinted at London by Thomas Este, dwelling in Aldersgate Street. 1598. 4to. 4 *leaves.*

In no list of Churchyard's productions is this little poetical tract included.[1] It clearly grew out of the Irish Rebellion, which Robert Earl of Essex very shortly afterwards was sent to Ireland to subdue, upon whose departure Churchyard wrote a " Fortunate Farewell," and whose return he greeted in a " Welcome Home," both dated 1599. It is the cause of the Earl's going that is treated in the work before us, which, as will be seen above, bears date in the preceding year. It only occupies a single sheet 4to, and, in order to include it in that compass, the dedication " To all the right noble of birth, or mynd, with the true hartted gentlemen, and loyall subjects of England," is printed at the back of the title-page. The whole, prose dedication and poetical appeal, is in

[1] We ought to have made an exception in favor of the list supplied by the industrious G. Chalmers, who mentions it in his " Churchyard's Chips concerning Scotland." 8vo. 1817. p. 63.

Churchyard's peculiar spelling, so that sometimes it is not easy to see at once the word he intends to use: thus *virtuous* is spelt "vertuos," *often* "offtten," *look* "loek," *perilous* "parrelos," &c. He tells the reader, "If thear wear no other president, maek Ierland an example what cursed callamitees aer set a broetch by theas wicked and unwelcom cawsis, canckers in a common weall, blayns and blotchis in a sound body, and gnawing worms and caetter pillars to every honest hart." He therefore prays them "with pacyence and sweet consitheracion (and no sowre senssuer) read what followeth in mield manner of vers, albeit somewhat byetting the gawlls of such, whoes wounds cannot be healed, but by som sharp and serching medson."

As the copy we have used is unique, we will make a few extracts equally uncouth, and not very edifying, but bearing in mind that the author in 1599 was a very old man, although he continued "to palter up something," in prose or verse, almost to the day of his death. He was born at Shrewsbury about 1520, and was buried at St. Margaret's, Westminster, 4th April, 1604.[1] His "Wished Reformation of wicked Rebellion" opens with this stanza: —

"Good men wear glad at Gods great glorie seen
(By speshall grace) on Englands joy to shyen,
Which grace prezarvd our quinttesenssed Queen
That skaeped saef from skaeth throw power deuien.
O falls forsworn, what ear you aer, giue place

1 We are obliged to Robert Cole, Esq., F. S. A., for the following copy of Churchyard's nuncupative will, dated only a few days before his death: it was obtained from a dealer in waste-paper, into whose hands it accidentally came.

"Thome Churchyard.

Memorandum the xxixth of Martch, Anno 1604. Thomas Churtchyard, Esquier, beinge of perfecte mynde and memorye, did dispose of his worldlye goods as followeth, in the presence of us hearunder written. Firste he gave to his brother Geordge the some of xxli. All the reste of his goods and chattles he gave unto Geordge Puslowe, whom he made his executor, that he should see him buryed like a Jentlemane.

ꝑ me Nathaniell Mathewe.
Gabriel Pope.
The marke of ✕ Jone Moore.
Silvester P Harlums marke."

"Proved, 8*th April*, 1604."

To mightty Iovs Lieftenant heer on earth.
O haetfull flock of traytors, heid your face
From rightfull Kings and Queens well boern by byrth.
Fy, tretcheros trash that wind will blo a way,
Pluck vp your sight, and see your own decay."

Besides his strange spelling, Churchyard has a peculiarity in his punctuation, for he places a comma after the fourth syllable of every line, as a cæsura, whether the sense do or do not require it: we will illustrate this point in another stanza where the old poet assails the Roman Catholics, and especially the Jesuits:—

" Hee preached peace, you sow discord and war,
All duety done, to Sesar Cryst dyd lyek,
But you in rage, and errors run so far
Yee care not whom, yee poyson, kill or stryek,
A shamelesse swarm, off Seminaries now
Disgisd lyek dogges, that whine before they bite,
Fills euery towne, with truthlesse traytors throw,
Whoes words lyke swords, are ready drawne to smite,
But blo of Axe, comes oft ere they bee waer,
And stryeks of head, and leaues the body baer."

Independently of punctuation, he observes no consistency, the very same word being spelt in different ways in different places. All the stanzas are in the spirit of those we have quoted, without a particle of information; and very near the conclusion Churchyard inveighs against the "sedishoes books and sawsy lybels" circulated so industriously by the Queen's enemies. At the end we read "Finis qd Thomas Churchyard"; and so desirous does he seem to have been that his name should not be passed over by the reader, that it appears, in one form or other, upon nearly every page.

CHURCHYARD, THOMAS. — The Wonders of the Ayre, the Trembling of the Earth, and the warnings of the world before the Iudgement day. Written by Thomas Churchyard Esquire, seruant to the Queenes Majestie. — Imprinted at London by Thomas Dawson. 1602. 4to. 12 *leaves.*

In both editions of Lowndes's *Bibl. Man.* it is stated that this tract is prose: a considerable part of it is verse, and the title is there given incorrectly. It is personally interesting because the writer, in his dedication to M. D. Sesar, (*i. e.* Master Doctor Cæsar, afterwards Sir Julius Cæsar,) acknowledges his obligations to him for "the little that I live upon, and am likely to die withall." Hence no doubt the title Churchyard here assumes of "servant" to the Queen. Here, too, he states that he had translated part of Pliny, but that "a great learned doctor, called doctor Holland," had translated the whole; and in fact it had come out in 1601. To this succeeds "The generall Epistle to the Reader," in two pages of long rhymes; and the Lord's Prayer, the Creed and Decalogue are added in verse, the whole being wound up by another page of poetry headed "Verses fitte for every one to knowe and confesse." The historical portion of the tract is, very consistently, in prose.

CHURCHYARD, THOMAS. — Churchyard's Good Will. Sad and heavy Verses, in the nature of an Epitaph for the losse of the Archbishop of Canterbury, lately deceased, Primate and Metropolitane of all England. Written by Thomas Churchyard, Esquire. — Imprinted at London by Simon Stafford, dwelling in Hosier lane, neere Smithfield. 1604. 8vo. 8 *leaves.*

This, as far as we know, was the last production of its author. In his "Charge," 4to, 1580, he tells us that he had been "servant" to the celebrated Lord Surrey; and we find by his "Fortunate Farewell," 4to, 1599, that, in the reign of Edward VI., he had been brought before the Privy Council for one of his writings, when he was befriended by the Duke of Somerset.

There is another piece by Churchyard, dated, like the present, 1604, "A blessed Balme to search and salve Sedition," but it was produced some time before the tract under consideration: it relates to the execution of Watson and Clarke, in November, 1603, while Archbishop Whitgift did not die until February, 1604. Churchyard was himself buried, as we have stated, the 4th of April, 1604.

Whitgift was succeeded by Bancroft Bishop of London, and to that prelate Churchyard dedicates his "Good Will." The following is the last stanza of this author's last poem: —

> "Croydon can shew his works, life, laud and all;
> Croydon hath lost the Saint of that sweet shrine:
> Lambeth may cry, and Canterbury may call
> Long for the like with wofull weeping eyne;
> But few, I feare, his like are left alive,
> The more our griefe — a great King so did say.
> Death stole, like theefe, the hony from the hive:
> Our great Primate in patience went away,
> Left stately Court and Countrey at the best,
> Because he hop't to sleepe in Abrahams brest."

The "great King" was James I., who deeply lamented the loss of Archbishop Whitgift. The eight leaves composing the tract are printed only on one side, and the poem is in six stanzas.[1] No other copy of it is known. In this tract Churchyard abandons the peculiar mode of spelling observed in many of his other productions.

[1] Churchyard had sufficient attainments in Latin to induce him to attempt, and to perform to a certain extent, a translation of Ovid's *De Tristibus*. It came from the press of Thomas Marsh in 1580, but there is no edition of 1578, mentioned by Dr. Bliss in his edition of Wood's Ath. Oxon. I. 734. Another perfect copy does exist, besides that in Earl Spencer's Library. At the back of the title-page comes "The occasion of this Booke," and on the next page the dedication "To his most assured and tryed Friende Maister Christopher Hatton, Esquire, Thomas Churchyarde wysheth continuaunce of Vertue," in which he familiarly calls the dedicatee "good maister Hatton." Here he mentions what he intended to be the contents of the second part of his "Chips": — "In my first booke shalbe three Tragedies, two Tales, a Dreame, a description of Frendship, a Farewell to the Court, the Siege of Leeth, and sondry other thinges that are already written. And in my seconde Booke shalbe foure Tragedies, ten Tales, the Siege of Saint Quintaynes, Newhaven, Calleis and Guynes; and, I hope, the rest of all the forrein warres that I have seene, or heard of, abroade shall follow in another volume." The first part of Churchyard's "Chips" had come out in 1575, but we never saw a copy of it. We are, of course, not to understand "Tragedies" in the popular sense of the word, but merely as tragical narratives: in this view Churchyard's "Shore's Wife," originally published in "The Mirror for Magistrates," and much enlarged by him in 1593, was a "tragedy."

Churl and the Bird. — Here foloweth the Churle and the byrde. n. d. B. L. 4to. 8 *leaves.*

This title is above a woodcut of two male figures, one in a flowing robe, and the other in a cloak, doublet, and hose: between them is a tree with a bird upon it. The colophon is, "Thus endeth the treatyse called churle & the byrde. Printed at Cantorbury in saynte Paules parysshe by Johan Mychel."

This tract was first printed by Caxton, and twice by Wynkyn de Worde, (*vide* Dibdin's Typ. Ant. I. 307, and II. 325,) but both Wynkyn de Worde's editions are unlike the present, regarding which Herbert had obtained some hint from a note by Ritson. Dr. Dibdin says, "at p. 1779, vol. iii., he (Herbert) notices an edition of it without date, printed by one Johan Nychel, [not Nychol,] on the authority of a MS. note by Ritson." This, "one Johan Nychel," is, of course, Johan Mychel, but no bibliographer seems to have been aware that this popular tract was printed at Canterbury. Besides the woodcut on the title, it differs in many respects from the editions by Wynkyn de Worde, as may be seen by comparing only the opening stanza, as here printed, with that given by Dr. Dibdin: —

"Problemes of olde lykenesse and fygure,
Which proved ben fructuous of sentence,
And have auctorites grounded in scripture
By resemblaunce of notable aparaunce,
With moralities concludynge on prudence;
Lyke as the byble reherseth by wrytynge
How trees somtyme chose them a kynge."

If Dr. Dibdin's statement be correct, that in Wynkyn de Worde's editions the poem contains fifty-two seven-line stanzas, and another of eight lines, by way of "Lenvoye," there is a very material variation beyond typographical changes; for, in Mychel's edition, printed at Canterbury, there are fifty-four seven-line stanzas, besides the terminating stanza of eight lines.

The author avows that the work is only a translation: —

"And here I cast on my purpose
Out of frenche a tale to translate,
Which in a pamflete I saw and redde but late;"

and it has usually been attributed to Lydgate, (Ritson's Bibliogr. Poet. 69,) although his name is nowhere mentioned in it. After a sort of prologue of six stanzas, vindicating the poetical license of giving speech to birds and beasts, the main subject of the performance thus commences: —

> " Somtyme there dwelled in a small vylage,
> As myn auctor maketh mencyon,
> A churle which had lust and corage
> Within hym selfe by dyligent travayle
> To aray his garden with notable aparayle,
> Of length and brede, in lyke square and longe,
> Hedged and dytched to make it sure and stronge."

Here the second line, " As myn auctor maketh mencyon," is clearly wrong, for the last word, according to the construction of the stanzas, ought to rhyme with " travayle " : it ought to run, "As myn auctor maketh *rehersayle*." The moral is very prettily conveyed. The Churl, morning and evening, hears a Bird sing joyously in a laurel-tree in his garden : he catches it in a trap, and is about to cage it, when the Bird remonstrates, declares it cannot sing excepting when free, and promises, if the Churl will first set it at liberty, to give him three most valuable pieces of advice. The Churl agrees, and the Bird, flying to its tree, warns the Churl against credulity, against impossible desires, and against immoderate grief for anything irrecoverably lost. The Bird follows up its advice by laughing at the Churl for letting it escape, seeing that it has a precious stone within it, which would make him inexhaustibly rich, &c. The Churl bitterly grieves that he has given so rare a creature its liberty, and the Bird proceeds to show him how little he has profited by the three pieces of advice he had received, the Bird having in fact no such treasure concealed within it. The fable terminates with these stanzas: —

> " Ye folke that shall this fable se or rede,
> Newe forged tales I counseyle you to fle;
> For losse of gooddes take never to great hede,
> Nor be nat sory for none adversyte;
> Nor covete thynge that may not recovered be;
> And remembre where ever ye gone,
> That a churles byrde is ever wo begonne.

"Unto my purpose this proved is fully ryve:
Rede and reporte by olde remembraunce,
That a churles byrde, and a knaves wyfe
Have oftentymes great sorow and myschaunce:
And who that hath fredome hath all suffysaunce;
For better is fredome with lytel in gladnesse,
Than to be thrall with all worldly rychesse."

"The Churl and the Bird" is reprinted in Ashmole's *Theatrum Chemicum*, 1652, under the title of "Hermes Bird." Pynson printed an edition of it, not mentioned by Dibdin; and the original, or what may have been the original, is to be found in the Latin *Gesta Romanorum*, No. 167. A modernization of it is inserted in Way's *Fabliaux*.

CLIMSELL, HENRY. — Londons Vacation, And The Countries Tearme. Or A lamentable relation of severall remarkable passages which it hath pleased the Lord to shew on severall persons, both in London, and in the Country in this present Visitation, 1636. With the number of those that dyed at London and Newcastle, this present yeare. With new Additions. By H. C. — London, Printed for Richard Harper, and are to be sold at his shop in Smithfield, at the Hospitall Gate, 1637. 8vo. 12 *leaves.*

The author of this singular tract, or more properly chap-book, was a well-known writer of ballads in the reigns of James and Charles I., and he seems to have survived until after the Restoration. Most of his productions, all of which, as far as they are known, are of a temporary character, bear only his initials, but upon some his name, Henry Climsell, is inserted at length. We do not find "Londons Vacation" anywhere mentioned, yet the words on the title-page, "with new additions," would indicate that it had been printed before. Excepting the address "To the Reader," and a particular account of the deaths by the Plague in London and Newcastle (which seems to have been specially afflicted, the deaths there amounting in 1636 to more than 5000, while in London they were 27,000), it is entirely in verse.

It consists principally of anecdotes connected with the prevalence of the Plague, and it is called "London's Vacation and the Country's Term," because at such times it was usual to adjourn the term, and to hold the courts of law out of town, at St. Albans, Hertford, and other places. The comprehensive woodcut on the title-page refers to some of the chief incidents narrated by the author: Time stands in the foreground with his scythe and a child in his arms; and near him is seen a man escaping over a brick wall, who had been mistakenly placed for dead under a coffin: in the background is a Sexton digging a grave for a person who is on his knees praying; and not far removed is a dead man, fully clothed, lying on his back.

The most remarkable part of the tract is an account of a cold-water cure for the plague, so early had its virtues been discovered, and applied in precisely the same way as of late years. A gentleman travelling in the country discovers, to his dismay, that he had "God's tokens," *i. e.* "blue spots" upon his arm: —

"He spurs his horse, and speedily he rides
To the next toun, and there all night abides.
But yet before he went to bed, 'tis said,
In 's chamber he a goode fire causde be made:
So, when the Chamberlain had made a fire,
A payle of water he did then desire:
Then cal'd he for the best sheet in the Inne,
The which he wet, and wrapt himself therein.
The sheet being wet, and he stark naked in it,
About his body he did strait way pinne it;
Which being done, away to bed he went.
The morning being come, and the night spent,
He found himself well, and his body cleare
From all those spots which before did appeare."

There is little doubt that the cure was effected by the profuse perspiration occasioned by the wet sheets; but Climsell, in the true spirit of modern brandy-drinking unbelief, exclaims, —

"But yet my doctor he shall never be;
Such physick, sure, would be the death of me;"

and it is not improbable that he had strong reasons for disliking water. He adds, what is as curious as the rest, that the gentleman having prudently procured the sheet to be buried, it was "covetously dug up," and those concerned in the operation died of the plague caught from the infected linen. Various other stories are narrated, and the precise dates are given to some of them. Under the head of "The Belmans call, or Thursday morning," we have the following: —

"This day the weekly Bils come out,
To put the people out of doubt
How many of the Plague do dye:
We summe them up most carefully.
But, oh, if our transgressions all,
Both how we sinne and how we fall,
God should take notice what they are,
Where should we sinfull men appeare?
We look upon the punishment,
But not upon the cause 'tis sent:
Remove the cause, & you shall see
The Plague shall soon removed be."

The last part of the production consists of a didactic poem or song, with the burden, "The Lord have mercy on us all," from which its character may easily be guessed. There can be no doubt that the materials of the tract were hastily collected, and as hastily put together, for the purpose of securing a temporary sale during the prevalence of infection.

Clinton, Purser and Arnold. — Clinton, Purser and Arnold to their Countreymen wheresoeuer. Wherein is described by their own hands their vnfeigned penitence for their offences past: their patience in welcoming their Death, and their duetiful minds to wardes her most excellent Maiestie. — London Imprinted by Iohn Wolfe and are to be sold at the middle shop in the Poultry, ioyning to S. Mildreds Church. 4to. B. L. 6 *leaves.*

Only two copies of this poetical tract are, we believe, at present known, one of them having come to light very recently.

It is not easy, perhaps not possible, to settle the date, but we may place it either in 1590 or soon afterwards, and we know that at least two of the persons named above were hanged as pirates late in the reign of Elizabeth. They are characters who are led out to execution in T. Heywood's drama, "Fortune by Land and Sea," which, although not printed until 1655, was unquestionably written while Elizabeth was still upon the throne. Our Chroniclers and Camden are silent regarding them,[1] and one of them, called Walton, *alias* Purser, in our tract, is named Tom Watton in the play.

Three copies of verses are included in the six pages, each of the prisoners being supposed (we take it for granted that they were not the real penmen) to contribute his share just before death. Walton begins (at the back of the title to save room, and to make the publication cheap) and gives thirteen seven-line stanzas. Arnold follows with sixteen stanzas in the same form; and Clinton concludes with fourteen similar stanzas — all three clearly by one hand. Walton opens with an address to "Lordings that list to heare a dreary tale," and thus narrates how they came to be captured: —

"Two lofty saile from out the lovely East
it was our hap unhappy to descry:
I wish they had bene further in the West,
when gracelesse we to greete them came so nie;
but who fares well whome Fortune doth defie?
We stoupt, we strake, and vaild when we had seene
The Armes of Englande and our noble Queene."

He ends with these lines: —

"As for my selfe I owe a due to Death,
and I respect it not in that I die;
Onely the manner of my losse of breath
is cause that I for some compassion cry.
My soule is sav'd, where ere my body lie.

[1] This is a mistake. Stow mentions the execution of Walton and Clinton on 30th August, 1583, which therefore, no doubt, was the date of the tract.

This makes me sigh — that faith unto my frend
Hath brought me thus to this untimely end.
Thomas Walton, *alias* Purser."

Arnold informs us that he was "an aged man of no great personage," and that he was by birth a gentleman of Hampshire: he accuses a priest of being the cause of his misfortune, by robbing him of his farm and other property, and then compelling him to take to the sea and piracy for a maintenance. Clinton dwells in his effusion upon the fickleness of Fortune: —

"Welth, worldly wit, ambition or renowne,
nor ought on earth so permanent abides,
But fickle Fortune sometime puls them down:
so vaine we are, so soone our honor slides,
so trustlesse she whose mirth to mischiefe glydes!
Our paines endure, our pleasures are but short;
But what availes the heedlesse to exhorte? * * *

"Then give me leave to breath abroad my moanes,
whose life or death my Prince may take or give;
And though they stand like stockes and senseles stones,
whome I have holpe whilst I in hap did live,
and sooner might have fild an emptie sive,
The time hath bene when they to please me prest;
But now they dare not, cause I am distrest."

It seems certain that, although three different names are appended to the several poems, they were all written by one man, and that man, as we conclude, some professional scribe, who took occasion, on the trial and conviction of the three pirates, to compose a tract that would command a sale from the interest and notoriety of the subject.

COKAYNE, SIR ASTON. — A Chain of Golden Poems, embellished with Wit, Mirth and Eloquence. Together with two most excellent Comedies, viz, The Obstinate Lady, and Trappolin suppos'd a Prince. Written by Sr. Aston Cokayn. — London, Printed by W. G. and are to be sold by Isaac Pridmore. 1658. 8vo. 262 *leaves*.

The above is the general title to this volume, and it is followed by a particular title to the shorter pieces: — "Small Poems of Divers Sorts. Written by Sir Aston Cockain — London Printed by Wil. Godbid, 1658." "The Author's apology to the Reader" serves by way of preface, and to it are added commendatory verses by Tho. Bancroft, and a list of *errata*. The poems then begin with "a Remedy for Love," and fill two hundred and eighty-four pages. "The Obstinate Lady," and "Trappolin suppos'd a Prince," have distinct titles, but the paging and signatures are continued to the end. The author's "Tragedy of Ovid" was not added to his other plays until 1662.

COKE, JOHN. — The Debate betwene the Heraldes of Englande and Fraunce, compyled by Ihon Coke, clarke of the kynges recognysaunce, or vulgerly called clarke of the Statutes of the staple of Westmynster, and fynyshed the yere of our Lord M.D.L. B.L. 8vo. 94 *leaves.*

The colophon, whimsically given by the author in four languages, runs thus: — "Fynished by me John Coke Le dernier Jour Doctobre, Den yaer ons here duisent vijf hundred negen en viertich. *Finis Laudat opus.* And Imprynted by me Rycharde Wyer, and be to be solde at his shop in Poules churche yearde. *Cum privilegio ad imprimendum solum.*" Hence we learn that the book was finished by the author on the last day of October, 1549, and printed by Wyer (though nowhere enumerated among the productions of his press) [1] in 1550. At the back of the title are three woodcuts, representing Lady "Prudence," (whom the author addresses) "The frenche Heralde," and "The englyshe Heralde."

The author purports to have written his book in answer to one he met with in Brussels, in which a French Herald exalted his country above England. The Herald of France, as may be ex-

[1] It is given by Dibdin (Typ. Ant. IV. 238) with a reference to his *Bibliomania*, p. 13. We inadvertently derived this error from the Bridgew. Catalogue, 1837, p. 66.

pected, is here worsted at every point, and Coke does not scruple to introduce among historical worthies Guy of Warwick, (quoting Lydgate as one of his authorities,) and Bevis of Hampton: of the last he says the story was extant in English, Dutch, and French. Farther on he enumerates among the "great clerks" of this country, Chaucer, Gower, Lydgate, Bongay, Grosdon, Payce, Lylly, Lynacre, Tunstall, Latymer, Hoper, and Coverdale; and then adds, — "Also we have dyvers gentylwomen in Englande, whiche be not onely well estudied in holy Scrypture, but also in the Greke and Latyn tonges. As maystres More, maystres Anne Coke, maystres Clement, and other, beynge an estraunge thing to you and other nacions." "Maystres More" was the daughter of Sir Thomas More, and she had "disputed of philosophy" before Henry VIII. (*Vide* Hist. Engl., Dram. Poetry, and the Stage, I. 113.)

The author winds up his work with eight stanzas of verse, headed, "The Message sent by John Coke, compyler of this smale treatyse, to such as be enemyes to our soveraygne Lord Kynge Edwarde the vi. and to his Realmes of Englande and Irlande." The following is the sixth stanza: —

"Drowned be he as was Narcisus,
Or syxe monethes kepte in a a Cage syngynge
By Lameth, Belsabub, Pluto and Aserberus,
That wolde hurte to our noble yonge kynge,
Edwarde the syxte, not yet twelve yeares olde,
Precioser to Englande then stone or golde.
Lorde, preserve his hyghnes from traytours popishe!
To whom prosperous helth cordyally I wysshe,
With longe lyfe, and that his puyssaunt hande
Maye subdue the vyle nacion Scottysshe,
Whiche desyre the dystruccion of Englande."

In the next stanza he expresses his hope that every enemy of England may be boiled in a caldron, like the maid in Smithfield for poisoning her master, and concludes by a stanza in French, mentioning the death of James IV. of Scotland, and the slaughter of Porrex, which in 1561 was made the subject of a tragedy by Sackville and Norton, and was printed in 8vo, 1565, under the title of "Gorboduc."

Coke was unknown to Ritson and other poetical antiquaries, and we learn nothing of his personal history.

Collins, Thomas.—The Teares of Love : or Cupids Progresse. Together with the complaint of the sorrowfull Shepheardesse, fayre (but unfortunate) Candida, deploring the death of her deare-lov'd Coravin, a late living (and an ever to be lamented) Shepheard. In a (passionate) pastorall Elegie. Composed by Thomas Collins, &c.—London, Printed by George Purslowe for Henry Bell. 1615. 4to. 28 *leaves.*

The word "Shepherd" having formerly been synonymous with "Poet," this piece was published to celebrate the death of one of the "fraternity of featherbrains." Who was meant by Coravin it is not perhaps possible now to ascertain, and the only point which could at all lead to the discovery is, that the author informs us (p. 20) that he died on St. Peter's day:—

"Untill the time that he was clad in clay,
Which (woe is me) was on St. Peter's day."

Of Coravin's skill in poetry Collins speaks as follows:—

"Then Candida (awhile) lay teares aside,
And tell what love-tricks did in 's life betide:
Tell how hee'd sit, and pipe so prettily
That all Swaines joy'd to heare his harmonie.
Each Nimph and Shepheardesse, that now remains
In any of these neighbouring groves or plains,
From fountaines and from fieldes would flock with speed,
To heare him play upon his Oeten Reed;
And as they daily used for to doe,
So would the Satyrs and the Dreiads too.
How oft have I my milke-white flocke forsooke,
And slily stolne downe to a silent brooke,
My Coravins sweet Songs and Oads to heare,
When he (poore Soule) thought little I was there."

The main subject of the poem is the apologue of Cupid exchanging arrows with Death, upon which elegant fancy James Shirley wrote a drama, and which in various shapes has been treated in French, Spanish, and Italian.

The poem is full of unnatural and forced conceits, and possesses very little pastoral simplicity, with much feebleness and dilation.

The opening, where Collins describes himself following some garlands thrown upon a stream, is the best part of the work. At the end the author apologizes for his imperfections, praises Sidney, Spenser, and Drayton, and alludes to Lodge.

But two other copies of this production are believed to exist. The dedication is to Lady Haddington, where the author mentions "some of his braines best-borne issues," which were yet concealed; and it is followed by fourteen lines "to those Readers that can and will conceive reason."

Commendatory verses, signed Jo. B[eaumont?], thus refer to other productions by our author: —

"From *Newports* bloudy battell (sung by thee)
With *Yaxley's* death (the flow'r of Chivalry)
As from thy well-pen'd *Publican*, to bee
Transported thus to fields of Arcady,
Shews that thy Muse is apt for all assayes," &c.

The "well-pen'd Publican" is the subject of our next article, but of the two other pieces we know nothing. The preliminary matter concludes with two stanzas by Samuel Rowlands "to his affected friend Master Thomas Collins."

COLLINS, THOMAS. — The Penitent Publican, his Confession of Mouth. Contrition of heart. Unfained Repentance. And fervent Prayer unto God for Mercie and forgivenesse. — At London, Printed for Arthur Johnson, dwelling in Paules Churchyard, at the signe of the white Horse, neere the great Northdooré of Paules Church. 1610. 4to. 25 *leaves.*

This, of course, is the poem referred to by Jo. B. in his lines at the close of the preceding article. Its extreme rarity forms its chief claim to notice. The dedication, subscribed Thomas Collins, and dated 6 of July, 1610, is to the Countess of Huntington, where he commends to her protection his "illiterate and little-worth labour," as he calls it, with some affected diffidence. However, it must be admitted to be superior to his later and feebler work in earnestness, which sometimes almost rises to eloquence: the Publican in one place exclaims: —

"Lord! I no presents, no oblations bring,
 Onely my selfe I offer unto thee:
A broken heart is all my offering,
 The which, although it far unworthy bee,
 Yet, Lord, accept it; for behold, and see,
In true devotion and in perfect zeale,
I, prostrate here, for mercy do appeale."

The printer seems, here and there, to have done the author injustice, and in the last line *doth* is put for "*do*." Another stanza, the latest of the whole, is as much as may be required in the way of specimen: —

"As thou art holy, heare my prayer, Lord!
 As thou art good and gracious pittie mee:
As thou art true and faithfull of thy word
 Forgive my sins (though infinite they bee)
 And let me live to laud and honour thee;
To whom be given all glory, power, and praise
Even to the end of never-ending daies."

Of Collins nothing appears to be known, and in these two productions of his pen he affords us no personal information: he takes pains, however, to inform Lady Huntington in his dedication that he is no Puritan; and he adds a sonnet "To the Reader whatsoever," which has no merit of any kind.

COLMAN, W. — La Dance Machabre, or Deaths Duel. By W. C. — London Printed by William Stansby. n. d. 8vo. 44 *leaves.*

This poem, in two hundred and sixty-one six-line stanzas, is without date; but, as the author complains at the end, that one Roger Muchill had anticipated his second title of "Deaths Duel" by printing a Sermon of Dr. Donne's under it, which Sermon bears date in 1633, we need not hesitate in fixing "La Dance Machabre" either in that year or in the year following. Not more than three or four copies appear to be known of it.

The title is excellently engraved by T. Cecil, and facing it are some lines headed, "The mind of the Front." The dedication is in French prose, *A la Royne*, and the tendency of the work may be seen by what the author says of it: *pour ayder aux hommes pervertis de cèst siecle corrompu à retourner de l'insolence à la crainte du Ciel, et de la debauche à la raison* — a considerable task for "an unpractised youth," as he calls himself in some preliminary lines signed W. Colman. To this succeeds "The Author to his Book," and commendatory verses by John Peashall, E. H., Thomas Veridicus, James Sherlie, and John Crompton. Opposite the commencement of the work is another plate of Death with a spade, leaning his elbow upon a rotten post, with this motto above, *Sum quod eris. Fui quod es*, and a translation in a couplet at the bottom. The principal poem consists of a series of not very novel moral reflections, without order or system.

Appended to the main poem are Elegies upon the Earl of Shrewsbury, the Marchioness of Winchester, Lord Paget, and Sir John Beaumont, the poet. A fragment of another edition seems to be in existence.

CONSTABLE, HENRY. — Diana. The praises of his Mistres, in certaine sweete Sonnets. By H. C. — London, Printed by I. C. for Richard Smith: and are to be sold at the West doore of Paules. 1592. 4to.

Few men of his day enjoyed a higher reputation, especially as a sonnet-writer, than Henry Constable; yet, as far as is known, it was built upon a very narrow foundation: the above is the title-page of the only separate work with which his name is connected; and bibliographers were until lately ignorant of the existence of such an edition: they apprehended (Ritson, Bibl. Poet. 172) that the impression of 1594 was the earliest. On this account we shall describe the one before us more minutely, although the pieces it contains (with one important exception) were again printed in 1594 (not 1584), 1597, and 1604. All editions are of extreme rarity, but that of 1592 is unique.

The dates of Constable's birth and death are alike uncertain, but having been born towards the middle of the sixteenth century, he survived into the seventeenth, so that he flourished in the time of Shakspeare, Spenser, Drayton, and Daniel: his first work appeared in the same year as the earliest production of the last of these distinguished poets, and his effusions were exposed to powerful competition. Our notion is, contrary to the received opinion, that he was a native of Scotland, but there is no distinct evidence upon the point, beyond the fact that he seems to have been in great favor with our James I., and that he had employed himself to write sonnets in that monarch's praise, and especially of his "Poetical Exercises" when they were printed at Edinburgh in 1591. Constable was an avowed Roman Catholic, and on account of his faith early retired to the Continent, and remained for some years abroad: he travelled in Poland and in Italy, and letters from him are extant dated from Rouen in 1596 and from the Tower in 1604. It is a peculiarity in the edition of his Sonnets of 1592, that they are all numbered in Italian, from *Sonnetto Primo*, to *Sonnetto Ultimo;* and though none of them are translations, they savor much of the flowers and soil where some of them, in all probability, were composed. At all events, they are in form more after the Italian model than the sonnets of most of Constable's contemporaries. They are rather elegant than impassioned.

The following sonnet, for some unexplained reason, was never reprinted after 1592, and it there immediately follows the title-page, and precedes a brief address from the Printer, or Stationer, of which we shall speak presently.

"To his absent Diana.

"Sever'd from sweete Content, my lives sole light,
Banisht by over-weening wit from my desire,
This poore acceptance onely I require,
That though my fault have forc'd me from thy sight,
Yet that thou wouldst (my sorrowes to requite)
Review these Sonnets, pictures of thy praise;
Wherein each woe thy wondrous worth doth raise,
Though first thy worth bereft me of delight.
See them forsaken; for I them forsooke,
Forsaken first of thee, next of my sence:
And when thou deignst on their blacke teares to looke,

Shed not one teare, my teares to recompence;
But joy in this (though Fates gainst me repine)
My verse still lives to witnes thee divine."

These fourteen graceful lines are quite equal to any others in the small volume; and some private cause, to which we have no clue, must have prevented their reappearance. The address "to the Gentlemen Readers" was also never repeated; but it is not necessary to say more of it than that it speaks of the sonnets as "orphans," as if the father were dead; the explanation probably being that Constable had at this date withdrawn to France, and had thus deserted his literary progeny. Richard Smith, the stationer, substituted in 1594 a sonnet of his own to the Queen's Maids of Honor for his prose address, and there again he speaks of Constable's "orphan poems."

The edition of 1592 contains only 22 sonnets, and after *Ultimo Sonnetto* we read, at the bottom of the page, the catch-word "Blame," with which, in fact, *Sonnetto terzo* had begun. Hence we might suppose that the impression is incomplete: but a small piece of paper seems originally to have been pasted over "Blame," as if this copy of the "Diana" had been intended to comprise no more. It may so have happened that Constable was obliged to quit the country, on account of his religious tenets, while his poems were actually going through the press, and that on this account Smith put forth the "orphans" without the accompaniment of their brothers and sisters, which, being added to the family in 1594, made in the whole 76 sonnets. That number was not afterwards increased.[1]

COPLAND, ROBERT. — Jyl of Breyntfords testament. Newly compiled. 4to. B. L. 8 *leaves*.

It is a new fact, connected with this ancient piece of broad and coarse humor, that it was twice printed by William Copland: in one impression it is called "Jyl of Braintfords Testament," and in

[1] In 1859 Mr. W. C. Hazlitt published a selection of Constable's Sonnets, and introduced them by a judicious memoir, which contains nearly all that is known of the author.

the other as we have spelt it above. The colophon is still more different, for in one it stands merely "Imprinted at London by me William Copland," and in the other, "Imprented at London in Lothbury over agaynst Saint Margarytes church by me Wyllyam Copland." The literal variations are innumerable, and sometimes important: thus in one we are told that Jyl of Brentford was "a widow of a holy sort," and in the other that she was "a widow of a *homly* sort": again, "pastyme" is changed to *pastaunce*, and "chyet" to *cheef*, the last being probably right, as it refers to the condition of a "scroll," or manuscript, the "chief" of which was "clene defaced." We take it for granted that the edition which has *homly* for "holy," and *cheef* for "chyet" is the latest, and that the corrections were made when the piece was set up in William Copland's workshop for the second time. None of our typographical historians or bibliographers have made us aware of these and many other changes of text, because they were, as we believe, ignorant that there existed more than one impression of the tract.

Robert Copland, who had been an assistant to Wynkyn de Worde, avows himself the author of "Jyl of Breyntfords testament"; but, according to our modern notions of decorum, and even of decency, there is little to be proud of in it. It is certainly in some parts very shrewd and droll, but it is impossible for us, without gross offence, to give an accurate notion of its import and contents. William Copland, who printed it, was in all likelihood younger brother to Robert Copland, who, after the death of his master and instructor, Wynkyn de Worde, followed the same business, and dying about 1547, left it to William Copland, who carried it on at all events until 1561; but some of the most curious and amusing productions of his press have no dates, and may have come out later. Robert Copland, besides "Jyl of Breyntfords testament," in a covert manner admitted his authorship of a tract, printed by Wynkyn de Worde without date, called "The Complaynte of them that ben to late maryed:" his two names form an acrostic just preceding the last stanza: this too is a fact not noticed by bibliographers, and only recently pointed out to us.

"Jyl of Breyntfords testament" is introduced by what is called the "Prologus of Robert Copland the auctor," so that there can be no mistake upon that point: his "Complaynte" about late marriage was unquestionably a translation from the French, but his "Jyl of Breyntford's testament" must have been original,[1] and certainly displays no great refinement, whatever may be said of its humor: humor of the lowest description it certainly contains in abundance, and such as in many cases it is impossible to transfer to our pages. The commencement of the Prologus may indeed be quoted, and we give it from what must have been the second and amended impression: —

> "At Brentford, on the west of London,
> Nygh to a place called is Syon,
> There dwelt a widow of a homly sort,
> Honest in substaunce and full of sport.
> Dally she cowd with pastim and Jestes
> Among her neyghbours and her gestes:
> She kept an Iñe of ryght good lodgyng
> For all estates that thider was comyng.
> It chaunced this wydow, as it is supposed,
> In her sport, and meryly dysposed,
> After her deth, for a remembraunce,
> Thought to have some matter of pastaunce,
> For people to laugh at in suche company
> As are dyposed to talke meryly,
> Mengled with many proper scoffes and boordes,
> Of sondry tauntes, with some mery woordes,
> The which I have hard at many seasons,
> Full of pastyme with prety reasons."

Robert Copland then quotes a proverb of anything but a delicate kind, the application of which he jestingly demonstrates by the assistance of one John Hardysay, whom he accidentally meets in Brentford. They adjourn "to the red lyon at the shambles end" (showing how ancient a sign it is in that town) for the purpose of discussing the proverb, and "a pot of good ale." Hardy-

[1] The first notion of "Jyl of Breyntford's Testament" may, however, have been derived from Chaucer's "Sompner's Tale," where the sick man, Thomas, bestows a corresponding legacy upon the friar, whose cupidity is similarly disappointed: —

> "The frere up starte, as dothe a wode lyon:
> A, false chorle! (qd the frere) for Goddes bones,
> This haste thou in dispyte do for the nones," &c.

say pretends to have discovered the origin of the proverb in an "old scroll": he says, —

"And truly now is come to my mynde,
Not long ago how I dyde fynde
An old scrow, all ragged and rent:
Beseming it is some mery entent,
And dyvers say that do it rede
But gallaunt toyes there semes in dede:
It is so antick broken, and so raced,
That all the cheef is clene defaced.
Take it; and I pray thee hartyly
Loke theron, and yf thou espy
That it be of any substaunce
Of myrth or of honest pastaunce:
And where thou spyest that it dooth want,
Or wher for lack the mater is scant,
To put it as is accordyng
To the mater in every thyng;
Bere it with thee, and take sume payne
The poore mare shall have his man agayn."

In these quotations the literal differences between the two copies are too numerous to be pointed out, and to an important verbal variation, "cheef" for *chyet*, we have already adverted: in the last line but one, also, *Keep* in one copy is "Bere" in the other; but the most noticeable line is the last, because it importantly illustrates a speech by Puck in "Mids. N. Dream," Act III. sc. 2; only in "Jyl of Breyntford" Hardysay, perhaps owing to the effect of the "pot of good ale," reverses the words. Puck speaks of it as a "country proverb," and so Hardysay uses it in his converse with Copland, who carries home the "old scrow," and pretends to give an account of its merry, and then popularly palatable, contents. It appears that Jyllyen, or Jyl of Breyntford, being at death's door, sent for the Curate, and while he was drinking a cup of her best ale, dictated to him her last will and testament. In it she makes an unsavory bequest to every person who is so foolish as not, in all cases, to do what is most to his own advantage and liking: —

"He that is ever way ward at hart,
And with every man is over wart,"

i. e., overthwart, is to have the benefit of her bequest. So again, still more humorously, —

> "He that lendeth a horse with all thynges mete,
> And on his own vyage gooth on his fete,"

deserves also to be remembered by a similar legacy. We need not go through the rest, but when the Curate (in the presence of some of the merry old dames' friends and neighbors) has concluded the will, old Jyl calls her servant: —

> "What maid! come hither, I shrew your neck.
> Bring us up shortly a quart of seck,
> A cuple of bunnes, and set us some cheese.
> Lo, freends! ye shall not your labour leese:
> I have, as now, no better cheer to make you.
> Be mery and welcome. To God I betake you!"

With which words she expires. After some abuse by Copland of the priest, for not taking his reward in good part, calling him "Sir John Whipdock," "Sir John Smelsmock," and "hedge curate," the piece closes with "an Exhortation," entreating the indulgence of the reader for "this little prety fantasy," which was clearly only calculated for the atmosphere of tap-rooms, and for the boisterous amusement of "bench-whistlers." It is, however, characteristic of the time, and mainly upon this account we have noticed it.

COPLEY, ANTHONY. — Wits, Fits and Fancies: or a generall and serious Collection of the Sententious Speeches, Answers, Iests, and Behauiours of all sortes of Estates from the Throane to the Cottage. Being properly reduced to their seuerall heads for the more ease to the Reader. Newly corrected and augmented, with many late true and wittie accidents. *Musica mentis, medicina Mæstus.* — London Printed by Edw: Allde, dwelling in little Saint Bartholomewes, near Christ-Church. 1614. 4to. B. L.

This work was originally published with the name of the author,

Anthony Copley, in 1595; but the impression before us is particularly valuable, inasmuch as it illustrates Shakspeare more than the earlier impression quoted by Malone, Sh. by Bosw. III. 73, and by Douce in his "Illustrations," I. 340. In 1614 all mention of Copley seems to have been studiously omitted, (as well as a poem called "Love's Owle" included in 1595,) possibly on account of his concern in Raleigh's Conspiracy, for which he and others were tried at Winchester, in Nov. 1603, (Stow's *Annales*, 1605, p. 1418.) The impression of which we have availed ourselves is entirely prose, and consists of jests, sayings, and anecdotes, for many of which Copley was indebted to the *Floresta Spagnola*, as Douce pointed out in 1807, and as the writer in Cens. Lit. (II. 127) repeated in 1815.

Pistol's exclamation in 2 Henry IV. Act II. sc. 4, *Si fortuna me tormenta, sperato me contenta*, will be well remembered; and Farmer referred to this old "Collection of Tales" as an authority for the true Italian wording. The following are the very terms Copley employs on p. 35 of "Wits, Fits and Fancies": "Hannibal Gonzaga being in the Low Countries overthrowne from his horse by an English Captaine, and commanded to yeeld himselfe prisoner, kist his sword and gave it to the Englishman, saying, *Si Fortuna me tormenta, il speranza me contenta*."

In the same work we meet with the famous proverbial saying regarding Venice (Love's Lab. L. IV. 2), but Copley puts it into English. In "Twelfth Night," Act III. sc. 2, Sir Toby tells Sir Andrew, "If thou *thoust* him some thrice, it shall not be amiss;" and on p. 28 of the work before us we read, "There was a certaine poore Gentleman, who, in regard of his poverty, every one *thowed*, and not any one vouchsafed him the title of Mastership: whereupon one that noted it said, — "This argueth that neither God nor the King ever created Mastership."

Ben Jonson, also, may hence have received a hint for the last scene of his "Every Man in his Humour," where Justice Clement, on the entrance of Babadil, and on being informed that he is a soldier, calls for his armor and sword, that they may be upon equal terms. In "Wits, Fits and Fancies," (p. 120,) this conduct is attributed to "a merry Recorder of London," meaning, no doubt, Fleetwood: —

"A souldiour comming about a sute to a merrie Recorder of London, the Recorder, seeing him out of the window, ran hastilie into an inner roome, and there put on a corslet and a head-peece, and then with a launce in his hand came downe unto him and said, How now, Sirra! are you the man that hath somewhat to say to me? Begin now when you dare, for behold (I trowe) I am sufficiently provided for you."

On p. 50 there is a remarkable anecdote of Henry Goldingham, the poet, (who wrote part of the Entertainment for Elizabeth at Norwich in 1578,) of which no notice has been taken, although very characteristic. Copley, who probably knew him, tells us that Goldingham "had long sued to her Majestie for her signet to his graunted suite, and her Majestie still saying that she had no pen and inke at hand to doe it, [he] at last humbled his bill to her Highnesse foote, and said, 'May it, then, please your Majestie but to step your royall foote hereupon, and I my selfe will then warrant it for good.' Her Majestie so well liked of his merrie conceipt, that presently, calling for her pen and inke, did daigne to signe it."

There are many jokes and stories in the volume that were transferred without acknowledgment to later collections, or perhaps had been derived from the same original. Such materials were considered common property, and the following, a full century after it appeared in English, was imputed to no less a man than Swift, as if in him it had originated: — "A famous preacher who had long sued for a Bishoprick, and could not attaine to any, used to say that, out of doubt, if it rayned myters, not any one would light upon his head." (p. 64.)

Stories that we meet with in 1595 were so soon adopted by others, that in 1604 one was introduced into "Mother Bunch's Merriments," and another into Dekker and Wilkins's "Jests to make you merry," 1607. (See *post.*)

As a poet, Copley is scarcely worth notice. His "Fig for Fortune," 1596, is good in little but in its pretentious and disappointing title: it is dull, and ill versified. The dialogue, — "Love's Owle," — in the first edition of "Wits, Fits and Fancies," 1595, is something better, and we quote the following stanza, in which Love says of an old man, —

"Though age be old and colde, I can
Re-young him to a lustie man,
And in his joyntes infuse a fire
To execute a kinde desire.
I can regenerate his dying yeere
By faire bepriesting him to a bonny feere,
Or els dispensing him such like good cheere
Elsewhere."

This is, perhaps, the best of all the stanzas of which the piece consists, and some of them, it must be allowed, run ruggedly and uncouthly. It may be doubted whether Copley's proposed remedy would be at all effectual: young "feeres," *i. e. wives*, have not usually lengthened the lives of old men.

CORYAT, THOMAS. — Coryats Crudities. Hastily gobled up in five Moneths travells in France, Savoy, Italy, Rhetia, commonly called the Grisons country, Helvetia, alias Switzerland, some parts of high Germany, and the Netherlands ; Newly digested in the hungry aire of Odcombe in the County of Somerset, and now dispersed to the nourishment of the travelling Members of this Kingdome &c. 1611. 4to. 453 *leaves.*

The engraved title, as above, by W. Hole, is followed by a printed title: "London Printed by W. S. Anno Domini 1611." The first two hundred pages are occupied principally by mock-panegyrics upon the author by Ben Jonson, Sir John Harington, John Donne, Christopher Brooke, Inigo Jones, Richard Corbet, Thomas Campion, Thomas Bastard, Michael Drayton, John Davies, Henry Peacham, &c. The "Crudities" themselves occupy six hundred and fifty-five pages, and to them are added *Posthuma Fragmenta Poematum*, &c. The Table is given on six leaves, and the work is concluded by a list of *Errata*, and an introductory address to it.

Coryat does not seem to have wanted knowledge nor cleverness, but he made himself the laughing-stock of the time by his gross deficiency in common sense and discretion. A complete copy of his "Crudities" ought to include, among other plates, a full length of the author welcomed by a Venetian Courtesan. Coryat afterwards travelled into the East, and died at Surat, in 1617. Such is Anthony Wood's statement, who goes into considerable detail regarding Coryat's later travels, which began in 1612, the year after he had published his "Crudities," having been encouraged to continue his vagrancy by the success of that singular and much ridiculed volume.

COSBY, ARNOLD. — The most horrible and tragicall murther of the right honorable, the vertuous and valerous Gentleman, Iohn Lord Bourgh, Baron of Castell Connell. Committed by Arnold Cosby, the foureteenth of Ianuarie. Togeather with the sorrowfull sighes of a sadde soule vppon his funerall: written by W. R. a seruaunt of the said Lord Bourgh. — Printed by R. R. 1591. 4to.

There were two impressions of this curious tract, by the same printer and publisher, in 1591, but the only difference in the title-page is the omission of the nonsensical Latin motto, *Tempus fortuna flent*, which was left out in what we consider the second edition. The title-pages of both speak of certain "sorrowfull sighes of a sad soule uppon his funerall, written by R. R. a servaunt of the said Lord Bourgh," which ought to be found in the tract; but such apparently was the haste in bringing it out, for the gratification of public curiosity on the melancholy event, that they were omitted in a copy sent to Lambeth Palace, though they are found in another exemplar of the same date which we have since examined. In other respects they do not materially differ; and though the "sorrowful sighs" are written in an ambitious style and strain, and fill no fewer than eight 4to pages, there really is very little in them worth notice. At the close of both is "Arnold Cosbie's *Ultimum Vale*," in which he laments his treacherous cowardice in slaying Lord Bourgh, while the latter, at Cosbie's instance, was stooping to unbuckle his spurs. This is in blank verse, a form of writing very unusual in 1591 in pieces not designed for the stage; and it is the more remarkable, because Shakspeare took from it Pistol's famous exclamation, "Death, rock me asleep!" 2 Henry IV. Act II. sc. 4. We quote the passage from the *Ultimum Vale:* —

> "Why do I kill my dolefull dying heart
> With sad rehearsall of this heavie chance?
> O death, rocke me asleepe! Father of Heaven!
> That hast sole power to pardon sinnes of men,
> Forgive the faults and folly of my youth,
> My youth misspent in wast and wantones;
> And for sweete Jesus sake forgive my soule,
> Fouly defiled with this above the rest,
> This wickednes, this hard unworthie deed!"

These lines were probably not by Cosby, but were written by some person employed by the publisher; and we feel considerable confidence, from the line "Forgive the faults and folly of my youth," that they were by Robert Greene, because that very expression occurs in one of his acknowledged pieces. The other verses, that is to say, "the sighs of a sad soul," were by some inferior scribe; but with this remarkable peculiarity, not belonging to any other poem in our language that we are aware of, that the first four lines of each stanza are blank verse, closed by a rhyming couplet; thus, —

> "The soveraigne of the Planets never rose,
> But in a cloudie vale did shrowd his head;
> His Chariote covered like a mourning hearse,
> Rejected quite his golden furniture:
> Ceres and Flora suffered such a dearth
> As never happened on the barren earth."

We add another stanza for its novelty, not for its merit: —

> "Thus is my spring become the leaves decaie,
> Where characters of endles griefe are writ:
> The dewfull teares doe trickle from the boughs,
> That lost their cloathing when I lost my love.
> And aye to me my sorrow writs the worst,
> My joyes are barren, and myselfe accurst."

The precise meaning we do not pretend to explain, but the

form is, we apprehend, without example.[1] These verses are divided under the heads, "The sighes of the Night," "The sighes of the Morning," "The third sigh of Winter," and "The fourth sigh of the Spring."

Cosby's *Ultimum Vale*, as it is called, was also printed as an appendix to the account of his execution, published by William Wright with the date of 1591. It consists of four leaves; and the only material fact is that the murderer, in his last and penitent moments, was attended by Dr. Fletcher, then Bishop of Bristol, the father of the dramatist, John Fletcher. The title-page of Wright's tract is "The manner of the death and execution of Arnold Cosbie &c. with certaine verses written by the said Cosby in the time of his imprisonment." He was hanged at "Wandsworth townes end," near where he murdered Lord Bourgh.

CRAIGE, ALEXANDER. — The Amorose Songes, Sonets, and Elegies: Of M. Alexander Craige, Scoto-Britane. — Imprinted at London by William White. 1606. B. L. 8vo. 84 *leaves.*

This author began to write, or rather to publish, in 1604, when his "Poetical Essayes" addressed to James I. appeared. They are more remarkable for their adulation than for their poetry, and they are overburdened with classical allusions, which perhaps rendered them acceptable to the king. The volume before us is dedicated to the Queen, whom the author styles "incomparably bountiful, incomparably beautiful, and so peerless Princess;" and the remark just made upon the character of his production of 1604 will apply equally to that of 1606. It seems that Craige was indebted to the Queen's "munificence," and that she had bestowed "frequent benefits" upon him; but he furnishes no particulars. After the dedication he inserts an "Epistle generall to Idea, Cynthia, Lithocardia, Kala, Erantina, Lais, Pandora, Penelopœ," to all of whom he also adds separate epistles. He apolo-

[1] See, however, article in Vol. III., BARNABE RICH, who in 1613 adopted a similar kind of stanza.

gizes "to the Reader" for "using the Scotish and English dialectes," but he is also fond of French terms, by which he thinks he gives a polish to his "rude rhimes," and he employs besides a number of affected words. The following Sonnet "to the Queene her most excellent Majestie" introduces the "Amorous Songes and Sonets." It is one of the best specimens of the author's style: —

"Apelles' man did all his wits imploy
To paint the shape of Lœdais daughter faire;
But when he saw his worke prov'd nought, poore boy,
He wept for woe and tooke exceeding care:
Then deck'd he her with jewels rich and rare.
Which when the brave Apelles did behold,
Paint on (quoth hee), poore boy, and haue no feare:
When beautie fayles, well done t' enrich with gold.
I am (faire Princesse) like the Painter's man;
As ignorant, as skant of skill as hee,
Yet will I strive and doe the best I can
To manifest my loving minde to thee.
But to supply the weaknesse of my skill,
In place of gold (great Lady) take good will."

This is only subscribed "Craige," but sometimes he adds "Scoto-Britain," and once "Banfa-Britain." He refers to his youth, and promises to present the lady he calls Lithocardia with "some better poem." These names probably have all an individual application, and in one of his sonnets Craige unequivocally tells us that Penelope is Lady Rich. Although he here and there speaks diffidently of his own powers, it is evident that he thought he was destined to immortality, and to give immortality to those whom he celebrates. A "Sonnet to Idea" begins, —

"My Muse shall make thy boundless fame to flie
In bounds where yet thy selfe was never seene;
And were not for my songs thy name had beene
Obscurelie cast into the grave with thee."

His notion of addressing a real or imaginary female under the name of "Idea" he had from Michael Drayton, who had done the same thing ten or twelve years before. On sign. K i, we come to a new prose dedication "To my honorable good Lord and maister (the true Mæcenas of my muse) George Earle of Dunbar, Lord

Barwick, high Tresurar of Scotland," ending with these words: "What I have heere set downe is for your sollace; and so I beseech your Honor to accept from the table of my Chamber, at your liberall charge and allowance, the 5 day of November 1606." In this part of the volume we meet with those imitations and enlargements of Christopher Marlow's well-known ballad, "Come live with me and be my love," and the answer to it by Sir Walter Raleigh, which the Rev. H. J. Todd has pointed out in his edition of Milton, v. 68. They consist of four poems between Alexis and Lesbia, the first beginning,

"Come be my love and live with me,"

the second, in reply:

"If all were thine that there I see."

The third is "a new persuasion":

"Once more I pray thee be my love;"

and the fourth,

"Oft have I pray'd thee be my love."

Few imitations can be less like the original, excepting in mere form, for all the natural and pastoral simplicity of Marlow is lost in trite, tedious, and repeated allusions to Parnassus, Castalian drops, Hippocrene, Aganippe, &c.

Craige cannot do without the heathen gods and goddesses at every turn, and he afterwards calls in the aid of Flora, Daphne, the Nereids, Apollo, and Cynthia, in the poem which opens thus: —

"Come be my Love and live with mee,
And thou shalt all the solace see,
That glassie gulfs or earth can bring
From *Vesta's* wealth, or *Neptuns* reigne.

"For we shall on the mountains go,
In shaddie umbers to and fro;
In vallies low, and on the bray,
And with thy feet the flowrs shall play."

The printer often does injustice to the author, who probably had no opportunity of correcting the errors of the press. The volume ends on sign. L iiii, with an English sonnet "to the Author," subscribed I. M., and two copies of Latin verses, *Cragio Suo*, and *De Alexandro Rupæo*, the first signed Robertus Aytonus, and the last Arthurus Gordonus.

Cries of London. — The Manner of Crying Things in London. 4to. 32 *leaves.*

This is a series of thirty-two copperplates, without date or engraver's name, and the above title is given to them in the handwriting of the second Earl of Bridgewater. They were perhaps by some foreign artist, and probably proof impressions; for on the margin of one of the plates is a small part of another, as if it had been taken off for a trial of the plate. It is impossible to assign a date to them with any exactness, but assistance may be derived from a black-letter ballad by W. Turner, called, —

> "The Common Cries of London Town,
> Some go up street and some go down."

Under the title of it is a woodcut of a man with a basket on his head. The only known copy is dated 1662, but it contains internal evidence, in the following stanza, that it was written in the reign of James I.

> "That's the fat foole of the Curtin,
> And the lean fool of the Bull:
> Since Shanke did leave to sing his rimes
> He is counted but a gull.
> The Players on the Banckeside,
> The round Globe and the Swan,
> Will teach you idle tricks of love,
> But the Bull will play the man."

Shanke, the comic actor here mentioned, was one of Prince Henry's players in 1603; and Taylor, the Water-poet, informs us that the Swan Theatre, mentioned above, had been abandoned by the players in 1613. The Curtain Theatre had also fallen into disuse before the reign of Charles I. The Globe and Bull were employed until after the Restoration. Several of Turner's "Cries of London Town" are so similar to those represented in the engravings before us, that we may conclude they were nearly contemporary. As this is, perhaps, the earliest known series of the kind, an enumeration of the "Cries," illustrating very curiously the manners of our ancestors, will not be unacceptable.

1. Lanthorne and a whole Candell light: hange out your lights heare! 2. I have fresh Cheese and Creame. — 3. Buy a Bresh, or a table Booke.

4. Fine Oranges, fine Lemons. — 5. Ells or yeards: by yeard or Ells. — 6. I have ripe strawburyes, ripe-straw-buryes. — 7. I have Screenes, if you desier; To keepe your Butey from ye fire. — 8. Codlinges hot, hot Codlinges. — 9. Buy a steele, or a Tinder Box. — 10. Quicke paravinkells, quicke, quick. — 11. Worke for a Cooper: worke for a Cooper. — 12. Bandestringes, or hankercher buttons. — 13. A Tanker bearer. — 14. Macarell new: Maca-rell. — 15. Buy a hone, or a whetstone, or a marking ston. — 16. White Unions, whitt St. Thomas Unions. — 17. Mate for a Bed, buy a Doore mate. — 18. Radishes or lettis, tow bunches a peny. 19. Have you any worke for a Tinker. — 20. Buy my Hartichokes, Mistris. — 21. Maribones, Maides, maribones. — 22. I ha' ripe Couccumber, ripe Couccumber. — 23. Chimney Sweepe. — 24. New flounders, new. 25. Some broken Breade and meate for ye poore prisoners: for the Lords sake pittey the poore. — 26. Buy my dish of great Smelts. — 27. Have you any Chaires to mend. — 28. Buy a Cocke, or a gelding. — 29. Old showes or bootes: will you buy some Broome. — 30. Mussels, Lilly white Mussels. — 31. Small Cole a penny a peake. — 32. What Kitchen-stuffe have you, Maides.

The figures, male and female, in the engravings are all three-quarter lengths, and they are furnished with the implements of their various trades, or with the articles in which they deal.

Other London Cries are mentioned by different authors, and a list of them, under the title of the "Cries of Rome," may be seen in Tho. Heywood's "Rape of Lucrece," 1608. The earliest notice of Cries, that we recollect, is in Laneham's "Letter from Kenilworth, 1575": "That is," says he, in his peculiar spelling, "a fresh cheaz and cream, and the common cry that theez milkwives make in London streetes yeerly betwyxt Easter and Whitsontide." In the old play of "The Three Lords and Three Ladies of London," 1590, it appears that woodmen went about with their beetles and wedges on their backs, crying "Have you any wood to cleave?" In "The Loyal Subject," by Beaumont and Fletcher, Act III. sc. 5, we find that in the reign of James I. potatoes had become so common, that "Potatoes — ripe Potatoes" were publicly hawked about the city. "The Cries of London" are enumerated in R. Brome's "Court Beggar," Act V.; and in Ben Jonson's Epigram, xcii., "the new cry" is spoken of. In a mock list of books, in what is called "The Instructive Library," printed for the Man in the Moon, 1710, we have the cries of "Knives to grind," "Old chairs to mend," "Pears to bake," "Milk a penny a quart," "Grey

Peas and Bacon," "Fresh Herrings," and "Shrewsbury Puddings."

Turner in his ballad, before mentioned, gives several "Cries" not included in the engravings, such as "The Waterman," "The Blacking Man," "The Pedlar," "Cherry ripe," "Buy a Mouse-trap," &c. The following are two more of his stanzas: —

"Ripe, Cherry ripe
  The Coster-monger cries;
Pippins fine, or pears.
  Another after hies
With basket on his head
  His living to advance,
And in his purse a pair of Dice
  For to play at Mumchance.

"Hot pippin pies
  To sell unto my friends;
Or pudding pies in pans,
  Well stuft with candles ends.
Will you buy any Milk,
  I heard a wench that cries:
With a pale of fresh Cheese and cream
  Another after hies."

In the British Museum is a series of "Cries of London," resembling those under consideration, but larger, and much coarser in the style of engraving. Tempest's "Cries of London" came out about 1680.

In 1628 Samuel Rowland (who, we apprehend, is not to be confounded with the popular comic poet, Samuel Rowlands) printed a pious production called "Heavens Glory, seeke it," &c., at the end of which he inserted, with a new title-page, "The Common Cryes and Sounds of the Bell-man," which only relate to what we now term "Bell-mans Verses": they are all of a serious and religious character, such as the following: —

"*For New-yeares Day.*

"All you that doe the Bell-man heare
The first day of this hopefull yeare,
I doe in love admonish you
To bid your old sins all adue,

And walke as Gods just law requires
In holy deeds and good desires;
Which if ye doe, youle doe your best:
God will in Christ forgive the rest."

There are many others, but of the same character, and they do not properly come under the designation of "Cries of London." The work was printed for Michael Sparke.

CROSSE, WILLIAM. — Belgiaes Trovbles and Trivmphs. Wherein are truly and Historically related all the most famous Occurrences, which haue happened betweene the Spaniards and Hollanders in these last foure yeares Warres of the Netherlands, with other Accidents, which haue had relation vnto them, as the Battels of Fleurie and Statloo, the losse of Gulicke and Breda, the Sieges of Sluce and Bergen, the Conquest of St. Saluador in Brasilia, and the taking of Goffe by Charles Lambert, &c. Written by William Crosse, master of Arts of St. Mary Hall in Oxford, and sometimes Chaplaine vnto Colonell Ogle in the Netherlands. — London, Printed by Augustine Mathewes, and John Norton, 1625. 4to. 39 *leaves.*

Of this poem we find no mention, and of its author we can give no account beyond what Wood says of him, who, however, knew nothing of the work before us. He took the degree of B. A. in 1610, and of M. A. in 1613: in 1612 he had contributed to the *Justa Oxoniensium*, and in 1613 to the verses of the University on the marriage of the Prince Palatine with the daughter of James I. Two years after the appearance of his "Belgia's Troubles" he produced a "Continuation of the History of the Netherlands" from the year 1608; and in 1629 he published a translation of Sallust.

"Belgia's Troubles" is a work of little talent, but of considerable pretension, divided into two books, the first dedicated to the

Earl of Essex and Lord Mountjoy, and the second to Lord Conway, Baron of Raggely, and to Sir Horatio Vere. Crosse admits, modestly enough, that he has written "rather a discourse than a poem," and professes to have treated events historically without the display of imagination. He begins by a personification of Bellona, who summons her Page Discord to inflame the hostile parties, but we afterwards hear no more of them, nor of any corresponding machinery. The performance looks the heavier because each book, of many hundred lines, forms a single paragraph. The whole opens thus grandiloquently: —

> "After the calmes of sweet-contenting Peace
> Well passed were, and that luxurious ease
> Had griped on those Armes, which fighting were
> Imbru'd with blood, with danger death and feare,
> Bellona, storming with a fatall rage,
> Out of th' Infernall Cells calls forth a Page
> Fell Discord hight, with whom she thus doth treat.
> Do not thy trembling vaines, deare Discord, sweat
> Whole stormes of wrath?" &c.

The author is often not very particular as to the exactness of his rhymes, but we seldom have met with so bad a set as the following: —

> "For those hote bloods which never could agree,
> Nor simpathize in congruous qualitie,
> Now mounted are, and ready for to make
> Upon their foes a second Flanders State;
> Their high-proofe Armour for their temper equall
> To Millans making, and to Siras mettall."

"The second booke" is as long, and as wearisome, as the first, and here and there the author repeats himself, as where he says, twice over, that a certain furious bombardment would have been sufficient to demolish the walls of "Ecbatane or Babylon." Perhaps the best couplet in the whole poem is to be found in the second book, where Crosse describes a field after a desperate battle:

> "The bullet-furrowd fielde with shot was sowen,
> And all the plaine with batterd corslets strowen."

He has also a curious and somewhat striking passage where he describes soldiers during the severity of the winter in Flanders frozen to death, some of them standing stark against trees, &c. It was the Spanish soldiers who patiently endured this extremity of cold, and the author generally, and generously, admits the valor and hardihood of the enemy, besides bearing testimony to his excellent martial discipline.

CROWCH, HUMFREY. — Loves Court of Conscience. Written upon two severall Occasions; with new Lessons for Lovers. Whereunto is annexed a kinde Husbands advice to his Wife. By Humfrey Crowch. — London, Printed for Richard Harper, and are to be sold at his shop in Smithfield, at the Hospitall Gate. 1637. 8vo. 16 *leaves.*

This is a pleasant unpretending production, by an author, we think, nowhere recorded in our poetical annals. The truth, however, is that he was a popular ballad-writer; and the work before us was merely a chap-book, price twopence, — a form frequently adopted when the subject was too long for the first and second part of a broadside. We know nothing of the history or occupation of Humfrey Crowch, but perhaps, like Martin Parker, whose contemporary he was, he lived wholly by his pen; or perhaps, like an earlier predecessor in ballad-writing, Thomas Deloney, the silk-weaver, he added to his means of subsistence, derived from his trade, by applying his rhyming propensity to any popular topic.

In this instance Crowch hit upon a very good title, and the interior of his small work does not contradict it either by dulness or insipidity. He opens with a supposed Court of Justice, where Reason, Grace, Truth, and Wit preside, and before whom a person, called Intelligence, produces the body of a young man who had destroyed himself for love. Wisdom seems to act as assessor to the Court, and Discretion, as *Amicus Curiæ*, enlarges and moralizes upon the subject of love and matrimony, giving five distinct "lessons," as they are termed, all tending to produce constancy in admirers, and affection in husbands and wives. Discretion introduces a ballad upon the amour of Dido and Æneas, which ends with the subsequent stanza: —

"Dido wept, but what of this?
  The Gods would have it so:
Æneas nothing did amisse,
  For he was forc't to go.
Learn, Lordlings, then no vows to keep
With false loves, but let them weep;
  Tis folly to be true.
Let this lesson serve your turn,
And let twenty Didoes mourn,
  So you get daily new."

The moral, such as it is, is hardly consistent with the professed purpose of the tract, but the ballad is followed by what is more consonant, and is headed "A kinde husbands advice to his Wife," in which, among many others, are the following lines: —

"Then, I am richer far then some that have
Gold in their purses, lands, and livings brave:
Yet I enjoy these blessings but in vain,
Because I love, and am not lov'd again.
O! would I did not love thee half so well,
I'de nere regard that firebrand of hell,
I mean your tongue, that doth afflict my heart;
For if a stranger should but act thy part
I would not care. I am of this belief
Where is great love, the greater is the grief,
If that he be repulst with evill speeches
By a curst dame that strives to weare the breeches.
Consider what I say, and be advis'd:
Silence in women kinde is highly pris'd."

There is not much attempt at poetry in the tract beyond the rhyme, but the lines run easily, and were intended to be of a familiar cast. A single copy of the chap-book is all we ever saw, or expect to see.

Daniel, Samuel. — The Worthy tract of Paulus Iouius, contayning a Discourse of rare inuentions, both Militarie and Amorous called Imprese. Whereunto is added a

Preface contayning the Arte of composing them, with many other notable deuises. By Samuell Daniell late Student in Oxenforde. — At London, Printed for Simon Waterson. 1585. 4to.

This is chiefly remarkable as being Daniel's earliest known work: he was at this date in his twenty-third year.[1] It is entirely prose, excepting one stanza from Ariosto, which is thus translated, but not in the form of the original: it refers to the dress and device of Bradamante: —

> "Her upper robe of such like colour was,
> As is the fading leaf of palish hew,
> When from the bowe the lively sap doth passe,
> Which nourish did the stock whereon it grew,
> Embrodered al with braunches thick aboue,
> And fading bowes of dolefull Cipresse tree;
> Which cut with deadly axe doth neuer proue.
> This habit with her griefe did well agree."

It certainly does not promise much, and the passage of the original —

> "*che mai non si rinfranca,*
> *Poi ch' ha sentito la dura bipenne*" —

is so badly rendered as hardly to convey the meaning of the poet.

Besides the translation from Paulus Jovius, there is a good deal of original matter, contributed chiefly by Daniel. The dedication

[1] Samuel Daniel was a Somersetshire man, as we learn from Lane's "Triton's Trumpet," a MS. dated in 1620; and it is stated that his father was a music-master at Taunton. A little earlier there was a John Daniel who was an author, and may have been related: he wrote, and dated "From my house in Saint Brides churchyard, the 13 of January, 1576," the following work, — "Jehovah. A free Pardon, with many Graces therein conteyned, graunted to all Christians by our most Holy and reverent Father, God Almightie, the principal high Priest and Bishoppe in Heaven and Earth &c. by John Danyel of Clements Inn. Printed at London by Thomas East for Andrew Maunsell," &c. It is a translation rom the Spanish. Samuel Daniel had a brother John, whom, in Sept. 1619, he left sole executor of his will: see that will in the Shaksp. Soc. Papers, iv. 156.

is to "Sir Edward Dimmock, Champion to her Maiestie," followed by an epistle of twelve pages, "To his good friend Samuel Daniel," subscribed N. W., to encourage him to print what he had thus rendered into English. Near the commencement he speaks of three works, one existing, one lost, and the third mentioned nowhere else, viz., Nicholas Breton's "Flourish upon Fancy," printed in 1577; Richard Tarlton's "Toys," entered for the press on 10th December of the same year, and no doubt published, though now extinct; and an "Interlude of Diogenes," of which we never hear elsewhere.

This notice of the three early productions is new, and a copy of Daniel's translation is extremely rare. The letter of N. W. goes learnedly, and somewhat pedantically, over the whole subject of the antiquity of Impreses and Emblems, and it is followed by an Epistle of 15 pages from Daniel, on devices in various parts of Europe, "to the friendly Reader." "The Discourses of Paulus Jovius" follow, and the work ends with 13 pages regarding "certaine notable devises, both militarie and amorous, collected by Samuell Daniell." They contain nothing worth extracting.

DANIEL, SAMUEL. — Delia. Contayning certayne Sonnets: with the complaint of Rosamond. *Aetas prima canat veneres postrema tumultus.* — At London, Printed by I. C. for Simon Waterson, dwelling in Paules Church-yard at the signe of the Crowne. 1592. 4to. 50 *leaves.*

This is the earliest edition of Daniel's "Delia," but it may be doubted, for reasons hereafter assigned, whether it is the first impression of "The complaint of Rosamond." At the back of the title-page (which is in an arabesque compartment) is a brief address "To the Reader," requesting him to correct in the Sonnets six errors of the press, which are pointed out. In the other impression of 1592 (the title-page of which is in an architectural compartment) these "faultes escaped in the printing" are rectified. The title-page of that second edition runs thus: —

"Delia. Containing certaine Sonnets: with the complaynt of Rosamond. *Ætas prima canat veneres postrema tumultus.* 1592. At London, Printed by J. C. for S. Watersonne." 4to.

We have been thus particular, because the two impressions of the work in 1592 differ very materially: for instance, the second of 1592 contains 54 sonnets, being four more than are in the first; and in the Bodleian Library there is a copy of an edition with the date of 1592, and with the "Rosamond," as usual, appended, in which (besides the correction of several errors, and minor changes) no fewer than 23 stanzas of the "Rosamond" are omitted. The pagination is also different, and it seems clearly a distinct impression, which makes three in the same year, showing the great popularity of the work. The corrections prove that this edition at Oxford must have been subsequent to the others; and if so, why were the 23 stanzas of the "Rosamond" omitted, when they are found in the two other 4tos of 1592, and in the 12mo editions of 1594 and 1595?

Our notion is, that none of the earliest editions of "Rosamond" were printed at the same time as the "Delia": the type is much coarser and thicker, and having first gone through the press, we apprehend that it was subsequently added to the sonnets inscribed to Delia. We are, however, aware of no extant separate edition of the "Rosamond," and that which follows the "Delia," in the Bodleian Library, must have been Daniel's original draught, before he added the twenty-three stanzas inserted in all the other copies, and forming an important part of the poem, although the sense is complete without them. As a specimen of the variations contained in the copy at Oxford, we may give the last line of a stanza not far from the end of the "Rosamond," which in the two other impressions of 1592 runs thus: —

"That overwhelms vs or confounds vs quite."

In the Oxford copy, of 1592, it stands, —

"Tongue, pen nor arte can neuer shew a right."

That copy has also a manifest improvement in the very last stanza, which absurdly begins, in the other copies of the same year, —

"So vanquisht she, and left me to returne;"

instead of —

> "So *vansht* she and left me to returne."

It is remarkable that the blunder is repeated in the 12mo edition of 1594, while it is corrected in the 12mo edition of 1595. There is much that seems inexplicable in the early impressions of Daniel's poems, partly owing, perhaps, to the fastidiousness of the author, and to the changes he from time to time introduced.

No other perfect copy of the first edition of "Delia" (which also promises "The complaint of Rosamond" on the title-page) is known but that now before us. It has been already observed, that, besides the correction of the errors of the press, the second edition, with the date of 1592, comprises four sonnets not in the first edition, and they are numbered respectively xxvii, xxviii, xxix (by mistake printed xxxi), and xxx: the other fifty sonnets are all in the first edition. The types are the same for both, but there are differences in the spelling: and, besides the mistakes pointed out in the *errata*, some valuable corrections are made in the second edition: in the first edition, for instance, in Sonnet x, Venus is called "Laughter-louing *Gods*," instead of *Goddesse*, which was afterwards substituted. Here and there emendations were adopted for the improvement of the metre, as in Sonnet xxxv, where the first edition defectively reads, —

> "And I, though borne in a colder clime,"

which the second edition alters to —

> "And I, though borne *within* a colder clime."

Again, in Sonnet xliiii, the first edition has —

> "Deckt with her youth, whereon the world smyleth;"

but the second restores the measure of the verse thus: —

> "Deckt with her youth, whereon the world *now* smyleth."

It is very certain that some of Daniel's Sonnets had appeared in 1591, at the end of the surreptitious impression of Sir P. Sidney's "Astrophel and Stella," edited by Thomas Nash. (See p. 42.) In fact, this forms Daniel's excuse for printing his "Delia." In the dedication to the Countess of Pembroke, Daniel tells her, — "Seeing I was betraide by the indiscretion of a greedy printer, and had some of my secrets bewraide to the world uncorrected, doubting the like of the rest, I am forced to publish that which I never ment;" and he adds that the same wrong had been done to Sidney, whom he designates as Astrophel. The "greedy printer" was Thomas Newman, who, not long before, had published the first and unauthorized impression of Sidney's poems.

Who Delia might be we have no information, but in the 48th Sonnet of the collection named after her, we are told that she lived on Shakspeare's river: —

"But Avon, rich in fame, though poor in waters,
Shall have my song, where Delia hath her seate:
Avon shall be my Thames, and she my Song;
Ile sound her name the Ryver all along."

The fact, first stated in the edition 12mo 1595, that the 44th Sonnet "was made at the Author's being in Italie," explains how it happened that he there speaks of Delia as residing in the North —

"My joyfull North, where all my fortune lyes."

However, in the very same series of Sonnets, Daniel avows his affection for another lady, whom he calls Cynthia, and who appears to have been very cruel; for, in Sonnet 40, he says of her, —

"Yet nought the rocke of that hard hart can move,
Where beate these tears which zeale and fury driveth;
And yet I rather languish in her love,
Then I would joy the fayrest she that liveth."

In the original, "which" is misprinted *with* in the second line, and the obvious error is not corrected in the later copy of 1592. From an author like Daniel it cannot be necessary to quote specimens, but we may point out a clear allusion to Spenser, and to his "Fairy Queen," which has been noticed in the "Life of Spenser," 8vo, 1862, p. ci: it is at the opening of Sonnet 46. The first three books of Spenser's work, in which, as Daniel says, were many "aged accents and untimely words," had been printed, as everybody is aware, in 1590.

It should be mentioned that in every edition, between the portion Daniel calls "Delia" and "The Complaint of Rosamond," is inserted "an ode," which was so popular as to be set to music in John Farmer's "First set of English Madrigals," 1599.

DANIEL, SAMUEL. — The First Fowre Bookes of the civile wars between the two houses of Lancaster and Yorke. By Samuel Daniel. *Ætas prima canat veneres postrema tumultus.* At London, Printed by P. Short for Simon Waterson. — 1595. 4to. 89 *leaves.*

This is the first edition of Daniel's "Civil Wars": a fifth book was added in 1599, but it is sometimes appended to the first four books in 1595. As far as regards the first four books, the edition of 1599 precisely agrees with that of 1595, having been printed from the very same types, and without even the correction of the errors of the press.

None of Daniel's biographers notice the fact that he had travelled in Italy, no doubt early in life, and perhaps in the capacity of tutor to the son of the Countess of Pembroke. That he had visited that country we have upon his own evidence. In the same year that he published the work before us, he reprinted his "Delia," "Rosamond," and a tragedy called "Cleopatra," in 12mo; and one of the sonnets in his "Delia" is there headed, "At the Author's going into Italie;" and another, as before shown, is thus introduced, "This Sonnet was made at the Author's being in Italie."

"The first four Books of the Civil Wars" were ushered into the world in 1595, without any dedication or prefatory matter. The probability is, that the copies did not then sell, as they were preceded by a new title-page, and followed by another book of the same poem in 1599.

DANIEL, SAMUEL. — The Civile Wares betweene the Howses of Lancaster and Yorke, corrected and continued by Samuel Daniel, one of the Groomes of hir Majesties most honorable Privie Chamber &c. — Printed at London by Simon Watersonne. 1609. 4to. 120 *leaves.*

The above is an engraved title-page by F. Cockson, containing a portrait of Daniel in the centre, followed by the dedication to the Countess Dowager of Pembroke, in which the author refers to the many impressions through which this work had passed, without the addition of two books (the third book being enlarged and divided) which are here for the first time printed, making eight books in the whole. It brings down the history to the marriage of Edward IV.; but Daniel, as he informs Lady Pembroke, meant to continue it "to the glorious union of Henry VII." This part of his task he never completed, but (as he proposed in the end of the dedication) commenced a history of England in prose.

The alterations in this edition of the "Civil Wars," even of those parts of the work professed to be republished, are very considerable; and Daniel omitted at the end of the second book an elaborate eulogium of the unfortunate Earl of Essex, which originally appeared in 1595, including the following stanza:

"Thence might thy valor have brought in despight
Eternall tropheis to Elizas name,
And laid downe at her sacred feete the right
Of all thy deedes, and glory of the same.
And that which by her powre, and by thy might,
Thou hadst attaind to her immortall fame,
Had made thee wondred here, admir'd a farre,
The Mercury of peace, the Mars of warre."

There seems to have been no political reason for excluding this, and other stanzas in the same spirit, after James I. came to the throne, but they were never reprinted.

DANIEL, SAMUEL. — The Works of Samuel Daniel. Newly augmented. *Ætas prima canat veneres, postrema tumultus.* — London Printed for Simon Waterson. 1601. folio. 193 *leaves.*

This is an unknown edition of Daniel's productions, but it agrees in all essential particulars with the common impression dated 1602. The poet seems to have printed his Works in 1601, upon large paper, as gifts to his patrons, and the present copy was accompanied by a private letter to Lord Ellesmere, then Sir Thomas Egerton, Keeper of the Great Seal.

After the title-page comes an address "To her sacred Majestie," in four octave stanzas: then "The Civil Wars," in six books, followed by "Musophilus." The folios, which are numbered, end with "The Civil Wars," and fresh signatures commence with "Musophilus." This portion is succeeded by "a Letter from Octavia to Marcus Antonius," and by "the Tragedie of Cleopatra." "The Complaint of Rosamond" precedes "Delia," consisting here of fifty-seven sonnets, to which are added "an Ode" and "a Pastoral," concluding the volume.

Daniel, Samuel. — A Panegyrike Congratulatory delivered to the Kings most excellent majesty at Burleigh Harrington in Rutlandshire. By Samuel Daniel. Also certaine Epistles. With a Defence of Ryme heeretofore written, and now published by the Author. *Carmen amat, quisquis carmine digna gerit.* — At London Printed by V. S. for Edward Blount. n. d. folio. 40 *leaves.*

Although there is no date on the general title-page of this volume, the title-page to the second portion of it, "Certaine Epistles after the manner of Horace, written to divers noble Personages," bears the date of 1603. There is a third title-page to the "Defence of Ryme against a pamphlet entituled Observations on the Art of English Poesie," without date, and this last portion of the work is sometimes, though rarely, found appended to the folio edition of Daniel's Works, 1602. The first and third title-pages are within ornamental compartments, with the royal arms at the top, and Queen Elizabeth's favorite motto, *Semper eadem*, below them.

Only two or three complete copies of this edition of Daniel's "Panegyric Congratulatory" and "Epistles" are yet known, and it was most likely printed for presents. We have that copy before us which he gave to Lady Pembroke, as is testified by her autograph. He also probably gave them to the "noble personages" whom he addresses in the "Epistles," viz., Sir Thomas Egerton; Lord Henry Howard; the Countess of Cumberland; the Countess of Bedford; Lady Anne Clifford; the Earl of Southampton; and the Earl of Hertford. The volume has an introductory dedication to the latter, which was not afterwards reprinted. This folio probably came from the press before James I. reached London, and the "Panegyric Congratulatory" was delivered to him in Rutlandshire.

Daniel very seldom reprinted a poem without making alterations, more or less important, in it. The 40th stanza of the "Panegyric," in the folio before us, reads as follows: —

> "We shall continue one, and be the same
> In Law, in Justice, Magistrate, and forme:
> Thou wilt not touch the fundamentall frame
> Of this Estate thy Ancestors did forme;
> But with a reverence of their glorious fame
> Seeke onely the corruptions to reforme:
> Knowing that course is best to be observ'de
> Whereby a State hath longest beene preserv'd."

In the 8vo edition, which must have come out just afterwards, it runs thus: —

> "We shall continue and remaine all one,
> In Law, in Justice, and in Magestrate:
> Thou wilt not alter the foundation
> Thy Ancestors have laide of this Estate,
> Nor greeve thy Land with innovation,
> Nor take from us more then thou will collate;
> Knowing that course is best to be observ'de
> Whereby a State hath longest been preserv'd."

It may be matter of speculation whether the author was induced to alter the stanza on account of any objection by persons in authority to the tone and spirit of its anticipations, or, because he himself disliked, as a matter of taste, that three lines should end with the syllable "forme." Spenser, Drayton, and many other contemporaries of Daniel, thought rhymes having precisely the same sound admissible.

The title-page in which Daniel claims that his Epistles are "after the manner of Horace" was omitted in the reimpression of 1603, in 8vo.

The "Observations in the Art of English Poesie," against which Daniel wrote his "Defence of Ryme," was the work of Dr. Thomas Campion, a physician, poet, and musical composer, and it was published with the date of 1602. We learn from an address preceding Daniel's "Defence," that he had written it in the form of a private letter to a learned friend about a year before, but of course subsequent to the date when he had first seen Dr. Campion's "Observations." When Daniel printed it, it was addressed "to William Herbert, Earl of Pembroke," who had been his pupil: of him Daniel says that he "in blood and nature is interested" to take part against Campion, who was the advocate of blank verse.

DANIEL, SAMUEL. — A Panegyrike Congratulatorie deliuered to the Kings most excellent Majestie at Burleigh Harrington in Rutlandshire. By Samuel Daniel. Also certaine Epistles with a Defence of Ryme &c. — At London Imprinted for Edward Blount. 1603. 8vo. 63 *leaves.*

This is substantially the same work as the folio which came out before it, but, as has been already pointed out, there are variations besides such as are merely typographical. The "Defence of Rhime" has a separate title-page, and occupies the last twenty-eight leaves.

DANIEL, SAMUEL. — Certaine small Poems lately printed: with the Tragedie of Philotas. Written by Samuel Daniel, &c. — At London Printed by G. Eld for Simon Waterson. 1605. 8vo. 110 *leaves.*

This volume consists of pieces formerly printed by Daniel, and of the tragedy of Philotas, which appeared here for the first time, with a dedication to Prince Henry, containing these lines, which are personally interesting: —

"And therefore, since I have outliv'd the date
Of former grace, acceptance, and delight,
I would my lines, late-borne beyond the fate
Of her spent line, had never come to light.
So had I not been taxd for wishing well,
Nor now mistaken by the censuring stage,

Nor in my fame nor reputation fell;
Which I esteeme more then what all the age,
Or th' earth can give. But years hath done this wrong,
To make me write too much, and live too long."

It seems that the story of Philotas received an application to some of the incidents of the life of the unfortunate Earl of Essex, and when the tragedy was reprinted it was accompanied by an "Apology," in which Daniel says: "And for any resemblance that, through the ignorance of the history, may be applied to the Earl of Essex, it can hold no proportion, but only in his weaknesses, which I would all that love his memory not to revive."

DANIEL, SAMUEL. — The First Part of the Historie of England. By Samuel Danyel. — London, Printed by Nicholas Okes dwelling neere Holborne bridge. 1612. 4to. 117 *leaves.*

This seems to have been a private impression of the earlier portion of Daniel's History of England, ending with the reign of Stephen. He intended to distribute some copies as presents, and that before us was doubtless given by him to Lord Ellesmere. At the end is a note, which shows that the work was not printed for sale in 1612.

Daniel had promised to write the History of England from the Conquest, in the dedication of his complete edition of the "Civil Wars" to the Countess of Pembroke; but he brought it no lower than the reign of Edward III., and printed it in folio as a private speculation about 1618. He died in October of the following year. The edition before us is dedicated to Viscount Rochester, and the first and third books (for it has three divisions) mention him in the opening paragraphs. After the disgrace of that nobleman, all allusion to him was omitted.

DANIEL, SAMUEL. — The Collection of the Historie of England. By S. D. — London, Printed by Nicholas

Okes dwelling in Foster-lane for the Author. *Cum Privilegio.* n. d. fol. 115 *leaves.*

Daniel's privilege to print this work and an " Appendix" (which never appeared) for his own benefit, is opposite the title-page on a separate leaf, and dated " 11 March, 15 James I." It never was regularly published, and the author opens his preface in these terms: — " This Peece of our History, which here I divulge not, but impart privately to such worthy persons as have favoured my endeavours," &c. One of these was the first Earl of Bridgewater, who no doubt followed up the patronage which his father, Lord Ellesmere, had extended to Daniel, and therefore took a large paper copy of this work. It has no date, but it must have appeared prior to the author's death in October, 1619, and subsequent to the date of the royal privilege. The author complains that ill-health had delayed his undertaking. It brings our history down to the end of Edward III.; and subjoined is a brief notice, concluding with these words: " And here I leave, unlesse by this which is done I finde incouragement to goe on." The work, in 1634, was continued to the reign of Henry VII. by John Trussell.

We may add that Daniel's will bears date on the 4th Sept. 1619. (See Shaksp. Soc. Papers, iv. 156.) In it he makes bequests only to persons of the name of Bowre, and to his brother John Daniel.

Darcie, Abraham. — Frances Duchesse Dowager of Richmond and Lenox &c. her Funerall Teares. Or Larmes Funebres de l'illustre Princesse Francoise Duchesse Dowagere de Richmond et de Lenox &c. pour la Mort et Perte de son cher Espoux, &c. Louis de Obegny Duc de Richmond et de Lenox &c. Qui deceda le 16 Februrier 1624 en la maison Royale de Whit-hall. &c. n. d. 8vo. 58 *leaves.*

No bookseller's name is to be found in any part of the volume, which was most likely printed by the author, Abraham Darcie, for, not always disinterested, presents. A copy was given to the

Earl of Bridgewater, and at the end of it is placed a large folded leaf, containing a poem on the deaths of his Lordship's two infant sons, James and Charles, to whom King James and Prince Charles had been godfathers: the one expired on the 30th of December, 1620, and the other on the 18th of April, 1623. The dates are filled up in MS. by the author, who in the introduction to his verses professed "to immortalize the noble memory" of the young persons he celebrated. The lines are in English and French, and they are placed in two columns, opposite each other. The English begins as follows: —

"Faire beames of short continuance, yet most bright,
If your wisht luster, and desired light
Hath had too sudden and untimely end,
Such destiny doth on faire things attend:
A morning is the Roses chiefest prime,
And flower-de-luces dye in blooming time."

These are the best out of the thirty-six lines of which the poem consists; and the corresponding French verses are these: —

"Beaux Rayons, plus clairs que durables,
Si vos lumieres desirables
On eut leur fin en commençant,
C'est le Destin des belles choses:
Un matin est l'aage des Roses,
Et les Lis meurent en naissant."

Darcie seems to have written with about as much facility in French as in English. The first five-and-twenty pages of his elegiac production on the death of the Duke of Richmond are in both languages, and the rest in English only, including twenty-four pages of prose at the end, entitled, "The World's Contempt," by which he means contempt for the world. In the first part of the tract is inserted a long and very particular account of the funeral of the Duke of Richmond, on which occasion the Earl of Bridgewater was one of the mourners. As a specimen of Darcie's versification, the subsequent lines are taken from that part of his work which has the running title of "Funeral Consolations": —

"God's Writt and Reason doth command to weepe,
And shed salt teares upon their Tombs which sleepe:

To be remorselesse in the death of friends
To natures inconveniency tends,
To savage temper too too neere affinity,
The eversion of the ground of piety,
Which is in others miseries to beare
Part of their sorrows, and a mutual share;
But as some griefe the Law of God's commanding,
So too much sorrow's want of understanding.
No sorrow is a sign of brutish state,
But yet too much proves one effeminate.
That mans account is to most goodnesse come,
Of which the golden mean's the totall summe."

It is to be hoped that the Duchess of Richmond had some better grounds of consolation than are afforded by such lines as these. Darcie's "Annales" of the reign of Elizabeth, translated from the French, because, as Fuller says, Darcie did not understand Camden's Latin, came out in 1625, 4to.

DAVIE, SAMPSON. — The ende and confession of Tho. Norton of Yorkshire, the popishe rebell, and Chr. Norton his nephew; which suffered at Tiburn for treason the 27 of May. — Printed by W. Howe. 1570. 8vo. 8 *leaves.*

The Nortons were "hanged, headed and quartered" two days after Felton had placed the Pope's Bull on the gate of the Bishop of London, so that the anti-papistical feeling was perhaps never stronger than at that moment. We may conclude that Sampson Davie's poems on the occasion, dated 1570, were published as soon as possible after the event they celebrate. They are of the utmost rarity.

The first poem, occupying two pages, is addressed "Unto the Christian Reader," and the second, filling about the same space, is thus headed, "The Confession and ende of Thomas Norton." The third is longer than those which precede it, and is entitled, "The ende and Confession of Christopher Norton." The fourth is called, "An exhortation to all true subjects, and a warning to the Papists." The last poem is headed, "To the Papists," and is not in the same ballad-metre as the other productions: we quote it entire: —

"You Popish route,
Looke well aboute
And warning hereby take,
Unless you swinge
In Tyburne stringe
As some did but of late.

"Your selves submit,
As it is fit,
Unto the Lorde above:
Then, as I deeme,
Our noble Queene
Ye cannot choose but love.

"Which doth maintaine,
I tell you plaine,
Gods word which is so pure:
Why do you, then,
Resist againe,
And treason so procure?

"I do not faine,
But tell you plaine,
If you do not amend,
Such plagues may fall
As will you gall;
And thus I make an end.
Finis qd Sampson Davie."

This was entered at Stationers' Hall by William Pickering just after the event, which gave rise to several other popular effusions: one of these, a broadside, was licensed to Henry Kirkham, and it had for title, "A description of Nortons in Yorkeshyre:" it has come down to us with the name of William Gibson at the end of it, and was printed by Alexander Lacy. Richard Jones also published, and William Howe printed, "The severall Confessions of Thomas Norton and Christopher Norton, two of the northern Rebels, who suffered at Tyburn and were drawn, hanged and quartered for Treason, May 27." Of this also we have seen a copy.

Davies, John. — Mirum in Modum. A Glimpse of Gods Glorie and the Soules Shape. &c. — London Printed for William Aspley. 1602. 4to. 42 *leaves.*

This seems to be the first printed work of its voluminous author;[1] but that he had written earlier we have evidence in his "Wittes Pilgrimage," 4to, n. d., which contains (sign. V i.) "A Dump upon the death of the most noble Henrie late Earle of Pembrooke," who died in 1601. "Wittes Pilgrimage" is a collection of many scattered pieces, which Davies had composed between the years 1600 and 1618, but which possess little merit or originality, and remained unpublished till shortly before the author's death: some account of them, and of various others, may be seen in Brit. Bibl. II. 247, where they receive more attention than they deserve. His *Mirum in Modum* is a very dull and unintelligible discourse, in various stanzas, upon the soul, its faculties, &c., and the author very appropriately placed these two lines by way of motto on his title-page: —

"Eyes must be bright, or else no eyes at all
Can see this sight much more then mysticall."

It is dedicated to the Earl of Pembroke, Sir Robert Sidney, and Edward Herbert, Esq., in a sonnet wherein the author devotes his understanding, will, and memory to them; and in the last couplet he parts between the three, his soul, his book, and his "broken heart." It does not however appear that he had met with any particular affliction at this period. He arbitrarily divides his subject; and the following stanza, which, from its reference to the literature of the time, is worth quoting, concludes his first division: —

"Halla! my Muse: heere rest a breathing while,
Sith thou art now arriv'd at Reasons seate;
To whom, as to thy Sov'raigne, reconcile
Thy straying thoughts, and humbly hir intreate
With her just measure all thy lines to meate;

[1] We ought to have said "first *separately* printed work," because in Vol. III. article William Parry, is given Davies's earliest printed work, namely, a Sonnet to W. Parry on his narrative of the Travels of the Sherleys.

Lest that, like many *Rimers* of our time,
Thou blotst much paper without meane or measure,
In verse whose reason runneth al to rime:
Yet of the Lawrell wreathe they make a seazure,
And doth Minerva so a shrewde displeasure."

DAVIES, JOHN. — Bien Venu. Greate Britaines Welcome to hir greate Friendes and deere Brethren, the Danes &c. — Imprinted at London for Nathaniel Butter &c. 1606. 4to. 12 *leaves.*

This rare temporary production is dedicated by John Davies of Hereford, in a sonnet, to Philip Herbert, Earl of Montgomery, and to Sir James Hayes, Knight. It was written to celebrate the arrival in London of the King of Denmark and his suite, and is entirely in the octave stanza. Of himself Davies querulously says: —

"But ah, (alas!) my short-wing'd Muse doth hant
None but the obscure corners of the earth,
Where she with naught but care is conversant,
Which makes her curse her case, and ban her birth!
Where she (except she would turne ignorant)
Must live, 'till die she must, in mournfull mirth;
Which is the cherishing the World doth give
To those that muse to die, not muse to live."

Davies seems to have entertained the notion that to rhyme was the chief art of poetry, although, above, he charges others with letting their "reason run all to rhime": of no man could it be more truly said than of himself, that he blotted "much paper without meane or measure." His thoughts are oftener far-fetched than new or appropriate; and he was overweening in his self-estimate.

DAVIES, JOHN. — הַדָּת÷ Summa Totalis or All in All, and the same for ever: Or an Addition to Mirum in Modum. By the first Author John Davies.

Those lines which all or none perceive aright
Have neither Judgment, Art, Wit, Life or Spright.

London Printed by William Jaggard dwelling in Barbican. 1607. 4to. 42 *leaves.*

This author's *Mirum in Modum*, to which the present work is an "Addition," appeared, as we have seen, in 1602. They are both of the same ethical and religious character: the most commonplace topics are handled with a tedious and important air of mystery, which the author seems to have mistaken for profound metaphysical reasoning. This production is dedicated to Lord and Lady Ellesmere in the following sonnet:—

"To the right Honourable mine approved good Lord and Master, Thomas Lord Elsmere, Lord Chancellor of England: and to his right noble Lady and Wife, Alice, Countesse of Derby, my good Lady and Mistresse, be all felicitie, consisting in the sight of the Objective Beatitude."

"The time, my duty, and your deere desert
(Deservedly Right Noble) do conspire
To make me consecrate (besides my Heart)
This IMAGE to you, forg'd with heavenly fire!
The backe-parts of his FORME, who formed this ALL,
(Characterd by the hand of loving Feare)
Are shaddow'd here: but (ah) they are too small
To shew their *greatnesse*, which ne'er compast were!
But though that *Greatnesse* be past *quantity*,
And *Goodnes* doth all *quality* exceed,
Yet I this Forme of formelesse DEITY
Drewe by the *Squire* and Compasse of our CREED.
Then (with your greater GUIFTS) accept this small;
Yet (being right) it's more then ALL in ALL!

Your Honors in all duety most bounden,
John Davies of Hereford."

"Squire," in the 12th line, is what we now call *square*, not a parallelogram, but a measure. Some old authors spell it "squire," and others *square*.

Davies was a writing-master by occupation, and in the Epitaph upon himself, in his "Wit's Bedlam," 1617, he tells us that he "loved fair writing," and had "taught it others": he resided in Oxford for this purpose, but was not (as Wood erroneously supposed, *Anth. Oxon.* II. 264, edit. Bliss) a member of that University. He has corrected the copy we use (which no doubt was presented by him to Lord Ellesmere) very neatly in several places, and has added some MS. marginal notes. It is singular that, when correcting it, he did not perceive that sheet G was a duplicate.

DAVIES, JOHN. — The Holy Roode, or Christs Crosse: Containing Christ Crucified, described in Speaking-picture. By John Davies.

> And who in passion sweetely sing the same
> Doe glorifie their owne in Jesus Name.

Crux Christi clavis Cœli. — London Printed for N. Butter. 1609. 4to. 40 *leaves.*

The date is not on the title-page, (which is in an arabesque compartment, with figures of Minerva and Diana on either side,) but at the end. The dedication is "to the Right Honourable, well accomplished Lady, Alice, Countesse of Derby, my good Lady and Mistresse: And to her three right Noble Daughters by Birth, Nature and Education, the Lady Elizabeth, Countess of Huntingdon, The Lady Francis Egerton, and the Lady Anne, Wife to the truely Noble Lord Gray, Lord Chandois that now is." On the fly-leaf is the following letter, not addressed to, but obviously intended for, Lord Ellesmere. It is in the handwriting of Davies, and it is a beautiful and elaborate specimen of his penmanship: —

"Amonge many worldly Crosses, no worldlie Comfort do I enjoy more comfortable then your Honours effectuall favour, beeing the onely helpfull Stay (under God) my poore tempest beaten fortunes ever found to repose them. Ah! my good Lord, your Honour hath wounded my Heart with the deepest dutifull affection, in that undesired (o, forcible favoure) you had that Care of me, as finding mee in the Subsedie-booke at x[li] Land, having not so much (god helpe mee) of mine owne in possession nor reversion as will bury mee, to ease me thereof with your owne honorable upright hand: for which and for all other your Honours not onely gracefull but helpfull favour towards myne unworthie self (my Venison often tymes receaved, but never by word remembred) not forgotten, I returne your Lo. a Crosse for your Comfort, and withall the Almes of a Beggar.

God blesse, and reward you.

ever remayning

Yor Honors most bounden

Vassall,

Jo: Dauies."

At this date Lord Ellesmere had been married nine years to the Countess of Derby, to whom (with her daughters, one of whom had married the son of Lord Ellesmere) the printed dedication is addressed: it is in alternate rhyme, but of no merit, and the whole poem is serious and tedious. It is preceded by commendatory verses by Sir Edw. Herbert, Michael Drayton, and N. Deeble: Drayton's sonnet may be quoted, on account of the celebrity of its author, and the peculiarity of its construction, the whole running upon only two rhymes:

"Such men as hold intelligence with Letters,
And in that nice and narrow way of Verse,
As oft they lend, so oft they must be Debters,
If with the Muses they will have commerce.
Seldome at Stawles me this way men rehearse
To mine Inferiours, nor unto my Betters:
He stales his lines that so doeth them disperce.
I am so free, I love not golden fetters;
And many lines 'fore Writers be but setters
To them which cheate with Papers; which doth pierse
Our credits, when we shew our selves Abetters
To those that wrong our knowledge: we rehearse
Often (my good John, and I love) thy Letters,
Which lend me credit, as I lend my verse.
Michael Drayton."

No other instance of such a poetical caprice seems to be known, and Drayton must have meant to commend Davies's subject, rather than the treatment of it. The poem itself is in two hundred and four six-line stanzas: at the end are eight pious sonnets of no greater merit than the rest of the volume. Davies's best work is unquestionably his "Scourge of Folly," consisting mainly of epigrams and satires, which is praised by H. Parrot in his *Laquei Ridiculosi*, 1613.

Davies, John. — A Scourge for Paper-Persecutors, or
Papers Complaint, compil'd in ruthfull Rimes,
Against the Paper-spoylers of these Times
By J. D. With
A continu'd just Inquisition
Of the same subject, fit for the season.
Against Paper-Persecutors. By A. H. — Printed at London for H. H. and G. G. &c. 1625. 4to. 17 *leaves.*

The first portion of this tract was originally printed about 1610, in "The Scourge of Folly," "by John Davies, of Hereford;" and on the title-page of the tract before us the plate used for "The Scourge of Folly," representing Folly on the back of Time scourged by Wit, is repeated. It attacks many of the most popular authors as Paper-persecutors, including Churchyard, (who had been dead some years,) Sir John Harington, and apparently Shakspeare in the following lines. Paper, personified, speaks:

"Another (ah! Lord helpe mee) vilifies
With Art of Love, and how to subtilize;
Making lewd *Venus*, with eternall lines,
To tye *Adonis* to her loves designes.
Fine wit is shew'n therein; but finer 't were,
If not attir'd in such bawdy Geare.
But be it as it will, the coyest Dames
In private reade it for their Closset-games."

In Cranley's "Amanda," 1635, 4to, Shakspeare's "Venus and Adonis" is spoken of as forming part of the library of a lady of pleasure.[1] Thomas Nash and Harvey are severely handled by Davies, especially the former, as the author of an indecent work still existing in MS. Robert Greene, Samuel Rowlands, Thomas Dekker, and others not so distinctly pointed out, come in for their share; after which the author gives a blow to old Stow and the Chroniclers, and, having made a passing stroke at the dedicators of trash to the nobility, (entirely forgetting how responsible he was himself on the very same score,) he concludes with some solemn reflections.

[1] Cranley's lines may be seen in Shaksp. pub. by Whittaker, 1858, Vol. VI. p. 481.

The name of the Continuator, A. H., is not known. Anthony Wood conjectures it to have been Abraham Hartwell; but he was mistaken (*Ath. Oxon.* II., 504, edit. Bliss) in assigning the earlier portion of this volume to Dr. Donne. A. H. goes over much the same ground as Davies, bringing the list of authors down to the year 1625. He excepts Ben Jonson and Michael Drayton from his censure, but does not spare John Taylor the Water-poet, nor the ballad-makers of the time, especially pointing out such as (like Darcie, p. 220) had written elegies on the deaths of the Duke and Duchess of Richmond. Several of these are preserved in the library of the Society of Antiquaries, and have little or no merit.

DAVISON, FRANCIS. — A Poetical Rapsodie, Containing: Diverse Sonnets, Odes, Elegies, Madrigals, Epigrams, Pastorals, Eglogues, with other poems, both in rime and measured verse. For varietie and pleasure the like neuer yet published.

> The Bee and Spider by a diuerse power,
> Sucke Hony and Poyson from the selfe same flower.

Newly corrected and augmented. — London, Printed by William Stansby for Roger Iackson dwelling in Fleet-street neere the great Conduit. 1611. 8vo. 112 *leaves.*

This was the last impression issued in the lifetime of the author-editor, Francis Davison, eldest son to unfortunate Secretary Davison, who died in 1608, leaving four sons and two daughters.[1] It is believed that Francis Davison himself died in 1619, before any of his brothers and sisters. The collection, which is even superior in some respects to "England's Helicon," 1600, was made in imi-

[1] In 1602 young Francis Davison was disappointed in his hope of going abroad as Secretary to Parry; and Chamberlain, in one of his letters dated June 8, 1602, says: — "Yt seemes young Davison meanes to take another course and turne poet, for he hath lately set out certain Sonnets and Epigrams." The allusion, no doubt, was to the first edition of the "Poetical Rhapsody."

tation of it, and first appeared in 1602. Such was its popularity that it was reprinted, with additions, in 1608, 1611, and 1621: in the last impression, after Francis Davison's death, the materials were rearranged. At the end of four leaves, containing the alphabetical contents, are the initials D. P., but why they were placed there, or what or whom they mean, is nowhere explained. The mere list was hardly worth owning.

We notice the volume here chiefly for the purpose of pointing out an important error that must have been committed in assigning one of the longest and most striking poems to a man who clearly could have had nothing to do with it. We refer to the first "Eglogue," which at the end has the initials F. D., which Sir H. Nicolas in his edition (8vo, 1826) enlarged to "Francis Davison"; but he could not have read the production without seeing at once that it contains passages which could by no possibility have been written by that young man, who was at most twenty-seven when they first appeared in print. It was evidently the authorship of a person who had long been in disgrace at Court, (or with Astræa, as he calls Elizabeth,) for he says, —

> "My night hath lasted *fifteene yeares*,
> And yet no glimpse of day appeares."

How could young Francis Davison have been fifteen years out of favor with the Queen? or how could he proceed to lament, —

> "But I that late
> With upright gate
> Bare up my head while happy favour lasted,
> Now old am growne,
> Now overthrowne,
> With woe, with griefe, with wailing now am wasted."

The whole is a personal production, referring to the previous advancement and subsequent sudden fall of the speaker; and our solution of the difficulty is, that the Eclogue was the production, not of Francis Davison, but of his father William Davison; but the MS. being in the handwriting of the former, the printer (to whom such matters were avowedly left) erroneously placed the initials F. D. at the end of it.[1] In 1602, when this Eclogue first

[1] The speculation that William Davison, and not his son Francis, was the author of the first Eclogue in the "Poetical Rhapsody" will not appear so unlikely, when it is mentioned that William Davison was poet-

appeared, it was exactly "fifteen years" since the death of Mary Queen of Scots, for hastening whose execution (though with the good will of Elizabeth) William Davison had incurred the well affected displeasure of the Queen. Whether our speculation be or be not adopted, it is quite certain that Sir H. Nicolas had no warrant for here extending the initials F. D. into "Francis Davison." Another explanation may be, that F. D. ought to be E. D.; and that Sir Edward Dyer, who complains that he had been long excluded from Court, was the author of the first Eclogue. How carelessly the printer (W. Stansby) performed his duty in other respects might be illustrated in many places, but we will take an instance from this very production, subscribed F. D., where the following couplet occurs: —

"My nightly rest[s] have turn'd to *detriment*,
To plaints have turn'd my wonted merriment."

Here "detriment" and "merriment" do not rhyme; but as *dreriment* was then a comparatively new word, (employed first by Spenser,) the printer did not know it, and composed "detriment" instead of it. In the second Eclogue he was guilty of a blunder of a different kind, omitting to mark the speech of "the Herdman," and thereby giving the conclusion of the Dialogue to "the Shepherd." This error also was never set right in ancient or modern editions.

Some of the best pieces in the Collection, especially "an

ically inclined, and that he has left behind him some specimens of verse. These are contained in Harl. MS. 290; and one of them is the following, by no means contemptible, epigram: —

"Virtue and learning were, in former time,
Sure ladders by the which a man might clime
To honor's seate; but now they will not hold,
Unless the mounting steps be made of gold."

The theme of another piece is *Semper eris pauper*. It is not at all unnatural to imagine that during his long confinement in the Tower, or while he was resident in disgrace at Stepney (where he was buried 24th Dec. 1608), he amused himself by poetical composition, a talent inherited by his son; who nevertheless may possibly have written the Eclogue in question in the person of his father. We are of opinion, however, as expressed in our text, that the piece was by the father, and that the initials of the son were erroneously appended to it.

Eglogue made long since upon the death of Sir Philip Sidney," are subscribed A. W., initials which nobody has yet been able to appropriate at all satisfactorily. Ritson's notion, that they were by Arthur Warren, shows that he was no good judge of poetry. Warren, from what he has left behind him, was wholly incapable of them. We do not recollect that the following has been quoted in reference to Spenser, but no one else can be meant by Collin, and personally the passage is very interesting: —

"*Perin.*

" Who else but Thenot can the Muses raise,
And teach them sing and dance in mournfull guise?
My finger's stiffe, my voice doth hoarsely rise.

" *Thenot.*

" Ah! where is Collin and his passing skill?
For him it fits our sorrow to fulfill.

"*Perin.*

" Tway sore extreames our Collin presse so neere
(Alas, that such extremes should presse him so!)
The want of wealth, and losse of loue so deere;
Scarse can he breath from under heapes of woe:
He that beares heauen beares no such weight, I trow.

" *Thenot.*

" Hath he such skill in making all aboue,
And hath no skill to get or Wealth or Loue?

" *Perin.*

" Praise is the greatest prise that Poets gaine,
A simple gaine that feeds them ne're a whit.
The wanton lasse for whom he bare such paine,
Like running water, loues to change and flit.
But if thou list to heare a sorry fit,
Which Cuddy could in doleful verse endite,
Blow thou thy pipe, while I the same recite."

It was just about the date of Sidney's death that Spenser, here named Collin, having obtained his grant of land in Cork, had gone to take possession of it. (" Life of Spenser," 1862, p. lii.) The " wanton lass," who was as changeable as water, must have been his poetical mistress Rosalind. Farther on, in relation to the death of Sidney, as the friend and patron of Spenser, A. W. says: —

"Ah! Collin, I lament thy case:
For thee remaines no hope of grace.
The best reliefe
Of Poet's griefe
Is dead, and wrapt full cold in filthy clay;
And nought remaines
To ease our paines,
But hope of death to rid us hence away."

We have briefly touched upon these points because, we apprehend, they are new, and have not been noticed in the various editions of the "Poetical Rhapsody."

DAVYS, SIR JOHN. — Orchestra, or a Poeme of Dauncing. Judicially prooving the true observation of tune and measure, in the Authenticall and laudable use of Dauncing. Ovid. Art. Aman. lib. i.

Si vox est, canta: si mollia brachia, salta;
Et quacunque, potes dote placere, place.

At London, Printed by J. Robarts for N. Ling. 1596. 18mo. 24 *leaves.*

In the "General Biographical Dictionary" by A. Chalmers, under "Davies," we are told that the first edition of Sir John Davys's Poem called "Orchestra," originally published in 1596, "has escaped the researches of modern collectors, and the poem, as we now find it, is imperfect. Whether it was, or was not so in the first edition may be doubted." This in our hands is the first edition, and the poem is in all respects complete.

The title is followed by a dedicatory sonnet, "To his very Friend, Ma. Rich. Martin." The circumstance is singular, recollecting that this Richard Martin was the very person whom, according to his biographers, Sir John Davys beat in the Middle Temple Hall, which occasioned his expulsion from the society in February, 1597–98. In *Polymanteia*, which was printed in 1595, it is stated that Davys was of Lincoln's Inn: why he changed to the Middle Temple does not appear, nor to what Inn of Court, if any, he went after having been expelled from the Middle Temple. The quarrel with Martin (afterwards Recorder of London) was of course subsequent to the Sonnet, which is written in extravagant terms of friendship and admiration. As it has never been reprinted, it deserves on all accounts to be quoted:

"*To his very Friend, Ma. Rich. Martin.*

"To whom shall I this dauncing Poeme send,
This suddaine, rash, halfe-capreol of my wit?
To you, first mover and sole cause of it,
Mine-owne-selves better halfe, my deerest frend.
O, would you yet my Muse some Honny lend
From your mellifluous tongue, whereon doth sit
Suada in Majestie, that I may fit
These harsh beginnings with a sweeter end.
You know the modest Sunne full fifteene times
Blushing did rise, and blushing did descend,
While I in making of these ill made rimes,
My golden howers unthriftily did spend:
Yet, if in friendship you these numbers prayse,
I will mispend another fifteene dayes."

When Sir John Davys republished "Orchestra" with his other pieces in 1622, he substituted for the above a sonnet addressed to Prince Charles; and at the conclusion of the poem he left a *hiatus* after the one hundred and twenty-sixth stanza, perhaps on account of his quarrel with Martin. In the edition of 1596, as has already been remarked, the production is complete, but some portions of the last five stanzas are at this distance of time obscure. Sir John Davys, however, pays tribute in them to his predecessors in English poetry, Chaucer, Spenser, Daniel, Chapman, Drayton, Sir Philip Sidney, &c. These terminating stanzas are numbered respectively from one hundred and twenty-seven to one hundred and thirty-one inclusive, and run thus:—

"Away, Terpsechore, light Muse, away,
And come Uranie, prophetesse divine:
Come, Muse of heav'n, my burning thirst allay,
Even now for want of sacred drink I tine.
In heav'nly moysture dip thys Pen of mine,
And let my mouth with Nectar overflow,
For I must more then mortall glory show.

"O, that I had Homer's aboundant vaine,
I would hereof another *Ilias* make;
Or els the man of Mantua's charmed braine,
In whose large throat great Jove the thunder spake.
O, that I could old Gefferies Muse awake,
Or borrow Colin's fayre heroike stile,
Or smooth my rimes with Delia's servants file.

"O, could I, sweet Companion, sing like you,
Which of a shadow under a shadow sing;
Or, like faire *Salue's* sad lover true,
Or like the Bay, the Marigold's darling,
Whose suddaine verse Love covers with his wing.
O, that your braines were mingled all with mine,
T' inlarge my wit for this great worke divine.

"Yet, Astrophell might one for all suffize,
Whose supple Muse Camelion-like doth change
Into all formes of excellent devise.
So might the Swallow, whose swift Muse doth range
Through rare *Idœas*, and inventions strange,
And ever doth enjoy her joyfull spring,
And sweeter then the Nightingale doth sing.

"O, that I might that singing Swallow heare,
To whom I owe my service and my love,
His sugred tunes would so enchant mine eare,
And in my mind such sacred fury move,
As I should knock at heav'ns gate above,
With my proude rimes, while of this heav'nly state
I doe aspire the shadow to relate."

This is followed by the word "Finis"; but yet the poet seems rather to have been about to begin a new subject than to finish an old one. It is now perhaps impossible to explain who is intended by "Salue's sad lover true," or who is figured under "the Bay, the Marigold's darling." "The Swallow" is probably *Martin*, the friend to whom the poem is inscribed, and who seems to have been himself a verse-maker. Excepting this interesting conclusion, the rest of the poem was exactly reprinted in 1622. Sir John Davys was, perhaps, an expert dancer earlier in life; but, in 1603, he had grown very corpulent, as appears by Manningham's Diary among the Harleian MSS. in the British Museum. (*Vide* "History of English Dramatic Poetry and the Stage," Vol. I. p.

320.) Sir J. Harington, in Epigram 67 of Book II., bears testimony to the same fact.

It is stated correctly by the biographers of John Davys that he was patronized by Lord Ellesmere, and among the papers of his lordship is preserved the following autograph Sonnet, which appears to have been addressed to the Lord Chancellor, on the death of his second wife in the year 1599: —

"You, that in Judgment passion never show,
(As still a Judge should without passion bee),
So judge your self; and make not in your woe
Against your self a passionate decree.
Griefe may become so weake a spirit as mine:
My prop is fallne, and quenched is my light;
But th' Elme may stand, when with'red is the vine,
And, though the Moone eclipse, the Sunne is bright.
Yet were I senselesse if I wisht your mind,
Insensible, that nothing might it move;
As if a man might not bee wise and kind.
Doubtlesse the God of Wisdome and of Love,
As Solomon's braine he doth to you impart,
So hath he given you David's tender hart.
Yr Lps in all humble Duties
and condoling with yr Lp most affectionately
Jo. Davys."

The following note is appended, also in the handwriting of Sir John Davys: — "A French writer, (whom I love well), speakes of 3 kindes of Companions, Men, Women, and Bookes: the losse of this second makes you retire from the first: I have, therefore, presum'd to send yr Lp one of the third kind wch (it may bee), is a straunger to your Lp, yet I persuade me his conversation will not be disagreeable to yr Lp."

DAVYS, SIR JOHN. — Nosce teipsum. This Oracle expounded in two Elegies. 1. Of Humane Knowledge. 2. Of the Soule of Man, and the immortalitie thereof. — London Printed by Richard Field for John Standish. 1599. 4to. 43 *leaves*.

This is the first edition of a very celebrated poem, which is said to have gained the author the favor of James I., even before he came to the crown. It is addressed in verse to Queen Elizabeth, and subscribed "John Davies," but the name of the author did not appear upon the title-page until it was printed for the third time in 1608. In the address to the Queen, Sir John Davys terms her

"Loadstone to Hearts, and Loadstarre to all eyes;"

a line not unfrequently quoted and imitated. A great deal has been said by bibliographers respecting the date of the address to the Queen. In the copy before us it has no date.

DAVYS, SIR JOHN. — Nosce teipsum, &c. Written by Sir John Davis his Majesties Atturney generall in Ireland. — London Printed by Henry Ballard for John Standish. 1608. 4to. 43 *leaves.*

This is the third edition. The second edition appeared in 1602. The variations between them are merely typographical.

The sudden death of Sir John Davys is usually said to have occurred in 1626; but if this be not an error, what is to be said of the following registration in the book of St. Mary Aldermanbury? —

"Buried Sir John Davyes, Knight. May 28. 1624."

We copy the following from the original in the S. P. O., and it deserves preservation, because it must refer to the presentation by Sir John Davys of a copy of his *Nosce Teipsum*, 1599, through Michael (afterwards knighted) Hicks.

"Mr. Hicks. I have sent you heer inclosed that cobweb of my invention which I promised before Christmas: I pray you present it, commend it, and grace it, as well for your owne sake as mine; bycause by your nominacion I was first put to this taske, for which I acknowledge my self beholding to you in good earnest, though the imployment be light and trifling, bycause I am glad of any occasion of being made knowne to that noble gentl. whom I honore and admire exceedingly. If ought be to be added, or alter'd, lett me heare from you. I shall willingly attend to doo it, the more speedily if it be before the terme. So in hast I commend my best services to you. Chancery Lane 20 Jan. 1600.

Yours to do you service very willingly,

Jo. Davys."

DEE, JOHN. — A Letter, containing a most briefe Discourse Apologeticall, with a plaine Demonstration, and fervent Protestation for the lawfull, sincere, very faithfull and Christian course of the Philosophicall studies and exercises of a certaine studious Gentleman: An ancient Servaunt to her most excellent Majesty Royall. n. d. 4to. 12 *leaves.*

This "certain studious gentleman" was Dr. John Dee, who subscribed the "Peroratio" thus: "Very speedily written this twelfth even, and twelfth day, in my poore Cottage at Mortlake: Anno 1595. currente à Nativitate Christi: ast, An. 1594. Completo, à Conceptione ejusdem, cum novem præterea mensibus, Completis.

Alwaies, and very dutifully,
at your Graces commandement
John Dee."

The whole is addressed to the Archbishop of Canterbury, and we learn from the dedication that, on the 9th of November, 1592, Dee had presented a supplication to the Queen at Hampton. Then follow lists of his works, printed and unprinted, an "Epilogue," and a copy of the Latin Testimonial given to him by the University of Cambridge in the year 1548. The date in the colophon of Peter Short, the printer, on the last leaf, is 1599.

On the title-page is a woodcut of Dee on his knees, a sheep, a wolf, and a many-headed human monster. Another edition of this tract was printed in 1604, 4to.

DEKKER, THOMAS. — The Seuen deadly Sinnes of London: Drawne in seuen seuerall Coaches, Through seuen seuerall Gates of the Citie Bringing the Plague with them. — *Opus septem Dierum.* Tho: Dekker. — At London Printed by E. A. for Nathaniel Butter, and are to be solde at his shop neere Saint Austens gate. 1606. 4to. B. L. 31 *leaves.*

We believe that the only scrap of biographical information regarding Dekker, to be met with in his works, is found in this tract, on sign. A 3 b, not far from the close of "The Induction to the Booke," where he says, apostrophizing London, — " O, thou beawtifullest daughter of the two vnited Monarchies! from thy womb received I my being; from thy brests my nourishment; yet give me leave to tell thee that thou hast seven Divels within thee," &c. We learn from the Registers of St. Saviour's Southwark that the person who probably was his father was buried there in 1594; and from the Registers of St. Giles Cripplegate, (where Henslowe's and Alleyn's theatre, the Fortune, for which Dekker wrote, was situated,) that Thomas Dycker, gent., had a daughter Dorcas christened there on 27th Oct. 1594, and that Thomas Decker, yeoman, had a daughter Anne christened there on 24th Oct. 1602. Neither of these might be our poet, and it was not usual to designate an author "yeoman." Thomas Dekker had a daughter Elizabeth buried there in 1598, and a son of Thomas Dekker was buried at St. Botolph's Bishopgate on 19th April in the same year. The widow of old Thomas Dekker, who died in 1594, was living in "Maid Lane," Southwark, near the Globe theatre, in 1596.

Thomas Dekker, the dramatist, was often, if not always, in difficulties.[1] We have no reason to think that he was, like Shakspeare, Ben Jonson, and others, also an actor; and the first we hear of him, in connection with theatres, is in 1597, when he was a writer for Henslowe's company: in 1598 he was in the Counter, and the old Manager advanced forty shillings to discharge him. In the same year he was arrested for money due to the association for which Shakspeare wrote. In 1602 he and Anthony Monday acknowledged a debt of £5 to Henslowe. Dekker seems to have lived from hand to mouth, supplying his necessities by his pen in the production of plays, pamphlets, and poems; but in 1613 he was in prison again, and perhaps several times in the interval. He was in the King's Bench in 1616; when he wrote and sent to Alleyne "a eulogium," as he called it, on the building of Dulwich College,

1 In September, 1616, he was a prisoner in the King's Bench, and from thence wrote a supplicatory letter to Edward Alleyn, which is preserved in Dulwich College, and was printed in the Memoirs of Alleyn (published by the Shakspeare Society in 1841), p. 131.

soliciting at the same time pecuniary aid. We hear nothing of him after 1638, and he is supposed to have died before the Civil Wars.

The tract in our hands was one of those which he produced on the spur of his necessities, and he makes it a boast on the title-page that it only cost him a week's work. In it he mentions his "Wonderful Year," another tract, no doubt composed with about as much speed, in order to take advantage of an attractive topic, "the Plague," which broke out in 1602, and which cost the lives of 30,578 persons in London, as the author informs us in a note in his "Seven Deadly Sins."

Respecting his "Wonderful Year," 1603, we have some curious information in the Registers of the Stationers' Company under the date of 5th Dec. Hence it appears that three publishers, Ling, Smithwicke, and Browne, had procured it to be printed by Tho. Creede, and then published it without any entry of it at the Hall. The following order was therefore made: —

> "Yt is ordered that they shall pay x^{s} a pece for their fines for printinge a booke called the Wonderfull Yere without authoritie or entrance, contrary to thordonances for pryntinge. Also that they shall forbeare, and never hereafter entermeadle to printe or sell the same booke or anie parte thereof. — Also that they shall presently bringe into the Hall, to be used according to thordanance in that behalf, so many of the said bookes as they, or any to their use, have left in their handes."

A note is added that the imprisonment of Ling, Smithwicke, and Browne was "respited till further order." It is not known what was done upon this order; but Dekker's tract, "The Wonderful Year," is very rare, and perhaps it became so because the copies sent in by the three booksellers were destroyed.

"The Seven Deadly Sinnes of London" is arranged, in some sort, like an old morality, or moral-play, and the names of the supposed allegorical impersonations are inserted at the end of the address to the Reader, viz.: 1. Politike Bankruptisme; 2. Lying; 3. Candle-light; 4. Sloth; 5. Apishnesse; 6. Shaving; 7. Crueltie. In conformity with the practice of our older stage, a Devil was also made one of the supposed actors; and the whole seven sins of London, one after the other, make their several entrances in triumph, the appropriate attendants and accompaniments being metaphorically and satirically described. What Dekker calls the "deadly sin of Candle-light" has a "nocturnal triumph," that is, he enters surrounded by torches; and here it is that we meet with the passage showing that in the time of Shakspeare a private theatre, like the Blackfriars, for which he wrote and where he acted, had windows, and was not, like public theatres, lighted by being uncovered at the top and open to the weather. The Globe, on the Bankside, was a theatre of this latter description. Dekker's words are, "all the Citty looked like a private playhouse, when the windowes are clapt downe, as if some nocturnal or dismall tragedy were presently to be acted before all the tradesmen."

The author goes through the vices prevailing in the metropolis, not without some tediousness, and in the course of his descriptions introduces various temporary allusions, such as to the two uncommonly successful plays, Marlowe's "The Rich Jew of Malta," and Kyd's "Spanish Tragedy." "Robin Goodfellow" is also spoken of; and the prodigious success of the players of London "at the comming of the ten Ambassadors" is recorded. Dekker does not put his friends, the actors, in very good company where he speaks of the followers of Sloth as "Anglers, Dumb Ministers, Players, Exchange-wenches, Gamesters, Whores and Fiddlers." As if determined not to lose any credit, or perhaps profit, by this production, Dekker not only placed his name prominently on the title-page, but he, somewhat unusually, subscribed it at the end, thus:—

"*Dii me terrent, et Jupiter hostis.*
FINIS.
Tho. Dekker."

The *Jupiter* and *Dii* were, perhaps, at this time a bailiff and his followers, in search of the author for the non-payment of some debt.

DEKKER, THOMAS.—The Double P P. A Papist in Armes. Bearing Ten severall Sheilds. Encountred by the Protestant. At Ten severall Weapons. A Iesuite marching before them. *Cominùs & Eminùs.*—London, Imprinted by T. C. and are to be sold by John Hodgets &c. 1606. 4to. 22 *leaves.*

This tract by Dekker (for a presentation copy of it with his autograph is in existence) has little but its rarity to recommend it: it is a violent, and, as far as we can now understand the allusions, not a very witty attack upon the Catholics, provoked by the Gunpowder Plot of the year preceding its publication. It is of the same character, though not so amusing, as John Rhodes's "Answere to a Romish Rime," 1602, who was also the writer of a tract printed in 1606, called "A briefe Summe of the Treason intended against the King and State," &c.

After a dedication in verse, so constructed as to represent a column, "To all the Nobility, Clergy and Gentry of Great Brittaine, true Subjects to King James," Dekker commences with the following, which he calls "A Riddle on the double P P.": —

"Upon the double P P. badder fruits grow,
Than on al letters in the Christ-Crosse-Row:
It sets (by reason of the Badge it weares)
The Christ-Crosse-Row together by the eares.
The reason is, this haughtie double P P
Would clyme above both A. B. C. and D
And trample on the necks of E. F. G.
H. I. (Royall K.) L. M. N. O. and Q,
Threatning the fall of R. S. T. and U."

"*The Resolution.*
P P = Pa Pa = the Po Pe.
Christ-Crosse-Row = Christendome.

A. B. C. D. E. &c., the States of the land; as Archbishops, Bishops, Councellors, Dukes, Earles, &c.
K. the King.
Q. the Queene.
R. Religion.
S. State.
T. Truth.
U. You all."

This (after "the Picture of a Jesuite," "A Papist in Armes," and some other matter of a like kind) is succeeded on sign. D iiii. by "The Single P: A Riddle on the single P.," in the same form, but of course of a character directly opposed to "the Double P." The tract concludes upon sign. F 2, with "The Papist Encountered." There was another edition of it in the same year, with some immaterial variations.

DEKKER, THOMAS. — A Knights Coniuring. Done in earnest: Discouered in Iest. By Thomas Dekker. — London, Printed by T. C. for William Barley, and are to be solde at his Shop in Gratious streete, 1607. 4to. 40 *leaves.*

There were three editions of this tract, the first under the title of "Newes from Hell, brought by the Divells Carrier," 1606, and two others (with the date of 1607, and without a date), as "A Knights Conjuring." It may be disputed, perhaps, whether the last was a reprint or only a reissue; but it is quite certain that there are very material differences between "Newes from Hell," and "A Knights Conjuring." The first contains important passages which were omitted in the last, and the last has some additions not in the first, while the whole (to give it, perhaps, the appearance of greater novelty) is divided into nine chapters.

All three impressions have reference to an extremely popular publication, about thirteen or fourteen years older, by Thomas Nash, and still read and reprinted when Dekker sat down to write what may be considered a sequel to it. Nash's tract was called "Pierce Pennilesse his supplication to the Devill," 4to, 1592; and in the second impression of it the author held out a sort of promise to write a continuation, but he died before 1600, without keeping his word. About six years after his death an anonymous author produced what he wished to be considered a sequel of the subject: he called it "The Returne of the Knight of the Post from Hell, with the Devils Answeare to the Supplication of Pierce Penniless." This was followed immediately by Dekker's "Newes from Hell," in which he criticizes the production of his rival, "The Returne of the Knight of the Post," and describes it as heavy and puritanical. Of course, Dekker intended his own work to be the reverse, but he was not altogether successful.

It may be supposed that the sale of "A Knights Conjuring," after the anonymous "Returne of the Knight of the Post" and Dekker's own "Newes from Hell," was not rapid in 1606; and in the following year a new title-page was printed to it, without any date, of which some copies have reached our day. One of those, with the date of the year 1607, is the subject of the present article.

The dedication to Sir Thomas Glover, and the address "To the Reader," both subscribed "Tho. Dekker," are not in "Newes from Hell"; but the last has a curious paragraph about Nash and Gabriel Harvey, which was subsequently suppressed — in all likelihood because it revived the memory of a literary contest regarding which the public authorities had interfered, and had ordered that the satirical and abusive pamphlets on both sides should be destroyed. Dekker, in his "Newes from Hell," thus breaks out in an apostrophe to Nash, who had been his private friend: —

> "And thou into whose soule (if ever there were a Pithagorean Metempsuchosis) the raptures of that fierce and unconfineable Italian spirit were bounteously and boundlesly infused; thou sometime Secretary to Pierce Pennylesse, and Master of his Requests, ingenious and ingenuous, fluent, facetious T. Nash, from whose abundant pen hony flowed to thy friends, and mortall Aconite to thy enemies; thou that madest the Doctor [Hervey] a flat dunce, and beatst him at his two sundry tall weapons, Poetrie and Oratorie; sharpest Satyre, luculent Poet, elegant Orator, get leave for thy ghost to come from her abiding, and to dwell with me a while, till she hath carows'd to me in his owne wonted ful measures of wit, that my plump braynes may swell, and burst into bitter invectives against the Lieftenant of Limbo, if he cashiere Pierce Pennylesse with dead pay."

Excepting the above, the most interesting part of Dekker's "Knight's Conjuring" is the conclusion, which relates to certain dead poets, whom the author must have known when living, (for he descends even to their personal appearance,) whom he represents enjoying the society of each other in the Elysian Fields. He first speaks of Chaucer, surrounded "by all the makers or poets of his time"; and then he introduces Spenser, Watson, Kyd, Atchlow, Marlowe, Greene, Peele, Nash, and Chettle, which last had only just arrived, so that we may presume he was only recently dead.

The passage regarding Spenser is more interesting than any other, because it decisively shows what has been doubted, namely, that he never wrote more of his "Faerie Queene" than has come down to us, and that there were in fact no six books, concluding the great subject, which were said to have been either lost at sea, on their way from Ireland, or destroyed by the carelessness of a servant. Dekker's words regarding Spenser are: —

> "Grave Spencer was no sooner entred into this Chappell of Apollo, but these elder Fathers of the divine Furie gave him a Lawrer and sung his Welcome: Chaucer call'de him his Sonne, and plac'de him at his right hand. All of them (at a signe given by the whole Quire of the Muses that brought him thither) closing up their lippes in silence, and tuning all their eares for attention, to heare him sing out the rest of his Fayrie Queenes praises."

It was because Spenser had never written "the rest of his Faerie Queene" that the Muses listened to hear the conclusion of the subject. Had "the rest" ever been composed, the Muses must have known it, and "tuning their eares" for attention would have been needless. (See "Life of Spenser," 1862, p. cxliii.)

In his "Knights Conjuring," Dekker purposely omitted all allusion to the anonymous writer of "The Returne of the Knight of the Post," whom he had mentioned with no great respect in his "Newes from Hell." Why he thus slighted him does not anywhere appear; and as "The Returne of the Knight of the Post from Hell" is a greater rarity than even Dekker's work, and as a copy of it is now lying before us, it may be worth while to note, that the author claims to have been one of Nash's intimate friends, and to have heard from him what he had intended to have said and done in a second part of "Pierce Penniless's Supplication." Upon that plan he pretends to proceed, but his work is not only dull and dry, but affectedly pious. He avails himself of the popular topic afforded by the recent discovery of the Gunpowder Plot, and introduces curious particulars regarding some of the actors in that conspiracy. He thus speaks of John Wright, brother to Christopher Wright, both of whom were implicated: —

> "The elder of these was infinitely proud, yet not so proud as ungratefull, for being utterlye without any certaine meanes more then the revenue of other mens purses, yet was his generall ostentation that he was beholden to no man. His vertue was a good oylie tongue, that with easie utterance beguiled many weake attentions, and a formall carriage, which, contemning others, heapt upon himselfe a selfe commendation: his usuall boast was that he scornd felt hats, he lovde doublets lined with taffata,

linnen of twenty shillings an elle, silk stockings, never under twenty angels in his pocket, and his horse at least of fortie pound reckoning."

The Knight of the Post, who has just returned from the infernal regions, finds Pierce Penniless walking in what was termed "the Intelligencers Walk," in St. Paul's Cathedral; and whoever was the writer of this tract (whom Dekker, in his "Newes from Hell," professes not to know) must have been a tolerable composer of verses; and near the end of his tract he introduces two specimens, which are far from contemptible, particularly the second, where he speaks of a person who

"in poverty no poorenesse knowes,
Nor feeles the strange diseases of the rich."

We may feel well assured that Dekker knew who and what he was, though he might not like to acknowledge him as an acquaintance.

DEKKER THOMAS, AND GEORGE WILKINS. — Jests to make you Merie: With The conjuring up of Cock Watt (the walking Spirit of Newgate) to tell Tales. Unto which is added, the miserie of a Prison and a Prisoner. And a Paradox in praise of Serjeants. Written by T. D. and George Wilkins. — Imprinted at London by N. O. for Nathaniell Butter, dwelling neere to St. Austins Gate, at the signe of the pide Bull, 1607. 4to. B. L. 31 *leaves.*

The fact has not been noticed, but it is nevertheless certain, that there were two poets of the name of George Wilkins, in the latter end of the reign of Elizabeth, and in the beginning of that of James I. Which of them was the author of the admirable drama, "The Miseries of enforced Marriage," 4to, 1607, it is impossible now to determine; but the natural conjecture seems to be that they were father and son. The father, as we suppose him, died in the summer of 1603, as is apparent from the ensuing entry in the burial-book of the parish of St. Leonard Shoreditch, where two of the public theatres were situated, and where so many dramatists and actors resided.

"1603. George Wilkins, the Poet, was buried the same day, 19 August. Halliwell Street."

Thus we see that he lived in Holywell Street; and as the plague was at that date raging in London, we may perhaps infer that his death was produced by it. That another George Wilkins, an author, if not a poet, survived him, we have evidence in the work before us, and in the additional fact, that in 1608 he put forth "The painfull Adventures of Pericles, Prince of Tyre," a novel avowedly founded upon Shakspeare's drama of the same name, which itself came from the press in 1609. A copy of this novel, wanting the dedication, (which alone supplies the information that it was by George Wilkins,) is in the British Museum. Another, and a complete, copy is in the public library of Zurich, and has recently been reprinted in Germany. That the two George Wilkinses were therefore distinct authors, is sufficiently obvious. It was the younger one who contributed to "Jests to make you Merry," and who had the aid of so popular a dramatic poet and pamphleteer as Thomas Dekker. We may be disposed to believe that Wilkins was the principal author and compiler, and that his coadjutor was called in mainly for the sake of additional attraction.

An address "To the Reader" is subscribed "T. D. and G. W.," and in two pages dwells much upon the difficulty of procuring of publishers who would buy books for the "Paules Churchyard walkers." They say, "Go to one and offer a copy: if it be merrie, the man likes no light stuffe: if it be sad, it will not sell. Another meddles with nothing but what fits the time." It ends thus in reference to satirists: — "Of those sharp-toothed dogs you shall finde me none. I hould no whip in my hande, but a soft fether, and there drops rather water then gall out of my quill: if you taste it and finde it pleasant, I am glad: if not, I cannot be much sorry." This sentence clearly alludes to such publications as Goddard's "Mastiff-Whelp," 1599, and to Marston's "Scourge of Villanie," 1598, where he boasts that he "holds in his hand Rhamnusia's whip." This address is in the first person throughout, though subscribed both by "T. D. and G. W."

A definition of "what a jest is," is followed by sixty specimens, good, bad, and indifferent, some of them by no means coming up to the standard laid down. The best of them, not so much as jokes, but as the means of conveying information, relate to plays, theatres, and actors. Thus, No. 16 mentions Middleton's comedy, "Blurt, Master Constable," which had been printed in 1602.

"A Player riding with his fellowes (in a yeare of Peregrination) up and downe the countries, resolved to be merry, tho they got little money; and being to passe through a Towne, hee gets a good way before the rest, crying (with his drawne Rapier in his hand) which is the Constables house? where is the Constable? The dogs of the parrish at the noise fell to barking, the threshers came running out with their flailes, the Clounes with rakes and pitch-forks, asking what the matter was? [He] cried still, And you be men bring me to the Constable! At last the wise gentleman appeared in his likenesse: Are you the Constable? saies the Player. Yes, that I am for fault of a better, quoth he. Why then Blurt, Maister Constable! saies the other, and clapping spurres to his horse gallopd away amaine, some of the companions laughing, others rayling, the Constable swearing, and the rest of the players that came behind post through the thickest of them, and laughing the whole Towne to scorne, as it had bin the foole in a Comedie; which made the hob-naile wearers stampe tenne times worse then they did before."

Here the jest is worth nothing. "A year of peregrination" was a season when plays were forbidden in London on account of the plague. There is humor, however, in the following, No. 22: —

"A paire of Players, growing into an emulous contention of one anothers worth, refusde to put themselves to a day of hearing (as any Players would have done) but stood onely upon their good parts. Why, saies the one, since thou wouldst faine be taken for so rare a peece, report before all these (for they had a small audience about them, you must note) what excellent parts thou hast discharged. Mary, saies the other, I have so naturally playd the Puritane, that many tooke me to be one. True, saies the first agen, thou playdst the Puritane so naturally that thou couldst never play the honest man afterwards; but I (quoth he) have playd the Sophy. The Sophy! replied the second: what a murren was he? What was he? saies the other: why he was a Turke: right, quoth his adversarie, get to play as many Turkes parts as thou canst, for Ile be hangd if ever thou playst a good Christian."

Most of the mere jokes have some novelty to recommend them, but here and there we meet with an anecdote which was stale even in 1607. The following, for instance, had been told in "Table Philosophy," in 1576 and 1583, and found a place also in S. Rowlands's "Night Raven," printed in 1618 and 1620; the original is Greek: —

> "A Company of theeves brake one night into a countrie schoole-maisters house, and he hearing them never stirrd out of his bed for the matter, but cried out aloude, You mistake your marke, my maisters: goe to the next house; thats a rich farmers. I wonder you will loose time to seeke any thing heere by night, when I my selfe can finde nothing by day."

At the close of the Jests we read *Nihil hic nisi seria desunt*, and we arrive at another heading, "The Discoveries made by Cock Wat, the walking Spirit of Newgate." He seems to have been a well-known personage of the time, who, in different prisons, had become well acquainted with all the frauds and shifts of cozeners, cut-purses, and conveyancers, and made revelations for the benefit of the public. This information is very commonplace, and such as Dekker had already inserted in several of his popular tracts. A third heading, "The miserie of a Prison and a Prisoner," and a fourth, "A Paradox in praise of Serjeants," present little or nothing worth extracting. It is hardly amusing, even as a picture of the manners and tricks of thieves and sharpers in the lower grades of society. We have it all in a more agreeable and intelligible form in Dekker's "Belman of London," "Lanthorn and Candle-light," &c., which came out not long afterwards, and much of which was itself drawn from earlier sources. (See the next article.)

DEKKER, THOMAS. — The Belman of London. Bringing to light the most notorious villanies that are now practised in the Kingdome. Profitable for Gentlemen, Lawyers, Merchants, Citizens, Farmers, Masters of Households, and all sortes of servants to marke, and delightfull for all men to Reade. *Lege, Perlege, Relege.* — Printed at London for Nathaniel Butter. 1608. 4to. B. L. 34 *leaves.*

Dekker's name is not found to this tract, but, in what may be considered a second part of it, "Lanthorne and Candle-light," 1609, he recognizes "The Belman of London" as his production. Its popularity was extraordinary, for it was printed three times in the first year. The edition under consideration is the earliest, and has on the title-page a woodcut of the Belman, with bell, lantern, and halbert, followed by his dog. On the title-page of "Lanthorne and Candle-Light," in the next year, he is represented in a night-cap, without his dog, and with a "brown bill" on his shoulder; and it is singular that, after the lapse of more than two hundred years, the very woodcut from which the impression was made in 1609 should have been preserved, and used as a head-piece to a ballad which we bought in St. Giles's in 1836.

"The Belman of London" is dedicated anonymously "to all those that either by office are sworne to punish, or in their owne love to vertue wish to have the disorders of the State amended." The greater part of the tract is borrowed *totidem verbis* from the "Caveat for Common Cursetors," (*vide* HARMAN, *post*,) but here and there curious additions are made, applicable to the time; and the following affords a useful note to Shakspeare's "King Lear," which came out in the year when "The Belman of London" was printed. Dekker is speaking of "Abraham-men," who pretended to be mad, and wandered about the country exactly in the way Edgar, in his disguised wretchedness, is represented to do: —

"He calls himself by the name of poore Tom, and comming neere any body cries out *Poore Tom is a-cold.* Of these Abraham-men some be exceeding merry, and doe nothing but sing songs fashioned out of their own braines: some will dance, others will doe nothing but either laugh or weepe: others are dogged, and so sullen both in looke and speech, that spying but a small companie in a house they boldly and bluntly enter," &c.

When Isaac Reed quoted this passage in a note to "Gammer Gurton's Needle," (Dodsley's Old Plays, II. 4, edit. 1825,) he seems not to have known of any edition of "The Belman of London" prior to that of 1616. The fact that it came out in 1608 renders the above passage peculiarly applicable to Shakspeare's great tragedy.

Samuel Rowlands, in his "Martin Mark-all Beadle of Bridewell," 1610, accuses the unknown author of the "Belman of London" of stealing from Harman's book. "At last up starts an old Cacodemicall Academicke with his frize bonnet, and gives them al to know that this invective was set foorth, made and printed above fortie yeeres agoe, and being then called a Caveat for Cursitors is now newly printed and termed the Belman of London." This exposure roused the ire of Dekker in his "Lanthorne and Candle-light," but he made no sufficient reply.

The allusions to temporary subjects are often curious, and the illustrations of manners very entertaining.

Dekker, Thomas.—The Dead Terme. Or Westminsters Complaint for long Vacations and short Termes. Written in manner of a Dialogue betweene the two Cityes of London and Westminster &c. By T. Dekker. — London, Printed and are to be sold by John Hodgets &c. 1608. B. L. 4to. 27 *leaves.*

The contents are at the back of the title-page, followed by a dedication to Sir John Harington, referring to his translation of Ariosto, first printed in 1591, (again in 1607 and 1634,) and praying him to "vouchsafe to view the labours of so dull a pen." It must be owned that this is one of Dekker's least humorous and amusing pieces. We have first "Westminster's speech to London," then "London's aunswere to Westminster," "Paule's Steeple's complaint," and finally "by what names London from time to time hath bin called, and how it came to bee divided into Wardes." The whole is prose, and very much derived from Stow's "Survey" and the old chroniclers.

Dekker, Thomas.—The Guls Horne-booke: Stultorum plena sunt omnia. *Al Savio meza parola Basta.* By T. Deckar.—Imprinted at London for R. S. 1609. B. L. 4to. 23 *leaves.*

This is unquestionably the most entertaining, and, exclusive of his plays, perhaps the best of Dekker's numerous works in verse and prose. It is full of lively descriptions of the manners of the beginning of the reign of James I., including accounts of, or allusions to, most of the popular and fashionable amusements. In an address "to the Reader," (which follows a mock dedication "To all Gulls in generall,") Dekker admits that his tract "hath a relish of Grobianisme," referring to Dedekind's "Grobianus and Grobiana," which had been versified by R. F. in 1605. (*Vide* SCHOOL OF SLOVENRY, *post.*) Dekker further states that he had himself "translated many bookes of that into English verse," but that he had abandoned the task, and "not greatly liking the subject, he had altered the shape, and of a Dutchman fashioned a mere Englishman." In this way he accounts for the "relish of Grobianisme," which he observes will be especially apparent in the beginning of his "Gull's Horn-book." Such certainly is the fact.

The work is entirely prose, and is divided into eight chapters, which are introduced by a *Proemium*. It was reprinted at Bristol, under the superintendence of Dr. Nott, in 1812, and it is often quoted by the commentators on Shakspeare and on our elder poets. Dr. Nott very injudiciously modernized the old spelling, and, in more important respects, was not faithful to the old text.

DEKKER, THOMAS.—The Ravens Almanacke. Foretelling of a Plague, Famine & Civill Warre. That shall happen this present yeare 1609 &c. With certaine remedies, rules and receipts &c.—London Printed by E. A. for Thomas Archer &c. 1609. B. L. 4to. 32 *leaves.*

A mock-prediction and a moral warning, drawn up with considerable humor and force, and intermixed with comic novels and incidents. The dedication is "To the Lyons of the Wood, (the young Courtiers) to the wilde Buckes of the Forrest, (the Gallants and younger Brothers) to the Harts of the field, and to the whole Country that are brought up wisely, yet prove Guls, and are borne rich, yet dye beggers," &c. It is subscribed T. Deckers, which was probably the printer's, certainly not the author's, mode of spelling his name. On sign. G 2 b. there is a good "song sung by an olde Woman in a Medowe." The tract contains several passages illustrative particularly of the dramatic amusements of the time. One of the author's objects was to ridicule the pretended prophecies of the almanac-makers.

We may here notice an imitation of this tract, published in 1618 by Lawrence Lisle, under the title of "The Owles Almanack," with a woodcut on the title-page of an Owl reading in his study. The tract is by no means without shrewdness and drollery, and, although not by Dekker, has a good deal of his style, but with more method than he gave himself time to observe. On p. 12 it mentions Marston's Play by the title of "the Fawn," Breton's "Pasquills Mad-cap," Dekker's "Bellman of London" and "Lanthorn and Candle-light," with various ephemeral productions and temporary allusions, among others to "Madame Vice, or Olde Iniquity in the Comedy." On the last page (57) the burning of the Globe theatre, and "the plucking down of the Cockpit" are mentioned, with a notice of Kempe's great achievement, "the horrible dance to Norwich," though why that epithet is applied to it is not explained. The whole is introduced by what is headed "The Owles Epistle to the Raven," where "the Raven's Almanacke" is termed "a hotch-potch of calculations." It enumerates many of the signs of shops in Cheapside, such as "the Ram, the Bull, the Crab, Capricorne, &c. only the young wench (called Virgo) would by no meanes sit in any shop in that streete, because so many Gallants lye over the stalls, courting every handsome woman there." It is full of variety, but nobody thought fit to own it.

DEKKER, THOMAS. — Lanthorn and Candle-light, or the Bell-Mans second Nights-walke. In which he brings to light a Brood of more strange Villanies then ever were till this yeare discovered &c. The second edition, newly corrected and amended. — London Printed for John Busby &c. 1609. B. L. 4to. 43 *leaves.*

The success of "The Bell-man of London," 1608, which Dekker published anonymously, induced him to write this second part, to the dedication of which "to Maister Francis Mustian of Peckham" he puts his name, while he also admits the authorship of the first part. This is the second edition of "Lanthorne and Candle-light," but it came out originally in the same year. From an address "To my owne Nation," it is evident that Samuel Rowlands's "Martin Mark-all the Beadle of Bridewell," though dated 1610, had been published before "Lanthorne and Candle-light." "You shall know him," says Dekker, speaking of a rival author whom he calls "a Usurper," "by his habiliments, for (by the furniture he weares) hee will bee taken for *a Beadle of Bridewell.*" No earlier impression than 1610 is, however, known of Rowlands's production.

The work before us is ushered by verses subscribed Io: Da: M. R. and E. G. On sign. F. 4. is a remarkable account of the modes in which poor pamphleteers of the time defrauded the rich out of money for pretended dedications: and after describing some of these tricks, Dekker observes: "Nay, there be other Birdcatchers that use stranger Quaile pipes: you shall have fellowes, four or five in a contry, that buying up any old booke (especially a Sermon, or any other matter of Divinity) that lies for wast paper, and is clean forgotten, add a new printed Epistle to it, and with an alphabet of Letters which they carry about them, being able to print any man's names (for a Dedication) on the suddaine, travaile up and downe most shires in England, and live by this hawking."

In the article on the "Buckler against Death," (p. 96,) it has been seen that Thomas Jordan played exactly this trick with that work. With his own productions he was in the constant habit of using "an alphabet of letters, which he carried about with him," in order to dedicate the same piece to as many separate patrons as would give him money for inserting their names.

Dekker, Thomas. — O per se O, or a New Cryer of Lanthorne and Candle-light. Being an Addition, or Lengthening of the Bell-mans Second Night-walke, &c. — Printed at London for John Busbie &c. 1612. 4to. B. L. 54 *leaves.*

This tract is mainly a reprint of "Lanthorn and Candle-light," 1609, with a repetition of the same woodcut on the title-page; but at the end comes a new division, consisting of fourteen leaves, called "O per se O," not in the former impression. The origin of this title is stated by the author to be a canting song of the beggars; and the tract concludes with another song in similar language, to which, "for the satisfaction of the reader," a translation is annexed. Previous to the year 1648, this production went through no fewer than nine distinct editions, varying only slightly from each other.

Dekker, Thomas. — A Rod for Run-awayes. Gods Tokens of his feareful Judgements, sundry wayes pronounced upon this City and on severall persons both flying from it and staying in it, &c. By Tho. D. — Printed at London for Iohn Trundle &c. 1625. 4to. 16 *leaves.*

This tract was composed by Dekker, who signs the dedication, no doubt in haste, during the plague of 1625, in order to take advantage of a temporary subject. The principal purpose is to censure those who fled from London in order to escape infection. On the title-page is a woodcut of London from the fields, where Death is driving a flock of citizens before him, who are welcomed by the country people with staves and pitchforks. It is one of the scarcest, but certainly one of the least interesting of this voluminous writer's productions.

DEKKER, THOMAS. — The Batchelers Banquet, or a Banquet for Batchelers. Wherein is prepared sundry dainty Dishes to furnish their Tables, curiously drest and seriously served in. Pleasantly discoursing the Variable humours of Women, their quicknesse of Wits and unsearchable Deceits &c. — London, Printed for Robert Bird &c. 1630. B. L. 4to. 39 *leaves.*

This tract has usually been attributed to Dekker, and from internal evidence it may be assigned to him, though it does not bear his name. No dedication is prefixed, and the body of the work commences immediately after the title-page. It professes to give the "humours," or dispositions of women, especially of married women, as a warning to all bachelors, that they may not "get into Lobs pound," by which the author means, obtain wives who will be their ruin or torment. It is divided into fifteen chapters, headed, "The humour of a young wife new married," "The humour of a Woman pranked up in brave apparel," &c., and contains a good deal of various description and narrative, all in prose, and all to the advantage of husbands. It is one of the most amusing and best compounded of Dekker's tracts.

The first edition, or at least the earliest known copy, is dated 1603, and the last 1679, but how often it was reprinted in the interval between those years it is impossible now to ascertain, but it must have been extremely popular, and often *thumbed* out of existence.

DEKKER, THOMAS. — Warres, Warres, Warres. *Arma virumque Cano.*

Into the Field I bring
  Souldiers and Battailes:
Boeth their Fames I sing.

Imprinted at London for J. G. 1628. 12mo. 8 *leaves.*

Only a single copy of this tract appears to be known; but the late Mr. Douce had a fragment of it, consisting of only two pages.

Up to the hour of his death he did not know to what publication they belonged, as he had never had an opportunity of seeing any perfect exemplar, with the name of the author, which happily is the case with that to which we have been indebted.

The dedication is by Tho. Dekker to Hugh Hammersley, Lord Mayor, and to the two Sheriffs of London and Middlesex for the year; in which he states that, as City Poet, he had been employed to write the pageant for Hammersley's Mayoralty, and he seems to have been not a little proud of it. He says, "What I offred up then was a Sacrifice *ex officio.* Custome tooke my Bond for the Performance; and on the day of the Ceremony I hope the debt was fully discharged." If it were ever printed, it has not survived; but that for the next year, 1629, on the Mayoralty of "the Right Honorable James Campebell," by Dekker, is extant, the only perfect copy being in the collection of the Duke of Devonshire. A copy wanting two leaves at the end, the only other known, the late Duke gave to the editor, who had been the means of procuring, at his Grace's no trifling cost, the perfect exemplar for him.

After four lines "To all noble Souldiers," "Warres, Warres, Warres" begins, and here the old dramatic poet could not refrain from deriving a figure from the stage: —

> "Brave Musicke! harke! The ratling Drum beats high,
> And with the scolding Fife deaffens the skye."

The word "scolding," applied to the fife, is not as descriptive as Shakspeare's epithets "wry-necked" and "ear-piercing"; but still the sound has some resemblance to the high accents of female objurgation. Dekker then speaks of the trumpet, and the theatre: —

> "The Brazen Herald in a shrill tone tells
> We shall have Warres (ring out for joy your Bels)
> We shall have Warres! when Kingdoms are at odds,
> Pitch'd Fields those Theaters are, at which the Gods
> Look downe from their high Galleries of Heaven,
> Where Battailes Tragedies are, to which are given
> Plaudits from Cannons: Buskind Actors tread
> Knee deep in blood, and trample on the dead.
> Death the grave theame of which is writ the story;
> Keene swords the pens texting (at large) the glory

> Of Generals, Colonels, Captaines and Commanders,
> With common fighting men (the hardy standers
> Against all hellish horrors) Souldiers all,
> And Fellowes (in that name) to th' General."

Dekker speaks of himself as an old man, and at this date he had been for more than thirty years a popular author of plays, poems, and pamphlets: —

> "For my heart danceth sprightly, when I see
> (Old as I am) our English gallantry."

The Lord Mayor, Hammersley, was at this date, as Dekker tells us, "sole and worthy Colonel of a brave company of Gentlemen in armes," and all the earlier portion of this trifling tract is devoted to a panegyric upon war. The writer proceeds afterwards, as Poet to the City, to praise the Aldermen in succession for their forwardness, and he adds at the end a very labored, if not a very happy, comparison between war and the sun. This is followed by what he calls "Warre his Zodiacke," in twelve short pieces of rather ingenious verse, and the conclusion consists of some vigorous, and doubtless acceptable, applause of the twenty "City Lieutenants."

Dekker seems, as we have elsewhere remarked, always to have been a struggler, and to have generally written on a sort of dinner-demanding emergency. Such was, no doubt, the case here, and as he had a ready pen, the composition of the tract before us could not have occupied as many hours as it takes minutes to read it.

DELONEY, THOMAS. — The Garland of Good Will. Divided into three partes. Containing many pleasant Songs and prety Poems to sundrie new Notes. With a table to finde the names of the Songs. Written by T. D. — Imprinted at London by E. A. for E. White, dwelling at the little North doore of Paules. 1604. 8vo. 64 *leaves.*

The above is the title-page of an edition of this favorite work twenty-seven years anterior to any that is now known. Unluckily it consists of only the first sheet. It was once in the editor's possession bound up with a copy of the second part of the same author's "Gentle Craft," of the date of 1598, (perhaps the earliest impression of that novel,) which he lent, thirty years ago, to a poor printer of the name of Connell, that he might reproduce it, but the original could never be recovered by its owner. The borrower is now dead, and the loan is mentioned for the purpose of identification, should the pieces have found their way into other hands. The oldest edition of Deloney's "Garland of Good Will," hitherto mentioned, is that of 1631, in the Bodleian Library, and that wants sheet G. Our first sheet of the copy of 1604, agreed (excepting in small variations in the title-page, and two or three words, to be specified presently) very exactly with the edition of 1631, which was "Imprinted at London for Robert Bird at the Bible in Saint Lawrence Lane." [1]

Having luckily transcribed the ballad, entitled, in the edition of 1604, "A mowrnfull Dittie of faire Rosamond, King Henry the seconds Concubine," before we lent the fragment; and having before us, besides the version in "Strange Histories," 1607, the impressions of 1662, 1678, and one without date, together with an exact collation of the copy at Oxford, we are able to point out some discrepancies in the text at different dates, which may be interesting to book-antiquaries, and to students of our early popular literature.

1 Deloney's "Garland of Good Will" was in being when T. Nash wrote as follows in his "Have with you" &c. 1596:—"Thomas Deloney, the balleting silke-weaver, hath rime enough for all Myracles, and wit to make *a Garland of Good Will* more than the premisses, with an Epistle of Momus and Zoilus: whereas his Muse, from the first peeping forth, hath stood at livery at an ale-house whispe, never exceeding a penny a quart, day nor night; and this deare yeare, together with the silencing of his looms, scarce that, he being constrained to betake him to carded ale." From hence Nash proceeds to assert that since a particular date Deloney had only published his "jig" of "John for the King," and ballads with the titles of "The Thunderbolt against Swearers"—"Repent England repent," and "The straunge Judgements of God." If these titles were not invented by Nash, none of the ballads have come down to us. By "carded ale" Nash seems to mean to pun upon *corded* ale, or ale obtained by bullads written upon hempen executions.

For "A fair and princely dame" of all other old copies, the edition of 1604 alone reads "*peerlesse* dame," and in the next line *matchlesse* for "peerless."

In the line, "Was known a mortal foe," of the editions of 1662 and 1678, in the copies of 1604 and 1631, the word is "*cruell* foe": it is also *cruell* in "Strange Histories," 1607.

In the line, "Unto a worthy knight," of the copies of 1662, 1678, and n. d., the epithet is *valiant* in the editions of 1604 and 1631, as well as in "Strange Histories," 1607.

Farther on, "For why," (i. e. *wherefore* or *because*, and not an interrogation,) of the copies of 1604, 1607, 1662, 1678, and n. d., is "For *while*" in the edition of 1631 only.

For "I must leave my fairest flower," of the editions of 1604, 1607, and 1631, the copies of 1662, 1678, and n. d. have "*famous* flower."

In the next stanza, Rosamond is called "the lady bright," in the three earlier copies, and "the lady *fair*," in the three later ones.

Again, for the lines, as they stand in 1604, 1607, and 1631,

"Full oft betweene his princely armes
Her corpes he did embrace,"

we have, in all the copies in and after 1662, these words,

"Full oft *within* his princely armes
Her *body* he did embrace."

In the next line but two, "Untill she had receiv'd againe," as we find it in 1604 and 1607, we read in all other impressions, "Untill *he* had *reviv'd* againe."

It would be tedious to carry this minute dissection farther, and we will only state generally, that in subsequent parts of the same ballad "annoy" of the older impressions is altered to *offend* in the more modern — "gallant" is altered to *royal* — "inward" is altered to *very* — "came" is altered to *went* — "lovely cheekes" is altered to *comely face*; and (without adverting to many other variations) at the close of the ballad, the burial-place of Rosamond is changed from "Godstow," as it is given in 1604, 1607, and 1631, to "*Wood-stock*," as it stands in 1662, 1678, and in the undated impression.

Were we to pursue this investigation through the small volume under review, we should, no doubt, meet with many other discordances of text. This course, however, would scarcely be desirable, even if we had been able to consult perfect exemplars of the editions of the " Garland of Good Will," in 1604 and 1631; but as the sheet that was once our own was merely a fragment, and the Bodleian copy wants sixteen entire pages, we have not the means of doing so. Collation of copies dated after the Restoration would only show that the author's language had been more or less corrupted, without at all establishing what he originally wrote.

So popular was this collection of ballads and poems during a century and a half, that, although very few copies of any date are now to be met with, it was so fast multiplied between 1596, when, we apprehend, it first appeared, and 1760, the latest date of any recorded reprint, that it must have gone through at least thirty impressions.

DELONEY, THOMAS.— Strange Histories of Songes and Sonets of Kings, Princes, Dukes, Lordes, Ladyes, Knights and Gentlemen. Very pleasant either to be read or songe: and a most excellent warning for all estates.— Imprinted at London for W. Barley, and are to be sold at his Shop &c. 1607. B. L. 8vo. 40 *leaves.*

This was doubtless a publication by Thomas Deloney, consisting principally of his own ballads, with a few compositions by other writers, whose initials are appended. There was another edition of it in 1612, but only one other copy of this earlier impression is known. What is called " The Table " commences at the back of the title, and includes twelve ballads, and " a speech betwenne certaine Ladyes, being Shepheards on Salisburie plaine," in prose. To these are added, without any list of contents applicable to them, Deloney's well-known ballad of Fair Rosamond; " A Sonnet;" a poem entitled *Sonetta*, with " *Finis* T. R." at the end; " A Maydes Letter," (" *Finis* A. C."); and " A new Dittie in prayse of Money," without any name or initials, containing, with seven others, the following spirited stanzas: —

"Vertue is nothing if Money be wanting:
 Vertue is nothing esteemed or set by.
Wisedome is folly and so accounted,
 If it be joyned with base povertie.
Learning's contemned, wit is condemned,
 Both are derided of rich Miserie.

"He that is wealthy is greatly regarded,
 Though he be never so simple a sot:
He that is needy, he is despised,
 Tho he have wisedome which th' other hath not:
Though he have wisedome (which many wanteth)
 Yet is his credit not worth a grot.

"When thou hast Money, then friendes thou hast many,
 When it is wasted their friendship is cold:
Goe by Jeronimo! no man then will thee know,
 Knowing thou hast neither silver nor gold.
No man will call thee in, no man will set a pin
 For former friendship, though never so old."

"Go by, Jeronimo," was an almost proverbial expression, from Kyd's "Spanish Tragedy," 1599, and instances of its use are innumerable. This poem "in praise of money" is succeeded by "An Epigram," to which "Finis quoth R." is appended, with several other short productions of the same kind, including what are termed four "Wise Sentences." The last two pages are thus headed: — "These Sentences following were set upon Conduits in London against the day that King James came through the Citie at his first comming to the Crowne." The following is the commencement of a poem which follows the ballad of "Fair Rosamond," and is called

"*A Sonnet.*

"All you yong men that faine wolde learne to woe,
And have no meanes nor know not how to doe,
Come you to mee and marke what I shall say,
Which being done, will beare the Wench away.
First, seeme thou wise and deck thy selfe not meanly,
For women they be nice, and love to have men clenly.

"Next, shew thy self that thou hast gone to schoole;
Commende her wit, although she be a foole:
Speake in her prayse, for women they be proud;
Looke what she sayes for troth must be aloude.
If she be sad, seeme thou as sad as shee;
But if that she be glad, then joy with merry glee.

"And in this mood these women must be clawde.
Give her a glasse, a phan, or some such gawde,
Or (if she like) a hood, a capp, or hatt:
Draw to thy purse and straight way give her that.
This being done, in time thou shalt her win,
And when that she is won, let tricks of love begin.

"If at the borde you both sit side by side,
Say to her this — That Jove hath no such bride.
Or if it chaunce you both sit face to face,
Say to her this — Her lookes alone sayes grace.
Such tricks as this use oft to her at meat,
For nought doth better please then doth a good conceit."

The remaining four stanzas are not nearly so good, and turn principally on indecent plays upon words. The following couplet of an Epigram, subscribed "*Finis* quoth R," has survived to our own day: —

"Dull sayes he is so weake he can not rise,
Nor stand nor goe: if that be true, he lyes."

DELONEY, THOMAS. — Thomas of Reading, or the sixe worthie Yeomen of the West. Now the fift time corrected and enlarged by T. D. — London Printed by W. I. for T. P. 1623. B. L. 4to. 38 *leaves.*

Thomas Deloney, the author of this novel, succeeded Elderton as the writer of ballads on every public occasion, when it was thought that such a production would be salable. Elderton ceased to write about the time when Deloney seems to have commenced, namely, 1585 or 1586. Between that date and 1600 his pen was very constantly employed, and he did not omit to avail himself of the excitement occasioned by the Spanish Armada, regarding which he wrote three extant ballads.[1] In the summer of 1596 one of his effusions on the dearth of corn was complained of by the Lord Mayor, who also mentioned his "booke for the Silke-weavers," of which we hear on no other authority (Wright's "Elizabeth and her Times," II. 462). Deloney was himself called "the ballading silk-weaver." "Richard Delonie sonne of Thomas Delonie" was christened at St. Giles, Cripplegate, on the 16th October 1586, and various other members of the same family and name resided in the parish.

There is no doubt that the work before us, which is a prose narrative interspersed with songs, came out prior to 1600, as Kempe, the comic actor at the Globe Theatre, in that year states that Deloney, chronicler of the memorable lives of the "Six Yeomen of the West," "Jack of Newbery," "The Gentle Craft," &c., had written ballads on the subject of his (Kempe's) Morris-dance to Norwich. As two plays founded upon "Thomas of Reading" were written by Day, Hathway, Smith, and Haughton in 1601, (*vide* Hist. of Engl. Dram. Poetry, III. 99,) it is most likely that the novel had been printed only a short time previously. From Kempe's testimony (had we no better) the same date might be

[1] The titles of the three ballads regarding the Armada are these: the first was entered at Stationers' Hall on 10th Aug. 1588, by John Wolfe, but without any mention of the name of the author:—"The Queenes visiting the Campe at Tilsburie with her Entertainment there: To the tune of Wilsons Wilde." The second was entered on the same day, and in the same manner, and the following is its title: "A joyfull Ballad, declaring the happie obtaining of the great Galleazzo, wherein Don Pietro de Valdez was the Chiefe, through the mightie power and providence of God, being a speciall token of his gracious and fatherly goodnes towards us, to the great encouragement of all those that willingly fight in the defence of his Gospell and our good Queene of England: To the tune of Mounseurs Almaigne." The third was entered, also anonymously, by Thomas Orwyn on 31st Aug. 1588, and its title was "A new Ballet of the straunge and most cruell Whippes which the Spanyards had prepared to whippe and torment English men and women; which were found and taken at the Overthrow of certaine of the Spanishe Shippes in July last past, 1588: To the tune of the Valiant Soldiour." The name of the author, Deloney, is only ascertained by his initials T. D. at the end of each broadside.

assigned to "The Gentle Craft," but an edition of it printed in 1598 is known, and it had been entered on the Stationers' Books on the 19th of October, 1597, as "a booke called the gentle Crafte, intreatinge of Shoo-makers."

"Thomas of Reading" was printed in 1612, for the fourth time. The fifth impression, we see, was not issued until 1623, and the sixth came out in 1632. In the edition of 1623 there is no introductory matter, but the story commences immediately after the title-page, and concludes on sign. K 2.

DELONEY, THOMAS. — The pleasant Historie of John Winchcomb, in his yonguer yeares called Jack of Newbery, the famous and worthy Clothier of England; declaring his life and love, together with his charitable deeds and great Hospitalitie &c. Now the tenth time Imprinted, corrected and enlarged by T. D. *Haud curo invidiam.* — London, Printed by H. Lownes, &c. 1626. B. L. 4to. 46 *leaves.*

This production was even more popular than "Thomas of Reading." That work only reached a fifth edition by 1623; but "Jack of Newbery" arrived at the eighth edition by 1619, and at the tenth edition by 1626. It was again printed in 1633. According to Warton (Hist. Engl. Poet. IV. 257, 8vo), it was entered for publication on the books of the Stationers' Company, March the 7th, 1596; but he mistook a year, because 7th March, 1596, was, in fact, 7th March, 1597.

In "Jack of Newbery," as the work before us is usually designated, is inserted the celebrated ballad of "Flodden Field," (Ritson's Ancient Songs, II. 70, ed. 1829,) which is highly appropriate, as John Winchcomb (according to Fuller, in his "Worthies of Berkshire") marched to it at the head of one hundred of his own men. He also feasted King Henry VIII. and Queen Katherine at his house at Newbery. A good deal of moderate poetry is interspersed.

DEMAUNDES JOYOUS. — The Demaũdes Joyous. [Colophon] Emprynted at London in Fletestrete at the signe of the Sonne by me Wynkyn de worde In the yere of our lorde M ccccc and xi. 4to. 4 *leaves.*

Ames, Herbert, and Dibdin never saw a copy of this extraordinarily rare tract — so rare that we doubt if a second exemplar be in existence. Ames copied Palmer, and Herbert Ames, while Dibdin was obliged to content himself with the account in Coles' MSS. (Typ. Ant. II. 165.) There are two figures upon the title-page representing men conversing, one bare-headed, and the other in a sort of doctor's gown: over them is the scroll, "The Demaũdes Joyous." There is no doubt, as Coles remarks, that it is a book addressed to the lower orders, and some portions of it cannot be quoted.

A defective reprint of it was attempted some years ago, from the unique copy belonging to the late Mr. Heber. There are four errors on the first page of it, and even the colophon is not given correctly, for Wynkyn de Worde is represented as carrying on business at the sign of the *Swan*, when everybody knows that his house bore the sign of the Sun. We may make a few unobjectionable citations from the original, which will remind the reader of Nicholas Breton's "Cross Answers," of which we have spoken on p. 13.

"*Demaunde.* What space is from ye hyest space of the se, to the depest? [Answer] But a stones cast. [D.] How many calues tayles behoueth to reche frome the erthe to the skye. [A.] No more but one if it be longe ynough. [D.] Whiche is the brodest water and leest jeoperdye to passe over. [A.] The dew. [D.] Why driue men dogges out of the chyrche. [A.] Bycause they come not vp and offre. [D.] What almes is worst bestowed that men giue. [A.] That is to a blynde man, for as he hathe ony thynge gyuen hym, he wolde with good wyll se hym hanged by the necke that gaue it hym. [D.] Wherfore be there not as many women conteyned in ye daunce of poules as there be men. [A.] Bycause a woman is so ferefull of herte, that she had leuer daunce amonge quicke folke than deed."

This of course refers to the famous painting of the "Dance of Death" in old St. Paul's, regarding which see Douce's work on the "Dance of Macaber," 8vo, 1833, p. 51, or Stow's "Survey," edition of 1599, p. 264. We make another brief quotation: —

"[D.] What was he that slewe the fourth parte of the worlde. [A.] Cayne when he slewe his broder abell, in the whiche tyme was but foure persones in the worlde. [D.] What man is he that geteth his lyvinge bacwarde. [A.] That is rope maker. [D.] What people be they that geteth theyr lyuynge most merylyest. [A.] They be prestes and fullers, for one syngeth, and the other daunceth."

Several of the questions and answers, as we have already stated, cannot in our day be repeated, but others have considerable and harmless humor, as for instance where the demand is "Why dooth a dogge tourne hym thryes aboute, or that he lyeth hym downe?" and the reply is "Bycause he knoweth not his beddes hede frome the fete." It is a curious popular relic, and well merits preservation; but in the reprint of it there are about fifty variations from the original, to which we have been fortunately able to resort.

The device of the printer fills the last page; but Cole, in quoting only the colophon, misrepresents the spelling of Wynkyn de Worde, though he does not go so far as to state that the old typographer carried on business "at the sygne of the *swane*," instead of the "sonne." That was a discovery made by the editor of the modern impression.

DICKENSON, JOHN. — Greene in Conceipt. New raised from his grave to write the Tragique Historie of faire Valeria of London. Wherein is truly discovered the rare and lamentable issue of a Husbands dotage, a wives leudnesse and childrens disobedience. Received and reported by I. D. *Veritas non quærit angulos, umbra gaudet.* — Printed at London by Richard Bradocke for William Jones, dwelling at the signe of the Gunne neare Holborne conduit. 1598. 4to. B. L. 67 *leaves.*

On the title-page is a woodcut representing Robert Greene, sitting at a table in his shroud, writing. The object of the author of "Greene in Conceipt" was to connect his pamphlet with the popular name of the writer of so many successful publications;

but in the dedication, signed John Dickenson, "to my deare friend Thomas White, of Corffe in Dorsetshire," he, with great emphasis, denies that he was an imitator of Greene, and yet nearly every page proves him to have copied his prototype. Dickenson in 1594 had printed "Arisbas: Euphues amidst his slumbers, or Cupids Journey to Hell," a title that sufficiently indicates the source of his inspiration; and here he promises his friend and schoolfellow, White, that he would in due time pen something better than "Greene in Conceipt," which he terms one of his "youth's follies."

In "an Advertisement to the Reader," the author tells him that he fell asleep while perusing Lucian's "Timon," and dreamed that he saw before him "the shape of a well proportioned man, suted in deaths livery," who said to him: — "I am he whose pen was first employed in the advancement of vanitie, and afterward in the discovering of villanie;" and after quoting his motto, *omne tulit punctum qui miscuit utile dulci*, Greene proceeds "boldly to affirm that my later labours have made a large part of amends for those former vanities." He then informs Dickenson that, by the aid of Mercury, he had come from Elysium in order to write the story of a female ghost he had seen; of whom he remarks, "I knew who she was, and remembred when she dyed: she lived at London in florishing estate, and as lewde a dame as anye in that Citye." Greene is only allowed by Mercury an hour to begin the novel, and he leaves the conclusion of it to Dickenson. The latter pleads incompetency, but Greene's ghost would listen to no excuse, and having dreamed out the conclusion of the tale, Dickenson awoke and wrote it down.

The prose, as we have stated, is an imitation of Greene; but the verse, if not better, is as good as any Greene himself wrote. Valeria is married to an old man named Geraldo, to whom she is unfaithful, indulging in every species of pleasure. The following is the beginning of a "Canzon," which she sings to her lute: —

"Happie lot to men assign'd,
Hartes with hartes in love combinde!
Love, the soule of earthly sweetes
When with mutuall love it meets;
Not consisting all in lookes

Like to idols, lay-mens bookes,
But who tries this true shall prove,
Action is the life of love.
Why slacke we, then, to bath in sweet delight,
Before our day be turn'd to endlesse night?

"Fairest things to nothing fade
Wrapt in deaths eternall shade:
Hence I prove it beauties crime
Not to reape the fruits of time:
Time which passeth swift as thought,
Time whose blisse is dearely bought,
Dearely bought so soone to faile us,
Soone, that should so long availe us.
Why slacke we, then, to bath in sweete delight,
Before our daye be turn'd to endlesse night?"

If not very original in thought, the wording is extremely harmonious, and the same praise may be given to another song, celebrating Valeria's birthday, by one of her illicit lovers: —

"Let others use what Calenders they please,
And celebrate their common holidayes,
My rules of time, my times of joy and ease,
Shall in my zeale blaze thy perfection's praise.
Their names and worth they from thy worth shall take,
And highly all be honoured for thy sake. * * *

"Haile, happy day! to whome the world doth owe
The blissefull issue of that influence,
Which from the force of best aspects did growe,
In luckiest house of heaven's circumference.
Haile, happy daie! that first did shewe this aire
To her whom Fairenes selfe doth yield more faire! * * *

"Such and so long may be to me her love,
As Ile this vow religiously maintaine:
So may my plaints her heart to pittie moove,
As from my heart I speake! let false hearts faine.
Haile, happie day! but, then, how happie shee,
Who makes this day thus happy unto me!"

But Dickenson is not satisfied with trying his hand at ordinary lyrical measures: he attempts some English hexameters; and however ill-suited to our language we may consider such verses, then somewhat fashionable by the examples of Sidney, Spenser, Dyer, Fraunce, and others, we cannot deny that Dickenson writes them quite as well as his rivals, with this additional merit, that he does not require us to sacrifice accent, which is the rule in English, to any fancied conformity to the quantities of Greek and Latin : *e. g.*,

"As when a wave-bruis'd barke, long tost by winds in a tempest,
Straies on a forraine coast, in danger still to be swallow'd,
After a world of feares, with a winter of horrible objects,
Heaven in a weeke of nights obscurd, day turn'd to be darknes,
The shipman's solace, faier Ledas twinnes, at an instant,
Signes of a calme, are seene, and seene are shrilly saluted:
So to my drooping thoughts, when sorrow most doth await me,
Your subduing lookes, in fayrenesse first of a thousand,
(Staine to the brightest star that gildes the roofe of Olympus)
Calm'd with a kind aspect, vouchsafe large hopes to releve me."

Here, with the exception of "subduing," there is no word to which any other than the ordinary modern pronunciation need be given for the sake of the measure; and even as to "subduing," the emphasis in Dickenson's day was frequently laid upon the first syllable.

Of the story of Valeria we really need say no more than that it is an example of the misery to which vice ultimately leads; for the once beautiful Valeria dies wretchedly, after having been succored and supported by one of her own servants. This copy is the only one we ever happen to have heard of.

Dobson, George. — Dobsons Drie Bobbes: Sonne and Heire to Scoggin. — London Printed by Valentine Simmes. 1607. 4to. B. L.

In bibliographical catalogues the date of 1610 is given to this work: it is an error, for both the known copies are dated 1607.[1] In an address "To the Reader," without name or initials, we are assured "that it is no forraine translation, but a home-bred sub-

[1] Mr. Bohn, in his second edition of the Bibl. Man. p. 654, incautiously followed the statement of Lowndes in the first edition.

ject, nor doth he (the writer) desire any other than his patrimony, which is, as being the eldest sonne of Skoggin, to be esteemed for no changeling." At the end we are told that the old joker is no other than George Dobson, "whose pleasant meriments are worthy to be registred among the famous recordes of the jeasting Worthies: yea, he hath proceeded farther in degree than Garagantua, Howleglasse, Tiell, Skoggin, olde Hobson or Code."

We may either suppose that "Tiell" is a misprint for Peele, whose jests were published soon after his decease in 1596, or that the confusion in the old printer's mind arose out of the fact that the other name of Howleglasse was Till: possibly, Howleglasse and Tiell changed places, and that we ought to read Tiell Howleglasse. "A mery Jeste of Howleglas" was printed by W. Copland. "Scoggin's Jests" were also in print long before the date of any edition that has reached our day. Hobson's Jests came out in 1607, but regarding Code we can give no information. "Dobson's Dry Bobs" is merely a collection of low, stupid, and often coarse jokes, not a few of them of long-established reputation, but fathered as infants upon George Dobson, for the sake of filling the volume.

Dove and Serpent. — The Dove and the Serpent. In which is conteined a large description of all such points and principles as tend either to Conversation or Negotiation. *Tuta velis; Tutus eris.* — London Printed by T. C. for Laurence L'isle, dwelling at the Tygres head in S. Pauls Church-yard. 1614. 4to. 50 *leaves.*

The "subjects" of the fifteen chapters into which this rather dull, but not prosy (for a good deal of translated verse is intermixed) work is divided, follow the title-page. The dedication to Sir Henry Mountagu, Knight, Recorder of London, is subscribed D. T., which some have taken for the initials of Thomas Dekker reversed. This is not the case. Our old poet, dramatist, and pamphleteer never transposed his initials, and could not have put together anything so commonplace. On the other hand, we may be pretty sure that D. T. was the same author who in 1608 and 1609 had published two small volumes of "Essayes politicke and morall," and "Essayes morall and theologicall." He was a man well read in classical authors, whom he quotes freely both in Greek and Latin, and some of his versified translations from Horace, Juvenal, Virgil, &c. are not amiss; but his own observations have no originality, and his style is wearisome. He once (p. 91) quotes four lines from Spenser's "Faery Queene," (B. I. C. 12, st. 42,) but without any accompanying praise, and merely by way of illustration of what he means by a tropical expression. Spenser is, however, the only English poet whom he condescends to mention; and on a single other occasion he refers to a topic of the time, when (p. 31) he blames the corruptions that prevail in "Great Britaines Court," by which "the prince's breath" is sold to "poore needy suppliants" at an excessive rate. As a specimen of some little skill in rendering the language of others into his own, we may extract his version of Martiall's well-known epigram, *Vitam quæ faciunt beatiorem, &c.*, and we will follow it by a similar effort by Ben Jonson, which has never been printed with his works, but which we met with in his own hand-writing at Dulwich. D. T. gives it thus: —

"The things that make man's life more happie seeme
Are these, delightfull Martiall, as I deeme.
Wealth not by labour got, but left by will;
A fruitfull field, a fier burning still;
Meane clothes, no strife the mindes rest to confound;
Indifferent strength, a body firme and sound;
Warie Simplicitie and equall friends;
An easie Diet, which no art commends;
The night not drunke, yet loose and free from care;
The bed not sad, though chaste beyond compare;
Sleepe which may make the longest darkes but short,
(Never disturbd with thoughts of worldly sort.)
Be still well-pleas'd to be that which thou art,
And let thy choyce affect no greater part:
Feare not the day which must thy life up-summe,
Nor wish the same before the time doe come."

We now subjoin, from his own MS.,[1] the terse and nervous manner in which Ben Jonson gives it: —

"The things that make the happier life are these,
Most pleasant Martial: Substance got with ease,
Not labour'd for, but left thee by thy Sire;
A soyle not barren; a continuall fire;
Never at law; seldome in office gownd;
A quiet mind, free powers, and body sound;
A wise simplicity; friends alike stated;
Thy table without art, and easy rated:
Thy night not dronken, but from cares layd wast;
No soure or sollen bed-mate, yet a chast;
Sleepe that will make the darkest houres swift-pac't;
Will to be what thou art, and nothing more;
Nor feare thy latest day, nor wish therefore."

D. T. supplies for comparison the words of the original, which Ben Jonson in many respects has so well imitated. His most defective line certainly is, *Nox non ebria, sed soluta curis*, in which D. T., we venture to think, has succeeded at least as well as our great master of Roman English. The amplifications of D. T. are detestable, and worst of all his gratuitous and superfluous parenthesis, —

"Never disturbd with thoughts of worldly sort."

DRAYTON, MICHAEL. — Idea. The Shepheards Garland. Fashioned in nine Eglogs. Rowlands Sacrifice to the nine Muses. *Effugiunt auidos Carmina sola rogos.* — Imprinted at London for Thomas Woodcocke, dwelling in Pauls Churchyarde, at the signe of the black Beare. 1593. 4to. 37 *leaves.*

This is Drayton's second known work, his "Harmonie of the Church" (printed in 1591 and 1610) being his first. Throughout he calls his mistress by the name of Idea; and from this publication he derived his own poetical appellation of Rowland, by which he was afterwards known and spoken of among his contempora-

[1] See also "Memoirs of Edward Alleyn," 8vo, 1841, p. 54.

ries. This edition deserves especial remark, because the work subsequently underwent numerous and important changes, and more especially because it contains several poems that were never reprinted by the author. One of these is an elegy, as it may be called, upon the death of Sir Philip Sidney, whom Drayton celebrates as Elphin. It is to be observed also, that in posterior impressions the arguments preceding the eclogues, and the mottos by which they are concluded, were omitted.

The dedication "to the noble and valerous gentleman, Master Robert Dudley," is subscribed Michael Drayton, but in the body of the work he never mentions himself but by his assumed and favorite name, sometimes only Rowland, or "little Rowland," and at others "Rowland of the Rock."

It is impossible to give an adequate notion of the many alterations subsequently introduced; but here and there they are so extensive as to give the whole pastoral an appearance of novelty. One of the most striking of these is "the sixt Eglog," where Drayton introduced some very high-flown praises of the Countess of Pembroke; among other things, speaking of her as a bird: —

"Delicious Larke, sweete musick of the morrow,
Cleere bell of Rhetoricke, ringing peales of love;
Joy of the Angels, sent us from above,
Enchanting Syren, charmer of all sorrow,
The loftie subiect [of] a heavenly tale,
Thames fairest Swanne, our summers Nightingale."

The word "of" is inserted in MS. by an old hand, and it was evidently omitted by error of the press. The same blunder occurs afterwards and is similarly corrected. There are several mentions of Spenser in the eclogues, by his assumed and well-known name of Colin: —

"And I to thee will be as kinde,
As Colin was to Rosalinde," &c.

It may be noticed that in the stanza we have just quoted, in praise of "Sidney's sister," Drayton adopts an expression Spenser had applied to Sir Walter Raleigh in 1590, in the sonnet to him appended to the first three books of "The Fairy Queen."

"To thee that art the summer's nightingale!"

The poem, contained in Drayton's fourth Eclogue, upon the loss of Sidney, which for some reason was not reprinted by the author in subsequent editions of his works, may be here fitly quoted at length : —

"Melpomine, put on thy mourning Gaberdine,
And set thy song unto the dolefull Base,
And with thy sable vayle shadow thy face:
with weeping verse
attend his hearse,
Whose blessed soule the heavens doe now enshrine.

"Come, Nymphs, and with your Rebecks ring his knell;
Warble forth your wamenting harmony;
And at his drery fatall obsequie
with Cypres bowes
maske your fayre Browes,
And beat your breasts to chyme his burying peale.

"Thy birth-day was to all our ioye the even,
And on thy death this dolefull song we sing:
Sweet Child of Pan, and the Castalian spring!
unto our endles mone
from us why art thou gone,
To fill up that sweete Angels quier in heaven?

"O, whylome thou thy lasses dearest love,
When with greene Lawrell she hath crowned thee,
Immortall mirror of all Poesie,
the Muses treasure,
the Graces pleasure,
Reigning with Angels now in heaven above.

"Our mirth is now depriv'd of all her glory;
Our Taburins in dolefull dumps are drownd;
Our viols want their sweet and pleasing sound:
our melodie is mar'd,
and we of ioyes debard:
Oh wicked world, so mutable and transitory!

"O dismall day, bereaver of delight!
O stormy winter, sourse of all our sorrow!
ô most untimely and eclipsed morrow,
to rob us quite
of all delight,
Darkening that starre which ever shone so bright!

"Oh Elphin, Elphin! Though thou hence be gone,
In spight of death yet shalt thou live for aye:
Thy Poesie is garlanded with Baye,
and still shall blaze
thy lasting prayse,
Whose losse poore shepherds ever shall bemone.

"Come, Girles, and with Carnations decke his grave,
With damaske Roses and the hyacynt;
Come with sweete Williams, Marjoram and Mynt,
with precious Balmes,
with hymnes and psalmes;
His funerall deserves no lesse at all to have.

"But see where Elphin sits in fayre Elizia,
Feeding his flocke on yonder heavenly playne;
Come and behold yon lovely shepheards swayne
piping his fill
on yonder hill,
Tasting sweete Nectar and Ambrosia."

In the eclogue, as he afterwards printed it, Drayton gave his lamentation for the untimely death of Sidney a totally different form. The above can hardly be the epitaph on Sidney spoken of by N. Baxter in "Ourania," 1606. (See p. 76.)

The encomium on Queen Elizabeth under the name of Beta, in the third eclogue, is much the same in the earlier and later impressions. The song in praise of his mistress, in the second eclogue, was not repeated after 1593, but another substituted; and the same may be said of the "doleful elegy" imputed, just afterwards, by Winken to Rowland. Rowland's description of "Idea," in the fifth eclogue, is nearly all new; and Borrill's denunciation of love, in the seventh eclogue, has little more than the termination of the same in subsequent editions. In early life Drayton was not so particular in the exactness of his rhymes as he had become when he republished his pastorals. Take for instance the following stanza in Eclogue VIII.

"The infant age could deftly carroll love,
till greedy thirst of that ambitious honor
Drew Poets pen from his sweete lasses glove,
to chaunt of slaughtering broiles and bloody horror."

The author subsequently made it stand thus : —

" That simple age as simple sung of love,
  Till thirst of empire and of earthly sways
Drew the good shepherd from his lasses glove,
  To sing of slaughter and tumultuous frays."

Many proofs to the same effect might be found in these pastorals. The tale of Dowsabell and the Shepherd, in the eighth eclogue, underwent little or no change.

The copy we have here used has the autograph of Robert Earl of Essex, Queen Elizabeth's beheaded favorite, upon the title-page. We dare not impute to him various MS. alterations, but they are most of them singularly judicious. For instance, in one place Drayton mentions Chaucer, —

" Or else some Romaunt unto us areed
  Which good old Geffrey taught thee in thy youth."

Here Geffrey is misprinted *Godfrey*, but altered to Geffrey in a handwriting of the time. Again, in Drayton's song in praise of Beta (*i. e.* Queen Elizabeth), we meet with this couplet : —

" And tune the taber and the pipe to the sweet violons,
And move the thunder in the ayre with lowdest clarions."

Here " move " ought probably to be *mocke*, and to that word it is amended in MS.

We never saw more than two copies of Drayton's " Shepheards Garland," 4to, 1593 ; one that belonged to the late Mr. Heber, and the other the exemplar we have employed.

Drayton, Michael. — Endimion and Phœbe. Ideas Latmus. *Phœbus erit nostri princeps, et carminis Author.* — At London, Printed by James Roberts for John Busbie. n. d. 4to. 25 *leaves.*

This is a production which Drayton thought fit wholly to suppress ; for the few lines he inserted from it in his " Man in the Moon," some years afterwards, cannot be said to contradict the general statement, that after the first appearance of " Endimion and Phœbe," he never acknowledged it as one of his works.

He dedicated it in a sonnet, subscribed with his name at length, "To the excellent and most accomplisht Ladie, Lucie Countesse of Bedford;" and although he rejected the poem it introduced, he did not suppress this sonnet, which appeared among the pieces he collected and printed in 1605. At the back of the sonnet is a laudatory effusion of the same kind with the initials E. P., (which we cannot satisfactorily assign,) and there Drayton is addressed by his poetical name of Rowland. It begins —

"Rouland, when first I read thy stately rymes
 In Sheepheards weedes, when yet thou liv'dst unknown,
Not seene in publique in those former tymes,
 But unto Ankor tund'st thy Pype alone,
I then beheld thy chaste Ideas fame," &c.,

clearly referring to his "Idea. The Shepheards Garland," of 1593. The poem before us has no date, but it must have been printed in 1594, because it is not only alluded to, but quoted by Thomas Lodge in his "Fig for Momus," which came out in 1595.

The sonnet by E. P. is succeeded by one entitled "To Idea," to which the initials S. G. are appended; and there is no writer of that period to whom they can be appropriated but Stephen Gosson, who continued a miscellaneous poet until 1595 and 1596, and who may then have been one of Drayton's admirers. S. G. says of Drayton,

"Borne to create good thoughts by thy rare woorth,
 Whom Nature with her bounteous store doth blesse,
More excellent then Art can set thee forth,
 Happy in more then praises can expresse."

The body of the poem, which is in couplets, (like Marlow's "Hero and Leander," written probably before Drayton began to print, although not published until 1598,) commences on the next leaf, marked with the signature B, thus: —

"In *I-onia* whence sprang old Poets fame,
From whom that Sea did first derive her name,
The blessed bed whereon the Muses lay,
Beauty of *Greece*, the pride of *Asia;*
Whence *Archelaus*, whom times historifie,
First unto *Athens* brought Phylosophie;
In this faire Region, on a goodly Plaine,

Stretching her bounds unto the bordring Maine,
The Mountaine *Latmus* over-lookes the Sea," &c.

We soon arrive at a passage which Drayton would, perhaps, never have written, had not Spenser printed something even better in Canto 12 of Book II. of his "Fairy Queen," st. 70 and 71. Drayton's lines are beautiful, and refer to the various songs of the birds: —

"The Nightingale, woods Herauld of the Spring,
The whistling Woosell, Mavis carroling,
Tuning theyr trebbles to the waters fall,
Which made the musicque more angelicall;
Whilst gentle *Zephyre* murmuring among
Kept tyme, and bare the burthen to the song."

It is quite needless to follow the story in which, in general, Drayton more imitates the style of Marlow than of Spenser. He seems, almost expressly, to avoid anything like a resemblance to Shakspeare, whose "Venus and Adonis," it will be remembered, had come out in stanzas in the preceding year, and whose "Lucrece," also in stanzas though of a different form, was printed in the same year as Drayton's "Endimion and Phœbe."[1] The following begins an account of a meeting between the two: —

"And comming now to her Endimion,
Whom heavy sleepe had lately ceas'd upon,

[1] In the edition of Shakspeare (Whittaker and Co. 1858), Vol. VI. p. 525, a mistake is committed, where it is said that Drayton, after the original impression of his "Legend of Matilda" in 1594, left out a stanza in which express reference was made, and praise given, to Shakspeare's "Lucrece," also published in 1594. The fact is that Drayton did not omit the stanza until after 1596, and two years, in a question of the kind, are highly important. The edition of 1596 bears the following title, and we will add to it the three stanzas as they are there given, which clearly allude to Daniel, Shakspeare, Churchyard, and Lodge: —

"The Tragicall Legend of Robert Duke of Normandy, surnamed Shortthigh, eldest sonne to William Conqueror, with the Legend of Matilda the chast, daughter to the Lord Robert Fitzwater, poysoned by King John. And the Legend of Piers Gaveston, the great Earle of Cornwall, and mighty favourite of King Edward the second. By Michaell Drayton. The latter two by him newly corrected and augmented. — At London, Printed by Ja. Roberts for N. L. and are to be solde at his shop at the West doore of Paules. 1596." 4to.

The stanzas, as they originally appeared in 1594, are thus repeated

Kneeling her downe, him in her arms she clips,
And with sweet kisses sealeth up his lips,
Whilst from her eyes teares, streaming downe in showrs,
Fell on his cheekes like dew upon the flowrs,
In globy circles like pure drops of Milk
Sprinckled on Roses, or fine crimson silk.
Touching his brow, this is the seate (quoth she)
Where Beauty sits in all her Maiestie!
She calls his eye-lids those pure christall covers,
Which do include the looking glasse of Lovers:
She calls his lips the sweet delicious folds
Which rare perfume and precious incense holds:
She calls his soft smooth Allablaster skin
The Lawne which Angels are attyred in."

---

in 1596: the first praises Daniel, the second Shakspeare, and the third Churchyard and Lodge:—

" Faire Rosamond, of all so highly graced,
Recorded in the lasting booke of Fame,
And in our Sainted Legendarie placed
By him who strives to stellifie her name;
Yet will some Matrons say shee was to blame,
Though all the world bewitched with his rime,
Yet all his skill cannot excuse her crime.

" Lucrece of whom proud Rome hath bosted long,
Lately reviv'd to live another age,
And here arriv'd to tell of Tarquins wrong,
Her chast deniall and the Tyrants rage,
Acting her passions on our stately stage,
Shee is remembred, all forgetting mee;
Yet I as faire and chast as ere was shee.

" Shores Wife is in her wanton humor sooth'd,
And modern Poets still applaud her praise;
Our famous Elstreds wrinckled brows are smooth'd,
Call'd from her grave to see these latter dayes;
And happy's hee their glory high'st can raise.
Thus looser wantons still are prais'd of many:
Vice oft findes friends, but vertue seldom any."

Therefore, if any quarrel ever occurred between Drayton and Shakspeare, which led the former afterwards to omit the stanza upon "Lucrece," it is probable that it did not happen until subsequent to 1596. We are the more anxious to set this matter right, because the question arose out of our original error in 1843. See the edition of Shakspeare's Works in that year, Vol. VIII. p. 411.

We have already stated that Lodge in his "Fig for Momus," 1595, expressly cites "Endimion and Phœbe"; and the Epistle where he does so is addressed "to Master Michael Drayton," whom he has also called Rowland in an Eclogue between Wagrin and Golde, — Golde being only the letters of Lodge transposed. The most interesting part of "Endimion and Phœbe," on some accounts is the latter end, where Drayton bestows high praise upon Lodge, by the name of Goldey, upon Spenser, by the name of Collin, and upon Daniel, by reference to his "Delia." It may be thought somewhat singular that he does not speak of Shakspeare; but he also omits Marlow, who was then recently dead, and of whose "Hero and Leander" Drayton's effusion most reminds us. His address to Spenser, Daniel, and Lodge runs thus: —

"Dear Collin, let my Muse excused be,
Which rudely thus presumes to sing by thee,
Although her straines be harsh untun'd and ill,
Nor can attayne to thy divinest skill.

"And thou, the sweet Museus of these times,
Pardon my rugged and unfiled rymes,
Whose scarce invention is too meane and base,
When Delias glorious Muse dooth come in place.

"And thou, my Goldey, which in Sommer dayes
Hast feasted us with merry roundelayes;
And, when my Muse scarce able was to flye,
Didst imp her wings with thy sweete Poesie."

The last line would indicate that Lodge, being an older poet than Drayton, had lent him some assistance by imping, or mending, the wings of his poesy. Lodge was certainly a writer ten years before we hear of Drayton, and perhaps the latter was indebted to the former for improvements introduced into his "Harmony of the Church," 1591, or into his "Idea. The Shepherds Garland," 1593. Daniel, who is referred to in the preceding quatorzain, had (as we have seen, p. 210) published his "Delia," with great applause, in 1592. Spenser's Pastorals had been before the world about fifteen years, and the first portion of his "Fairy Queen" about four years.

But a single perfect copy of Drayton's "Endimion and Phœbe"

remains to us; but an exemplar, wanting the title-page, has been long in the possession of the editor. It is said in Lowndes's Bibl. Man. edit. 1858, p. 672, that "a unique copy is in the Bridgewater Collection": this is a mistake. The error arose out of the fact that the editor of the "Bridgewater Catalogue," 4to, 1837, mentioned "Endimion and Phœbe" only by way of illustration. The only copy he then knew of was his own, wanting the title-page; but he has since discovered another, which is quite perfect. Various works are, in the same manner, mentioned in the Bridgewater Catalogue which were not, and are not, in the Earl of Ellesmere's library.

DRAYTON, MICHAEL. — The Owle. By Michaell Drayton Esquire. *Noctuas Athenas.* — London Printed by E. A. for E. White and N. Ling, &c. 1604. 4to. 27 *leaves.*

The author states, in an address "to the Reader," that "this small poem was lastly finished," almost a year before it was printed, and that it was postponed to his gratulatory effusion on the arrival of King James. He dedicated it in a sonnet to his "most esteemed patron Sir Walter Aston, Knight," and there refers to his "Barons Wars," which had already been about ten years in type. For some reason not explained, "The Owl" was not included in the collection of Drayton's works which he published in 8vo, 1605, but it was inserted in the folio of 1619, and in all subsequent impressions.

It appears by Sir David Murray's account of the Privy Purse expenses of Prince Henry, preserved in the Audit Office, that Drayton was an annuitant to the extent of £10 a year. The document applies to two years, and Joshua Sylvester's annuity of £20 is entered for both years, while Drayton's is only for one year. Perhaps his name had only been recently placed upon the list.

On the title-page of "The Owl" is a woodcut representing that bird surrounded by "chattering pyes." It is from end to end a satirical apologue, and passages might easily be pointed out that possibly gave offence. That it was popular we need not doubt; and it is twice spoken of by N. Baxter, in his "Ourania," 1606, (see p. 76,) as "Madge Howlet's Tale."

> "And every Stationer hath now to sale
> Pappe with a Hatchet and Madge Howlet's Tale."

And again afterwards, —

> "Learned Drayton hath told Madgehowlet's Tale
> In covert verse of sweetest madrigale."

It certainly is "covert verse," but in ten-syllable couplets, without any lyrics such as madrigals were usually composed in.

DRAYTON, MICHAEL. — The Legend of the Great Cromwel. By Michael Drayton Esquier. — At London Printed by Felix Kyngston and are to be sold by I. Flasket &c. 1607. 4to. 25 *leaves.*

This fine poem is gratefully inscribed by its author "to the deserving memorie of my worthy Patron, Sir Walter Aston, Knight"; and the dedication is followed by two pages of notes, which Drayton states ought to have been placed in the margin, had not the type, without his knowledge, been chosen too large. The last of these notes deserves remark: "The 34. page the 1. stanza, *Pierce the wise Plowman* &c. The morall of Contrition and the Frier, the matter of which is Pierce Plowmans in his vision, the workmanship therof wholly mine owne, containing about 10. stanzas." It is in fact substantially taken, necessarily with much alteration and considerable improvement, from *Passus Vicesimus* of "Pierce Plowman's Vision," and Drayton has introduced it with great ingenuity and good effect. All the rest is the poet's sole composition, the incidents being adopted from the history of Cromwell, Earl of Essex, who is made to narrate his own life in the same manner as the heroes of "The Mirror for Magistrates." Prefixed to the "Legend" are commendatory lines by I. Cooke, Henry Lucas, and Christopher Brooke.

DRAYTON, MICHAEL. — Poems by Michael Drayton Esquyer. Collected into one Volume. With sondry Peeces inserted never before imprinted. — London printed for John Smethwick. 1619. fol. 247 *leaves.*

There is no date on the general engraved title-page of the volume, but each division has a separate printed title, and all are dated 1619, the year when the collected impression of Drayton's poems made its appearance. Nevertheless, it does not contain all that Drayton had previously published, as he never reprinted the whole of his "Idea's Mirror," 4to, 1594, (a collection of love sonnets,) nor any part of his "Phœbe and Endymion," excepting the few lines inserted in "The Man in the Moon," which is the last piece in the volume before us. There is little doubt that it was printed under the supervision of Drayton.[1]

[1] We may here insert a copy of the title-page of the unique volume:— "Ideas Mirrour. Amours in Quatorzains. *Che serve é tace assai domanda.* — At London, Printed by James Roberts for Nicholas Linge. Anno. 1594." 4to. It consists of 51 sonnets, some of which were afterwards reprinted by Drayton, but many of them never again saw the light. The second line of the following dedicatory sonnet to Anthony Cooke, Esq., shows that the pieces included in the volume had been written some time:—

"Vouchsafe to grace these rude unpolish'd rymes,
Which long, dear friend, have slept in sable night,
And, come abroad now in these glorious tymes,
Can hardly brooke the purenes of the light.
But sith you see their destiny is such,
That in the world theyr fortune they must try,
Perhaps they better shall abide the tuch,
Wearing your name, theyr gracious livery.
Yet these mine owne: I wrong not other men,
Nor trafique further then thys happy clyme;
Nor filch from Portes, nor from Petrarchs pen,
A fault too common in thys latter tyme.
Divine Syr Phillip! I avouch thy writ,
I am no pickpurse of anothers wit."

The last line is Sidney's in one of his sonnets in "Astrophel and Stella." It is not so clear to whom Drayton alludes when he says that they had "filched" from Desportes and Petrarch. Spenser had printed sonnets avowedly from Petrarch and Bellay. We subjoin Drayton's last sonnet

DRAYTON, MICHAEL. — The Battaile of Agincourt. Fought by Henry the fift of that name, King of England &c. The Miseries of Queene Margarite &c. Nimphidia, the Court of Fayrie. The Quest of Cinthia. The Shepheards Sirena. The Moone-Calfe. Elegies upon sundry occasions. By Michaell Drayton Esquire. — London, Printed for William Lee &c. 1627. fol. 116 *leaves.*

A portrait of the author by William Hole follows the title-page, and facing it is Drayton's Dedication "to the gentlemen of England." "The Vision of Ben Jonson on the Muses of his friend M. Drayton" introduces other complimentary poems by I. Vaughan and John Reynolds, related perhaps to the Henry Reynolds to whom Drayton addressed his Epistle "Of Poets and Poesy." What are called "Elegies upon Sundry Occasions," which close the volume, are in fact, with a few exceptions, merely epistles. Only five can be termed "elegies," in the common acceptation of the word.

DROUT, JOHN. — The pityfull Historie of two louing Italians, Gaulfrido and Barnardo le vayne: which ariued in

in this "Amours in Quatorzains," chiefly because he ever afterwards excluded it from his collected works: —

> "Go you, my lynes, Embassadors of love,
> With my harts trybute to her conquering eyes,
> From whence if you one teare of pitty move
> For all my woes, that onely shall suffise.
> When you Minerva in the sunne behold,
> At her perfections stand you then and gaze,
> Where in the compasse of a Marygold,
> Meridianis sits within a maze.
> And let Invention of her beauty vaunt
> When Dorus sings his sweet Pamelas love,
> And tell the Gods Mars is predominant,
> Seated with Sol, and weares Minervas glove:
> And tell the world that in the world there is
> A heaven on earth, on earth no heaven but this."

This is not now very intelligible; but, of course, Dorus and Pamela are two of the characters in Sidney's "Arcadia."

the countrey of Grece, in the time of the noble Emperoure Vaspasian. And translated out of Italian into Englishe meeter by Ihon Drout, of Thauis Inne Gentleman. *Anno* 1570. — Imprinted at London by Henry Binneman, dwelling in Knightrider streete, at the signe of the Mermayde. 8vo. B. L. 32 *leaves.*

This is a new, and not very euphonious, name to be added to the list of our early English versifiers. The poem has only comparatively recently been discovered, and it has not been noticed by any bibliographer. Malone, in a note upon "Romeo and Juliet," (Shaksp. by Bosw. VI. 4,) speaks of the entry of it at Stationers' Hall in 1570, adding, "I suspect that it was a prose narrative of the story on which our author's play was constructed." He was wrong in both conjectures; for it is not prose, and it has not the remotest connection with the incidents of "Romeo and Juliet."

It was mentioned, however, in connection with "Romeo and Juliet" in the earliest instance in which it is alluded to. We refer to that remarkable collection, published by I. C., called "A poore Knight his Pallace of private Pleasures," 1579, where, on sign. Bii b, we meet with the following lines: —

> "Verona path we lefte, where Romeus doth lye,
> Where Juliet with Iconia injoy a place thereby:
> Gaulfrido lyeth in Venis, Barnardo doth the same,
> And the Arestons only child which Gnosia hath to name."

This quotation shows that the tale had attracted attention not very long after its publication by Drout. Of him we know absolutely nothing; but we may speculate, in the irregular spelling of names at that period, that he was descended from the John Droyt who in the household-book 20 and 21 Henry VIII. is enumerated as one of the minstrels attending upon the court, who were each paid 40*s.* quarterly. Yet at the end of the piece in hand we read, "Finis q^{d} Iohn Grout Gent.," which may lead to the belief that the author's name was really *Grout*, and not Drout.

Four introductory copies of verses, by W. W., R. W., T. F., and T Smith, afford no personal information, but Drout himself, (for so we shall spell his name,) in a prose "Preface to the Reader," speaks of his contemporary Underdowne, who, we know, was the writer of a poem on "Theseus and Ariadne," in 1566, and who we gather was also the author of some work upon the friendships of Titus and Gesyppus, Orestes and Pylades, &c. The title-page before us states that "Gaulfrido and Barnardo" was a translation from the Italian; and the use there of the word "arrived" for *happened*, and other circumstances, may strengthen our belief of the fact; but we are not aware of the existence of any foreign original for the few incidents of the story, in the course of which, when speeches occur, they are marked, as in a play, by prefixes. This is unusual in narrative poems; but when Achelley printed his "Didaco and Violenta" in 1576, (see p. 5,) he followed the precedent. Drout concludes his prose preface by this couplet:—

"Reade ere thou judge, then judge thy fill,
But judge the best, and mende the yll."

This "pitifull History" is sad indeed, for no person concerned in it escapes death; even the mariners of a ship that conveyed one of the two heroes are all drowned, while the rival friends, Gaulfrido and Barnardo, the lady they are in love with, as well as her father and mother, all come to untimely ends. Nobody survives. The tale, as far as a trial for murder is concerned, reminds us of the incidents of Titus and Gesyppus, and some parts of it are not badly told; but the conclusion, and the annihilation of all parties, no matter how remotely connected, is nothing short of ridiculous. The two friends Gaulfrido and Barnardo, who had been unexpectedly parted, meet again as unexpectedly, and one of them, on an early page, thus narrates the grief he had experienced at the separation:—

"Thus would I vewe, and dayly thinke
that thou wouldst after hye.
Now would I thinke unto my selfe
thy shippe for to espye;
But all for nought: the longer I
did gaze in open ayre,
The farder still thou wast from me,
so much the more my care.
When as I had in memorie
our parents that be dead,

Our mothers kind which pampered us,
  and long ago had fed
Both thee and me with milke so sweete,
  then was I like a stone;
Then was my hart even like to burst,
  my senses they were gone."

Drout observes no poetical propriety in the telling of his story, and mixes up the most incongruous materials and absurd images. The following is worth quoting, as it gives a glimpse of the manners of the time, where a party begin to dance: —

"The minstrell he was called in
  some pretty jest to play;
Then Robin hood was called for,
  and Malkin ere they went,
But Barnard ever to the mayde
  a loving looke he lent;
And he would very fayne have daunst
  with hir, if that he durst:
As he was offering, Galfryd caught
  hir by the hand at furst." &c.

It was this dance that led to the catastrophe. Gaulfrido being successful with the lady, Barnardo kills himself, and Gaulfrido, finding his friend's dead body, stabs himself with the same sword. Charina, beloved by them both, follows the double example, and her parents seem to think that they can do no less. After "Finis q[d] John Grout, gent." comes the following epilogue to the whole subject, which, as we have explained, has been somewhat dramatically treated: —

"These will bee had in memorie
  of all that have them seene.
Now they be dead, let all men say
  God save our noble Queene:
That she may vanquishe traytors all
  whiche seeketh hir decay;
The good and godly so I knowe
  continually will pray."

The recent execution of Felton, the Nortons, &c., is here, no doubt, referred to, and the words "now they be dead" must relate to them, and not to the characters engaged in the story. There seems no particular reason why the Queen should be prayed for, in consequence of the slaughter of Gaulfrido, Barnardo, Charina, Tisbine her father, her mother, and all the innocent mariners.

DRUMMOND, WILLIAM. — Forth Feasting. A Panegyricke to the Kings most excellent Majestie. *Flumina senserunt ipsa.* — Edinburgh, Printed by Andro Hart, 1617. 4to. 8 *leaves.*

This is an anonymous publication by W. Drummond of Hawthornden, afterwards included in his works; but in the sale catalogues of various periods we only find a single trace of it. Heber had no copy.

It is a favorable specimen of the versification, rather than of the genius, of Drummond, for the images, like the general subject, are violent, and it opens with one of the most extravagant, where the poet supposes the mountains to stand on tiptoe to witness the arrival of James I. in Scotland. The Forth speaks: —

> " What blustring noise now interrupts my sleepe?
> What echoing shouts thus cleave my chrystal Deep,
> And call mee hence out of my watrie Court?
> What melodie? what sounds of joye and sport
> Be these heere hurl'd from ev'rie neighbour Spring?
> With what lowd rumours do the Mountaines ring,
> Which in unusuall pompe on tip-toes stand,
> And (full of wonder) over-looke the land?"

For the mountains to stand on tiptoe on the occasion was certainly very "unusual pomp." The Forth afterwards addresses the King in these commonplaces of poetry: —

> " To virgins flowrs, to sun-burnt Earth the raine,
> To mariners faire winds amidst the maine;
> Coole shades to pilgrimes, which hote glances burne,
> Please not so much, to us as thy returne."

The following ends with an absurd and impious piece of flattery: —

"Eye of our westerne world, Mars-daunting king,
With whose renowne the Earths seven climats ring,
Thy deeds not only claime these Diademes
To which Thame, Liffy, Taye subject their streames,
But to thy Vertues rare, and gifts is due
All that the Planet of the yeare doth view:
Sure, if the world above did want a Prince,
The World above to it would take thee hence."

Afterwards the poem proceeds better and more naturally : —

"Ah! why should Isis onlie see Thee shine?
Is not thy Forth, as well as Isis, thine?
Though Isis vaunt shee hath more wealth in store,
Let it suffice thy Forth doth love thee more.
Though shee for beautie may compare with Seine,
For swannes and Sea-Nymphs with Imperiall Rhene,
Yet in the title may bee claim'd in Thee,
Nor shee, nor all the world can match with mee."

It concludes with some of the most pleasing lines in the tract:

"O! love these bounds, whereof thy royall Stemme
More than an hundreth were a Diademe.
So ever gold and bayes thy browes adorne,
So never Time may see thy race out-worne;
So of thine owne still mayst Thou bee desir'd,
Of Strangers fear'd, redoubted, and admir'd:
So Memorie the praise, so pretious Houres
May character thy name in starrie flowres;
So may thy high exployts at last make even
With Earth thy empire, Glorie with the Heaven."

We may doubt whether we ought not to read above "So Memorie *thy* praise": if not, the line is hardly intelligible. This is the poem which Ben Jonson told Drummond, for the sake of pleasing King James, he wished he had written, — "yett that he wished, to please the King, that piece of Forth Feasting had been his owne." — Conv. with Drummond, (Shaksp. Soc. edition, by D. Laing, 1842,) p. 7.

The copy we have used is the more interesting because it has the author's autograph at the end. Perhaps it was a gift to some friend — not to Ben Jonson, or he would also have placed his name upon it.

Dyer, Sir Edward. — Sixe Idillia, that is Sixe small, or petty Poems, or Æglogues, chosen of the right famous Sicilian Poet Theocritus, and translated into English verse. *Dum defluat amnis.* — Printed at Oxford by Joseph Barnes. 1588. 4to. 8 *leaves.*

This work, though unquestionably by Sir Edward Dyer, has never been mentioned by any bibliographer, nor does it appear to have been known to any poetical antiquary. The same may be said of a prose production, no doubt also by Dyer, published three years earlier under the title of "The Prayse of Nothing," which came from the press of Hugh Jackson. Of each only a single copy remains to us. Edward Dyer, who was not knighted until 1596, was born at Sharpham Park, Somersetshire, but the year is not recorded in the registers of the parish. The date of his death, at a very advanced age, has not hitherto been ascertained, but we give it from the register of St. Saviours, Southwark, in the following terms: —

> "11 May 1607. Sr. Edward Dyer, Knight, buried
> in the Chancell Ground — xxvjs viijd."

A search in the Prerogative Office has not procured his will, or any copy of it; but we learn from the original records formerly preserved in the Chapter House, Westminster, that in 9 Jac. 1, Catherine Dyer, his widow, commenced a suit in the Court of Requests against John Earl of Mar to enforce the payment of a rent-charge of £100 per annum upon the Manors of Middlegowey and Othery, in Somersetshire, granted to her by her late husband, Sir Edward Dyer. The result does not appear among the Decrees and Orders. In 1598, as we learn from the Token-books of St. Saviours, Sir E. Dyer lived in Winchester House, and he was in the habit of giving a buck annually to the church-wardens. He was made Chancellor of the Order of the Garter in the year he was knighted (1596), and in his official capacity, on 7th May, 1598, he addressed a letter to the Earl of Shrewsbury (preserved at Lambeth) on the subject of the Feast of which his lordship was

Lieutenant.[1] He never published anything that bore more than his initials, which, as M. D. (*i. e.* Master Dyer), are inserted at the end of a poem in " The Paradise of Dainty Devices," 1576. In 1582 a collection of Italian Proverbs, &c. was dedicated to him by John Florio, but we believe they were not printed, (Sale of Bright's MSS. June, 1844 ;) and in February 1583, according to a letter from N. Fant to Anthony Bacon, Dyer returned to England from a mission with which he had been charged to the Low Countries. In 1585 he wrote and printed his " Prayse of Nothing," a specimen of paradoxical playfulness, and it was followed by the work the title of which stands at the head of the present article. His initials are given in the following form at the back of the title-page.

"E. D.
Libenter hic et omnis exantlabitur
Labor, in tuæ spem, gratiæ."

Although Dyer was one of those who, with Spenser, Sidney, and

[1] As Dyer's autographs are very rare, we quote the hitherto unprinted letter: —

" Right honorable. It is the office off the Register to register those actes which this last feast, and since, have been or shall be doon. And I doubt me, under your L. correction, whether the tyme of your L. Lieutenancie be quyte expired, or no ; bicause the woords of the Commission ar but for three dayes — that is the xxij, xxiij and xxiiij dayes of this present moneth, and only for the celebrating of the ceremonies during that tyme. Therfore I thinke your L. may well cast off the care off such enregistering, as belonging to the Dean of Wyndsore properly. Neverthe-les, iff it please your L. to have me send in your L. name, I am at commandm^t in this, and in all the services that I can performe.

" The vij off Maye 98. EDWARD DYER."

The above is from Lambeth MS. No. 706. On 1st May, 1598, according to Stow, (edit. 1605, p. 1307,) the ambassadors had returned from France. We apprehend that Sir Edward's father was Sir James Dyer, the celebrated judge who died in 1582, and of whom the following anecdote is told in MS. Harl. 5353: — " Upon a time, when the late Lord Treasurer, Sir William Cecil, came before Justice Dyer in the Common Pleas, with his rapier by his side, the Justice told him that he must lay aside his long pen-knife, if he would come into that Court. This speech was free, and the sharper because Sir William was then Secretary."

By a letter from N. Faunt, also preserved at Lambeth (MS. 647), it appears that on 28th Feb. 1583, Sir E. Dyer " had returned from his employment in the Low Countries."

Gabriel Harvey, in 1580 and 1581, endeavored to introduce the classic metres into English, and although in 1585 he printed a specimen (one of the very earliest in our language) of undramatic blank-verse in his "Prayse of Nothing," he translated these "Idillia" of Theocritus in rhyme. They are the 8th, 11th, 16th, 18th, 21st, and 31st Idyls, and in various measures. The following, in twelve-syllable lines, concludes the first Idyl in the volume: —

"O Daphnis, what a dulcet mouth and voice thou hast!
'Tis sweeter thee to heare than honie-combes to tast.
Take thee these pipes, for thou in singing dost excell.
If me, a Goatehearde, thou wilt teach to sing so well,
This broken horned Goate on thee bestow I will,
Which to the verie brimm the paile doth ever fill.
So then was Daphnis glad, and lept and clapt his handes,
And danst as doth a fawne when by the damm he standes.
Menalcas greev'd, the thing his mind did much dismaie,
And sad as Bride he was upon the mariage daie.
Since then among the Shepeheardes Daphnis chiefe was had,
And tooke a Nimphe to wife, when he was but a lad."

The second Idyl in the volume (the 11th of Theocritus) opens thus jiggingly: —

"O Nicias, there is no other remedie for love,
With ointing or with sprinkling on, that ever I could prove,
Beside the Muses nine: this pleasant medsun of the minde
Growes among men, and seems but lite, yet verie hard to finde."

In the last Idyl Dyer again varies to six-syllable lines, rhyming in couplets, a measure that afterwards, for lyrical pieces, became somewhat popular, having been adopted by Shakspeare; and it is devoted to the fable of Venus and Adonis, a subject our great dramatist also adopted, but in a totally different form and manner. Dyer gives it thus: —

"When Venus first did see
Adonis dead to be,
With woeful tatter'd heare,
And cheekes so wan and seare,
The winged Loves she bad
The Bore should straight be had.
Forthwith like birdes thay flie,

And through the wood thay hie.
The woefull beast they finde,
And him with cordes thay binde."

The Boar is accused and accurst by Venus, but he excuses himself by asserting that he only wished to kiss and not to wound Adonis. He calls upon Venus to deprive him of his offending tusks, and here we meet with an unusual triplet.

"Wherfore these teeth, Venus,
Or punish or cut out.
Why beare I in my snowt
These needless teeth about?
If this may not suffice,
Cut off my chaps likewise."

"Snowt" and "chaps" are not very well-sounding words in English poetry, and Dyer might easily have avoided them had he wished it. The piece, which consists of only forty-seven lines, concludes thus: —

"To ruth he Venus moves,
And she commands the Loves
His bands for to untie.
After he came not nie
The wood, but at her wil
He followde Venus still,
And cumming to the fire,
He burnt up his desire."

"*With* desire" would perhaps be more intelligible. We may add that the specimen of undramatic blank-verse of which we have spoken, in Dyer's "Prayse of Nothing," is not in the usual ten-syllable iambics, afterwards constantly employed, but only differs from twelve-syllable rhymes in not having the jingle. It was, however, a novelty in its way in 1585, and on this account it principally merits notice. It is a version of a small part of Petrarch's "Triumph of Death," and reads more like plain prose than measured verse.

East Indies. — The Journal, or Dayly Register, contayning a true manifestation, and Historicall declaration of the voyage, accomplished by eight shippes of Amsterdam, under the conduct of Jacob Corneliszen Neck Admirall, and Wybrandt van Warwick Vice-Admirall, which sayled from Amsterdam the first day of March, 1598. Shewing the course they kept, and what other notable matters happened unto them in the sayd voyage. — Imprinted at London for Cuthbert Burby and John Flasket: And are to be sold at the Royall Exchange, and at the signe of the black beare in Paules Church-yard. 1601. 4to. B.L. 63 *leaves.*

This tract is principally curious from its rarity, for the details of the voyage of these Dutch ships present few incidents of interest. The title-page has a woodcut of a ship in full sail (the stern towards the spectator) with the wind, represented by a face in the clouds, blowing strongly. "The Journal" commences immediately afterwards; and it is, at the beginning, more in the form of the log-book of a ship than anything else. As we proceed, the information is more general, and on fol. 5 b. we have "a description of the Island de Cerne, which was now named Mauritius, lying 21 degrees to the South of the Equinoctiall line"; from whence we gather that these visitors were the first to give the island De Cerne the name of Mauritius. Afterwards we have descriptions of the town of Tuban in Java Major, of the island of Amboyna, of the islands of Banda, Ternate, &c.; but the most remarkable portion of the pamphlet is the early Malay vocabulary it furnishes, which is thus introduced: —

"Some words of the Malish speech, which language is used throughout the East Indies, as French is in our countrie, wherewith a man may travell over all the land."

Taking this literally, it serves to show how common a medium of communication French was at the end of the reign of Elizabeth. It does not appear that the tract was translated from the Dutch, but it may have been so. The whole of the information seems to be minute and authentic, making allowance for the simplicity and ignorance of some of the sailors and natives from whom it was derived. We are told, among other things, that the island of Cerne was uninhabited, and that the birds upon it were so unused to the sight of men, or to expect injury from them, that the crews caught, and knocked down with their hands, as many as they liked.

EDWARDS, RICHARD. — The Paradyse of daynty deuises. Conteyning sundry pithy preceptes, learned Counsels, and excellent inuentions, right pleasant and profitable for all estates. Deuised and written for the most part, by M. Edwardes, sometimes of her Maiesties Chappell: the rest, by sundry learned Gentlemen, both of honor, and worship, whose names hereafter folowe. — Imprinted at London, by Henry Disle, dwelling in Paules Church-yard, at the Southwest doore of Saint Paules Church, and are there to be solde. 1578. 4to. B.L.

That in our hands is the only known copy of this edition of a highly popular and valuable miscellany. By the following enumeration of the various impressions it appears to have been the third — viz., 1576, 1577, 1578, 1580, 1585, 1596, and 1600. There was also an edition, "printed by Edward Allde for Edward White," without date, but probably between 1596 and 1600.

The edition of 1578 is especially interesting, not merely on account of its rarity, but because it contains some poems not in any other impression, earlier or later, because it includes others for the first time inserted in the work, and because it ascribes several pieces to authors to whom they were not before imputed. It is to be lamented, therefore, that it wants one leaf, or possibly two leaves, at the end. In its present state it has 40 leaves, of course including the title. The names of the contributors, which we are told on the title-page "hereafter follow," are thus inserted at the back of it, with the arms of Lord Compton (to whom H[enry] D[isle], the publisher, dedicates the work) above them: —

"Saint Barnard E. G. Lord Vaux, the elder W. Hunis	"Iasper Haywood F. Kindlemarsh D. Sand M. Yloop."

When the reprint of the "Paradise of Dainty Devices" was made in 1810, Haslewood had seen, and only seen, (as he himself states,) the edition of 1578, of which, however, he professes to give the title-page, but with various errors, no doubt from haste in transcription. His note upon it is as follows: —"The above is the title of edition 1578, with the sight of which I have been favoured. Subsequent collation may enable me hereafter to give a more minute account of its contents; at present, I can only undertake to say, that it appears to vary from all other editions, and to contain a poem by George Whetstone no where else to be met with." This note refers to the very copy now before us, which we proceed to describe.

The dedication is the same in the impression of 1578 as in those of 1576 and 1577; and there the printer speaks of Edwards as having "not long since departed this life." The precise year of his death is nowhere stated; but Barnabe Googe, in his lines "Of Edwardes of the Chappell," printed in his most rare volume, "Eglogs, Epitaphes and Sonettes," 1563, (see *post*,) speaks of him as then living, and we know that he attended Queen Elizabeth on her visit to Oxford in 1566, as a gentleman of the Chapel Royal, and master of the singing-boys belonging to it. We do not recollect to have seen Googe's verses anywhere quoted, and they are not even referred to by Haslewood, or by his coadjutor, Sir Egerton Brydges. We insert them in connection with the biography of a distinguished poet and dramatist: —

"Of Edwardes of the Chappell.

"Devyne Camenes, that with your sacred food
Have fed and fosterde up from tender yeares
A happye man, that in your favour stoode,
Edwardes, in Courte that can not fynde his feares,
Your names be blest, that in the present age
So fyne a head by Arte have framed out,

Whom some hereafter, healpt by Poets rage,
Perchaunce may matche, but none shall passe (I doubt).
O Plautus! yf thou wert alyve agayne,
That Comedies so fynely dydste endyte;
Or Terence thou, that with thy plesaunt brayne
The hearers mynde on stage dydst much delyght,
What would you say, syrs, if you should beholde,
As I have done, the doyngs of this man?
No worde at all, to sweare I durst be bolde,
But burne with teares that which with myrth began;
I meane your bookes, by which you gate your name
To be forgot, you wolde commit to flame.
Alas! I wolde, Edwards, more tell thy prayse,
But at thy name my muse amased stayes."

It is certain, however, that Edwards was dead when Turberville printed his "Epitaphs, Epigrams, Songs and Sonnets" in 1567,[1] because that author has an Epitaph upon him;[2] and in the same volume is another poem, subscribed "Tho. Twine," (the finisher of Phaer's translation of Virgil,) which is of more value, inasmuch as it touches some points of the biography of Edwards, and mentions two of his dramas, "Damon and Pythias" and "Palamon and Arcite," by name. From the following passage in it we may conclude that Edwards died in London: —

"His death not I, but all
good gentle harts doe mone:
O London! though thy grief be great,
thou didst not mourne alone."

Anthony Wood informs us (*Ath. Oxon.* edit. Bliss, I. 353) that Edwards was first of Corpus Christi College, and afterwards of Christ Church; and this is confirmed by Twine, who exclaims, —

"O happie House! O place
of Corpus Christi, thou
That plantedst first, & gavste the roote
to that so brave a bowe;
And Christ Church which enjoydste
the fruite more ripe at fill,

1 There was also an edition in 1570.

2 See Vol. IV., article TURBERVILLE, GEORGE.

Plunge up a thousand sighes, for griefe
your trickling teares distill," &c.

The subsequent mention of his two dramas also deserves remark, coming, as it does, from a contemporary: —

" Thy tender Tunes and Rimes,
wherein thou woonst to play,
Eche princely Dame of Court & Towne
shall beare in minde alway.
Thy Damon and his Friend,
Arcyte and Palemon,
With moe full fit for Princes eares,
though thou from earth art gone,
Shall still remain in fame," &c.

Its printer informs us that the poems in " The Paradise of Dainty Devices" were "penned by divers learned Gentlemen, and collected togeather through the travell" of Edwards; who has various poems of his own in the volume, more (according to the copy in our hands) than have been hitherto ascribed to him. Thus, "The historie of Damacles and Dionise," "A yong man of Ægipt and Valerian," "Zeleuch and his sonne," which are anonymous in other impressions, are assigned to him at length in the edition of 1578. The following couplet, in reply to W. H.'s lines headed " The fruites of fained frendes," is also attributed to him, and is omitted in other copies of the work. They stand thus: —

" If suche false Shippes doe haunte the shore,
Strike doune the saile and trust no more
M. Edwardes."

Again, the poem "Being importunate, at the length, he obtaineth," on the same authority, is the property of Edwards, and not of M. B., to whom it had been given in 1576 and 1577. In the impression of 1578 it bears this title, "A Dialogue betwene a Gentleman and his Love." How far these ascriptions are to be relied upon is another question; but, at all events, they show that between 1577 and 1578 the printer had seen grounds for making the changes. This fact of itself establishes the importance and interest of the copy of 1578.

Disle, or his editor, pursued a similar course with other authors, when they had reason to believe that the ascriptions in the two first editions were erroneous. We will take an example from Churchyard, whose name is not met with in the editions of 1576 and 1577, but who, according to the edition of 1578, wrote a poem entitled "He persuadeth his friend from the fond effects of love," which is anonymous in other copies. Moreover, the subsequent important addition is made to it in the impression of 1578: —

"First count the care and then the cost,
And marke what fraud in faith is found;
Then after come and make thy bost,
And shew some cause why thou art bound:
For when the wine doth runne full low,
You shall be faine to drinke the lies,
And eate the flesh, ful well I know,
That hath ben blowne by many flies.

"We see, where great devotion is
The people kneele and kisse the crosse;
And though we find small fault of this,
Yet some will gilld a bridles bosse.
A foole his bable will not change,
Not for the septer of a king;
In lovers life is nothing strange,
For youth delightes none other thing.
FINIS. Tho. Churchyard."

To those who are aware that Churchyard began writing in the reign of Edward VI., and that he was a most prolific versifier, it seems strange that Edwards should have omitted to select any piece by him. The same observation may be made upon George Whetstone, whose name appears first in the impression of 1578, at the end of a long poem entitled "Verses written of 20 good precepts, at the request of his especiall good freend and kinesman, M. Robart Cudden, of Grayes Inne." Of Cudden, as a kinsman of Whetstone, we hear on no other authority. The poem itself is much too long to be quoted at length here, but we give the opening: —

"Old frendship binds (though faine I would refuse)
In this discourse to please your honest mind;
For, trust me frend, the counseling words I use
Are rather forst of cause, then come of kind."

After twenty other stanzas it concludes thus : —

> "*Thinke on thy end:* the tyde for none doth waight;
> Euen so pale death for no mans wil doth stay:
> Then, while thou mayst, thy worldly reckning straight,
> Least when thou wouldest, Death doth goodwil dismay.
> *G. Whetstones. Formæ nulla fides.*"

The "precept" enforced is placed in Italic type at the commencement of each stanza. On the evidence afforded by this edition we may, perhaps, assign a poem headed "No pleasure without some payne" to Sir Walter Raleigh, for his initials are placed at the end of it, instead of E. S., as they stand in the two earlier impressions. E. S. is also subscribed to "Of sufferance cometh ease," which in fact appears, on early authority, to belong to Lord Vaux. From Lord Vaux we must, however, take "Beyng asked the occasion of his white head, he aunswereth thus," which is said to belong to W. Hunnis. Such also will be the case with a poem entitled "Of the meane estate." The poem, which is anonymous in other editions, headed "No foe to a flatterer," is likewise attributed to Hunnis. He has property also in a poem that has no title, and is given to M. B. in the impressions of 1576 and 1577, but which is called in the impression of 1578 "He assureth his constancie." The Earl of Oxford, on the same evidence, may claim "Beyng in love he complaineth," and not M. B. to whom it is elsewhere imputed ; while that the initials E. O. apply to him is proved by their standing E. Ox. in the copy of 1578. It not unfrequently happens that names and titles are there put at length, which in earlier and later impressions stand only as initials; and on the whole the information as to authorship is much more precise in the copy which we now for the first time bring under notice in any detail. It is impossible, without consuming a much larger space than we can afford, to point out all the important differences : we have necessarily contented ourselves with some of the most remarkable.

EGERIA, THE LADY. — The Adventures of the Ladie Egeria. Containing her miserable bannishment by

Duke Lampanus her husbande, through the inducement of Ladie Eldorna, the harlot, and Lord Andromus the Flatterer: who for his perjurie and softe insinuation was by a wonderfull judgement utterly subverted and devoured. The Combat fought by Lord Travenna (with Necto the Slave, in steade of Andromus the Flatterer) obtayning the victorie was afterwards bannished. The grave Letters, wise and sentencious Orations of the Counsaile, Judges and others. The bannishment of the Dukes two children. Lastly the Duke himselfe bannished by Pasifer the Flatterer, and Eldorna the harlot: the bloudy murther of Eldorna by her owne bastarde sonne Rastophel, who through their meanes usurped the governement: with a wonderfull description of other Flatterers and insolent persons: with many other memorable accidents, contayning wisedome, discretion and pollicie; no lesse renowmed then profitable. Published by W. C. Maister of Art. — At London, Printed by Robert Walde-grave. 4to. B. L.

The longest title to a work of the kind that is, perhaps, to be found in our romance literature. It was clearly intended to be a puff of the contents; but however various the materials, the story is full of the grossest improbabilities, and on the whole extremely tedious. It has no date, but we may place it between 1580 and 1590. The word "published," before the initials W. C., are no doubt to be taken in the same sense as "published by I. C." on the title-page of "A poore Knight his Pallace of private Pleasures," which came out in 1579. In both cases W. C. and I. C. must, we think, be held to be the names of the writers, and not merely of the editors of the volumes.

"The Adventures of Lady Egeria" require only a brief notice. They are dedicated by W. C. to Lady Cicely Buckhurst, but without any information as to the author, or as to the origin of his story, which certainly reads without that constraint and use of foreign idioms that sometimes belong to mere translations. At the end is placed a colophon which it is necessary to notice, because it states that it is "the end of the Duches Egeriaes first adventures"; as if the writer, when he printed it, contemplated a continuation, which, if ever published, is not now extant. The probability is that, in spite of the loquacious and descriptive title, the work did not sell, and that no second part was ever called for by Waldegrave, or the public. The running title throughout is "Lady Egeria to her Adventures." The work extends to sign. S 2. We only know of the existence of two copies of it, and it is entirely prose.

Elizabeth, Queen. — The Poores Lamentation for the Death of our late dread Soveraigne, the high and mightie Princesse Elizabeth, Queene of England, France and Ireland. With their Prayers to God for the high and mightie Prince James, by the grace of God King of England, Scotland, France and Ireland, defender of the Faith. — Imprinted at London for Thomas Pavier, &c. 1603. 4to. 6 *leaves*.

This is a unique tract, the existence of which has been long known, but which, we apprehend, has never been critically noticed. A brief memorandum regarding it is all that will be deemed necessary. The author does not give his name, and we are aware of no clue to it, although the verses are not utterly despicable — as good perhaps as many of the rhyming effusions on the demise of Queen Elizabeth. The publisher was probably desirous of putting forth something on the occasion, and employed a ballad-writer of the day to supply him. It treats the commencement of Elizabeth's life historically, deriving the materials from ordinary popular sources. Thus near the opening are the following narrative stanzas: —

"In the beginning of Queene Maries raigne
Her grace at Ashridge at her house did lie;
Sore sicke, God wot, and very full of paine,
Not like to live but very like to die:

To her in all the hast Queene Mary sent
To have her brought to her incontinent.

" Three of the Council to that end did ride,
With twelve score horse-men in their company,
And every one his weapon at his side,
To Ashridge posting they in hast did hie:
Yet it was ten a clock within the night
When they were at the gate for to alight.

" Straight to her chamber they in hast did goe,
And with her grace demaunded for to speake.
Answere was made them, that the cause was so
That she in bed that time was very weake;
And did request them stay till the next day,
Who answered, that the Queene they must obey."

They insist that, " alive or dead," she should go with them, and they carry her away early in the morning to the Court, where she was detained fourteen days before Mary would see her. From thence Elizabeth was sent to the Tower, and afterwards to Woodstock. Here the same plain narrative style is continued, the object being to afford information to the two-penny purchasers: —

" During the time that she at Woodstock lay
With life she often escaped very neere,
For many ways Stephen Gardiner did assay,
As in the story it doth plaine appeare,
To bring that godly Lady to her end
But God above her Grace did still defend."

This is just such a production as would have been printed as a penny broadside, if it had not been too long. The writer finally consoles himself for the loss of Elizabeth by thinking, that, while she has ascended to heaven, such a successor as James I. has ascended the throne: he concludes thus: —

" Then feare the Lord and honour still thy King,
Joyne all in one the trueth for to defend;
Then peace unto our land will plenty bring,
And all our feeble states shall then amend.
Then let us all with ecchoing voices crie,
The Lord preserve his Royall Majesty!"

Elliot, George. — A very true report of the apprehension and taking of that Arche Papist Edmond Campion, the Pope his right hand, with three other lewd Jesuite priests, and divers other Laie people, most seditious persons of the like sort. Conteining also a controulment of a most untrue former booke, set out by one A. M., *alias* Anthonie Munday, concerning the same, as it is to be proved and justified by George Elliot, one of the ordinary yeomen of her Majesties Chamber, Authour of this booke, and chiefest cause of the finding of the sayd lewde and seditious people, great enemies to God, their loving Prince and Countrie. *Veritas non quærit angulos.* — Imprinted at London at the three Cranes in the Vintree by Thomas Dawson. 1581. 8vo. B. L. 14 *leaves.*

George Elliot, who puts his name at the end of this tract, complains, in an address "to the Reader," that he had been "very vilely slaundered" by Anthony Munday in the account published of the discovery and capture of Campion and his confederates. Munday took all credit to himself in the transaction, whereas Elliot insists that he was the chief means of finding, and consequent apprehending of the Jesuits. It is not worth while to enter into the claims of the candidates; but Elliot admits that he came forward very late with his pamphlet, and he makes a merit of having been a Roman Catholic, and of now turning against the friends of his former faith. His tract is entirely prose. It is remarkable that, while Elliot's answer to Munday is dated 1581, Munday's "Discourse," to which it is an answer, has "29th of Janua. 1582" upon the title-page, — the printer, Edward White, making the new year 1582 begin in January. Elliot's answer was of course issued in 1581-2, making the year 1582 commence on the 25th March.

ELLIS, G. — The Lamentation of the lost Sheepe. By G. E. — London, Printed by W. Jaggard dwelling in Barbican. 1605. 4to.

The only existing copy of this poem, that we know of, wants a page, sign. E 3; but the writer has a sheet of the same work, which, unluckily, does not supply the deficiency. It is entirely of a religious cast, and the versification has so much general excellence as to make it very readable, and even persuasive.

The dedication supplies the name of the author, for it is signed G. Ellis, which in catalogues has been interpreted George Ellis, but it may have been any other name beginning with G. We have nothing else to guide us, for he left no other work behind him that has survived, and this, as we have said, has reached us only in a mutilated state. The dedication is "to Sir Francis Castillion, Knight, a Gentleman Pentioner to his Majesty," who is also addressed in an acrostic. By "the lost Sheep" the author means himself, a repentant sinner, and he says near the commencement, —

"[I] humbly come with sorrow-rented hart,
With blubbered eies, and hands upreard to heaven,
To play a poore lamenting Lost Sheepes parte,
That would weepe streames of bloud to be forgiven,
So that heavens joyes may not from me be reaven.
But (oh) I feare mine eies are drained drie,
That, though I would, inough I cannot crie."

Farther on he ascribes his sinfulness to —

"Ill Companie, the cause of many woes,
The sugred baite that hideth poysoned hooke,
The rock unseene that shipwrackt soules ore-throwes,
The weeping Crocodile that kils with look,
The Siren that can never vertue brooke,
The readiest step to ruine and decay,
Graces confounder, and hels nearest waie."

After eighty-one numbered stanzas the author winds up thus: —

"I sing not I of wanton love-sick laies,
Of tickling toies to feede fantastick eares;
My Muse respects no glozing tatling praise:
A guilty conscience this sad passion bears;

My straying from my Lord hath brought these tears:
My sinne-sick soule, with sorrow al besprent,
Lamenting thus a wretched life mispent.

Finis.

Omnem crede diem tibi diluxisse supremum."

There is an air of sincerity throughout, and we are inclined to think that Ellis was not hypocritically, though poetically, repentant.

ELVIDEN, EDMUND. — The most excellent and plesant Metaphoricall Historie of Pesistratus and Catanea. Set forth this present yeare by Edm. Elviden Gentleman. — Imprinted at London by Henry Bynneman. *Cum privilegio.* n. d. B. L. 8vo. 95 *leaves.*

Although "this present year" is mentioned on the title-page, no date is to be found in any part of the volume: it may, however, be fixed about 1570; and in 1569 the same author printed a work called "The Closet of Counsells," (see the next article.) The dedication of the poem before us is to the Earl of Oxford, Lord Great Chamberlain of England, to whom Elviden offers "this present rude and grosse conceite, wherin I have, to my slender abilitie, bestowed the fruits of my willing labour." In the same spirit he requests the Reader "to accept this my simple indevour, and it shall be the redy way to incourage a gros conceit to somewhat better fertility"; adding that this work "requyreth rather the judgement of the gentle, than the prayse of the slaunderous, or sentence of the capcious." "The Argument" of the poem follows, but in his endeavor to be concise, the author has hardly rendered himself intelligible: —

"In Grecian soyle two brothers born there is:
They father have, Agenetos, whose blis
In happie time the children had attainde.
The father died and valiant sons remainde.
The eldest sonne, he Kenedoxus hight,
The other namde Pesistratus: they fight
With auncient foes, who, Tetimetians callde,
Were (caitifs al) to martial brothers thralde:

And, conquest got, the brothers fal to strife
For spoile of foes, wheron ech seekes the life
(In pointed place) of other to suppresse.
Pesistrate conquerour departs, and in distresse
He brother leaves, whose fatal wound, he thought,
With cursed blade his cruel hand had wrought.
Wheron into Italian partes he flies,
And wel retainde, a seemely Ladie spies,
Whom, loving long, the joyfull man at last
His Ladies love attainde, his dollors past.
From ruling roome then Kenedox deprivde
In native soile, to Tarent towne arivde,
Where brother was: of treason he accusde
The lovers both; and Champion not refusde,
In combat fought: the Kenedox was slaine,
And lovers thus were rid from former paine.
Then, Champion dead, was Pesistrate exild
From Ladies sight, whose chaunged robes beguild
His foes despight: then proclamation made
That Pesistrate to proper soile should vade,
He there arivde, prepard a valiant hoste,
Wherewith returnde into Italian coast,
He slew the fo in open chalengde fight,
That erst had wrought the troubled man such spight;
And Lady woonne, he tooke hir to his mate,
And livde at ease, and dyde in happie state."

This extract, of course, is not a fair specimen of the author's talents as a versifier, and we shall select a passage from the body of his production, which is terminated by a colophon in Bynneman's secretary-type: — "Imprinted at London by Henry Binneman, dwelling in Knightrider streate at the Signe of the Mermaid," his device occupying the last page. The poem, some part of which is allegorical, is rather arbitrarily divided into six unequal parts, and in the course of it several love-letters, which pass between the hero and the heroine, are inserted: these are not drawn out unnecessarily, but most of the speeches are of tedious length, and the story moves slowly and heavily, the more so on account of the author's laborious versification, which, excepting in the instance of one song, is without any variety. Precipater, brother to Catanea, slays Antropos, a traitor, in single combat, and the author thus describes the consequences: —

"Wheron with strained loftie voice
the people movde such cries,
That through their hie conceived joyes
they shakt, I thinke, the skies.
And now the lovers were so glad,
as though their lives renewd
Their happy state with heavenly joyes
and pleasures were indude.
But little deemed Pesistrate
the riddance of his paine
To come by death of Kenedox,
his brother that was slaine.
Wheron they cravde to see the face
of viliant him, that so
Had saved their lives, and maintaind truth,
and vanquished the foe.
And when, his helmet laide aside,
the lovers sawe to be
Precipater, and people viewd,
and knew that it was hee,
O! how the people vaunst his fame,
and joyed to see their Lorde
So valiant Knight, and yelded prayse
to him with one accorde:
As though their voices would have raisde
the man from mortal case
To hiest heavens for his desert
amongst the Gods to place.
And so the lovers joyd in hart,
requiting endlesse thankes
For his aboundant courtesie,
and manly martial prankes;
That it doth farre excel my power
to paint in proper wise,
I therefore yeeld it to conceit
of eche man to devise."

The cant phrase, therefore, of all poverty-stricken penmen, "which can better be imagined than described," is of ancient origin in English. There is one point deserving note in this poem, which may aid in fixing its date: a song written by Pesistratus is introduced on sign. C, and in the margin we are told that it is "To the tune of Damon and Pythias." This alludes to a song of the same measure in Edwards's Play of "Damon and Pythias," which must have been written and acted before 1566, although it was not printed until 1571. Pesistratus was a much better knight than poet, or he never would have gained the hand of Catanea. His song runs thus: —

"Oh, heavie hart dismaid!
oh, stomacke stuft with paine!
Oh, woful wight! oh, cursed wretch!
why shouldst thou not complaine?
Art thou in pleasant state,
or hast thou cause to joy?
No, no, thy fates are frounst in feares:
come, death, and ridde my ceasles anoy.

"Oh, cruel carelesse wretch!
doest thou deserve thy life,
Since thou thy gentle brothers breast
hast pearst with cursed knife?
What, meanest thou to live?
and wilt thou life enjoy?
No, no, thy fates are frounst in feares:
come, death, and ridde my ceasles anoy.

"You fatal sisters all,
you twisters teare my threede:
With fatall knife my fatal knott
to share in hast proceede;
For I, unhappie wretch,
am cleane exilde from joy,
And live in woes, in griefes and feares:
come, death, and ridde my ceasles anoy."

As far as research has yet extended, the present is the only existing copy of "Pesistratus and Catanea." Of the personal history of the author nothing whatever has been collected.

ELVIDEN, EDMOND. — The Closet of Counsells, conteining the advice of divers wyse Philosphers, touchinge sundry morall matters, in Poesies, Preceptes, Proverbes and Parables, translated and collected out of divers aucthors into Englishe verse: by Edmond Elviden Gent. Whereunto is anexed a pithy and pleasant discription of the abuses and vanities of the worlde. 1569. — Imprynted at London in Fleetstreat, at the signe of the Saint John Evangeliste, by Thomas Colwell. 8vo. B. L.

The date of the publication of this rather wearisome work is, as we imagine, anterior to that of the preceding article, and it is by a different printer. Bynneman, however, who put "Pesistratus and Catanea" into type, printed a new impression of "The Closet of Counsells" in 1573. It was therefore acceptable to readers of the day.

The dedication is to the author's nephew, for whom perhaps the "Poesies, Preceptes, Proverbes and Parables" were collected; and although Elviden, in his address "to the Reader," apologizes for his "worke, barbarous, rude and unpollished," he seems to have ransacked Plato, Pythagoras, Socrates, Seneca, Plutarch, &c. for materials, which fill the first seventy-seven folios of his book. We then arrive at "A pithy and pleasante discription of the Abbusions and Vanities of the Worlde," which is a very prosy affair, though in verse: it is certainly not "pithy," for it occupies forty pages; and it is not "pleasant," inasmuch as it is more remarkable for "dullness than delight." There is not a syllable to render it applicable to the state of manners or society of the time. In one place Elviden says, —

"Viewe therefore from the top to toe
 of every such degree,
And wisely ponder of the same,
 and thou shalt plainly see,
That in conclusion each and all
 is bent to care and payne,
And yet doth tende to no good ende,
 but frustrate and in vayne."

It terminates thus, which, being the conclusion, is certainly the most welcome part of the book.

"Who therfore gladly would receave
 the happy life and time,

Must in his mortall race avoyde
the motions unto crime:
Regarding each thing in this vale,
as I have said before,
To be but frustrate, vayne and fonde,
no better, nor no more.
For mortall trace a passage is
unto another life,
Which is not mortall, but devoyde
of foolish mortall strife.
And therfore, he that willingly
would other life attayne,
Must seeke for to reforme this life,
because it is but vayne."

It is saying more for the patience than for the poetry of the age, when such tedious commonplaces went through at least two distinct impressions in four years.

ELYOT, SIR THOMAS. — Pasquyll the Playne. Anno M. D. XL. — [Colophon] Londini in ædibus Thomæ Bertheleti typis impress. *Cum privilegio ad imprimendum solum.* Anno M. D. XL. 8vo. B. L. 22 *leaves.*

We have never seen any earlier edition of this semi-serious argument on the subject of loquacity and silence, but it was first published in 1533. A supposed edition in 1539 is in fact only the impression of 1540; but the work must have been popular. It is in the form of a dialogue between Pasquil, Gnatho, and Harpocrates, and it is introduced by an epistle "to the gentile reders" by Sir Thomas Elyot, who explains what the characters are, and afterwards deprecates the censures of "venemous tunges and overthwart wittes." The dress of Gnatho as described by Pasquil is worth quoting: —

"A cappe full of aglettes and bottons! This longe estrige fether doeth wonderly well: the tirfe of the cappe towrned downe afore, like a pentise, hath a marvailous good grace; but this longe gowne, with strayte sleves, is a *non sequitur*, and lette you to flee; and than your fethers shal stande you in no stede, and soo, moughte you happen to be combred, yf ye shulde come in to a stoure."

This contradiction in Gnatho's dress is equally contradicted in its accompaniments, for Pasquil detects two books about him, and they appear to be copies of the New Testament and of Chaucer's tale of "Troylus and Chreseid."[1] Here we may remark that the whole tract has a decidedly Protestant tendency, and that the conversation between the three is conducted with the most perfect freedom. Among other things, Pasquil is thus made to speak against confession: — "Wenest thou that I was never confessed? Yes; I have tolde a tale to a friar, or this tyme, with a grote in my hande, and have been assoyled forthwith without any farder rehersall, where, if a pore man had tolde halfe so moch, he should have been made equall with the divell."

Pasquil swears continually by St. John, St. Paul, and other saints, while Harpocrates indulges in similar asseverations, and several times invokes the Saviour. From Gnatho such exclamations might be expected. The question discussed is, when men ought, and when they ought not to speak, Gnatho beginning with a quotation on the point from Æschylus. He handles the matter so well that Pasquil admits that Gnatho, while dressed otherwise like an extreme fop, deserves also to wear a doctor's gown. We may cite as a specimen the following curious picture of the manners of the time.

"In olde tyme men used to occupy the mornynge in deepe and subtile studies, and in counsailes concerninge the commune weal, and other matters of great importaunce. In lyke wise, than to here controversies and gyve judgementes. And if they had any causes of theyr owne, than to treate of them; and that didde they not without great consyderation, procedynge bothe of naturall rayson, and also counsayle of phisyke. And after diner they refreshed theyr wittes eyther with instrumentes of musyke, or withe redinge, or heringe some pleasant story, or beholdinge some thinge delectable and honeste. And after theyr diner was digested, than eyther they exercysed them selfes in rydinge, runnynge on fote, or shotynge, or other lyke pastyme, or went with theyr haukes to se a flight at the

[1] Hence we might infer, and it is not very improbable, that Sir T. Elyot referred to some separate publication of Chaucer's "most cunningly amplified" poem, as Speght justly describes it. It would not have been easy for Gnatho to have carried the large folio of Chaucer's Works in his bosom.

ryver, or would se their grehoundes course the hare, or the dere; whiche they didde as well to recreate theyr wittes, as also to get them good appetite. But, lo! nowe all this is tourned to a newe fascion; God helpe ye! the worlde is almost at an ende; for after noone is tourned to fore noone, vertue into vyce, vice into vertu, devocion into hypocresie, and in some places menne say, fayth is tourned to herisye."

Gnatho is the advocate of talking, and Harpocrates of silence, while Pasquil agrees with neither, and throughout is very plain-spoken in his severe remarks: in fact, in some places the dialogue assumes the character of a prose satire. After his two companions have left him, Pasquil, who is represented as an old talking statue in the streets of Rome, concludes in these terms: —

"Nowe, whan these two felowes comme to theyr maister, they wyl tell al that they have hard of me: it maketh no matter, for I have sayd nothyng but by the way of advertisement, without reprochyng of any one person, wherewith no good man hath any cause to take any displesure. And he that doth, by that whyche is spoken he is soone spied to what parte he leaneth. Judge what men lyst, my thought shall be free."

The whole is extremely amusing, and the argument sometimes so subtle that Gnatho hardly seems to understand it: neither he nor Harpocrates are convinced, but soliloquizing Pasquil is left in possession of the field — or rather of the street.

ENGLAND'S HOPE. — Englands Hope against Irish Hate. *Sint Mæcenates et non deerunt Marones.* — At London, Printed by W. W. for Thomas Hayes. 1600. 4to. 14 *leaves.*

This poem has, we believe, never before been heard of, but it is of little merit. At the end only are placed the initials J. G. E., the last being probably put for Esquire, so that the writer appears not to have been himself very proud of his performance. "The Epistle Dedicatorie" is addressed to nobody and signed by nobody, and in it the author recommends his reader "not to measure the matter by the man, nor proportion the worth of my labour with the unworthiness of my selfe," which is saying about the same thing twice over, although hardly worth saying once. J. G. E. especially attacks Tyrone, but also the Irish generally, as well as the Spaniards, in this and similar verses: —

"But if the sinnewes of their strong assaultes
The just revenger have in sunder crackt;
If so their huge Armados in the vaults
Of vast Oceans kingdome have been wrackt,
Leaving the world to descant on their faults:
If all their boasting threates away were blowne,
And they supprest, then why not now Terone?"

The whole is in the same stanza, and each stanza separated from its fellows by a line across the page. The author afterwards describes what he calls the "Traitor Passant," the "Traitor Regardant," the "Traitor Couchant," and the "Traitor Rampant," and asks, —

"But if Throckmorton, Campion and the rest,
With those their deadly sinnes in number doubling,
All agents to the triple wreathed Beast,
With plodding feete our spring of gladnes troubling,
Fell in their owne mudd errours groveling,
If their blood paceing tracts were quickly knowne,
And they supplanted, Why not then Terone?"

Many of the stanzas terminate with this inquiry. He praises Walter Earl of Essex, Lord Grey of Wilton, (Spenser's Patron,) Sir Henry Sidney, and Sir W. Fitzwilliam, who in 1600 were all dead; but had they been alive, it is not likely that they would have been very anxious for J. G. E.'s laudation.

ENGLISH-WOMEN, HABITS OF. — Ornatus Muliebris Anglicanus, or the severall Habits of English Women from the Nobilitie to the contry Woman, as they are in these times. Winceslaus Hollar, Bohemus, fecit Londoni. A. 1640. Cum privilegio Regis. 4to. 27 *leaves.*

The first leaf is a plain engraved title-page as above, after which come twenty-six most exquisitely engraved copperplates, representing the female dresses of all classes in the reign of

Charles I. They are all but the last numbered at the corner, and upon each (excepting the third, seventh, thirteenth, and twenty-third) is the name of the artist, who might well be proud of his performance. The first, third, thirteenth, and twenty-third are without dates; and eighth and fourteenth are dated 1638; the fourth, fifth, sixth, seventh, tenth, eleventh, and twelfth are dated 1639, and the remainder 1640. The difference in the character of every face, and the individuality of the representations, seem to establish that most of them were from the life, beginning with Queen Henrietta Maria.

ESSEX, EARL OF. — A True Coppie of a Discourse written by a Gentleman employed in the late Voyage of Spaine and Portingale: Sent to his particular friend, and by him published, for the better satisfaction of all such, as hauing been seduced by particular report, haue entred into conceipts tending to the discredit of the enterprise, and Actors in the same. — At London Printed for Thomas Woodcock dwelling in Paules Churchyard, at the signe of the blacke Beare. 1589. 4to. B. L. 31 *leaves.*

The chief interest of this very rare tract depends upon the Earl of Essex, and upon his concern in the Expedition to Spain and Portugal in 1589, under Sir Francis Drake and Sir John Norris. However, it adverts to the whole undertaking from its commencement to its termination, and the object, as the title-page explains, was to justify it, and to show, by its results, that it had much tended to the glory and advantage of England, as well as to the renown of all the leaders concerned in it. It was evidently founded upon official documents and information, brought forward to remove the prevailing impression against the undertaking and its issue. It deserves notice that the word "particular" in connection with "report" on the title-page was probably a misprint, and in an old handwriting it has been altered, in the copy before us, (the only one we have been able to examine,) to *partiall*, which is most likely what was intended.

An address "To the Reader" states that this "report of the late voyage into Spaine and Portingall" had been nearly four months in the hands of the party who put it forth, placed there by his near friend, a gentleman who had been employed in the enterprise, who had desired him "to reserve it to himself." He had nevertheless disobeyed the injunction, in order to remove the opinion some held of the action, and to show how much honor the nation had gained by it.

The writer sums up what had been accomplished in the outset in these terms: — "In this short time of our adventure wee haue wonne a Towne by *escalade*, battred and assaulted another, overthrowen a mightie Princes power in the field, landed our Armie in three severall places of his kingdom, marched seaven daies in the hart of his Countrey, lyen three nights in the Suburbes of his principall Citie, beaten his forces into the gates thereof, and possessed two of his frontier Forts."

He first gives the highest possible character to Sir John Norris as a soldier, and to Sir Francis Drake as a sailor, and then goes over all the details from the landing of the troops at the Groyne on 20th April, 1589, to the return of the expedition in the beginning of July; and he takes care to make the most of everything that tells in favor of the English. The Earl of Essex, his brother Walter Devereux, Sir Roger Williams, Sir Philip Butler, and Sir Edward Wingfield (having escaped from England, to the Queen's vehement displeasure, a circumstance not mentioned by this writer) did not join the fleet until after it had quitted the Groyne; but the Earl afterwards always led the vanguard, in company with Sir Roger Williams, by consent of the Generals. In the account of the affair at Peniche nothing is said of the killing of a man by Essex single-handed, as stated in some advices. The troops came to Lisbon on May 25th, and the Earl of Essex chased the enemy, who made a sally, "even to the gates of the high Towne." Meanwhile Drake made himself master of Cascais, and thither the English army marched; and here it was that the Earl of Essex sent his challenge to meet any equal singly, or six, eight, ten, or more on each side, in order to decide the victory.

On 6th June the Earl, "upon receipt of letters from her Majestie," took his departure for England. The great sickness of the troops followed soon afterwards, and the particulars, when Essex was gone, are unimportant and uninteresting. The forces under Norris returned to Plymouth on the 2d July, where he found Drake and nearly all the Queen's ships.

The pamphlet is a very able one, and in the latter part of it the writer dwells at large upon the triumphs that had been accomplished by a comparatively small force, and illustrates his subject by various references and examples. Nearer the close there is a mention of the railing of Martin Marprelate, and an enlargement upon the happiness and security of England, in spite of the efforts of all her enemies. The only point on which the author indulges a complaint relates to the small estimate in which the military profession was held: — "But it is true," he says, "that no man shall be a Prophet in his countrey; and for my owne part, I will lay aside my armes, till that profession shall have more reputation, and live with my friends in the countrey, attending either some more fortunate time to use them, or some other good occasion to make me forget them."

The date at the end is — "From London the 30 of August 1589;" so that, if it be true that the person who caused the tract to be printed had had it nearly four months in his hands before he sent it to press, it could not have been published until the latter end of December.

Stowe, in his Chronicle (edition of 1605, p. 1261), gives all the details of the shipping, their names, commanders, &c., but is silent respecting the disobedient resolution of the Earl of Essex to escape from court and join in the enterprise.

EVANS, LEWIS. — The Castle of Christianitie, detecting the long erring estate as well of the Romaine Church, as of the Byshop of Rome: together with the defence of the Catholique Faith: Set forth by Lewys Evens. [Texts from Eccl. 21, Hieron ad Paulum &c.] — Imprinted at London by Henry Denham. 8vo. B. L. 88 *leaves.*

Lewis Evans was the author of a sprightly but satirical ballad[1] entitled "How to wyve well," which was printed by Owen Rogers about the year 1560 or 1561. It is preserved in a unique broadside, and opens thus: —

"Wher wyving some mislike,
And women muche displease,
The women frowarde be,
And fewe men can them please."

Thence he proceeds to enlarge upon the consequences of marrying a Shrew, and after twenty four-line stanzas he ends with this piece of good advice: —

"You maydens al, that wives do mind
In time to come to be,
Endever your selfe that eche of you
A faythfull wyfe may be."

The work before us is of a far different character — sombre and severe; but, as a sort of intermediate production, we may mention Lewis Evans's translation of "The fyrste two Satars or Poyses of Orace," entered by Thomas Cobwell, the printer, in 1564–5, the second only of which, as far as we know, came from the press. If, as is most likely, the "first satire" was also published, it has not come down to our day. The translator was a schoolmaster, and from the dedication of his "Castle of Christianitie" to the Queen (at what precise date it was written has not been ascertained) we learn that he had been a refugee on account of his adherence to the Roman Catholic religion, but by "her Majestys great clemency" had been allowed to return to England on becoming a convert to the Protestant faith. To it is added an Epistle "to his loving friends" whom he had abandoned in faith, and who, he feared, would now abandon him in friendship. He tells them that his duty to God, to the Queen, and to his country had required him "to renounce obstinacie, to knowledge the right way, and to bid defiance to idolatrie." He

[1] The whole of it may be found in the Percy Society's first publication, "Old Ballads, from early Printed Copies," 1840, p. 37.

goes on: — "I have therefore in this treatise, though not eloquently, yet faithfully, brought forth reason, authoritie and Scripture, and that to defende the Catholike fayth, and to chase away the smoke of hell, the mist of Antichrist, and the false, long-mayntayned merchandise of Satan."

This must of course have been written after 1565, when he was in Antwerp, and just as violent an assailant of the opposite side of the question; and the colophon, at the end of the work before us, settles the year when Lewis Evans (upon what, if any, inducement does not appear) came to his senses on the subject of religion, for it is in these terms, "Seene and allowed, according to the order appoynted: Anno 1568." The "order appointed" related to the due licensing of works of controversial divinity; and it was obviously necessary to be careful as to what Evans might write, for in 1565 he had printed abroad "The betraying of the beastliness of Heretics," and in 1570 published in England a small work entitled "The hatefull hypocrisy and rebellion of Romish Prelates." (*Ath. Oxon.* I. 411, edit. Bliss.) He seems to have been equally violent and virulent on both sides; but in general, in the work in our hands, as it appeared at a middle date, so it took a middle course, and in some places was not so furious as such a convert might be expected to have been. It is not necessary for us to enter into an examination of his "Castle of Christianitie," which was clearly intended to propitiate persons in authority, and which handles the usual topics without any novelty in argument, or peculiarity in style. It is not at all certain that Lewis Evans did not ultimately revert to Popery and die a Roman Catholic; but it could not be of much importance to anybody, but himself, to what party so versatile and volatile a person ultimately adhered.

EVANS, THOMAS. — Oedipus: Three Cantoes. Wherein is contained: 1 His unfortunate Infancy. 2 His execrable Actions. 3 His lamentable End. By T. E. Bach: Art. Cantab. *Oedipus sum, non Davus.* — London, Printed by Nicholas Okes. 1615. 12mo. 39 *leaves.*

It is possible, as there is no bookseller's name on the title-page, that this production was not printed for sale. It is, however, dedicated and subscribed at length to "Mr. John Clapham Esquire, one of the Sixe Clarkes of the Chauncerie"; and in a preliminary address, "savouring much of the academy," the author says that it is his "first child, but not the heyre of all the fathers wit: there is some laid up to enrich a second brother, to keepe it from accustomed dishonesty, when I shall put it to shift into the world; yet if this prove a griefe to the parent, I will instantly be divorc't from Thalia, and make myself happy in the progeny from a better stocke." Probably the divorce from Thalia, *a mensâ et thoro*, took place, as we hear of no second offspring.

A general "argument" to the three Cantos precedes the first Canto in these lines:—

"Oracles counceld to preserve, a sonne
Exposed is to death, reserv'd by chance,
Doth all that to him's destin'd to be done.
In Father's bloud he steepes his impious lance,
Partakes incestuous sweetes through ignorance.
Untill, truth knowne, he teares out both his eyes,
So killes his mother, and by lightning dies."

Each canto contains about six hundred lines, rhyming alternately, and sometimes flowing with ease, but without any originality of invention. The whole story is thus summarily wound up: the author is speaking of the last meeting between blind Œdipus and Jocasta:—

"So having all the office of his eye
Discharg'd by th' other foure, his guidlesse feet
Are usher'd by his hands; when suddenly,
His wife, his mother, both in one, him meets.
Son, husband (cries she) would not both, or neither,
My wombes *Primitiæ*, my beds second Lord!
Why turnst thou hence thy hollow circles? whither
Those rings without their jewels? hold this sword.
Looke on my bosome with the eyes of thought;
Lend thou the hand and I will lend the sight:

My death thou mayst, that hast a fathers wrought.
Strike thou but home thou canst not strike but right.
Why dost thou stay? Am I not guilty too?
Then beare not all the punishment alone;
Some of't is mine; on me mine owne bestow:
A heavy burden parted seemeth none.
Oh! I conjure thee by these lamps extinguisht,
By all the wrongs and rights that we have done,
By this wombe lastly, which hath not distinguisht
Her love betwixt a husband and a sonne.
Ore-come at length he strikes with one full blow:
Her life it selfe to a long flight betakes.
He wanders thence, secur'd in dangers now,
Made lesse already then fate lesse can make.
Long liv'd he so, till heaven compassion tooke:
Revenge herselfe saw too much satisfied.
Jove with unwonted thunder-bolt him strooke,
Into a heape of peacefull ashes dryed.
His sonnes both killing warres, his daughters fate,
To following buskind Writers I commit:
My Popinjay is lesson'd not to prate,
Where many words may argue little wit."

This specimen shows that the author is not very strict in his observance of the exactness of rhyme; and other parts of his poem tend to the decided conviction that it was never meant that he should arrive at immortality by the road over Parnassus.

EVORDANUS. — The first and second part of the History of the famous Euordanus Prince of Denmark. With the strange Aduentures of Iago, Prince of Saxonie: And both theyr severall fortunes in Loue. — At London, Printed by J. R. for R. B. and are to be sold in Paules Church-yard at the signe of the Sun. 1605. 4to. B. L.

An English romance which has never been examined. Although the "first and second part" are mentioned on the title-page, the only copy hitherto discovered concludes at the end of the "first part." It is certainly not a translation, but in various respects an imitation of the style of Robert Greene. It professes to have been derived from the Chronicles of Denmark, but by whom is not stated, and we apprehend cannot now be ascertained. It may be a question how far the success of Shakspeare's "Hamlet," in 1602, 1603, and 1604, may have led writers of fiction to pretend to have resorted to similar sources.

Correct geography is not affected to be observed; for Mayence is represented as the capital of Denmark, Flanders is stated to be part of the same kingdom, and Dantzic one of its chief cities. The heroine is supposed to be the daughter of the King of France, with whom Prince Edward of England falls in love, and he obtains the prize at a tournament, where the lady is thus described:—

"Emilia, sitting amongst the rest seemed like Cinthia placed amongst the lesser starres, being in the fulnes of her power: or like Diana following her chase thorow the woods and launes, accompanied with her traine of Nimphs, whose paine in pursute had raised in her Alablaster cheeks a lively vermilion die. So seemed the beautifull Princesse, having in her well proportioned face the lovely rose and lilly striving for maisterdome."

It cannot be worth while to enter here into a story so commenced. Evordanus and Iago are of about the same age, and in their youth have been instructed not only in their own language, but, what is unusual, in Greek and Latin. The two young Princes require to be knighted in order that they may draw a magic sword from its scabbard, but the Duke of Saxony objects to comply with their request on account of their youth:—

"All which could not cause them to desist from their sute, but still more earnestlie they craved the same, alleaging many sundry examples of those who at younger yeares had inured themselves to as great labours; as Reynaldo at the age of fifteene yeares, stealing from his father's Court, went into Palestina to the Christian Armie, where, under great Godfry of Bullen, he obtained to be the chiefe scourge of the Sarasins, and without whom it had been impossible to have wonne the holy Citty of Jerusalem."

The above passage occurs near the end of Chapter XX., which is the last of the first part of the Romance. The author elsewhere shows that he had some acquaintance with Italian literature; as for instance where, following Dante, he observes, "in misery there is no greater griefe than to call to minde forepassed pleasure." (*Inf.*, Canto V.)

EUPHUES SHADOW. — Euphues Shadow, the Battaile of the Sences. Wherein youthful folly is set downe in his right figure, and vaine fancies are proved to produce many offences. Hereunto is annexed the Deafe mans Dialogue, contayning Philamis and Athanatos: fit for all sortes to peruse, and the better sorte to practice. By T. L. Gent. — London, Printed by Abell Jeffes, for John Busbie, and are to be sould at his Shop in Paules Churchyard, neere to the West doore of Paules. 1592. 4to. B. L. 50 *leaves.*

It seems to us so uncertain whether this production was by Thomas Lodge, or by Robert Greene, that we have preferred to place it under its own title. Our belief is that it was by Greene, but that his own name having been so often before the public, and Lodge having, precisely at this period, taken a long voyage with Cavendish (or Candish), Greene, for the sake of variety, thought fit to publish "Euphues Shadow" as the work of his poetical contemporary. It is in all respects identical with the style of Greene; and if Lodge really wrote it, it was an intentional and successful imitation; all Greene's peculiarities, for which in or before 1592 he had obtained celebrity, are here to be abundantly noted.

In his dedication to Viscount Fitzwaters, Greene tells his patron that Lodge had left this tract behind him for publication; and such may have been the fact; but he at the same time informs the "Gentlemen Readers," that he had already "put forth so many of his own labours" that they might be weary of his name. This statement tends to confirm the notion that he resorted to the expedient of palming "Euphues Shadow" upon Lodge, who was absent and could not contradict him; and who, if he had been then actually resident in England, would not have had much reason to complain that so popular an author as Robert Greene had paid him the compliment. Until some further evidence is produced, and we know not from whence it is to come, it must remain undecided whether the tract be by one or by the other. Greene was determined that his instrumentality in the matter, whatever his share may have been, should not be imputed to any other person, and therefore subscribed the dedication with the addition of the county from which he was known to have come — "Rob. Greene *Norfolciensis.*" In the year of the appearance of the tract under consideration, Greene said of himself, "I neede not make long discourse of my parentes, who for their gravitie and honest life is well knowne and esteemed amongst their neighbors, namely in the Cittie of Norwich, where I was bred and borne." (*Repentance*, 1592.) He professed to Lord Fitzwaters that Lodge, "in his last letters," had enjoined him to print "Euphues Shadow"; but it is more than doubtful whether Lodge did write, or could have written, to Greene in the interval since his sailing with Cavendish, and the whole affair reads more like a pretext than a reality. However, in our day it is a matter of little consequence, and certain it is that there is nothing in the production itself that should have made Lodge very anxious to own it. On the other hand, if the publication were a failure, Greene by this expedient had avoided all responsibility; and the more positive he represented Lodge in his directions to have "Euphues Shadow" printed, the more Greene shifted any weight from his own shoulders.

After the address "to the Gentlemen Readers," the story, such as it is, commences, but the few and commonplace incidents are not worth detailing; and the language, we feel assured, was the language of Greene, with precisely his thoughts, his images, and his modes of expression. The sort of epistle from "Philautus to his sonnes living at the Court," with which the piece commences, is exactly like Greene's composition, and it serves to introduce certainly one of the dullest performances of the period: as if Greene, having written it, was unwilling to avow it, while his necessities drove him to the sale of it, not under his own name, but under that of a poet with whom he was known to have been acquainted. The artificial style in which this and other pieces of the kind were composed was excellently ridiculed at this date by R. W., in his "Martin-Marsixtus," 1592, where he exclaims, —

"Fie upon this wit! thus affecting to be famous they become notorious * * * and when with shame they see their follie, they are faine to put on a *Mourning Garment* and crie *Farewell.* If any man be of a dainty and curious eare, I shall desire him to repayre to those authors: every man hath not a pearle-mint, a fish-mint, nor a bird-mint in his braine: all are not licensed to create new stones, new fowles, new serpents, and to coyne new creatures."

Here we see Greene's "Mourning Garment," 1590, and his "Farewell to Folly," 1591, distinctly mentioned; but it was not in those, so much as in others, that he resorted to his invention, and, for the sake of apt similes, imputed to pearls, fishes, birds, and beasts, properties which they did not possess.

Three small productions in rhyme are interspersed, but of as little merit as the prose; and it is evident that the whole was put together under that sort of pecuniary pressure to which Greene and his associates were constantly exposed. The lines run smoothly enough, as if by a practised versifier; but though words are abundant, thoughts are deficient; and the following is the only specimen at all worth quoting; it is headed,—

"The Epitaph of Eurimone.

"Heere lies ingravde, in prime of tender age,
Eurimone, too pearlesse in disdaine;
Whose proud contempt no reason might asswage,
Till Love, to quite all wronged lovers paine,
Bereft her wits, when as her friend was gone,
Who now lyes tombed in this marble stone.

"Let Ladies learne her lewdnes to eschew,
And whilst they live in freedome of delight,
To take remorse, and lovers sorrowes rew,
For why contempt is answered with dispight:
Remembering still this sentence sage and ould,
Who will not yonge, they may not when they would."

We have seldom read a more disappointing production, considering that two such names as Greene and Lodge were connected with it. It is, we think, unworthy of either, and we notice it chiefly on account of its extreme rarity. Only two copies (one of them imperfect) have been preserved. It was Nash's opinion (expressed in his "Strange Newes," 1593, sign. L 4) that Greene "came oftener in print than men of judgment allowed of"; and it was some feeling of this kind that perhaps induced Greene to father "Euphues Shadow" upon Lodge: still, it may have been Lodge's production after all.

www.ingramcontent.com/pod-product-compliance
Lightning Source LLC
LaVergne TN
LVHW020210110826
845151LV00003B/662